PHILOSOPHY,
CULTURE AND RELIGION

Ethics and Epics

PHILOSOPHY, CULTURE AND RELIGION

The Collected Essays of Bimal Krishna Matilal

Ethics and Epics

Edited by

Jonardon Ganeri

OXFORD
UNIVERSITY PRESS

OXFORD
UNIVERSITY PRESS

Oxford University Press is a department of the University of Oxford. It furthers the University's objective of excellence in research, scholarship, and education by publishing worldwide. Oxford is a registered trademark of Oxford University Press in the UK and in certain other countries

Published in India by
Oxford University Press
22 Workspace, 2nd Floor, 1/22 Asaf Ali Road, New Delhi 110002, India

First published 2002
Oxford India Paperbacks 2015
12th impression 2025

ISBN-13: 978-0-19-946095-3
ISBN-10: 0-19-946095-7

Printed in India by Manipal Technologies Limited, Manipal

Contents

VOLUME II

Mind, Language and World

PART I

Dharma, Rationality and Moral Dilemmas

1

Moral Dilemmas and Religious Dogmas

When does an act become moral? When does an act become religious? Can a moral act be religious by the same token? What is meant by the word 'religious'?

Suppose Mr X is a very rich man. He gave some money, a large sum, to an orphanage. As a consequence, a large number of orphans were fed, clothed and taken care of. Now should we say that Mr X has performed a noble, morally admirable act? I know there will be people who would disagree. It will be said, for example, 'Well, Mr X is actually a vain man,' or 'He is a *kālobājārī*, he made money in an unfair way,' or 'He is a *punjipati*, he made money by exploiting the labour group.' They will continue: (1) as a vain man he is now trying to show others how 'big' he is, to make an impression; (2) as a *kālobājārī*, he is trying to make up for his past sins, immorality, and guilty conscience; (3) he is trying to please God to get some religious merit (*puṇya*), he is bribing the Divinity to avoid hell; or (4) he is simply trying to avoid income tax, etc., etc.

We can thus go on imputing motivation after motivation to poor Mr X. Maybe, all of them are true, at least to some extent. Take the last insinuation. He may be afraid of the inland revenue, the tax man. That is why he gave this money. But he could have just paid the taxes, and forgotten about the orphanage. Or, he might have hired a tax-accountant to avoid taxes. Or, he could have bribed some officials. Has he not, therefore, done something better than that? Is he not slightly better, say, morally and religiously, than another, Mr Y, who follows an alternative course of action open to him? Is not the consequence of Mr X's action, whatever his motivation may be, good and beneficial to humanity?

Those moral philosophers who are consequentialists would say that this act saves a lot of human lives and so on. Hence we have to give him some moral credit. He is not a saint, but he is certainly better than some others.

Can we gauge his act in our barometer of religiosity? Well, we would say, he has done a *secular* act by helping an orphanage, and this *may be* a moral act, depending upon the motivation or its consequences, but it is not a religious act.

Is this a true picture of what has happened here? What is a religious act? What quality must an act have in order to be religious? Several answers may be forthcoming:

(1) A religious act is one that pleases God. Well, how do we know what pleases God? Well, one *knows*, one can tell, one just *feels*.
(2) A religious act is one that is enjoined in the scriptures.
(3) A religious act is one that brings one nearer to one's religious goal: *mokṣa, nirvāṇa*, or salvation.
(4) A religious act is one which is *Not Immoral*, and has one or all of the three characteristics mentioned above (God, scriptures, *mokṣa*).

Why this double negative 'Not Immoral'? There may be some religious acts which are neither moral nor immoral, for example, collecting flowers for daily puja. And there are, of course, some so-called religious acts which are definitely immoral, for example killing someone because he is not a believer. The purpose here is to include the former, and exclude the latter.

To return to Mr X, could we say what he has done has pleased God? Is God pleased, if twenty of His helpless creatures are clothed, fed, taken care of and saved from painful, premature death? *How do we know*?

Suppose Mr X does not believe in God. He may believe in a religio-moral system like Buddhism or Jainism. He is a non-theist but not an atheist or an indifferent man. Or he may be a humanist. He does not do his puja, does not say his prayers, and makes no attempt to bribe his way into heaven, for he does not believe in them. Would that particular act of his be still *religious*? It would still be moral, I suppose, but what more is needed to make it religious?

Let me explain the point. Suppose there is a God, in spite of what the non-believers say and argue. Should we then say that God would be highly displeased with Mr X and punish him, in the way only He can punish, because he does not believe in Him? Is God like a despot, a monarch or a dictator who would punish anybody who does not show Him respect? Is God like the Queen of Hearts in *Alice in Wonderland*, who used to shout, at the slightest provocation, 'Off with his head', 'Off with her head'? This will not be a very happy picture of God even for the religious, truly religious, persons.

A religious person may say that Mr X will certainly not go to heaven for his act. But can we send him to hell, even if he does not believe in it? He does not go to heaven because he does not believe in it, but can we blast him in hell? Where would he go? Does he have to go anywhere after death?

So far we have talked in terms of God. How about the second formulation? A religious act is what is approved by the scriptures, scriptures of any great religion. Of course, Mr X's act would be approved as a *good* act by the scriptures of any great religious tradition. I do not know of any great religion that would disapprove of the action of Mr X. But suppose he does not belong to any such religion. Should he then be excommunicated and condemned by his fellowmen, as the great philosopher Spinoza was? Would his act lose its intrinsic or inherent goodness, because he does not belong to any religious tradition? Would gold lose its intrinsic qualities, its brightness and beauty, when we suddenly change from the gold standard? Would it lose all its value? If so, then so much the worse for our scriptural pandits!

How about the third formulation? Can Mr X be drawn nearer to his *mokṣa* or *nirvāṇa* or salvation or whatever religious goal we believe to *be* there, even if he does not believe in any?

The fact is that our best moral intuition declares that the act of Mr X *is* a moral act (barring motivational complications). But could it not be a religious act by the same token? Our fourth formulation of the definition of a religious act brings us closer to the most pertinent question: Can an act be simply moral without being religious in any sense? Would a religious man admit that his notion of religion is so narrow as to exclude acts like that of Mr X? Should we say that our religion could not care less if somebody does something to help and save some of his fellow human beings?

How about a more disturbing question: Can some 'religious' acts be amoral and immoral? Can we give up morality in this way for the pursuit of religion? Is it possible to support a genocide, a blood-bath, a bloody war, a crusade, or a jehad in the name of religion?

Plato in his book *Euthyphro* has raised a very central question about religion and morality: Is it that gods love what is morally right? Or, is a thing morally right because gods love it? This presupposes a polytheistic religion. But we can easily substitute 'God' for 'gods'. But, maybe, to accommodate such non-theistic religions as Buddhism and Jainism (perhaps Vedānta also), we should put it as follows: Is a moral act a religious act (i.e. would it automatically have religious approval) by the same token? Or, is an act morally good because it is religious, that is, has religious approval? In other words, the dilemma is between the 'religious-because-moral' theory and the 'moral-because-religious' theory. If the first is true, our Mr X is a religious man. If we take the second, to kill Mr X, a non-believer, would be a virtue, a religious act! I have put the proposition in an extreme form, but I think my point is clear enough.

Let us now explain what we understand by moral dilemma. Some well-known philosophers have doubted whether there could exist such things as moral dilemmas, just as some religionists would doubt whether there could be any religious dilemmas. But I believe there are genuine action-guide dilemmas, which are not simply the products of confusion, and for which, to be sure, there are no clear-cut rational solutions. For me, a moral dilemma is a species of such action-guide dilemmas.

What is an action-guide dilemma (religious or moral)? A dilemma can be defined here, perhaps, in terms of obligation and evaluation principles. An action-guide dilemma arises in a situation just in case an agent cannot do everything that is obligatory for him to do in that situation. He feels obliged to do, say, both *X* and *Y*; but it is impossible to do both of them. For the situation is such that doing *X* would be undoing *Y*, and vice versa. You cannot cook your goose and have it alive at the same time. This is that kind of a situation.

Suppose several actions are possible in a situation that are both absolutely and unconditionally (not merely prima facie) obligatory, and at the same time, suppose that the performance of one precludes the performance of all others. It is a situation where you cannot 'kill the snake and *not* break the stick' at the same time. If we do not break the stick, we cannot kill the snake. But the dictates for both actions seem obligatory. Yet the principles which dictate them seem equally indispensable and absolute and not prima facie.

(1) A well-known case of moral dilemma is, I think, the *Bhagavad-Gītā* situation. (I will not bore you with the high philosophy of the *Gītā*, but only with the moral dilemma.) We all know the story. Should Arjuna fight the bloody battle and kill his venerable grandfather, teacher, uncle, brothers, etc., etc.? Or, should he not? It is obligatory, I should say, morally obligatory, for Arjuna as a man, as a human being, as a member of a family and a human society, to feel revulsion about a bloody battle that would lead to the senseless killing of his own venerable relatives, his

near and dear ones. At the same time, as a Kṣatriya, as a royal prince, it is his duty to fight wars when challenged, to recover the lost throne, and to see that his elder brother Yudhiṣṭhira wins the war. It is what we call an 'impossible' situation, an apt illustration of the 'action-guide' dilemma that I am talking about. He must kill and must not kill.

Aho ata mahat pāpaṃ kartuṃ vyavasitā vayam;
Yadrājyasukhalobhena hantuṃ svajanamudyatāḥ.

Alas! we have resolved to commit a great sin, inasmuch as we are endeavouring to slay our kinsmen out of a craving for the pleasures of dominion. (*Gītā*, ch. I, verse 45).

An incidental comment: The enigmatic *Gītā* has sometimes been criticized as a very *violent* text, one that incites violence and killing. It tells you to kill not only fellowmen but also relatives and superiors. In addition, it was Oppenheimer who apparently quoted from chapter XI of the *Gītā* after the first successful test explosion of the atom bomb! The most damaging and repulsive use of the *Gītā* has been made by the notorious cult-leader and killer Charles Manson, who in his defence against the charge of the most cruel and inhuman murder of an innocent pregnant woman, filmstar Sharon Tate, quoted:

Nainaṃ chindanti śastrāṇi nainaṃ dahati pāvakaḥ;
Na cainaṃ kledayantyāpo na śoṣayati mārutaḥ.

Him weapons cut not, Him fire burns not, and Him water wets not; Him wind dries not. (*Gītā*, ch. II, verse 23).

We can reject all these as gross misinterpretations. But the fact remains. What kind of religious text is this, which incites senseless killing, and a sort of amoral, if not wholly immoral, behaviour?

Without being an apologist, I would like to say that the *Gītā* can, paradoxically, be treated as a text that discourages violence or bloody battles. It may also show the futility of all such battles. Let us ask: Was Kṛṣṇa really doing anything wrong by asking Arjuna to forget all human concerns, noble sentiments and moral qualms, so that he could fight and kill? I think Arjuna's noble and moral concern for the life of his near and dear ones came to him when it was already too late, when daggers were drawn, and bows were strung and fitted with arrows in the battlefield of Kurukṣetra. And who was Arjuna? The entire Bhārata war was for Arjuna. It was his game and he should play. Throughout his life he has been preparing himself for this moment of truth. His whole life has been organized so as to be the best archer (*Pārtha eva dhanurdharaḥ*), the best warrior, the best fighter—which means the best killer. Arjuna was in Kurukṣetra by his own choice. He did not choose to be a monk, and so how could he say now that he would rather be a beggar (*bhaikṣyamapīha loka—Gītā*, ch. II, verse 5)? The point is that Arjuna could not stop midway. He could not make the arrow released by himself stop in mid-air and not hit the mark. The battle had to be fought, for he was responsible for it to begin with. The best way to avoid a bloody battle is to give up the preparations for it. Hence Kṛṣṇa could say:

Kṣudraṃ hṛdayadaur-balyaṃ tyaktvottiṣṭha parantapa.

Cast off this mean faint-heartedness and arise, O scorcher of thine enemies. (*Gītā*, ch. II, verse 3).

But could we really condemn Arjuna for showing such moral concerns? Was he merely acting? Was it a sort of a melodrama? My answer is *no*. For this only typifies the moral dilemma of an agent. Arjuna, by showing this side to his mind, becomes before our eyes more of a human being, not a gigantic killing machine. He had to do the killing, for the die was already cast and all was over, but he had also to weep for those he was killing. His dilemma was genuine, but the resolution was only through a pragmatic concern forced upon him by the situation in which he found himself, and for which he was also partly, if not fully, responsible.

Daṇḍiter sāthe daṇḍadātā kānde yave samān āghāte sarvaśreṣtha se vicār.

Justice reaches its noblest height when, in meting out punishment to a wrongdoer, the punisher sheds tears, being as much hurt as the one punished.

Why would such a situation arise and why would the agent *not* be fully responsible? My answer would be in terms of human limitations, human imperfections, and human frailties. We humans sometimes do bargain for more than what we expect and can take. This is an imperfect world.

(2) My second example is from a Greek source. The story of the Greek general Agamemnon runs as follows: The general was going to lead an expedition against the enemy, but it so happened that in order to win the battle he had to sacrifice his innocent, dearest daughter to perform a religious ritual. Either he had to save the country by sacrificing his own daughter or he had to lose the battle. Another 'impossible' situation. He sacrificed his daughter but should he *not* regret doing so? He did regret it as Arjuna did. Both were humans. It is another example of a moral dilemma (we may even call it a 'religious' dilemma) where only a pragmatic ad hoc resolution was reached.

(3) For my third example, I go back to the *Mahābhārata*. It is a story of, again, Kṛṣṇa and Arjuna—a story that once generated a very well-publicized controversy, toward the end of the last century in our country, between two great minds, Bankimchandra and Rabindranath. At the centre of the controversy there was a genuine moral dilemma, and the dispute was about how best to resolve it. In the great Bhārata war, in the *Karṇa-parvan*, Yudhiṣṭhira was once so humiliated in the battle with Kṛṣṇa that he 'blew his top'. He lost his calm (falsifying the meaning of his own name!) and insulted Arjuna by condemning his *Gāṇḍīva*, asking Arjuna to give up his famous weapon. Now Arjuna's promise was to kill anybody who would insult his *Gāṇḍīva*. Hence he took his sword and was about to do the most foolish thing, when Kṛṣṇa intervened, as usual. The dilemma was presented as 'Should I lie and not kill Yudhiṣṭhira, or should I kill him and be faithful to my promise?' (Promise-keeping is identified with truthfulness in almost all cultures.) So Kṛṣṇa tells a story, that of a sage, Kauśika. He had taken a vow of telling the truth always. A group of gangsters, in hot pursuit of some innocent men, came to ask him which way they had fled. Should he break his vow and tell a lie and save the men's lives, or should he not? Remember: a sage is a very religious person. He told the truth, and the men were chased and killed. Kṛṣṇa now has the last word. He said that when Kauśika died, he did not go to heaven or to his *sādhanocita dhāma*, for he had put his selfish religious dogma over the selfless, morally admirable action. Truth-telling may be morally admirable and hence certainly a religious virtue, but not under all conditions. One of the certain marks of morally superior (and in my scheme, 'religiously' superior) action is its non-self-regarding character, as philosophers in the Kantian tradition have no doubt emphasized. It seems to agree with the moral and religious intuition which Kṛṣṇa includes in his instructions to Arjuna.

The problem, however, cannot be so easily resolved. It may be that Kṛṣṇa again gave a pragmatic solution depending upon the situational constraints. Hence when Bankimchandra depicted Kṛṣṇa thus in his *Kṛṣṇa-caritra*, young Rabindranath protested with the zeal of a religious purist:

Konokhānei mithyā satya hay nā. Śraddhāspada Bankimbabu balileo hay nā; svayaṁ Śrīkṛṣṇa balileo hay nā.

Falsehood can never be true under any circumstances—even if respected Bankimbabu or Śrīkṛṣṇa himself says it can be. (*Bhāratī*, Agrahāyaṇa, 1291, p. 347).

What young Rabindranath insisted upon here was curiously enough in complete agreement with a strange and tortuous argument of Immanuel Kant in support of truth-telling. Kant talked about a situation which had an uncanny similarity with the *Mahābhārata* story (Kṛṣṇa's story). I quote from Kant's essay 'On a Supposed Right to Tell Lies for Benevolent Motives', *Critique of Practical Reason and Other Works on the Theory of Ethics*, Appendix (1889, pp. 361, 362–3):

The moral principle that it is one's duty to speak the truth, if it were taken singly and unconditionally, would make all society impossible. We have the proof of this in the very direct consequences which have been drawn from the principle by a German philosopher, who goes so far as to affirm that to tell a falsehood to a murderer, who asked us whether our friend, of whom he was in pursuit, had not taken refuge in our house, would be a crime. [This passage was quoted as the comment of a French philosopher on Kant.]

[Kant remarks]: '. . . if you have strictly adhered to the truth, public justice can find no fault with you, be the unforeseen consequence what it may. It is possible that whilst you have honestly answered *Yes* to the murderer's question, whether his intended victim is in the house, the latter may have gone out unobserved, and so not have come in the way of the murderer, and the deed therefore have not been done; whereas if you lied and said he was not in the house, and he had really gone out (though unknown to you), so that the murderer met him as he went, and executed his purpose on him, then you might with justice be accused as the cause of his death. For if you had spoken the truth as well as you knew it, perhaps the murderer, while seeking for his enemy in the house, might have been caught by neighbours coming up and the deed been prevented.

Both Kant and Rabindranath, I must admit, are my heroes. Kant was a great moral philosopher, perhaps the greatest of them all. But here, in this particular respect, I would beg to disagree with both of them. The above seems to give the impression of a tortuous argument, a desperate attempt to show that truth-telling is a 'moral absolute'. It would be comparable to the religious absolutes of religious people. Kant continued and concluded: 'To be *truthful* (honest) in all declarations is therefore a *sacred unconditional* command of reason, and not to be limited by any expediency.' (Mark the word 'sacred'. Is it not the return of the repressed, to use Freud's phrase, to analyse Kant? Kant was the first and foremost to take morality away from religious sanction.) Rabindranath was a little more resourceful here. In his debate with Bankimchandra, he said that Kauśika should have said, 'Yes I know, but I won't tell you.' Bankimchandra, in reply, asked, 'It was possible. But was it probable?' Given the fact that Kauśika was a human being with human frailties and imperfections, he could have been subject to inhuman physical torture, and, truth, in this way, could have been elicited from him in the end. If the gangsters said, 'We will kill you, if you do not tell,' in that case Rabindranath's suggested way out would have been appropriate. Kauśika could have saved the lives of the innocent men by giving his own life. But that was not the case.

I have already indicated that my inclination here is to support Bankimchandra, and not Kant or the stance of a religious purist that was represented by Rabindranath. (Rabindranath changed his view later, to which I will come back at the end.) On being truthful and keeping promises regardless of consequences, Bankimchandra commented:

Yadi keha prāte uṭhiyā satya kare ye āji divāvasāner madhye pṛthivīte yata prakār pāp āche—hatyā, dasyutā, paradār, parapīḍan sakali sampanna kariba—tānhāder mate ki ihār sei satya pālan-i ucit? Yadi tānhāder semat hay, tabe kāyamanovākye prārthanā kari, tānhāder satyavād tānhāderi thāk—ekhāne satyacyuti-i dharma. Mithyā-i satya.

Suppose a person after getting up in the morning swears that he will commit by dusk all kinds of crime under the sun—murder, robbery, and so on. Now, do they [religious purists] really subscribe to the view that the person in question should be faithful in translating his words—an utterance of even this nature—into action? If they think so then I should have nothing to do with their idea of adherence of truth. I would say, in this case *dharma* or righteousness consists in disregarding the utterance made. Here falsehood becomes truth.

What 'the unconditional command of reason' (to use Kant's expression) is, is very difficult to know in every situation with the required clarity. But truth-telling under the above circumstances is certainly not one of them (*pace* Kant and Rabindranath). For then we inadvertently turn a moral principle into a moral dogma. And there would be little fundamental difference between a *moral* dogma and a religious dogma. Remember that Kauśika was trying to keep to his religious principles, as he understood then.

(4) My last example is from Rabindranath's *Devatār Grās* (The Lord's Debt). Remember the crisis in the middle of the stormy ocean in that story. A shipful of people would apparently be drowned by the storm. The so-called deity wants the sacrifice of an innocent, helpless boy, the son of Mokṣadā. For without it, the boat would go down, or so it was believed. A pious brahmin Maitra was in charge. Let me quote. The poet says:

Maitra śuska pāṁśumukhe
cakṣu mudi kare jap. Jananīr buke
Rākhāl lukāye mukh kānpiche nīrave.
Takhan vipanna mājhi ḍāki kahe save,
Bābāre diyecha phānki tomāder keu,
yā meneche dey nāi tāi eta ḍheu—

Face shrunken and pale, Maitra sat with eyes shut and muttered his prayers. Rākhāl, in a cold tremor, hid his face in his mother's breast.

The boatman, desperate, suddenly called out, 'One in this boat has cheated the Lord, has offered Him a gift but has not kept his word. That explains this untimely storm and unruly waves.'

Yār yata chilo
artha vastra yāhā kichu jale pheli dilo
nā kari vicār. Tabu takhani palake
tarīte uṭhila jal dāruṇ jhalake.
Mājhi kahe punarbār, 'Devatār dhan
ke yāy phirāye laye, ei belā śon.'
Brahman sahasā uṭhi kahilā takhani
Mokṣadāre lakṣya kari. 'Ei se ramaṇī
devatāre sanpi diyā āpanār chele
curi kare niye yāy.' 'Dāo tāre phele'
ekvākye garji uṭhe tarāse niṣṭhur
yātrīsave. Kahe nārī, 'He dādāṭhākur,
rakṣā karo rakṣā karo.' Dui dṛḍhakare,
Rākhālere prāṇpaṇe vakṣe cāpi dhare.

The pilgrims threw overboard whatever they had—money and clothes and all, but to no avail. The waters again rushed fiercely on the boat.

'Listen before it is too late,' the boatman cried again. 'Who is it that is taking back what belongs to God?'

Suddenly the Brahmin rose and pointed to Mokṣadā, 'There's the woman who offered her child to God and is taking him back.' She had angrily said to her disobedient child that he would be thrown into the sea, but had not meant it.

Hearts merciless with fear, the pilgrims cried with one voice, throw him overboard.

'Save him, 'O save him,' cried Mokṣadā, clasping Rākhāl to her breast. 'Save him, *Thakur*, in the name of God save him.'

Imagine the situation:

Balite balite yata mili mājhi dāndi
bal kari Rākhālere nila chinḍi kāḍi
mār vakṣa hate. Maitra mudi dui ānkhi
phirāye rahila mukh kāne hāt ḍhāki.

Dante danta cāpi bale.
Ke tāre sahasā
marme marme āghātila vidyuter kaśā
daṁśila vṛścikdaṁśa. 'Māsi! Māsi! Māsi!'
bindhila vahnir śalā ruddha karṇe āsi
nirupāy anāther antimer ḍāk.
Citkāri uṭhila vipra Rākh rākh rākh.
'Phirāye āniba tore' kahi ūrdhvaśvāse
brāhmaṇ muhūrta mājhe jhānp dila jale
ār uṭhila nā. Sūrya gela astācale.

Even as she cried, the boatmen and the pilgrims tore Rakhal from her arms and threw him into the raging water. With set jaw and closed eyes, Maitra turned his face away, covering his ears with his hands.

'Aunt, O aunt,' screamed Rākhāl and suddenly Maitra felt lightning lash his heart. A hundred scorpions bit him as the helpless infant's last cry pierced into his ears like an arrow of fire.

'Hold! Hold!' the Brahmin shouted as his eyes rested for a moment on Mokṣadā who had fainted at his feet.

'I'll bring you [Rākhāl] back' cried the Brahmin and plunged headlong into the water.

Why did Maitra jump in the sea? This is an example of a true dilemma. But where Kauśika failed, Maitra succeeded. Here both truth and humanity have won. This probably approximates the 'ideal' resolution of the dilemma, by which I mean the *poetic* resolution of the dilemma. A truly religious man can transcend his so-called religious dogma and put moral concerns over narrowly religious ones.

2

Srī Rāmakṛṣṇa: Simplicity with Profundity

Srī Rāmakṛṣṇa Paramahaṃsa was a very unusual person. It is good to remember our 'Past Masters', to re-examine their teachings, their thought, if only to derive insights from such teachings in order to apply them to our present-day problems. That is why we celebrate centenaries, bicentenaries and 150 years. This is to remind us about the treasures of wisdom that we have inherited, but nevertheless might have forgotten. It is to make us self-conscious, in fact to arrest the drift.

I have said that Srī Rāmakṛṣṇa was a very unusual person. Using western terminology, people have called him 'a saint'. But he was not a saint in the usual Christian sense. He was in a sense 'illiterate'. But we have to change the definition of literacy (or illiteracy) if we really wish to apply the term 'illiterate' to describe him. He did not go to any college or university. He did not receive any formal education. But we cannot deny that he was a man of supreme intelligence. He was a man of wisdom. But, again, it was not the usual or even the Socratic kind of wisdom. It was wisdom for which the Sanskrit term *prajñā* is more suitable. It is more insight, not reasoned conclusions. He had a view of reality which was not necessarily metaphysical. Yet it was simple but profound enough to undervalue or devalue money, pleasures, power, fame and mundane happiness and at the same time enabled many to add meaning to their life.

He was a moral man, deeply committed to what was morally right or justified. He had an intuitive grasp of what was good or right. But in resolving the moral dilemmas of those who came to him he used to formulate moral arguments characterized by the same admirable qualities: simplicity and profundity. In fact, being in a sense an 'illiterate', he had the archangel's capacity to provide an exemplary moral reasoning in favour of what he considered good, just and fair. He was in a way an embodiment of Practical Reason.

Above all, he was committed to a deeply religious life. A religious life meant for him a life dedicated to the service of God, and to be dedicated to the service of God was spelled out for him as dedication to the service of suffering mankind. Within this type of simple ideal, religion and ethics melted into each other. What was ethical was also religious and what was religious was to some extent ethical. This also forces us to change the definition of 'religion'. Ethics and religion were indistinguishable in his teaching. To serve man is to serve God, and for God look no further. Kindness and compassion for the suffering humanity go hand in hand with godliness, or awareness of experiencing God's or the deity's or Kālī's, the mother's, compassion everywhere. If suffering is a fact of life, kindness or readiness of men to help each other in suffering is also a fact of life. Why should we accept one as more real than the other?

Some described him as the Vedānta Incarnate. He did not have any training or formal education in the intricacies of Vedānta philosophy. And yet, he was the embodiment of Vedānta. Of course he received some instruction in yoga and Vedānta much later in life. But that was like carrying coals to Newcastle, completely unnecessary.

Could we substantiate these claims? Let us try. His dialogues with others are recorded. They constitute an enormous body of literature. They are like the Sūtras of the Buddhist literature. They were simple, direct but profound. They supplied *ad hoc* and pragmatic resolutions of the situational paradoxes. A general notion of morality may not be developed out of these cases, but they certainly offer the challenge. Not all the problems of life are universal. They may of course be common or commonly shared by a few or many. Hence the pragmatic resolutions would not be universally valid, but they would certainly be applicable to a few or many as the case may be.

His untutored discussions were full of charm and poetic similes. One well-known Bengali author, Achintya Kumar Sengupta, compared his aptitude for simile with that of Kālīdāsa: *upamā Kālīdāsasya*—so goes the well-known Sanskrit adage, and it can also be said *upamā Rāmakṛṣṇasya*. (The title of a book about him was *Kavi Śrī Rāmakṛṣṇa.*) To use one of his similes to illustrate a difficult point of the Vedānta metaphysics: 'If a doll made of salt goes to measure the depth of the ocean, what will happen?' One may recall here that to measure is also to know, for in

Sanskrit the root *mā* means both to measure and to know. In Bengali, he also used the root *māpā*. Perhaps this was not a coincidence. It was suggestive—a *dhvani*. Raising the above question, he continued, 'Of course, the depth will never be measured in this way, for the depth is unmeasurable! Why? Because before the doll reaches the bottom to measure, its *salty* body will melt completely into the saline water of the ocean. And what will happen? In this way, there will be a complete loss of identity of the measurer (or knower) and total merging of the doll into the undifferentiated mass of water.' This is the merging of the individual identity into the undifferentiated mass of consciousness which is called Brahman. The line between the experience and the object of experience, sometimes called the subject-object duality, will be lost for ever. The agent, action and object will be in one unbroken line. The measurer, measuring and the object of measurement will melt into one whole unity. This is called Brahman experience. Can there be any simpler, any more direct, and at the same time any more convincing example than this one? It goes straight into the heart. It need not be filtered through the intellect because it is already filtered! A thousand lines of abstract philosophical discourse could be opaque to the readers. But this presentation, this explanation, is crystal clear. The doctrine of the dissolution of subject-object duality may sound enigmatic to a common man. But the simile dispels the enigma and even the common man can *see* the meaning of the doctrine.

Of many ethical dilemmas, let me talk about one at least, to illustrate Rāmakṛṣṇa's own way of resolving it. Today we talk about non-violence. Mahatma Gandhi is supposed to be a champion of this cardinal virtue. The recent success of the film *Gandhi* in the western world has revived the issue of non violence even in this nuclear age. Hence the issue is not entirely outdated. Nor is it irrelevant. This is perhaps one of the hardest principles to abide by, and yet it is implicitly or explicitly endorsed, recommended and glorified by most religious-ethical traditions of the world. 'Thou shalt not kill' is one of the principal commandments. We may universalize it to get rid of any sectarian tone. In the Buddhist prayer, the first *śikṣāpada*, the very first sentence is *pāṇātipātā veramaṇī sikkhāpadaṁ samādiyāmi*, which means 'we must by all means avoid taking life of others'. The Jainas are well-known extremists, and have in some modern quarters achieved some notoriety in observing the moral rule of non-violence (non-killing) in the strictest possible manner. It was noticed that the early Vedic religion encouraged religious violence by prescribing killing of sacrificial animals. Kumārila Bhaṭṭa tried to defend ritual violence (*vaidhī hiṁsā*). But others revolted. Later Hinduism, during its different sectarian movements and along with the rise of *bhakti* and Vaiṣṇavism, emphasized the glorious moral principle: *ahiṁsā paramo dharmaḥ* (non-violence is the best virtue). Even in the *Yoga-Sūtra*, one of the five cardinal virtues to be practised by a yogi is mentioned as *ahiṁsā* (non-violence).

But now let us examine. How can you respond only in a non-violent way when you are provoked, even attacked, by a violent enemy and your life is in danger? If somebody without provocation points a gun at you in order to kill, would you not be forced to adopt violent means in order to survive? Specially when peoples, countries, groups or individuals try to dominate and crush you with violent aggression, can you afford to be non-violent and non-aggressive? Sometimes, non-aggression and non-violence can be regarded as marks of weakness (maybe mistakenly so), and that will send an invitation to aggressors. The situation may be: Act with courage and respond with violence or you will be trampled and crushed. Of course, there is courage in remaining non-violent and taking punishment from the aggressors in order to show them that you refuse to play their game. And Gandhiji accepted this principle. But there are situations where this type of argument may not hold water. Once Gandhiji was confronted with such a question from Raychanbhai Mehta. It runs like this. Suppose a snake has come to bite me, shall I not kill it?

An idealistic answer was given in this way. Let the snake bite. Oh, maybe it is not poisonous and you will experience some pain but you will not die. It will be a small price to pay in order to save your life's principle of non-violence. Non-violence is after all a principle of life around which all your activities and thoughts will be interwoven. Or you may die because the snake is poisonous. But can you really give up your life's principle for fear of death? If you die for the sake of maintaining this glorious principle, you will certainly be better in your own life after death. From the Hindu point of view (and Gandhiji was a Hindu) one can say that you will have a better life in your *next birth*, for you are dying for a noble cause. It needs great courage to accept death in this way, and great moral courage is the most adorable (ethical) virtue on earth. Non-violence, in spite of its political overtone and past involvement, is not or need not be an instrument for achieving some goal, it is the goal itself. It is its own reward.

The above position has impeccable logic in its support. But it may be a bit unrealistic under the given circumstances. Sacrificing one's life for a noble cause is of course a good thing but voluntarily allowing a miserable creature to end your life is too uninviting to retain the quality of nobleness in the case under consideration. Hence another, more practical, answer is: Try to kill the snake and break your vow of non-violence for the moment. Although moral laws should be universalizable, prudential cosideration sometimes do impose limitations on an activity. Further, there are other considerations. If you can save your life even by this minimal act of violence (assuming the snake to be the embodiment of pure evil), you may be able to perform a lot of other-regarding activities and do good for others. It may sound presumptuous but it is possible that you are morally good and hence may dedicate the rest of your life to many moral, philanthropic and religious activities. For a Hindu believer there is the further argument that although killing is morally reprehensible, and you may be doing some *adharma* by killing this snake, all this will be more than compensated by your good acts afterwards. Your merit will outweigh your demerit. Such arguments seem to be given in utilitarian vein.

Srī Rāmakrṣṇa's moral intuition seems to suggest a possible third alternative, which is more pragmatic. His dialogues contain a slightly different story or parable but it is certainly relevant here. A snake was instructed by his guru to live a saintly life ('Change your evil nature, transform yourself into a saint, don't bite and kill others'). Giving such instructions, the guru went away. The snake became *non-violent*. Children started throwing stones at the snake; when it did not retaliate, they grew bold and started beating the snake severely. It was almost dead. The guru returned in the end. He asked 'What happened?' The snake, who was in great pain, replied, 'Sir, I followed your instruction. And this is the result.' The guru said, 'But why didn't you frighten them away at least. I told you not to harm them. But if they were harming you, you could have at least frightened them away. Your moral principle of non-violence would still be intact. And you would not have been half-dead as you are now. There are many ways to thread a needle (*upāya-kauśalya*)'. This is admittedly a pragmatic resolution.

I am not changing the point. If Srī Rāmakrṣṇa were told about the story that Gandhiji had to deal with, he could have said the following: 'Oh, there are many ways of getting rid of an attacking snake instead of killing it outright. Have you tried them all? Have you used all rational means to avoid breaking your vow of non-violence? As the above story of Srī Rāmakrṣna exemplifies, there may be other ways by which one can avoid final catastrophe—simple but practical advice, and a situational resolution of the conflict.

3

Moral Dilemmas: Insights from Indian Epics

1. INTRODUCTION

Dilemmas are like paradoxes. Genuine paradoxes are seldom solved. They are, generally speaking, resolved or dissolved. Those philosophers and logicians who have tried over the centuries to solve the well-known logical and semantical paradoxes, have more often than not created new problems elsewhere in the conceptual apparatus, which exposes the non-existence of a universally accepted solution. Paradoxes in other areas of knowledge have been more troublesome. Sometimes it has been conceded by people that paradoxes are what we learn to live with. Can moral dilemmas be put into the same category as those unsolvable paradoxes?

Theologians, ethicists and 'strong-minded' moral philosophers have often been reluctant to admit the reality of moral dilemmas; for if there can be genuine unsolvable moral dilemmas in a moral system, then it would be as good as courting defeat in our attempt to formulate rational moral theories. That is, it would be conceding inconsistency in a 'rational' moral system. It is assumed, therefore, that there must always be a right solution, a right path leading us out of the maze. Whether we can always find it or not, a solution exists. Moral dilemmas, on this view, are like ordinary mathematical puzzles, for which solutions are there, but we probably need a supermathematician to work them out.

It takes some courage to talk about moral dilemmas with regard to the great epic, the *Mahābhārata*. Indological scholars have often argued that Hindu orthodoxy would seldom agree that there are dilemmas in the teaching of the *Mahābhārata*. For is it not the case that Lord Kṛṣṇa is always in the *Mahābhārata* to play the role of the supermathematician and resolve the dilemmas for Arjuna? Is it not the case that Vidura is there to give the right kind of advice whenever the old, blind king Dhṛtarāṣṭra is in any dilemma, whether or note the blind kind, being blind in more sense than one, pays any heed to the well-meaning and ever-righteous brother? Does not the deity Dharma, natural father of Yudhiṣṭhira, have to appear in many different forms—a mongoose, a stork, a *vakṣa*—and so on—in order to instruct and teach Yudhiṣṭhira the right path whenever dilemmas have presented themselves? It would be improbable to argue, on such a view, that there could have arisen any genuine dilemmas in the *dharma*-ethical system that has been delineated in the *Mahābhārata*.

One may further argue that no dilemmas were left dangling or unresolved except perhaps the unique case of Draupadī's question in *Sabhāparvan*. The situation can be unmistakably pinpointed as the turning point of the entire story. It is uniquely described in the very beginning, the *Ādiparvan*, in *Dhṛtarāṣṭra-Vilāpa*:

> I did not hope for victory, O Sañjaya, when I heard poor Draupadī was dragged into the royal court with voice choked with tears wearing only a single piece of clothing. She had five husbands but still she was as if without protector and hence publicly humiliated.

But the question that Draupadī asked was more concerned with the rights or legality of her husband's action that with the morality of the situation. Did Yudhiṣṭhira, having first lost his own freedom (as well as the freedom of the four brothers) and thus becoming a slave of the Kauravas, have any right to gamble again with Draupadī as the stake? The question reveals an intricate point of law or the legal convention of the community, and also makes a social point, the point of a social rebel, presumably of a non-conformist. In the story, the question was met by either silence or side-long glances. Bhīṣma, the oldest of the Kauravas, only recognized that this was 'a very good point'; but was unable to answer it. Only Vikarṇa, an insignificant character, sided with Draupadī. Society still did not allow the wife any freedom or autonomy as an independent person. It regarded wives as 'properties' of husbands, which hence can be staked in a gambling match. The incident seems to have a deep significance. If Draupadī questions were properly answered, it would have required a 'paradigm shift' in India's social thought.

Both legal and social codes were designated by the pervasive term *dharma*, as were the moral principles or moral codes. The intentional ambiguity of the world *dharma*—its often-emphasized subtlety and ever-elusive nature (as Bhīṣma emphasized on this occasion)—is too well known to be mentioned here. Draupadī, on the other hand, was standing up for the rights and autonomy of the entire womanhood of that time, although she had to conform at the end, and the situation was saved by a miracle.

Let us take a close look at the dilemmas within the structure of the *dharma*-ethics as propounded in the epic. The main point, as I understand from the immense popularity and widespread discussion of such epic episodes, is to show that some of these moral dilemmas presented in the epic are illustrations of perennial problems in moral philosophy. Some of them have no satisfactory solution, although, in each case, an *ad hoc* practical action-guide was devised in the original story while the main problem remained unsolved. Over the ages we notice that various episodes and subplots of these epic stories have been retold with great ingenuity in various regional and vernacular versions of the epics, in folktales, plays, dramas, etc. Each new version may be regarded as a novel attempt to resolve the dilemma inherent in the original version. In what follows, I shall concentrate particularly upon certain aspects of the *Mahābhārata*.

2. THE *MAHĀBHĀRATA*: ITS GREATNESS

I shall start with a remark V.S. Sukthankar made in 1942: 'Whether we realize it or not, it remains a fact that we in India still stand under the spell of the *Mahābhārata*. There is many a different strand that is woven in the thread of our civilisation, reaching back into hoary antiquity.'[1] In the same lecture series, posthumously published, he called this epic a 'dateless and deathless poem . . . which forms the strongest link between India old and new' (ibid.). After forty-five years, I do not think we can in any way challenge or differ from this great scholar of our country.

The *Mahābhārata* is a unique creation of India, one of its kind which has no equal in world literature. Thanks to the laudable efforts of Peter Brooks, the story, the underlying unique human drama, has been staged in cities like Paris, New York and Glasgow in recent years with great success. Its popularity is no longer restricted to the geographical boundaries of India. This is the epic, which well-known Indological scholars like Hermann Oldenberg[2] and E. Washbrook Hopkins[3] have called 'the most monstrous chaos' of an epic narrative, 'a text that is not a text'. It represents a corpus of some 200,000 lines, eight times the size of the *Illiad* and the *Odyssey* put together, that has influenced and captivated the minds of almost all Indians for about two millennia. The puzzlement of the older

Indologists is understandable. Not only were the philological problems of their 'higher criticism' insuperable, and attempts to discover an *Ur-Mahābhārata* getting rid of everything else unsuccessful, but they seemed also to have seen the great paradoxes which this enormous text presents. It is, however, doubtful whether they really understood or enjoyed these paradoxes.

It suffices to say that, despite the untiring and life-long attempts of many worthy philologists and indologists, the 'epic nucleus' has never been discovered (unless we take the idiosyncratic solutions of some scholars at face value), for obviously a mere process of stripping off whatever one or the other scholar regards as interpolations cannot lead to a pure and unalloyed 'core' (peeling off onion skins does not lead to any core, as we all know). Besides, why should there be only one 'core' and not a multitude of 'cores' or sources from which this multifaceted cultural epic might have developed? Search for the original epic nucleus, in this case, may very well be like the search for the original, virgin meaning of the text, which, according to some post-structuralist philosophers, did not exist in a unified way even at the origin.

For my purpose, I would take the *Mahābhārata* as a whole, the text that the critical edition has given us after the pruning away of a lot of unnecessary overgrowths. And I shall deal with the moral issues as treated in various episodes and sub-plots of the epic. I have taken some time to convince myself that the great epics, apart from being the source of everything else, constitute an important component of what we may term as moral philosophical thinking of the Indian tradition. Certainly, there exists a lacuna in the tradition of Indian philosophy. Professional philosophers of India over the last two thousand years have been consistently concerned with the problems of logic and epistemology, metaphysics and soteriology, and sometimes they have made very important contributions to the global heritage of philosophy. But, except some cursory comments and some insightful observations, the professional philosophers of India have very seldom discussed what we call moral philosophy today. It is true that the *dharmaśāstra* texts were there to supplement the Hindu discussion of ethics, classification of virtues and vices, and enumeration of duties related to the social status of the individual. But morality was never discussed as such in these texts. On the other hand, the tradition itself was very self-conscious about moral values, moral conflicts and dilemmas, as well as about the difficulties of what we call practical reason or practical wisdom. This consciousness found its expression in the epic stories and narrative literature which can, therefore, be used for any illuminating discussion of moral philosophy in India. I propose to take this line of enquiry. The moral dilemmas presented in the *Mahābhārata* are in some sense universal, for most of them can be effectively used even today to illustrate arguments in moral philosophy.

Before I proceed any further I wish to make another point about my attitude towards the text of the *Mahābhārata*. Indologists have often distinguished between the narrative material and the didactic material in the epic. The implicit idea was that the didactic material was added to the narrative material and sometimes the narrative to the didactic, so that modern scholarship could separate one from the other. This seems to me a very artificial distinction as far as the text of the *Mahābhārata* is concerned. The so-called narrative and didactic material are found inextricably fused together in the text, such that often they cannot be differentiated. Sometimes the narrative itself imparts the moral lesson without any deliberate efforts on the part of the narrator. In other words, the medium itself is the message here.

3. WHAT IS A MORAL DILEMMA?

Let me first explain what I mean here by the term moral dilemma. A shallow critic might say: 'Well, since there was no concept of morality in Sanskrit, except "only a strict status compartmentalization of private and social ethics" (Max Weber),[4] how can there be moral dilemmas?' This was, however, not exactly the view of Max Weber. What I take here to be a view of the shallow critic can be regarded as a hypothetical construal of an opponent's view, a *pūrvapakṣa*. It is true, however, that morality is not an Indian term and its Sanskrit equivalent is not easy to find. The nearest that you can get is to use the rather ubiquitous and enigmatic term *dharma*. However, the basic assumption of the above question is wrong, for one cannot argue that, if a particular term was not used in a particular tradition, then the social or political reality denoted by the term would not also exist in that tradition. For, in that case, one might as well argue that, since the term 'religion' did not have a Sanskrit equivalent in ancient India, the social reality that you call religion did not exist in ancient or classical India.

Moral dilemmas are, in fact, very common in everyday life. Stories in classical and contemporary literature are full of such cases. Most moral dilemmas seem to remain unresolved in such stories. Very roughly, such dilemmas arise when the agent is committed to two or more moral obligations, but circumstances are such that an obligation to do *x* cannot be fulfilled without violating an obligation to do *y*. Dilemmas present irreconcilable alternatives, and the actual choice among them becomes either irrational or is based upon grounds other than moral. Moral philosophers have generally denied that such dilemmas are even possible, for an adequate moral theory is supposed to resolve such dilemmas; that is to say, it will show that such dilemmas are not genuine. In fact, today we may say that moral philosophers are divided into camps: those who think that such dilemmas are not genuine and those, a tiny minority, who think that such dilemmas are both possible and actual.

Some ethicist-philosophers believe that there are probably readymade recipes for avoiding conflicts in the moral domain. But the question is whether such recipes are available when needed. There is no easy answer. Besides, weakness of the will plays an important role in the agent's final decision-making procedure. Can we think of two types of genuine dilemma? In the case of one, what ought to be done has remained unsettled for the agent even when he has considered all the relevant information *known* to him in the situation. If we regard our weakness of will as incontinence *à la* Davidson, then we believe that, if the deemed informational constraint is removed, the dilemma will dissolve. But this is conceded to be only a matter of hope.

According to another type, what ought to be done remains unsettleable even after the exercise of all rational means. Here, if the informational constraints are removed, it may not help the decision. Philosophical controversies have been more interesting when they arise around this second type of dilemma. My concern is primarily with the second type.

I personally believe that certain moral dilemmas are genuine, and also that the occurrence of such dilemmas does not present any problem for moral realism. I shall not argue for these views here, but refer to other philosophers who have maintained such positions. My purpose here is to discuss certain striking and stimulating examples to be found in the great epics of India, specially in the *Mahābhārata*. My analysis will show that they were genuine dilemmas, and also that traditional wisdom, as I have emphasized, maintained an ambivalent attitude towards the ad hoc resolutions described in the ancient texts. Sometimes the same episodes were retold throughout the ages in plays, poems and in different local versions of the epics. In these later versions, the ad hoc resolutions of the dilemmas were differently conceived, which probably reflects the changing pattern of the social ethos of the narrator's time.

4. A TYPICAL CASE IN THE EPIC

A typical case of moral dilemma is presented by Arjuna's question at the beginning of the *Bhagavad Gītā*. Was Arjuna faced with a genuine moral dilemma? I shall come back to the question later on. Let us take another clear case of moral dilemma in an episode in the *Karṇaparvan*. Arjuna was faced with a choice between two irreconcilable obligations: promise-keeping and avoidance of fratricide. The incident that led to this is the following. On the very day of final encounter between Karṇa and Arjuna, Yudhiṣṭhira fled the battlefield after being painfully humilated by Kṛṣṇa in an armed engagement. When Arjuna came to the camp to pay a visit to him and asked what really had happened, Yudhiṣṭhira flared up in anger and told Arjuna that all his boastfulness about being the finest archer in the world was a lot of nonsense, because the war was dragging on. He reminded Arjuna that he had claimed to be capable of conquering everybody and thus end the war within a few days. In a rage, he not only insulted Arjuna but also slighted the *Gāṇḍīva bow*, the most precious possession of this valiant warrior. The bow was a gift to Arjuna from Agni, the fire-god. He held it so dear to his heart that he had promised to kill anyone who would ever speak ill of it. Hence Yudhiṣṭhira's words put Arjuna in a very difficult situation: either he would have to kill his venerated elder brother or break his promise. When his Kṣatriya duty (*dharma*) made him choose the first alternative, Kṛṣṇa (his *alter ego*) appeared. On being asked Arjuna explained: he was obliged to commit fratricide in order to fulfil his obligation to keep his promise. Arjuna had full knowledge of the gravity of the crime he was about to commit but like a *mistimed* Kantian he had already taken a conflict-free decision to meet the Kṣatriya obligation of promise-keeping. A quotation from Kant's *Introduction to the Metaphysics of Morals* (1797) may be relevant here:

> Because . . . duty and obligation are in general concepts that express the objective practical necessity of certain actions and because two mutually opposing rules cannot be necessary at the same time, then if it is a duty to act according to one of them, it is not only not a duty but contrary to duty to act according to the other.[5]

For Kant it seems that the objective rules should form a harmonious whole, a system characterized by consistency, much like a system of true beliefs. The moral conflict, which no doubt arises in the minds of moral agents, cannot, therefore, be genuine. It would be at best a confusion, at worst an illusion. It conflates, according to Kant, a genuine duty with a *ground* of that duty. Hence, in a so-called dilemma, one horn is a genuine duty, and the other is merely a ground of duty. There may be conflict between grounds but not between duties. Hence, in Kantian ethics, no agent can be forced to violate his duty. This is at least one of the interpretations of Kantian thought. Hence Arjuna might be said to be anticipating the Kantian model.

Kṛṣṇa, however, was not Kant. When he intercepted and started a discourse with Arjuna, he obviously turned an apparently moral conflict into a genuine moral dilemma. Promise-keeping is, indeed, a strong obligation. Plato is supposed to have described a typical case of dilemma, in which the return of a cache of arms has been promised to a man who, intent on starting mayhem, comes to claim them. Conflict was generated here by two opposing principles, that of promise-keeping and that of benevolence.[6] In fact, promise-keeping is regarded as equivalent to truth-telling. In Sanskrit, promise-keeping is sometimes classed as 'protecting the truth' (*satya-rakṣā*). Hence, both in India and the West, the two obligations are invariably connected. There is no cultural relativism here. In Kantian ethics, truth-telling gets the highest priority. Kṛṣṇa, however, continued to argue that promise-keeping or even truth-telling cannot be an unconditional obligation when it is in conflict with the avoidance of grossly unjust and criminal acts such as patricide or fratricide. Saving an innocent life is also a strong obligation, saving the life of an elder brother would naturally be an equally strong obligation, if not stronger. Hence, in fact, according to Kṛṣṇa, two almost equally strong obligation or duties are in conflict here.

5. KṚṢṆA'S STORY TO SUPPORT HIS ARGUMENT

Kṛṣṇa related a story to illustrate his point. A hermit, Kauśika by name, once took a vow of telling the truth throughout his life. One day he faced the following dilemma. Some bandits were chasing several travellers with the intention of killing them. Kauśika was sitting nearby at the crossroad. The travellers passed by, and requested him not to show the miscreants which way they had fled. Kauśika did not answer. Soon the bandits arrived, and, knowing that the hermit would not lie, asked him about the travellers; and Kauśika told the truth. As a result, the travellers were caught and killed. Kṛṣṇa added that Kauśika did not reach heaven after his death (his much-coveted reward) just because of this act of cruelty. Although he abided by his principle of truth-telling throughout his life, it came to no effect. The major point was that, under situational constraints, there might be stronger grounds for rejecting truth-telling as a duty and accepting the stronger duty of saving an innocent life. This encapsulates a very strong moral insight, although it is not Kantian.

For Kṛṣṇa, *dharma* is at least sometimes dictated by the constraints or the contingency of the situation (*Āvasthika, Mahābhārata*, xii, 36.2). But this is no defence of opportunism. Truth-telling has been extolled as one of the highest virtues in the tradition. We should not have any illusion, despite frequent criticisms to the contrary, that the tradition of the *dharmaśāstras* or the religious texts of India underplayed the importance of truth-telling as a virtue and a value. *Āpastaṃbha* says plainly that every perjurer goes to hell. Thus, there does not seem to be any religious, textual or *dharmaśāstric* support for sweeping comments such as 'all Hindoos are compulsive liars' (Lord Curzon). But it must be admitted that excusable untruths were permitted by such writers of *dharmaśāstras* as Gautama and Manu. Thus, perjury to save life was permitted as a *dharma*. Hence Kṛṣṇa's story is compatible with the general dictum of *dharmaśāstras* (*dharma*-ethics).

6. KṚṢṆA AND R.M. HARE

There are several intricate issues of moral philosophy that can be discussed here in connection with this epic story. There are those philosophers who admit the factuality of moral dilemmas and insist that our commitment to consistency would require us to modify the system by reordering priorities or by discarding certain principles. For example, R.M. Hare believes that our moral precept, 'do not lie', can be reformulated in light of wartime experience as 'do not lie except to the enemy in time of war', which will be the more adequate principle and make the system consistent by resolving a conflict situation.[7] Alternatively, moral conflicts can be resolved with a 'higher' type of critical thinking. Hare has distinguished between two types of cases: the intuitive perception or the intuitive level of thinking done by one whom he calls 'the Prole', and the critical level of thinking done by a more exemplary figure whom he calls 'the Archangel'. Oddly enough, this may just fit the episode described in the *Mahābhārata*. It is tempting to say that Arjuna was acting like 'the Prole', while Kṛṣṇa intervened and became 'the Archangel'. Hare's system acknowledges progressive revision of our moral principles in the light of conflict situations that are bound to arise. It may be suitable to some extent to regard Kṛṣṇa as an anachronistic exemplar of the Harean model. But I believe the problems we face at various stages of the epic are much deeper than what would fit such simple explanations.

7. KṚṢṆA AND SARTRE

Jean-Paul Sartre gives a striking example of practical conflict where a young man must choose between his patriotic duty to join the French

Resistance and his filial obligation to care for his aging mother.[8] Sartre, like Hare, acknowledges the reality of this conflict, but uses such *hard* cases as evidence to draw the conclusion that it is useless for a moral agent to form an ordered system of ethical principles and to try to live by it. The agent, according to Sartre, is *condemned to be free*. Sartre takes man to be *condemned*, because 'he did not create himself'; yet he is *free*, because 'from the moment that he is thrown into this world he is responsible for everything he does'. He, therefore, should use his radical liberty, and improvise his choice according to the situation without regret or remorse. In the *Mahābhārata* episode, we again see a resonance of the Sartrean advice in Kṛṣṇa's advice to Arjuna. Kṛṣṇa said to Arjuna, after relating the story of Kauśika, that Arjuna, unlike Kauśika, must not regret his failure to keep the promise when the concrete situation would otherwise require him to commit fratricide. Again, in the *Gītā*, a Sartrean reading of Kṛṣṇa is possible, but perhaps we should avoid the temptation. The situation is comparable in respect of the recommendation of the unregretted choice to be reached (*māsucaḥ*) but not so, as far as the complete rejection of the search for a consistent ethical system is concerned. Kṛṣṇa also would not say that humans are *condemned* to be free. Sartre's example has been much discussed by others. Sartre himself says that the agent is 'hesitating between two kinds of morality' (*Speech Act*, p. 296), which neither Christian doctrine nor Kantian ethics can help him resolve.

8. SUBTLETY OF DHARMA-ETHICS: DHARMA AND LUCK

Let us discuss some details of the *Mahābhārata* episode. Kṛṣṇa emphasized the fact that it is very difficult but not impossible to understand the extremely subtle ways of *dharma* or duty (*dharmāṇāṃ gatiṃ, śūkṣmaṃ duranvayam*).[9] He also said that even Bhīṣma or Vidura or Kunti would have been able to resolve the dilemma for Arjuna. To sum up Kṛṣṇa's argument:

> It is true that truth-telling is the highest virtue but there are mitigating circumstances such as destruction of innocent lives and loss of all possessions under which to tell a lie may be a duty ('where telling a lie may be as good as "truth" and truth-telling may be as good as lying').[10]

Before telling the story of Kauśika, Kṛṣṇa told another story about an innocent hunter called Balāka. Balāka used to hunt animals to feed his blind parents. He was innocent and simple-hearted. But he had a rare skill. He could hunt an animal even when it was outside the range of his sight, simply by listening to the noise made by the animal drinking water from a river. One day, by chance, he hunted in this manner a ferocious creature called Andha. But as soon as Andha was killed, gods showered flowers from heaven, and the celestial chariot came to fetch Balāka to heaven. Why? For Balāka unknowingly did a great service to the lord's creation, because this Andha had grown up to be a terrible creature who was almost unkillable. Having received a boon from Lord Brahmā, he went on killing all the creatures. He was in a way out to destroy all creatures. Although Balāka was unaware of this fact, he was somehow able to kill this evil creature, and thereby obtained his just reward. This story sounds like the case of 'moral luck'. The goodness of a good human life is not always dependent on the things that the moral agent can control. There is 'external contingency' or luck coming to the agent from the word which is not under his control. But this contingency cannot be totally eliminated. Sometimes such contingencies would generate moral dilemmas, for the agent. Balāka was a good person in his own modest way, but external contingencies made his moral reward far greater than what he had dreamt of. By contrast Kauśika had a project for life which included the covetable moral reward, heaven, but external contingencies intervened and Kauśika was faced with a situation in which he was forced to act. But, according to Kṛṣṇa's ethical system, he acted stupidly, and chose the alternative that ruined his dream totally. Kṛṣṇa said that although Kauśika wanted to do his duty (*dharmakāmaḥ*), he was unwise (*apaṇḍita*) and a fool (*mūḍha, Mahābhārata*, 8.49.32).

9. TYPES OF CONFLICT: MORAL AND NON-MORAL

We have to discuss a whole spectrum of cases where some conflict of duties invariably arises; but, as we all know, some conflicts are more serious than others, for not all conflicts of duties can be raised to the status of a moral dilemma. Let us note four types of case where conflict arises. In all cases, the agent wants to do *x* as well as *y*; but, since both cannot be done because of contingencies of circumstances, he does *x* and foregoes *y*.

CASE 1 : What is foregone, that is, *y*, is a reward or a possession.

CASE 2 : *y* may be simply an omission or failure to pursue a desired project. (Let us note two subvarieties, at least.)

CASE 2*a* : When the desired project is not central to the agent's final commitment in life, that is, it is a luxury.

Case 2*b* : When the desired project is central to the agent's final commitment in life.

Case 3 : When *y* is something that, if it is not done, the omission is harmful. Two subvarieties again.

Case 3*a* : When it is harmful to the agent.

Case 3*b* : When it is harmful to others.

Case 4 : When non-doing of *y* does harm to the agent or to others, but is reparable.

Both epics, the *Rāmāyaṇa* and the *Mahābhārata*, are full of episodes which would present conflict situations of one or the other kind. The above list is not exhaustive.[11] However, it can help our discussion of the Kauśika incident as well as the dilemma that was faced by Arjuna. Was Kauśika faced with a real moral dilemma? I believe opinions will vary. If Kauśika belonged to our case 1, one would hardly think that it was a moral dilemma. In fact, one would say that it should have been more moral for him to save the lives of others even by foregoing his reward in heaven. This would be similar to the case where the captain of the ship throws his valuable cargo into the ocean in order to save the lives of the passengers.

How about case 2? Kauśika may properly belong here. He had a life-plan, a project that was central to his life. So his case would be similar to case 2*b*, for truth-telling was central to his life-plan. Would he then be justified in foregoing this duty so central to his life-plan, and tell a lie to save travellers? Is this what Kṛṣṇa's ethics demanded? It is not difficult to see, in this case, that Kauśika had a genuine dilemma, and that that dilemma was moral. If truth-telling was only peripheral to Kauśika's life-plan, that is, if he belonged to our case 2*a*, then, of course, one could easily say that Kauśika chose the wrong alternative from a moral point of view. But case 2*b* makes the conflict more evenly balanced. Hence a theory of ranking the alternative becomes necessary. Kṛṣna's ethics demanded such ordering of priorities. It was said by Kṛṣṇa that, according to him, saving the lives of the creatures should get the highest priority (*prāṇinām avadhas tāta sarvajyāyān mato mama, Mahābhārata*, 8.249.20 cr. ed.). He clearly ranked the value of saving a life higher than telling the truth. Here Krṣna clearly deviated from Kant, or even from the ideal that was sometimes upheld by Rāma in the *Rāmāyaṇa*. In other words, anachronistically speaking, Rāma was more Kantian. But I believe Kṛṣṇa's ethics had a concern for a richer scheme of values, moral or non-moral, presupposing a very complex societal and familial structure. It also envisions a society when saving innocent lives has a higher priority.

10. KṚṢṆA AND KANT

When Kant asserted that truth-telling should unconditionally get the highest priority, it is interesting to note that an example was cited which was similar to the Kauśika story of Kṛṣṇa. A contemporary French philosopher criticized it and said that if a murderer had been chasing a person who had taken shelter in the house of a moral agent, it would not be the obligation of the agent to tell the truth to the murderer. Kant, in reply, argued that truth-telling would be an unconditional obligation, and, therefore, the contingency of the situation should not affect it at all.[12] Kant, however, made some comments in the appendix of his *Critique of Practical Reason* which are worth mentioning. Kant argued that truth-telling, in that case, would not necessarily lead to murder. For it might not have been easy for the murderer to locate the person who was hiding. Or the victim might have fled by the back door. Or, when the murderer would be searching for the victim, the police or other neighbours might rush in as a group to stop the murderer and arrest him. These remarks of Kant are of interest to us, for they show that even a great philosopher like Kant was trying to find a way out of the tight corner which had arisen as the combined result of his rigid ethical principle and sound logical reason.

Our case 3*a* would also be easy to decide, if we believed in the notion of morality that is concerned with other-regarding actions. For example, Kauśika had actually four choices open to him. He could (*i*) tell a lie, (*ii*) remain silent, (*iii*), courageously tell the bandits that he would not help them; and (*iv*) tell the truth (which he did). He would have saved an innocent life, if he followed any one of the first three choices. By lying he would have to accept some harm coming to him, that is, moral culpability. But he had desired heaven. Hence this adherence to truth may not be a genuine moral stance. For, according to some philosophers today, the moral claim is a claim that cannot be avoided even by eliminating desires.[13] If he had eliminated his desire for heaven, he would have lied to save innocent lives, for that would then have been his *moral* obligation.

The second or the third choice would have been more risky, but they were morally more attractive, for a great deal of moral courage would have been necessary. The Davidsonian idea of weakness of the will as 'incontinence' might supply a relevant point here. The bandits might have tortured the hermit, if he remained silent or explicitly refused to tell them the truth. Kṛṣṇa himself refers to such alternatives. He says that, if, under such circumstances, one could get away by remaining silent, one should remain silent.[14] But if one saw that one could not remain silent, it would be better for one to lie and mislead the miscreants.[15] The third choice, however, seems to be morally the most attractive one. But this also takes account of the moral character of the agent himself. A person must be ready to accept inhuman torture to save the lives of others. This would have pleased a Kantian. The Kantian ethic says that we must never regard another person as a means but always as an end. Hence it is difficult to see how by telling the truth Kauśika avoided treating the travellers as means. For the same reason, it is difficult to see how truth-telling as a duty can never be subject to external contingency.

11. KṚṢṆA'S RESOLUTION: REMORSE AND REGRET

If Kauśika had chosen the third way, he could have been tortured to death by the bandits. But this would have been at least a moral victory. Giving up one's life to save the lives of others was also regarded as the highest virtue in the epic tradition of India, as other epic episodes such as that of Dadhīci would clearly show.

Case 4 needs some further comments. It seems to be particularly relevant to our epic story, where breaking a promise may be *reparable*. It is somewhat amusing to note that, when Arjuna was not only regretful but also remorseful, having foregone his obligation for truth-keeping or promise-keeping, Kṛṣṇa suggested that this omission was reparable. When Arjuna promised to *kill* the person who would insult his *Gāṇḍīva* bow, he was obviously not thinking of Yudhiṣṭhira as his victim. Now, since Yudhiṣṭhira was the intended victim who was also his revered elder brother, he could even keep his promise without actually killing him physically. Since insult and harsh words to such an elder brother would be as good as killing him in spirit, Arjuna could now insult Yudhiṣṭhira and use harsh words, and thus keep his promise. This type of 'face-saving' solution was suggested by Kṛṣṇa and accepted by Arjuna. A childish solution to the problem posed by a childish sort of promise! But I do not think the semantic issue raised by Kṛṣṇa can be totally ignored, even when he acknowledged its levity; for a promise-maker has to articulate his promise in the sentence of some natural language, where the relevant semantic rules must apply. And, according to a prevailing philosophical view, the intention of the speaker is also a factor for determining the meaning of a sentence.[16] Apart from the levity, we must also note that truth-keeping was not given up as a moral obligation for a person like Arjuna. I believe the dilemma has not been trivialized here. The moral agent's sentiment as well as his commitment have rather been respected. What was recoverable is salvaged from the conflict.

According to modern philosophers, genuine moral dilemmas generate what may be called the 'tragic cases' which are characterized by remorse or guilt which the agents experience after having acted in conflict situations. This feeling of *guilt* must be genuine, and it must be distinguished from the feeling of simple *regret*. We have seen that those who want to deny the reality of moral dilemmas would deny such moral sentiments on the part of moral agents. But, in the case of genuine dilemma, the agent, while doing *x* would be invariably overwhelmed with a feeling of remorse for not doing *y*. Hence, in a moral system, which acknowledges moral dilemmas, such moral sentiments are unavoidable, and neither of the conflicting obligations is permanently given up. The obligation that is overridden is only rendered temporarily ineffectual by the constraints of the particular situation. Arjuna had his share of remorse both in the beginning of the battle of Kurukṣetra and here. Hence the system that is outlined here makes room for genuine moral dilemmas with the attendant moral sentiments, remorse, regret and so on as I have tried to show above. Hence I believe there was a genuine moral dilemma at the beginning of the *Gītā* with which Arjuna was confronted. But this is not the place to enter into this issue.

12. CONCLUSION

The nature of our practical wisdom has a sort of malleability, which is comparable to the ever-elusive nature of *dharma*-ethics to be found in our epic literature. It has been said that *dharmasya tattvaṃ nihitaṃ guhāyām* (the truth of *dharma* lies in the dark cave). It cannot be completely known by us as universally fixed. But the acknowledgment of possible flexibility does not mean that the fixity and universality of ethical laws will be entirely negotiable. Situational constraints may require some bending, but by allowing genuine moral sentiments like remorse or guilt it makes up for occasional lapses. A moral agent exercises his practical wisdom, and also learns from the experiences he passes through during his life. He has an *enriched* practical wisdom when it is informed by his experiences of genuine moral dilemmas. A moral agent needs also a character which is nothing but a disposition to act and react appropriately with moral concerns. His later desires would be informed by the experiences he passes through, and he would, therefore, react appropriately when confronted with further moral dilemmas. This is the kind of moral insight that can be derived from a scrutiny of the Kṛṣṇa-ethics in the *Mahābhārata*.

In our review of the history of moral thought of mankind as a whole, we usually come across two different types of moral persons as paradigmatic. One is the dutiful fulfiller of universal obligations *à la* Kant. In India, we have Rāma whose moral ideals would fall into this category. The nature of *dharma* idealized by Rāma (or Yudhiṣṭhira) seems to have been very rigid. It seldom bends. The other paradigmatic person we meet in the moral field can be described as an imaginative poet. He becomes a perspectivist and understands the contingency of the human situation. He realizes the necessity of 'paradigm shifts' much like the revolutionary scientists in Thomas Kuhn's description of the nature of scientific revolutions.[17] He looks at the particularity of the situation but also looks beyond it. He is our Kṛṣṇa. So Kṛṣṇa allows for flexibility in *dharma*. But this flexibility never means the 'anything goes' kind of morality. He is the *poet* who accepts the constraints of metres, verses and metaphors. But he is also the strong poet who has absolute control over them. He uses metres, verses and metaphors to produce the music which you cannot but admire. He governs from above but does not dictate.

It is interesting to note that, towards the end of the nineteenth century, there was an important dispute on this very issue between Bankimchandra Chattopadhyay and Rabindranath Tagore wherein Bankimchandra supported the ethics of Kṛṣṇa and commented that truth-telling cannot be an unconditional value. Young Rabindranath, however, protested and said that this only showed how devious a follower of Kṛṣṇa would have to be. The arguments and counter-arguments of these two stalwarts rolled on for a while in the pages of the contemporary Bengali periodicals. It was young Rabindranath who somewhat unconsciously supported a Kantian moral stance. Both agreed that the third alternative (Kauśika saying, 'I know but I'll not tell you') would have been the best. A few years later, another story was reported in the gossip column of a Calcutta newspaper which concerned another famous man, a professor belonging to the Brahmo Samāj, Heramba Maitra. Apparently, he was asked by a traveller about the location of the Star Theatre. But since he morally disapproved of what went on in the Star Theatre, his first reaction was to say that he did not know. When he realized that this was a lie, he came back, called the traveller and told him: 'Look, I know where the Star Theatre is but I will not tell you.' All this shows how concerned our present-day moral thinking still is with the dilemmas presented in the traditional epics.

Notes and References

1. V.S. Sukthankar, *On the Meaning of the Mahābhārata*, Asiatic Society, Bombay, 1957, p. 32. Lectures delivered in 1942 at the University of Bombay.
2. Herman Oldenberg, *Die Literatur Des Alten Indien*, J.G. Cotta, Stuttgart and Berlin, 1903.
3. E. Washbrook Hopkins, *The Great Epic of India*, Yale University Press, New Haver, 1901.
4. Max Weber, *Wirtschaft und Gesellschaft*, Krepenheur & Witsch, Colonge and Berlin, 1964, 1, p. 366.
5. Immanuel Kant, *Groundwork to the Metaphysics of Morals*, academi edn., p. 293.
6. See R.B. Marcus, 'Moral Dilemma and Consistency' in *Journal of Philosophy*, 77 (1980), pp. 121–36.
7. R.M. Hare, *The Language of Morals*, Clarendon Press, Oxford, 1986.
8. J.P. Sartre, *L'Existentialisme est un humanisme.* My reference is from Walfer Kaufman, *Existentialism*, Beaconi Press, Boston, 1959, p. 295.
9. The *Mahābhārata* (critical edn., various editor, Bhandarkar Oriental Research Institute, Poona, 1928–70.
10. Ibid., 8.49.29.
11. Most of these varieties are noted in Martha Nussbaum's *The Fragility of Goodness*, Cambridge University Press, Cambridge, 1986, pp. 27–50. In what follows I have derived several points from her book to illuminate my discussion and analysis of the Indian epic stories.
12. See Immanuel Kant, *Critique of Practical Reason* (Abbott's translation), Appendix, pp. 361–3.
13. See B. Williams, *Problems of the Self*, Cambridge University Press, 1973, pp. 166–86.
14. *Mahābhārata*, 8.49.51.
15. Ibid., 8.49.52.
16. In many ordinary situations in our life we use the word 'kill' loosely in a wider sense. For example, a mother may tell the child, 'If you do this, I will kill you.' This, of course, leads to the problem of literal versus metaphorical uses of the word—an intricate issue which I do not wish to enter into here. This may also not be relevant to the context.
17. For a clear notion of 'paradigm shifts', see Thomas Kuhn's *The Structure of Scientific Revolutions*, University of Chicago Press, 1962. However, I am using the term in an extended sense.

4

Elusiveness and Ambiguity in *Dharma*-Ethics

It has been asserted by some writers, such as F.S.C. Northrop (1946), that, in Asia, religions, aesthetics and ethics—all have remained well-integrated. This seems to be a positive appreciation. The same point may be negatively put as a devastating criticism. For those who have been used to the modern 'analytic' method, to sharp distinctions, precision and exactitude, it can and sometimes has been said that the Asian or the Indian mind lacks the power of sharply distinguishing one concept from another. The blurring of concepts is then either a case of muddled thinking, or evidence of the survival of some 'primitive' or 'infantile' stage, where everything was 'entangled' with every other thing (and not *integrated*, as Northrop put it). The matter can be nicely put as an exclamation the echo of which I once found in the statement of a first-year Western student of Sanskrit: 'Oh, Sanskrit is a wonderful language—every word has its own meaning, plus it means sometimes its opposite, plus it is also a name for God, Brahman!' Thus, what is identified as a serious flaw from one point of view can be regarded as an admirable trait from another.

Northrop himself was after a contrast; besides, he was conscious that from the point of view of synthetic visions, the integration of religions, ethics and aesthetics may constitute a better alternative towards human understanding. Part of the problem is connected with translatability or interpretability of concepts across cultural boundaries. Must we not all speak the same language, if we are to understand each other and deal with each other? The unfortunate fact is that we do not, and there may be or might have been something providential about it, as the Tower of Babel story indicates. Linguistic compartmentalization is only the tip of the iceberg which is cultural compartmentalization. The question, however, is not one of lumping together, or non-separation, in some so-called infantile culture, of a number of concepts found to be distinct, separate and well-articulated in some other cultures, for that would be getting the matter upside down. The problem is one of coming to terms with incommensurability or under-commensurability of certain concepts between cultures; each seems to be characterized by a set of interrelated concepts, not always matched by the other.

Dharma is an intelligible concept on its home ground, in spite of its ubiquity, ambiguity and multivalent character. It makes sense in relation to other interrelated concepts, such as *artha, karma, duḥkha, kāvya* and *rasa*. In various contexts, the word *dharma* may mean: law, justice, custom, morality, ethics, religion, duty, nature, or virtue. Yet it is not usually regarded as a homonym. This almost breathtaking complexity (and, I venture to add, richness) of the *dharma*-concept seems to underline links between ways of living, ways of seeing and ways of relating to life's ultimate issues. It may be puzzling, even repulsive, to one used to an atomistic and compartmentalized view of life. And yet one cannot be entirely dismissive of it by calling it a muddle, or regarding it as something totally unintelligible and thereby giving support to a pernicious form of relativism. For undoubtedly there seem to be prominent family resemblances among the set of terms listed above as possible translations of *dharma* in different contexts. And if we believe Wittgenstein, and are permitted also to read him backwards, this family resemblance would offer us enough grounds for justifying the use of the same term for a variety of different items.

'*Dharma* is', P.V. Kane writes in the beginning of his monumental work, *History of Dharmaśāstra*, 'one of those Sanskrit words that defy all attempts at an exact rendering in English or any other tongue' (1930, p. 1). Kane adds another comment in this connection: 'That word has passed through several vicissitudes' (ibid.). Although this is generally true of many important key terms of Indian culture (*karma, Brahman, saṃsāra, niyatī*, etc.), perhaps it is more true of the word *dharma*. Its meaning has changed over the ages from the Vedic period up to the present day. The difficulty of translation is no less caused by such fluctuations in the meanings, nuances, contextual connotations of the original term.

Perhaps the etymology of the word *dharma* will be of some help here in unfolding the meaning of the term. It is from the root *dhṛ*, meaning 'up hold, support, sustain' (*dhṛ dhāraṇa-poṣaṇayoḥ*). So the meaning would be 'that which upholds and sustains.' But this is too general and hence too vague to be useful. It does not take us very far, thus proving the truth of the grammarians' dictum that established meaning must take precedence over etymological meaning.

The word is found in the *Ṛg-Veda* (I.187.1) and *Atharva-Veda*. There it might have meant 'merit acquired by the performance of (religious) rituals'. In the *Aitareya Brāhmaṇa* (xi.9.17), the expression *dharmasya goptā* 'protector of *dharma*' is used, and *dharma* might here mean the whole body of ritual prescribed by the scriptures. In *Chāndogya Upaniṣad* (2.23.1) three groups of *dharma* are mentioned: rituals (*yajña*), study of the scriptures (*adhyayana*) and austerities (*tapas*). *Vedāntasūtra* (III.4.18–20) refers to this passage and discusses it. In the famous 'convocation' instruction, *satyaṃ vada dharmaṃ cara*, it must have meant both duties and obligations of a man in a ritualistic society. It gradually came to mean man's standard of conduct, his religious-ethical duties, and other principles by which one should live as a member of the prevalent society.

A question lurks at this point. The philosophical texts of classical India (*darśanas*) had, unlike their Greek counterparts, surprisingly precious little to say about moral philosophy, although they had plenty to say on epistemology, logical theories and metaphysics. Why? The answer may be very simple if it comes from a follower of Max Weber's sociology of religion. He wrote in *The Religion of India* (English trans. 1958, p. 144).

> There was no universally valid ethic, but only a strict status compartmentalization of private and social ethic, disregarding the few absolute and general ritualistic prohibitions (particularly the killing of cows). This was of great moment. The doctrine of *karma* deduced from the principle of compensation for previous deeds in the world, not only explained the caste organization but the rank order of divine, human, and animal beings of all degree. Hence it provided for the coexistence of different ethical codes for different status groups which not only differed widely but were often in sharp conflict.

However, this is both simplistic and wrong. Even Manu, that celebrated champion of group-relative virtues and ethical relativism, and even a philosopher like Praśastapāda, talked about a number of universal virtues and ethical duties of all human beings (*sādhāraṇa-dharma*), which did reveal something like a universal ethic (and prohibition of cow-slaughter was not among them). A more informed answer should take account of the complexity of the matter. The tradition in India was extremely self-conscious about moral conflicts and disputes about ethical principles, commitments and priorities, and moral emotions, love, passion and self-control. This becomes crystal clear once we look at the great epics and other narrative literature. What philosophers failed to do was accomplished by the epic writers and other story-tellers. Indeed the epics were not just heroic tales. If anything, they were also practical lessons in morals and *dharma* deliberations. The *dharmaśāstras* supply only a skeletal account of *dharma*. The epic stories and narrative literature add flesh and blood to this skeleton. The richness and ambiguity of the concept of *dharma* is interwoven with the narrative at every step.

Even Weber himself was aware of this counter-evidence, as he added in a footnote (after saying 'it excluded forever the rise of social criticism, or nationalistic speculation') that traces of the concept of 'natural law' were indeed often found in the epic literature, in for example, in the complaint of Draupadī. But in his eagerness to prove a theory, he did not see the implication of the epic literature, which even today holds considerable sway over the Indian mind. I am, of course, not attempting to 'deconstruct' Weber. His gripping influence on modern thinking about comparative ethics and sociology, sometimes through indirection, is still visible. He was a great historiographer of cultures, asking us to develop a synthetic and transdisciplinary insight. While for Marx, the conduct of man is usually shaped and sustained by the economic and political condition of the society, for Weber this causal horizon is extended to included belief-systems, world-views, religions and rituals. However, as far as Hinduism was concerned, Weber's over-rationalization of the rather chaotic and confounding data, selectively gleaned from the Orient-alists' writings on caste, *karma* and *dharma*, contributed to his (mis-)understanding of the evidential support he was looking for, that is, support for his general (and debatable) thesis regarding the rise of capitalism and the Protestant ethic. One cannot afford to ignore the evidence of the epic and narrative materials in India. If the sociologist ignores them, he ignores India; that is, the reality, the turmoils, the conflicts, the clashes, the protests and above all the forced rationalizations and the ad hoc solutions.

Paradoxically, Weber saw in caste-*dharma* and in its tie-in with the *karma* doctrine of just deserts, a completely unique concept; the combination produced for Weber 'the most consistent theodicy ever produced' (1958, p. 121). Here Weber seemed to hit upon a right chord. There was one component, caste, that was avowedly anti-rational in virtually sanctioning inequalities, and another that was a commendable expression of ethical rationalism, the *karma* component of *dharma*. I believe the story or history of Hindu thought has been the tension and reaction between these two opposite tendencies. The seemingly tension-free perpetuation of the hierarchical social ethos for millennia is simply a myth. For almost the same set of reasons, I believe the Indologist's frequent construction of a 'neo-Hinduism', distinct and distinguished from 'traditional Hinduism' by the influx of Western ideas and ideology, (usually ascribed to Vivekananda, Bankimchandra Chattopadhyay, etc.), is also to be taken with a pinch of salt. The tradition was self-conscious. It has been interpreting and re-interpreting itself over the ages. It is hardly a new phenomenon. The myth is tied up with the Indologist's romantic search for a classical, pure form of Hinduism (or Buddhism as the case may be), and is little better than a dream, which even attracts some sinister fundamentalist sects of India today.

While for Weber the caste-*dharma* apparently denied the 'natural' equality of man (1958, p. 144), for Louis Dumont it embodied, presumably in an imperfect manner, another value, hierarchy. Dumont argued that '[t]o adopt a value is to introduce hierarchy, and a certain consensus of values, a certain hierarchy of ideas, things and people, is indispensable to social life' (1980, p. 20). If Dumont is right, Weber's characterization of caste-*dharma* as 'anti-rational' must have been wrong. According to what Dumont terms 'sociological apperception', that is, the apperception of man as a social being, hierarchy or a sort of 'inequality' is not only a social reality but can arguably be a value. Hence, if some well-known society 'valorizes' it consciously, a study of such a phenomenon may well open our eyes to the realities of modern societies. Besides, Dumont says, hierarchy integrates the society with reference to its values, as it did in India (p. 252). A further allure is suggested here, that hierarchy in India begat tolerance in Hinduism. The Hindus, when they were faced with a neighbour of a different and unfamiliar sort, assign a rank, while people in the West would either approve or exclude, thus only intensifying tensions.

To take the last point first, hierarchy can indeed generate values in the way indicated, but apart from being a social reality almost everywhere, whether it is a value in itself can be argued. But even the tolerance of the Hindu, if it is based simply upon the perception of *differentness* of the neighbour's culture, cannot be a pure value, for ranking or underranking a neighbour's culture becomes unavoidable and inevitable. In fact, pure pluralism in this way generates a pernicious form of relativism, one which may be rationalistic but cannot be rational. The valuehood of hierarchy is contained in some of its pragmatic consequences. But this is also reminiscent of the usual Weberian (and Indologist) mistake: that the caste-*dharma* was tension-free for ages. Again, analysis of the epic and narrative material would prove how wrong the assumption is. There was always some quiet revolution at some time or other. That is why the nature of *dharma* was never unambiguously formulated. Rather, its intractable and ever elusive nature has always been stated and extolled.

In the *Mahābhārata*, the mythical Dharma appears in many personified forms, sometimes as the father of Yudhiṣṭhira, sometimes as a *yakṣa* (another mysterious creature), sometimes as a stork, sometimes a mongoose. On the last day of the Pāṇḍava's exile in the forest, Yudhiṣṭhira said in reply to the 'riddle' question of the *yakṣa*:

> The scriptures are many and are divided; the *dharmaśāstras* are many and different. Nobody is called a sage until and unless he holds a different view. The truth of *dharma* lies concealed in the dark cave (of the human heart?). Therefore, the way to *dharma* is the one that is taken by *mahājana* (great persons or a great number of persons).

Even the story that led to this incident is interesting and revealing. It starts with a problem about *dharma*. On that day, a brahmin came to Yudhiṣṭhira with a complaint. The two sacrificial sticks used to produce 'ritualistic' fire were missing. They had got stuck, accidentally, to the horns of a deer, and the deer had fled. If the sacrifice were not started on time, *dharma* would be violated. It was the duty of Yudhiṣṭhira, as a king and a *kṣatriya*, to protect *dharma* and let the *agnihotra* sacrifice continue. So Yudhiṣṭhira, along with his four warrior brothers, rushed away and chased the deer. But the deer disappeared. The Pāṇḍavas had now 'had it'—the breach of a promise, the violation of so-called caste duties, and the failure to catch an insignificant deer adding insult to injury. They gave up the chase in despair, having become exhausted and thirsty. One by one Nakula, Sahadeva, Arjuna and Bhīma were all sent to fetch water from a pond. Nobody returned. Yudhiṣṭhira finally went near the pond himself, only to discover a total disaster. All four brothers lay dead on the ground.

As Yudhiṣṭhira descended to get water, a terrifying voice said: 'Do not be rash, O Prince. This lake belongs to me. I am a stork. Your brothers did not listen to me and descended to get water without answering my questions. Hence they are dead. You should answer my questions before you touch the water.' Yudhiṣṭhira wanted to know who he was. 'A *yakṣa*,' was the reply. A *yakṣa* is a mysterious creature. In the *Kena Upaniṣad*, Brahman appeared in the form of a *yakṣa* before some gods who were celebrating their victory over the demons. The gods did not know who this creature was. They were awe-struck and rendered powerless. The *yakṣa* finally taught the gods a lesson. It was Brahman who empowered the gods to win, so they should not be too self-congratulatory. In the *Mahābhārata* story, a similar *yakṣa* appeared in the form of a stork, who finally revealed himself as Dharma, father of Yudhiṣṭhira. In the form of the deer, he had stolen the sacrificial sticks. All these deeds were to teach Yudhiṣṭhira a lesson—about the intractable and the ever elusive nature of *dharma*. The brahmin's sacrifice or *agni*-ritual may be violated, and the *kṣatriya* may thereby fail to perform his duty or *dharma*. All this happens before a superior force which humans cannot control, but in all this *dharma* gets fulfilled in novel and mysterious ways.

The whole narrative here is an amplification of the nature of *dharma*, of its ambiguity and the ambivalence of the person following *dharma*. In the epics, the narrative material is not always easily separable from the ethical deliberation of the author, which the Indologists sometimes misleadingly call 'didactic material'. The two are not always separable because they form a whole together: the story and its moral or its message. For here, as elsewhere, the medium is also part of the message.

Robert Lingat (1973) has said that *dharma* is not imposed but proposed. Emphasis on this open-endedness of *dharma* has much to recommend it. Dumont captured the spirit when he said that *dharma* reigns from above without actually governing the world. Or, as J. Heesterman has remarked, it is a 'wide-open problem' (1985, p. 197). Paradoxically, Dumont has argued that hierarchy may be deemed as more 'natural' not only because most societies of the past have believed themselves to be based in the order of things, but because they have also believed themselves to be *natural*, and equality is something imposed by the so-called 'rational' society, recognizing only the 'individual', that is, seeing 'reason' only in the particular man (p. 253). While we may concede that hierarchy is perhaps ineliminable even in an egalitarian society, Dumont's implicit argument still seems to be fundamentally flawed. If in our contrast between nature and convention, hierarchy, that is, 'inequality', falls on the side of nature and equality falls on the side of man-made convention, the well-known parable of the Bostonian's garden perhaps captures the critical point nicely. A clergy man, while appreciating the beautiful garden of a Bostonian citizen said, 'Congratulations! God above and you below have created a beautiful garden.' To this, our Bostonian gravely replied, 'Yes, you should have seen it when it was left only to God's hand.' Here I think God or nature is put exactly in his or her place. Hierarchy may indeed be 'natural' in society, but when left to nature alone, it may not be a very pretty sight.

Does hierarchy spell out a principle of unity of different groups in the society as a whole? Dumont claimed this to be so. But this assumption is also of a piece with the notion that a peaceful, tension-free co-existence of different hierarchies has been possible for a long time in a given society, for example, in India. I have argued that this is broadly mistaken. Inner conflict is not always visible to an external observer. Tension-free tradition, on the other hand, becomes a piece of dead wood.

Weber asserted that the Hindu linkage of caste and *karma* is a pure product of rational ethical thought. Recently, Heesterman (1985, pp. 194–202) has said that the combination of the opposites (anti-rationality of caste and rationality of *karma*) made the whole system of *dharma* 'volatile', for it was 'paradoxical' (something Weber did not see). But after this comment, Heesterman went on to say that surprisingly this combination gave coherence and stability to the social order. This is again a misconception. The rightly emphasized volatile nature of the *dharma* system created tensions at various levels. We can witness it only when it bubbles up to the surface, and the muted group succeeds in making an oblique expression of its discontent. The tradition became volatile, but the rationality of the *karma*-ethics, a late-comer in the history, came to its rescue. Caste and *karma* relativized *dharma* and gave it the required appearance of coherence (hence it was deemed 'rational'), but I doubt whether it also gave it stability. The system was more destabilized than we think it was, by internal conflict, inner oppression, covert violence and muted torture. Coherence should be distinguished from stability.

Recently a form of moral relativism has gained currency among philosophers. Gilbert Harman, among others, has formulated it on the basis of a distinction between moral 'oughts' and other types of 'oughts', and on a separation of the 'right' from the 'good' by focusing upon the agent's frame of reference: what one ought or ought not to do, not what is good or bad (Harman, 1982). On this view, a Hitler or a member of Harman's 'Murder Incorporated' cannot be judged as a wrong-doer, but can only be called *evil* in our vocabulary. For they are *right* in doing what they do, since they reach their inner moral judgements *rationally* from their group-related moral frame of reference. This type of moral relativism would be perfectly applicable to the *varṇa*-related *dharma*-ethics resulting from the volatile combination of *karma* and caste. The *Bhagavad-Gītā* of the *Mahābhārata* can provide a classic example of this ethical relativism. Here Arjuna, the great warrior, is torn by conflict as to whether he ought to fight and kill his relatives, including his dearest grandfather Bhiṣma and his revered teacher Droṇa, in order to recover his kingdom, or quit the battle-field and become a recluse. Kṛṣṇa advises him to fight by appealing, among other things, to the *agreed-upon* moral code of the *kṣatriya* caste to which Arjuna belonged. This might instantiate perfectly the Harmanian notion of inner moral judgement. For here someone S (Kṛṣṇa) says that A (Arjuna) *morally* ought to do D (fighting, killing of relatives), and S assumes that A intends to act in accordance with an agreement (the moral code of *kṣatriya* caste), and thus A has reasons to fight—reasons endorsed by his group-related moral frame of reference.

Elsewhere, I have criticized such moral relativism on the basis of the repugnant consequences that it inevitably leads to (Matilal, 1989). But here my point is slightly different. The caste-society obviously accommodated pluralism (which simply meant recognition of the *other*), but it did not just stop there, for hierarchy became part and parcel of it and therefore tension followed. Thus, propounding a group-related ethics, in short, relativism, was the way to make the *dharma*-ethics coherent. Does it resolve the tension altogether? Hardly. Even Dumont argues that 'equality can, in our day, be combined with the recognition of difference, so long as such differences are morally neutral' (1980, p. 257). But the question is: can difference or otherness be made *morally neutral*? Do we not *rank* it, automatically showing very implicitly approval or disapproval? People are seldom indifferent to difference. Even the argument for relativism based on the incommensurability of standards of evaluation flies in the face of the Davidsonian objection to a duality of scheme and content. This objection may be answered but that would not give any *exciting* form of relativism that would necessarily induce indifference to difference.

The richness and ambiguity of *dharma*-ethics, as well as the ambivalence of the moral agent with the discourse of *dharma*, in a significant and telling way, culminated in the contradictions and controversies generated by various deeds, dicta, doctrines and arguments of the two celebrated 'god-man' characters of the epics: Kṛṣṇa and Rāma. Tradition regarded them as the two human incarnations of the deity, although the two characters were very different from each other. Kṛṣṇa has always an enigmatic smile on his face when he speaks about *dharma*. Rāma is presented as straightforward and strong; he kills with his right-hand-side and weeps for the killed with his left-hand-side (see, for example, Bhavabhūti, 1964). Hinduism accommodated both forms of the deity; the story of Hinduism is therefore the story of the tension between these two poles.

The activities of Rāma and Kṛṣṇa, as depicted in the original epics, became the subject matter of close scrutiny and sustained controversy in the tradition. Their inner contradictions were brought to the surface. Constant attempts were made to fill the gaps in the argument, by retelling, modifying, restructuring and reconstructing the stories. Thus, Bhāsa's Rāma appears in a different shade compared to that of Vālmīki, Bhavabhūti's picture or Kālidāsa's picture of Rāma have even different shades. So with that of Kṛttibās, or Tulsidās. It would be an enormous and for-midable task to underline all these differences, which, nevertheless, reflect the truth about the history of the changing ethos of the community over the ages. Historians cannot afford to ignore them. Only a few specimens will suffice to show that the tradition has always been self-conscious and self-critical, trying to effect rationalization, sometimes with false moves and sometimes with right ones. Even the human incarnations of the deity Viṣṇu were not spared criticisms, which must have preceded the efforts of the later writers to endorse or vindicate them.

Rāma killed Vālin from behind with an arrow, while the latter was engaged in a fight with his brother Sugrīva. More pertinent: there was no direct hostility between Rāma and Vālin (later tradition described Vālin as a great devotee or *bhakta* of Rāma). Rāma's act was highly immoral or unethical by all relevant moral standards. Not only was the heroic code of war ethics broken (see the beginning of *Bhīṣmaparva* in the *Mahābhārata*), it was an utterly cruel killing, by a 'stab-in-the-back' method, of a celebrated warrior king, who was not even posing a threat to Rāma. The first one to protest against Rama's immorality was Vālin himself while dying. Rāma's answer as given in the critical edition was anything but convincing. Of the three main reasons adduced by Rāma, the first was probably the strongest, but it was invalid due to an obvious inner contradiction. He claimed that Vālin deviated from *dharma* by driving his brother away from the city and marrying by force his sister-in-law. This was invalid on at least two counts. First, Sugrīva was guilty of almost the same offence, which infuriated Vālin into returning the favour. Besides, the practice was not at all an instance of *a-dharma* in the Vānara society. Was Rāma, the imperialist, trying to introduce the norms of his own 'civilized' society? No—he let Sugrīva continue with the norms of the Vānara society after Vālin's death. Second, you cannot punish a wrong-doer by killing him from behind. Was a hero like Rāma afraid to fight Vālin face to face? Rāma's second excuse was a claim that this act was necessary to rescue Sītā, stolen by Rāvaṇa, and thereby to save his *kula-dharma*, the 'prestige' of the family. This is another lame excuse, for you cannot break one *dharma* (the warrior's duty) for an utterly selfish reason, saving your own and your family's face. Rāma could have asked Vālin to help him to rescue Sītā. In fact, in the Kṛttibās version, this point was emphasized. Vālin, before his death, took Rāma to task for not coming to him directly. For according to the later version, the almost invincible Rāvaṇa was once defeated by Vālin and could have been defeated again.

Rāma's last excuse was even more strange. Vālin was an animal, a monkey. To hunt an animal from behind was not immoral or unethical in human society. This was not simply a 'lame' excuse—it had no leg to stand on. Even Vālin (in the southern version especially) promptly replied that he was not like a deer whose meat would provide food (sustenance) for survival to Rāma, for, Vālin insisted, monkey-meat could not be eaten by Rāma.

I have shown that even the tradition was highly critical from the early period. Apart from the *Rāmāyaṇa* and Vālin, the earliest critic of the immoral action of Rāma was no other than Arjuna of the *Mahābhārata*. In the *Droṇaparva*, Arjuna ruefully commented that the so-called 'indirect' or 'white' lie of Yudhiṣṭhira, which killed the great teacher Droṇa, was an indelible black spot in Yudhiṣṭhira's *dharma*-inspired character, and comparable to the immoral act of Rāma's killing Vālin from behind. (I would not enter here into the relative chronology of the *Rāmayana* and the *Mahābhārata*, but it is obvious that the Rāma story became well-known, if not the Vālmīki version as we have it, at the time this portion of the *Mahābhārata* was written.) The poet Kṛttibās tried his best to uphold the idea that Rāma was an *avatāra* or 'incarnation' of Lord Viṣṇu, but nevertheless did not absolve him of this glaring act of immorality. He called it a 'grave error' on the part of Rāma: 'I, Kṛttibāsa Paṇdit, feel sad. Why did you, Lord Rāma, commit this error?' Tulsidās, who came after Kṛttibās, was more ingenious. His Vālin was a great devotee of Lord Rāma. So when Rāma felt embarrassed (in Vālmīki, Rāma apparently was not embarrassed) at the admonition received from the dying Vālin, he said, 'If you so wish, Vālin, let me restore you to life.' To which Vālin replied, 'No, my Lord. Where shall I get this unique opportunity again—to die while looking at the face of my Lord.' In other words, for a devotee this was the best way of dying one may wish for. The theology of *bhakti* absolved Rāma here of any immorality in the act, which the tradition over the generations had found hard to explain. A hint of such a theological move is also found in the southern recension of the *Rāmāyaṇa*.

Yudhiṣṭhira's underhand lie, which Lord Kṛṣṇa himself encouraged, in order to save the army as well as the battle of the day from the merciless beating by Droṇa, was never found justifiable in the tradition. Arjuna himself was the first critic, as I have already mentioned. Besides, the story-teller made Yudhiṣṭhira lose all the privileges he used to enjoy for being truthful always. And towards the end, he was made to have a visual experience of hell, presumably as a punishment for that immoral behaviour. Both Rāma and Yudhiṣṭhira were extolled as the almost perfect upholders of *dharma*. But their human weakness or 'weakness of the will' left unanswerable blemishes on their characters, which added human interest to these stories and dramatized the acuteness of moral struggles and moral conflicts. These great epics are great, in fact, in more than one sense.

With Kṛṣṇa we would have a different story. Rāma's *dharma* was rigid; Kṛṣṇa's was flaccid. Rāma's policy was punitive; Kṛṣṇa's logic was permissive. The same Kṛṣṇa who advised Arjuna to fight the bloody war and kill his great grandfather for it was his duty as a *kṣatriya*, prevented Arjuna on another occasion from killing his elder, Yudhiṣṭhira, although that involved breaking the same code of conduct of a *kṣatriya*: truth-keeping. Transgression of *varṇa-dharma* was prohibited in one situation but recommended in another. For Kṛṣṇa, *dharma* is, at least sometimes, situational (*dharmo hi āvasthikaḥ smṛtaḥ, Mahābhārata* 12.36.2). Truth-telling and truth-keeping (promise-keeping) were extolled as among the highest virtues in the tradition as well as in the *dharmaśāstras*. Even Āpastamba says plainly that every perjurer goes to hell, Lord Curzon's celebrated remark at the convocation of Calcutta University, that 'all Hindus are compulsive liars,' not withstanding. But various untruths were permitted by the *dharmaśāstra* authors such as Gautama and even Manu. Perjury to save a life was permitted. Kṛṣṇa related the story of Kauśika to make the point and convince Arjuna. The story of Kauśika anticipated an example of Kant, although not Kant's solution. In Kant's ethic, truth-telling got the highest priority; in Kṛṣṇa's ethic, saving an innocent life got the ultimate priority. Of course, in an ideal world, we can do both, as Kant insisted. But Kṛṣṇa probably conceded that all we have is an imperfect non-ideal world. In Kṛṣṇa's world, when one *dharma* is violated to keep another equally important *dharma*, the intrinsic value of neither is diminished thereby. The situation only reflects imperfect human solutions in an imperfect world.

To come back to Harman's moral relativism. We do not know whether the member of 'Murder Incorporated' or a Martian or a Hitler would be at all torn by conflict as he does what, according to him, has to be done. But an Arjuna or a Rāma will always be unsure and torn by conflict as he kills. Even Kṛṣṇa has his moments of doubt. Weber saw ethical rationality in the *karma* doctrine (1958, p. 121). Dumont argued for the 'natural necessity' for caste-hierarchy (1980, pp. 19–20). Heesterman insisted that there was a 'fault-line' in *dharma* which could not stop intermixture of castes (1985, p. 198). I have argued that the general assumption common in all these three about the presence of a tension-free hierarchical society in India was more a dream than reality. It is like the dreamland or utopia called *Rāmarājya*.

Notes and References

Bhavabhūti (1964), *Uttarāramacarita*, edited by P.V. Kane (Bombay: Nirnay Sagar Press).

Dumont, Louis (1980), *Homo Hierarchicus: The Caste System and Its Implications*, translated by Mark Sainbury, et al., Complete Revised English Edition (Chicago: The University of Chicago Press).

Harman, Gilbert (1982), 'Moral Relativism Defended', in J.W. Meiland and M. Krausz (eds), *Relativism: Cognitive and Moral* (Notre Dame: University of Notre Dame Press), pp. 189–204.

Heesterman, J.C. (1985), *The Inner Conflict of Tradition: Essays in Indian Ritual, Kinship and Society* (Chicago: University of Chicago Press).

Kane, P.V. (1930), *History of Dharmaśāstra*, vol. 1 (Poona: Bhandarkar Oriental Research Institute).

Lingat, Robert (1973), *The Classical Law of India*, translated by J.D.M. Derrett (Berkeley: University of California Press).

Matilal, B.K. (1989), 'Ethical Relativism and Confrontation of Cultures', in M. Krausz (ed.), *Relativism: Interpretation and Confrontation.* (Notre Dame: University of Notre Dame Press), pp. 339–62.

Northrop, F.S.C. (1946), *The Meeting of East and West: An Inquiry Concerning World Understanding* (New York: Macmillan).

Weber, Max (1958), *The Religion of India: The Sociology of Hinduism and Buddhism*, translated by Hans H. Gerth and Don Martindale (New York: The Free Press).

5

Dharma and Rationality

1. INTRODUCTION: PRIMITIVE FORM OF RATIONALITY AND FREE RIDERS

I wish to confess to my readers at the outset that some of the stories I heard in my childhood still hold a certain fascination for me. Although this may be tantamount to bias, I nevertheless wish to start with such a story, which is often heard in the rural parts of Bengal. For I believe that the morals of this story and other similar tales often contain rudiments of some primitive theory of rationality.

One day, a king wanted to create a lake of white milk, because he was tired of looking at pools and lakes full of muddy water. He imagined what it would be like to watch the beauty of the milky waves glittering in the sunshine. Besides, people would be able to have milk to drink whenever they wanted. So the order was given, and thousands of diggers got busy digging in order to create the lake. The digging was successfully completed, but the final ingredient was still missing: the milk. Where could one locate a quantity of milk huge enough to fill the lake? (Remember, the dairy industry was at a very primitive stage in those days, and there was not even enough milk to feed the babies!) But, since the king wanted it, an order was given that, on a certain day, every citizen had to pour a bucketful of milk into the lake so that the lake that had been dug would be filled with milk. This meant that about one hundred thousand bucketfuls of milk were expected to come from the citizens. But, what happened the next day? Each citizen thought to himself, 'Since milk is so dear and so scarce, I will pour a bucketful of water into the lake in the darkness of the night, and when my little bit of water is mixed with all the milk the others will pour in, nobody will be any the wiser'. Next morning, when the king woke up he went to take a look at his new lake of milk, but what he saw instead was a huge lake full of muddy water. Why? Because not a single drop of milk had come from any of the citizens, since everybody had thought that the others were dealing with the milk and that he could therefore silently slip into their group without paying the price. In other words, everybody wanted to be a 'free-rider'! But everybody acted with rational self-interest in mind.

Let us assume that everybody wanted the lake of milk to be created because it would have been 'good' for the society in general—since it would create a common resource from which 'free milk' would be distributed to everybody—and not just because it would fulfil the king's whim. Then, one could say, at least from the point of view of this primitive theory of rational behaviour, that, by pouring in water instead of milk, every citizen acted not only immorally but also irrationally. For, based upon this so-called rational self-interest, the argument of each citizen was in fact irrational, since, among other things, everybody knew that everyone else could take the same line of action—based on the same argument—and that, if everybody did this, nobody's self-interest would be served because nobody would receive the intended benefit.

From the moral point of view, we cannot say anything very different. If it is assumed that each citizen was reasonably capable of making the sacrifice—contributing a bucketful of milk—and that in making that contribution none would have been subjected to unbearable hardship or a great deal of suffering, then, according to any moral theory, it would be considered immoral to be a 'free-rider'. Indeed, in accordance with one of the most well-entrenched and widely held views of morality today—Utilitarianism—'free-riders' such as those described in the story are clearly immoral because this action is irrational. In spite of many objections that have been raised against classical Utilitarianism, it unquestionably enjoys popularity and the support of many today because of the prime importance it gives to reason or rationality. In the past, Utilitarianism fought against the 'intuitionists' in political and moral fields, by emphasizing an impartial rational test for judging the existing moral principles and traditional social institutions. In many modern, modified versions of Utilitarianism, there is one common thread, that is, adherence to the principle that moral issues must be decided by rational tests. In fact, it has been even claimed that any theory of morality should itself be part of a general theory of rational behaviour.

By the term *dharma* in the title of this essay, I understand nothing short of moral virtue, or rather, a theory of moral behaviour, as it is found implicit in India's traditional wisdom. Thus, I prefer to call the attempt to be a 'free-rider' an *a-dharma*, or a violation of *dharma*. For, in the wider tradition of India, *dharma* stands for neither 'religion' nor the narrower caste-oriented duties. The best evidence for my claim are the frequent discourses on *dharma*, found throughout the two great Indian epics, the *Rāmāyaṇa* and the *Mahābhārata*—in all their different versions, composed at different periods of history and in different regional languages—as well as in many folktales, stories and fables told at different times.

2. *DHARMA* AND ITS RATIONAL CRITIQUE

Dharma is a popular subject of inquiry, often found in all this narrative literature. The nature of *dharma* is often hotly debated and argued about; no other principle has been regarded as sacred. This need not be very surprising, for neither in Buddhism nor in Jainism, or even in Hinduism, was God cited as the authority on *dharma*. Hence the search for a rational basis of *dharma* is often compatible with these religious traditions. There were, of course, the Hindu scriptures. But these scriptures proved to be flexible, sometimes to the point that they seemed to have meant whatever their interpreters chose to make them mean. Furthermore, even when the literal text of the scriptures was taken seriously, the interpreters of the Mīmāṃsā school undertook to make a rational examination (*mīmāṃsā* means rational examination) of the meaning of the Vedic (scriptural) statements.

It is true, of course, that, in those days, the search for a rational basis for mental or social behaviour was not free from unconscious bias and inherited prejudices; very few are unbiased, even in our own day. The supposedly rational argument often turned into a form of 'rationalization' or 'apologia'. The point, however, is that the tradition did not have to wait until something like the Age of Enlightenment came in order to question the basis of moral and religious beliefs. Even some of the actions of Kṛṣṇa and Rāma—who were regarded as incarnations of God on earth—were subjected to rational criticism over the ages. There is enough textual evidence to prove it.[1]

My claim so far has been that the *dharma* tradition developed through an attempt at rational criticism of itself. Another piece of evidence in support of this claim can now be briefly cited. Consider the caste-hierarchy that is almost as old as Vedic Hinduism. The *Śramaṇa* tradition provided a rational critique from outside. But, even within the domain of Vedic Hinduism, there occurred a search for a rational basis. What resulted was an interpretation of the *karma* doctrine that was intended to provide a 'rational' basis for the apparently irrational practice of caste-hierarchy or social inequality.

It was Max Weber who, in 1920, characterized the caste-*dharma* as 'anti-rational', because it denied the 'natural' equality of man.[2] But,

Weber then went on to pay a glowing tribute to the *karma* doctrine of Hinduism, for he saw how the latter provided the rational basis of the caste-hierarchy. For him, the *karma* doctrine of Hinduism was 'the most consistent theodicy ever produced in history'.[3] The caste-hierarchy was, it may be assumed, historically prior to the development of the full-fledged *karma* doctrine with its rebirth hypothesis. There is some justification for this conjecture, for the *Puruṣa-Sūkta* in the *Ṛg-Veda* clearly refers to the caste-hierarchy. But, although the rudiments of the notion of *karma* or 'just deserts' may be found scattered in various places in the Vedic hymns, it was explicitly referred to as a doctrine (although still deemed an esoteric or secret doctrine) in the *Bṛhadāraṇyaka Upaniṣad*. It was Yājñavalkya, the well-known philosopher of the day, who mentioned the *karma* doctrine in the court of King Janaka, in reply to a question from Ārtabhaga. Yājñavalkya did not, of course, expound the doctrine publicly.

This is how it is supposed to have happened. All the well-known brahmin scholars (both men and women) and priests assembled in the court of Janaka, and the one who could prove himself to be the best among the scholars gathered would win a prize of one thousand cows and ten thousand coins.[4] When Yājñavalkya claimed supremacy, a very tense session of debate, a form of question-and-answer session among the brahmin scholars, took place, all the others asking questions that tested the depth of Yājñavalkya's knowledge, and the latter endeavoring to satisfy them. When Ārtabhaga rose, he started asking questions on matters concerning various rituals.[5] But then he asked a very important question: 'Assuming that the person survives his bodily death, what substratum would the person have when his material body dies and dissolves into all its [material] ingredients?' Yājñavalkya replied: 'Hold my hand and let us go to a secluded place. Only two of us will consider [and know] the answer, not the others present here.' Then the two retired to a secluded place for a while. What they discussed has not been reported in the text. Only a brief account of the meeting has been given, in four lines. It is said that they talked about *karma*—a doctrine that should be admired by everybody, 'For good deeds earn merit for the person while bad deeds earn demerit' (or, the person becomes good in his next life through good deeds, and he becomes evil through evil deeds).[6] This was the outline of the primitive *karma* theory which was later developed in the tradition. And this is how the tradition itself rationalized the ever persistent caste-hierarchy in Hinduism: the birth of each individual is predetermined by his or her *karma* in previous births. Such rationalizations, however, are not often seen as very rational from our modern point of view (they often amounted to apologias). But the point that I wish to insist on is that the search for a rational basis was considered, at least implicitly, necessary for supporting an existing moral principle, and the caste-*dharma* unquestionably had a moral dimension since it legitimized social inequality.

It should be mentioned here that, while people like Louis Dumont 'valorized' the Hindu caste-system and considered it to be a 'value',[7] Max Weber hailed the linkage between caste and *karma* as a pure product of 'rational ethical thought', even quoting from *The Communist Manifesto*, for he was struck by the obvious similarity in logic: the pious Hindus of low caste were in the same situation as the proletariat; they had nothing to lose, and it was open to them to climb up the ladder of caste-hierarchy gradually, and even to become a god in future life, through good deeds in this one. Although I hesitate to share Weber's enthusiasm regarding the implication of the *karma* doctrine, it cannot be denied that the doctrine did have that sort of significance. I also disagree with Dumont when he considers the Hindu caste-hierarchy as a 'value' and also a 'rational' practice.[8]

Another illustration of the linkage between *dharma*-ethics and the search for a rational basis may be in order here. I shall refer to another ancient text, the *Chāndogya Upaniṣad*, for another story. Satyakāma grew up with his mother Jabālā, and he wanted to have an education. He approached the well-known teacher of his time, Sage Gautama, for initiation and to join the groups of pupils. For the initiation ritual, Gautama wanted to know the name of Satyakāma's father or his *gotra*, that is, his family name. Unfortunately, Satyakāma did not know who his father was. He said that he would come back after asking his mother. But Jabālā had been a maid who had had to sell her body in order to survive. Thus, she did not know the name of Satyakāma's father. Jabālā told this to Satyakāma, who went back to teacher Gautama and told the truth about his birth in the presence of all the other young pupils. There was a ripple of suppressed laughter out of contempt from the assembled pupils. But Gautama had to make a decision—a moral decision. He got up, embraced the boy and announced: 'Now I have no doubt that you belong to the highest caste, that you are a brahmin, for such courage, firmness and truthfulness can only be the constitutive qualities of a brahmin. I would accept your mother's name as your family name. You will henceforth be called Satyakāma Jabālā. Come, I will initiate you.'[9] Jabālā Satyakāma became a famous Upaniṣadic sage. Here, again, a moral decision was made on the basis of a rational argument. Caste-*dharma* does not always depend upon birth; possession of moral virtues should also be a criterion for one's claims to supremacy.

The above is reminiscent of an episode in the epic, the *Mahābhārata*, where a similar problem of *dharma* was posed, and the decision or rational preference was made on similar grounds. I shall refer to it only briefly, as I have already discussed it elsewhere.[10] In the *Vanaparva* of the epic, a discourse on *dharma* took place between Yudhiṣṭhira and King Nahuṣa who, under a curse, took the form of a huge python. (As I have already noted, such discussions on *dharma* are frequently found in the epic literature, which only showed the arguability of any *dharma*-preference.) When asked to define brahminhood, Yudhiṣṭhira said emphatically that what constituted brahminhood was not birth but a collection of moral virtues such as truthfulness, generosity, forgiveness, goodness, kindness. For, each birth was accidental due to the copulation of a man and a woman out of lust (*rāga*), over which the person born had little control.[11] This, too, shows the ambivalence of the later tradition to accept as entirely rational the prevalent resolution of caste-hierarchy in terms of the *past karma* of the individual. In the *Bhagavad-Gītā,* Lord Kṛṣṇa says, 'I have created the four *varṇas* (castes) in reliance upon the division of qualities and actions.'[12] This can be read more as a critique of the birth-based division of caste rather than as an endorsement of it.[13]

3. *DHARMA*, ITS NON-THEISTIC BASIS AND MORAL CONSCIENCE

I have said above that, in the Indian *dharma* theory of ethics, authority was seldom ascribed to God. Let us now turn briefly to the *dharmaśāstras* to examine their version of what the authorities had to say about *dharma*. I shall use the most well-known: *Mānava-dharmaśāstra*, or *Manu-saṃhitā* for reference. Verse 1 of chapter 2 says:

> Listen [my pupils], I shall describe *dharma*—it is always honoured by the honest and the wise [of the learned]; it is followed by those who are above attachment [greed] and aversion [hatred]; and it is approved by their hearts.[14]

Different commentators have given varying interpretations of some of the epithets, but all have agreed that they constitute a general definition of *dharma* (Kullūka, e.g., *dharma-sāmānya-lakṣaṇa*). In those days, any 'learned' person would have to be, among other things, an expert in Vedic studies. Hence, the commentators, being eager to connect the basis of *dharma* with the Vedas in some way or other, interpreted *vidvān*, or 'the learned', as *vedavit*, or 'versed in the Vedas'. However, the later (commentorial) tradition was aware already that everything enjoined in the Vedas was not a moral duty or a *dharma*. Commenting upon this verse, Kullūka, for example, quoted from the *Mīmāṃsā-sūtra* 1.1.2 of Jaimini, where *dharma* was defined as '*codanā-lakṣaṇo'rtho dharmaḥ*'.[15] But he noted immediately that, although *codanā* means Vedic injunctive statements by which the *dharma* duties would be signified (*lakṣaṇaḥ lakṣyate anena*), there is the word *arthaḥ*, which means *śreyaḥ-sādhanam*, or 'that which is conducive to good.' Hence Kullūka explains:

> Both are meant by 'injunction in the Vedas' [*codanā*]: good acts that bring about good, e.g., the *jyotiṣṭoma* ritual, and evil acts [*an-artha*] that bring about evil or moral lapses [*pratyavāya*], e.g., *śyena*, or ritual. Hence the meaning of the [Jaimini's] *sūtra* is this: only such Vedic injunctions signify *dharma* as are conducive to good, such as the *jyotiṣṭoma* ritual.[16]

It should be noted that, although they were enjoined in the Vedas, since rituals such as *śyena* or *abhicāra* were meant for harming others, it was immoral to perform them. This is another piece of evidence on how a rational critique developed within the tradition itself to separate the morally unjustifiable injunctions or action-guides from those that were morally justifiable or even morally neutral, for example, the quest for personal good such as perfect bliss, without harming others. This last type of action-guide may, therefore, be put among those that were rationally justifiable.

The other qualifications in the verse of the *Manusaṃhita* quoted above are somewhat self-explanatory. For our point of view, it is significant to note that *dharma*-ethics, or the *dharma*-prescriptions, cannot be based upon personal greed or hatred. Impartiality is an essential ingredient in the constitution of *dharma*, as it should be in any viable theory of rational behaviour. *Dharma*-morality can hardly be assessed from a self-centred or emotionally biased, partisan point of view. We need the viewpoint of an impartial observer, just as equity and justice are commonly symbolized by a lady blindfolded and holding a scale.

The last qualification in the verse quoted is also important. It enlightens us about the human side of *dharma*-morality. Whatever action is prescribed by *dharma* must also meet the approval of the heart of the honest and the wise; hypocrisy can never be a part of the *dharma* behaviour. Traditional commentators, however, suggest several explanations. Kullūka thinks that the prescribed action must lead to something good (*śreyas*), for then it will be the natural inclination of the mind to perform such acts.

Govindarāja interprets it as an absence of any doubt in the mind of the learned with regard to a particular action. Kullūka gives a taunting reply in rejecting this interpretation. He says that, according to this interpretation, if a Vedic scholar decided to travel to the countryside and had no doubt in his mind for reaching such a decision, then that would also be called *adharma*—an absurd consequence. Medhātithi first agreed that it meant 'approval of the mind', but then suggested a queer alternative: he interpreted 'heart' (*hṛdaya*) as the Vedas (for the Vedas had to be learned by *heart*), and then—in an awkward manner—claimed that the phrase meant that *dharma* was approved by the Vedas. This was somewhat embarrassing to the commentators, for the verse, while giving an almost impeccable definition of *dharma*, did not make any explicit reference to the scriptures or the Vedas. Hence various exegetical devices were used to establish the connection between the Vedas and *dharma*. (It may be that the definition was intended to be general enough to be acceptable to the Vedic and the non-Vedic people.) Medhātithi's alternative explanation, however, was too far-fetched to be true. As I have already explained, I believe that this last epithet was intended to establish the vital connection between *dharma* and the role of moral emotions, as well as the moral inclination of the person in determining the *dharma*. In this way, it supplements the impartiality criterion (see above) of rationality with the requirement of sympathetic understanding of the situation under which a moral decision is taken.

We may pursue this point a little further. As I will note presently, it was widely recognized that there was a strong connection between the dictates of moral conscience and *dharma*. Life presents us with many moral conflicts, some of which even amount to genuine moral dilemmas. In genuine moral dilemmas, rational arguments in favour of either prescriptions or actions (where both cannot be done, for the doing of one is the undoing of the other) are equally balanced. Hence if the rational agent is forced to take action, it is usually under unresolved conflict, and the agent may suffer from such emotions as regret and remorse. The Indian epics, especially the *Mahābhārata*, supply numerous illustrations of such genuine moral, or *dharma*, dilemmas, as I have argued elsewhere.[17] Some moral conflicts may be resolvable, but due to lack of enough information or informational constraints in the situation, a rationally arrived at decision may seem difficult or even impossible. But, since a decision has to be taken, for the situation demands it (and human beings cannot, like Buridan's ass, show an asinine preference for death by starvation over reaching a decision under unresolved conflict and picking either haystack, not *neither*), the agent may appeal to his own moral conscience, being impartial and not biased by any baser emotions such as greed, and his mental inclination will reveal his preference. I believe many moral (as well as other) conflicts are resolved in this way, through the 'heart's approval', and this is exactly what is implied in the last qualification found in the general definition of *dharma* in the verse quoted from the *Manusaṃhitā*.

It is easy to support the above interpretation by referring to the original text itself. In verse 6 of the same chapter of the *Manusaṃhitā*, five authorities on *dharma* are cited (where, by the way, Manu did not forget to mention the Vedas):

> The roots of *dharma* are (1) the entire Vedas, (2) the *dharmaśāstras* as well as the (3) virtues cultivated by the Vedic scholars, (4) the good conduct of the honest, and (5) satisfaction of the mind (of the agent).

Six verses later, in verse 12, the same idea is repeated; this time, however, four authorities are mentioned instead of five, for, as the commentaries explain, the virtues cultivated by the Vedic scholars and the good conduct of the honest are merged into a single authority:

> The following, they say, are the direct characteristics of *dharma*: (1) the Scriptures, (2) the *dharmaśāstras*, (3) the conduct of the good, and (4) satisfaction of the mind.

In both lists, our interest lies, of course, in the last item, which is similar to the 'heart's approval' of the previous general definition in verse 1. In his commentary on verse 6, Kullūka says clearly that this authority is appealed to where a conflict of *dharma* duties arises. He even quotes a line in support of his claim from Garga, another author of *dharmaśāstras*:

> Satisfaction of the mind is the only authority in cases of conflicting alternatives.

Thus, it is clear that the tradition accepted several other authorities on *dharma*-morality besides the scriptures and the *dharmaśāstras*. This openness bespeaks of the rational stream of the tradition as well as the lesser importance accorded to blind faith. Appeal to the mental inclination of the generally upright person in conflict-situations that are not rationally resolvable due to informational or other constraints, should not be confused with an appeal to inherent bias or blind faith. In his play, *Abhijñāna-Śākuntala*, the poet Kālidāsa put a similar argument in the mouth of his hero, King Duṣyanta: In matters where doubt intervenes, the [natural] inclination of the heart of the good person becomes the *pramāṇa*, 'authority' or the decisive factor.[18]

4. *DHARMA* AND SCEPTICISM

I have said that *dharma* was a subject of rational inquiry, not a matter of blind faith, except in the case of the Hindus, where the Vedas were given the supreme authority. But even these Vedas were subjected to rational investigation. (cf. *mīmāṃsā*). Two further points need to be made here. First, the Vedic injunctions cover only a very small part of our normal behaviour at the social and personal level. Hence the necessity arose for guidelines—from the conduct of the good as well as from appeal to good conscience—to achieve rational resolution of conflict-situations. The second point is that medieval authors of the *dharmaśāstras* such as Manu and Yajñavalkya were fully aware of the role of rationality in determining various moral or *dharma* preferences. This may sound a bit odd to some of us moderners, since these authors achieved notoriety for their narrow-mindedness, for 'irrational' rationalization of the same existing unjust social institutions such as inequalities in caste discrimination, and for resisting the change that was bound to come along with the change of time and environment. However, it is undeniable that these same authors also realized that the full extent of *dharma*-morality can be sustained only if it can be given a rational basis. Besides, the stream of critical rationality in the tradition was already alive and active. There were dissident voices not only from the low castes but also from the higher strata of the society, the brahmin priests, etc. We hear frequent stories in the epics and the *purāṇas* of a certain Cārvāka—an adherent of a philosophy sceptical of religious tradition—who, having entered the assembly of the brahmin priests (he was sometimes described also as a brahmin), used to ask questions and challenge the validity of the Vedic rituals, using *tarka* or *hetuśāstra,* the 'science of reasoning'. Some of his questions were so radical that satisfactory answers were hard to find. The episode usually ended in turning him away from the assembly. He probably represented the radical rebels of those days.

In the *Rāmāyaṇa* we read the story of Sage Jābāli, who was one of the brahmin-advisers of King Daśaratha.[19] He came to see Rāma in exile along with Bharata and others from Ayodhyā, and tried to persuade Rāma to return to his kingdom, for he claimed that it was a false *dharma* (according to Jābāli) to abandon his kingdom in order to keep some old promise that his dead father had made to Kaikeyī. The sage expounded elaborately a philosophy of materialism and a hedonistic ethic in support of his argument. Of course, Rāma rejected the advice, but that is not the point here. Even traditional authors of *dharmaśāstras* occasionally referred to such a hedonistic ethic as well as to the arguments of those who challenged the authority of the Vedas. Manu, for example, recognized the persistence of such brahmins who used to condemn the Vedic rituals by using reasoning, when he said (chapter 2, verse 11):

Such a 'two-born' [= brahmin, *dvija*] person as would condemn the root of *dharma* [i.e., the Vedas], having recourse to the 'science of reasoning' [*hetuśāstra*], should be turned away by the good people, for he vilifies the Vedas and is a 'Negativist' [*nāstika*].

The commentators pointed out that logic, or the science of reasoning, can be used in two ways: (1) to support and give a rational explanation of the Vedas, and (2) to reject it and thereby overthrow its authority. Obviously, it was claimed that the first was 'right' or 'the good way', which was acceptable to followers of the *dharma*-ethics, and the second was 'bad' and hence unacceptable.

Towards the end of the *Mānava-dharmaśāstra,* the rational basis of *dharma* was again emphasized. Chapter 12, verse 105, says in unambiguous language:

The person who wishes to 'purify' the *dharma*-ethics must be very well-acquainted with such *pramāṇas*, 'means of knowledge' as perception, inference and various *śāstra* and texts [sources of verbal testimony].

The commentators noted that the three well-known *pramāṇas*—perception, inference and verbal testimony—are mentioned here as essential requirements for determining any controversy regarding *dharma*. The next verse (106) makes it clearer:

Only he comes to know the *dharma*—he who examines in the light of reason (*tarka*) any instruction of *dharma* by the sages, and examines them so as not to contradict the Vedas—not anybody else.

In the case of dispute over *dharma*, where it is not easy to decide which course of action should be followed, or by which action *dharma*-morality would be sustained, Manu suggested another method which undoubtedly foreshadowed the upholding of the 'rational-democratic' principle. In verse 110 of chapter 12, it was said:

['What is to be done?' if such a doubt arises with regard to a conflict of *dharmas* where the texts such as the scriptures of the *dharmaśāstra* have not laid down anything—verse 108 supplies this context] an assembly of not less than ten persons, or [if ten are not available] not less than three persons, should deliberate and reach a decision on *dharma*, and that *dharma* [thus arrived at] should not be transgressed.

In verse 111, a selection procedure for these ten members was given:

The ten-member assembly will be constituted by three scholars versed in the three Vedas (Ṛg, Yajur, and Sāman, one logician [*haituka*, versed in *hetu-vidyā*], one dialectician or arguer [*tarkī*, versed in *tarka* 'dialectics' or hypothetical reasoning], one expert in semantics and etymology (*nairukta*), one scholar of the *dharmaśāstras*, and three laymen from three different groups, one celibate student [probably a young man studying under a teacher], one house-holder [a married man or a man with a family] and one *retired* person [a considerably senior man who has retired into the forest after leading a full family life].

This seems to be a good combination of people, whose combined wisdom will usually be an effective way to decide the *dharma* democratically in matters of dispute. Both terms, *haituka* and *tarkī*, may stand for 'logician'. Obviously, they were talking about two types of 'logician', one who was expert in the science of evidence, or *pramāṇaśāstra*, and the other who was expert in the *prasaṅga* or *reductio* type of argument. Kullūka, however, took one to mean a Naiyāyika, versed in Nyāya-type thinking, and the other to be a Mīmāṃsaka, versed in the Mīmāṃsā-type cogitation. My own interpretation is, however, not very different.

5. *DHARMA* AND MORAL WEAKNESS

Admission of moral conflicts or genuine moral dilemmas (or *dharma*-dilemmas; they are given various names: *dharmasaṃkaṭa, dharma-vikalpa, kṛtyākṛtya-viveka-nirṇaya, kiṃkartavya-vimūḍhatā*) requires using some method for making a rational choice. It is obvious that some sort of pre-ordering or ranking of principles helps such rational deliberation. In matters of ritual-orientated *dharmas*, when conflict arises, the Mīmāṃsā school has determined a fixed rule of pre-ordering, and has given a rational argument in favour of such ordering. Unfortunately, in all practical cases of value conflict or ordinary *dharma*-orientated conflict, it is extremely difficult to establish priorities in the same way. Many epic stories that illustrated such practical *dharma*-conflicts show that the practical resolution of such conflict does not always fix priorities according to the same pattern. It appears to me that this respect for the difficulties encountered in real life is not a mark of irrationality or inconsistency, but emphasizes that we sometimes face moral predicaments for which we cannot find a simply rational solution.

One kind of moral conflict or *dharma*-conflict is the struggle against temptation, or what is called weakness of the will. It is typified by the oft-quoted verse that follows:

jānāmi dharmaṃ na ca me pravṛttiḥ/
jānāmy-adharmaṃ na ca me nivṛttiḥ//

I know what is dharma, but I cannot persuade myself to act accordingly. I know what is a-dharma [evil], but I am unable to refrain from it.

This type of struggle is well illustrated in the ancient epic, the *Mahābhārata*, which tells of a struggle between two families, the Pāṇḍavas and the Kauravas. The leader of the Pāṇḍavas, Yudhiṣṭhira, was addicted to gambling, while the leader of the Kauravas, Dhṛtarāṣṭra, had a blind affection for his son Duryodhana, an affection which led him to allow (by not discouraging) the latter to go to war against the Pāṇḍavas. Yudhiṣṭhira was called Dharmarāja, 'the King of *dharma*,' for his righteousness and moral behaviour. But his addiction to gambling was almost proverbial—a fatal flaw in his character. He lost everything, his kingdom, his four brothers, his wife (and his wife Draupadī was publicity humiliated while he himself was present), at the first of his gambling matches. Rescued from this situation, when the second invitation (or challenge) for gambling came, he had the option to refuse. Now, in those days, gambling was explicitly recognized as a vice among the princes, and it was not unknown to Yudhiṣṭhira that it was an *a-dharma*. Besides, he had the fresh experience of the humiliation and shame after his first defeat—not to speak of the immorality of placing his beloved and innocent wife, as well as his four brothers, in a morally unbearable situation of shame. But he was like the celebrated gambler of the *Ṛg-Veda*.[20] This proverbial gambler said (verse 5, *The Gambler's Hymn*, 10th Maṇḍala):

Vainly I decide not to go gambling even when all my [gambling] friends left, but at that very moment I !isten to noise made by the throw of dice, and then I have to rush to reach there just as a fallen woman runs [to meet her paramour].

Yudhiṣṭhira's behaviour was in no way different. The second invitation came, and he ran to accept it. The temptation was great. Of course, he gave a reason in favour of this: as a prince, he must accept the so-called challenge. But a man under temptation can always argue himself into finding reasons that support his action. Thus, a bank-employee about to embezzle funds may indeed find reasons for his action (e.g., to counteract the injustice done by the capitalistic system to poor and middle-class people like himself). And there was no moral (or *dharma*-centred) obligation on the part of Yudhiṣṭhira in this case, as he himself admitted much later on, in the *Vanaparva* of the *Mahābhārata*. In the *Vanaparva*,

Bhīma once raised the question: 'What is the use of our gaining the kingdom back even though we would have to fight for it? For, my dear brother, I know you well, and I believe you will again be tempted to gamble away everything if the challenge comes for the third or the fourth time, and so on.' To this blunt accusation of Bhīma. Yudhiṣṭhira gave a significant reply: Yes, he would. He admitted that he would again be unable to check his temptation, for in this matter he had no control over himself.

There was a challenge all right—a challenge of a different kind—in the case of Yudhiṣṭhira. The challenge to him was to do what he himself (as Dharmarāja) recognized he ought to have done when desire, fear, temptation and the irrational hope that this time he might win after all, all inclined him to do the opposite. There was not the slightest doubt about what he ought to have done.

Dhṛtarāṣṭra's case was similar. He knew that his son Duryodhana was doing something completely immoral. Duryodhana's conspiracy to kill the Pāṇḍavas by setting fire to their house while they were asleep was quite serious, although even this might be ignored as an instance of the young prince's foolishness. Dhṛtarāṣṭra always looked the other way. He never tried to control his son or teach him any moral lesson. The father knew very well what his son had been doing, and he did not lack knowledge of the *dharma* or moral understanding of the situation. Each time he felt the pangs of his conscience, he would call upon Vidura to explain the *dharma*-ethics to his son. But he seldom listened to Vidura's advice. Anyway, in the two cases of gambling described, Dhṛtarāṣṭra made restitution to the Pāṇḍavas. He returned all their gambling losses to them. He also gave Yudhiṣṭhira Pandu's share of his kingdom after he learned that the Pāṇḍavas and their mother were alive and in exile. But Duryodhana could not reconcile himself to this outcome. The last act of Duryodhana was unpardonable. According to the conditions of the gambling match, he should have kept his part of the bargain and returned the Pāṇḍavas' share of the kingdom. But he wanted an all-out war with the Pāṇḍavas. Although there were several attempts to negotiate a deal in order to prevent a most devastating war between two lines of the same royal family, Dhṛtarāṣṭra could not do anything to persuade his son to listen to the voice of reason. He just let it happen. His blind affection for his son led him to ignore the advice of all well-meaning persons. It was not until almost the end of the war, after almost everybody was killed except for ten warriors (seven on the side of the Pāṇḍavas and three of the Kauravas), that Dhṛtarāṣṭra admitted his weakness and regretted it.

Philosophically speaking, this moral weakness or weakness of the will may require some explanation, for it may be argued that it is impossible for rational beings knowingly to do wrong. In fact, Plato made such a claim in the *Protagoras.*[21] And, in *Ethica Nicomachea*, Aristotle raised the question again, to discuss it:

Now we may ask how a man who judged rightly can behave incontinently.[22]

Aristotle argued that the Socratic (Plato's) claim that there is no such thing as 'incontinence', and that people act so only by reason of ignorance, was indeed a puzzle that needed some philosophical explanation. For, according to Aristotle, this view plainly contradicted the observed facts. Of the several explanations suggested in Aristotle, one may be stated as follows: it is observed that a person behaves incontinently with knowledge, but perhaps, here 'knowledge' is used in a slightly different sense—'for both the man who has "knowledge" but is not using it and he who is using it are said to know'.[23] Thus, one might say that the incontinent person has 'knowledge', but is not exercising it. Some philosophers put the matter more strongly. Human beings (and not lower animals, as Aristotle reminded us)[24], are able to, and often do, act against their sincerely held moral principles, with full knowledge and deliberation, and this is simply a fact about ourselves. As I have already noted, the predominant view in classical India is that people do, in fact, act against their moral convictions.

Another point should be made before we leave the subject. In the New Testament (Romans 7), our weakness of the will is seen as a consequence of our sin, and hence it is not philosophically puzzling. Indeed, the following quotation sounds almost similar to the Sanskrit verse I have quoted a few pages earlier: 'For I do not do the good I want, but the evil I do not want is what I do. Now if I do what I do not want, it is no longer I that do it, but sin which dwells within me.'[25] Here, the first part of the sentence coincides with the meaning of the Sanskrit verse. But the attitude the sentence conveys is not prevalent in the Indian tradition. Let me give an example. When the author of the *Mahābhārata* dwelt upon the similar cases of Yudhiṣṭhira and Dhṛtarāṣṭra, he did not refer to the question of sin. Also surprisingly, there was no explicit mention of the *karma* doctrine in this connection, to explain the obvious puzzle. Both Yudhiṣṭhira and Dhṛtarāṣṭra were fully aware of the weakness of their own character and occasionally felt bewildered by it. It may be contended that, according to classical Indian wisdom, weakness of the will is part of human nature (*svabhāva evaiṣa bhūtānām*), and is not ascribed to sin. Here, we can refer back to the *Manusaṃhitā* for an insight:

It is not a vice to eat meat, to drink liquor, or to have sexual intercourse, for they constitute the natural inclination of the creatures; but (judicious) refraining from such acts generates good consequences.[26]

Kullūka explains *pravṛtti* as the 'natural *dharma*'. This, I believe, illuminates a great deal about the attitude of the classical Indians towards the issue.

6. PHILOSOPHICAL ISSUES IN *DHARMA* DILEMMAS

We may now turn to the other kind of moral conflict: genuine moral dilemmas. Although several well-known philosophers today may disagree here, I believe that, in cases of moral dilemmas, weakness of the will does not have a large part to play in the philosophical analyses of such situations. Genuine dilemma arises when what ought to be done, all things considered, is as yet unsettled or even unsettlable. It may argued that if the informational constraints are removed and impartial rationality is allowed its full play, then such dilemmas will never arise, provided the agent is not suffering from *akrasia*, or weakness of the will. As opposed to this, one may hold that there may be equally strong and equally admired moral principles which prescribe actions that are in conflict, so that the doing of one is the undoing of the other, so that there is no third choice, for example, the complete withdrawal from action. This, then, would be a case of genuine dilemma, where, we may add, decisions are no doubt made, but such decisions are *ad hoc* and not arrived at fully rationally. To go back to ancient examples: in the beginning of the *Bhagavad-Gītā*, Arjuna faced a similar dilemma when he was torn between two *dharma* principles: the *dharma* of his Kṣatriya caste to fight on, and his family *dharma* infused with such admirable moral sentiments as love, devotion and respect for his grandfather Bhiṣma and esteemed teacher Droṇa. Arjuna himself suggested the third way out—that of complete withdrawal from action—as he said, 'I would rather accept the life of a mendicant' (cf. *bhaikṣyam apīha loke*). But it was more than obvious that it was decidedly too late for such a course of action to be undertaken. At Kṛṣṇa's advice, Arjuna decided to fight, but still, he regretted it many times in the later part of the epic.

Similarly, Yudhiṣṭhira was in a moral dilemma on several occasions. One was when he had to decide between telling a lie (only once in his whole life) and thereby winning the war which he morally deserved to win, and not being untruthful (even for once in his life) and thereby suffering defeat and humiliation by letting Duryodhana win, even though the latter choice would have meant that overall justice would not have been maintained. On the one hand, there was the strong moral principle of telling the truth throughout his life, and on the other, was the equally strong principle of justice—justice for the utter humiliation of innocent Draupadī. Yudhiṣṭhira was torn between the two. At the persuasion of Kṛṣṇa, and with great regret and reluctance, Yudhiṣṭhira decided to tell a lie.

How did the tradition look upon such cases? I believe there is strong evidence that it regarded them as genuine dilemmas. Both Arjuna and Yudhiṣṭhira suffered from the moral emotions of guilt and shame for violating the *dharma* principles that they did violate. Both of them held the principles they violated very dear to themselves. Tradition believed that one met moral retribution if one violated any important moral principle. The author of the *Mahābhārata* describes how Yudhiṣṭhira immediately lost the privilege he had enjoyed for upholding the high moral principle of truthfulness throughout his life. (During a war, his chariot used to travel a few inches above the ground due to his merit or excellence in *dharma*. This was only one lapse; however, a lapse was a lapse and he had to pay for it. Thus, his chariot symbolically came down to the level of all the rest.) Even Arjuna was greatly humiliated towards the end. He lost his prized possession, the invincible Gāṇḍīva bow, which had been a gift from Agni. When the war was finally over, his famous chariot was reduced to ashes as soon as Kṛṣṇa dismounted. Besides, towards the end (when Kṛṣṇa died), this great hero of the famous battle of Kurukṣetra suffered a crushing defeat and humiliation at the hands of ordinary tribal warriors and robbers, who kidnapped the women of the Yādava clan who were under his protection. When the battle of Kurukṣetra was over, both Arjuna and Yudhiṣṭhira regretted the loss of millions of lives and doubted whether the throne had been worth fighting for. After all, what kind of kingdom was it in which only old people, widows and children were alive? Whatever moral decision the moral agent might have taken in the case of genuine dilemmas, the violation of the conflicting principle was regarded as a violation by the tradition, and hence the talk about retribution seemed justified.

7. *DHARMA* AND MORAL EMOTIONS

I wish to regard the above cases as genuine dilemmas for a slightly different reason. I believe that, in the case of a genuine dilemma, the agent has to suffer from certain appropriate moral emotions, such as regret and remorse, guilt and shame, since he cannot rationally justify his preference for one principle and the resultant violation of the other. In the epic stories, both of our moral heroes suffered from such appropriate moral emotions. Regret is not enough; the morally sensitive agent usually feels remorse as well. Both guilt and shame are appropriate feelings for the morally alert agent. The by-now-well-known Rawlsian distinction between guilt and shame may be mentioned here to make a minor point.[27] According to Rawls, guilt invokes the concept of right, while shame appeals to the concept of goodness. Guilt can be relieved by reparation, it 'permits reconciliation' through forgiveness. Shame invokes aspiration and ideals, that is, certain forms of moral excellence the agent wishes to attain. In the case of our epic characters, they felt both the appropriate guilt and shame, although, as the texts testify, at some times, it was more guilt than shame and at others it was the other way around. For example, when Arjuna had to violate his principle of promise-keeping and refrain from killing his own venerable elder brother, Yudhiṣṭhira, he experienced more a sense of guilt than shame.[28] Hence, when Kṛṣṇa suggested a way for him to relieve himself of the guilt by reparation, Arjuna readily followed his advice. Rāma, in the *Rāmāyaṇa*, also felt more guilt than shame over his controversial acts, such as the abandonment of Sītā. But Yudhiṣṭhira was a different sort of person. After lying to Droṇa, he was overwhelmed with more shame than guilt; after the battle was over his self-shame, contempt and derision knew no bounds. He aspired to a sort of moral excellence and had the same ideals as Dhṛtarāṣṭra, that is, the King of Dharma. But the war was finally won by not very glorious means, and, as Kṛṣṇa made clear to him, it had to be done that way, for there was no other possible alternative. Bhavabhūti's Rāma, however (in his *Uttara-Rāmacarita*)[29], was more like Yudhiṣṭhira, a tragic hero, than the original portrait of him by Vālmīki.

8. *DHARMA*, ITS VULNERABILITY AND ELUSIVENESS

The epic stories presented the *dharma* morality in a novel light. They were dealing with practical problems of everyday life. I claim that sometimes there was more realism in these old epic stories than they are given credit for today. They underlined the two most prominent aspects of *dharma*: the vulnerability of moral virtues and the ever-elusive nature of truth in the moral domain. I shall conclude with another story from the *Mahābhārata*. Yudhiṣṭhira had to participate in *dharma* discourses several times, under various odd situations. The following was one of them.

On the last day of their exile, the Pāṇḍavas found themselves all of a sudden in a very strange situation. A brahmin-priest came and informed them that a deer had run away along with the two sacrificial sticks, used to light the sacrificial fire, stuck into its horns. The ritual would be stopped if the deer was not found in time, and *dharma* would be violated. Hence it was the moral duty (*dharma*) of the Pāṇḍavas, of the warrior caste (the *kṣatriyas*), to find the deer and recover the sticks. It was indeed a very small matter for warriors like Arjuna or Bhīma to recover the sticks. But as luck would have it, the deer had disappeared. The Pāṇḍavas searched and left no stone unturned, but they only got exhausted, showing that, even with the best of intentions and sincerest of efforts, people may be unable to obey *dharma*.

This was the case with the Pāṇḍavas. They became thirsty in the middle of the forest, and Nakula (the fourth brother) observed from a treetop that there was a lake nearby. Each of his four brothers was sent by Yudhiṣṭhira to fetch water, one after another. But nobody returned. Hence Yudhiṣṭhira finally went near the lake to see what the matter was. He saw all his four brothers dead near the lakeside. As he was descending to get some water, a voice spoke: 'Please do not be rash, O Prince. First you must answer my question and then touch the water. Your brothers did not listen and you can see what happened to them. The lake belongs to me.' In utter surprise, Yudhiṣṭhira asked: 'May I know who you are?' 'I am Yakṣa,' was the answer. Yudhiṣṭhira agreed and a question-and-answer session followed. Of the many tricky questions asked by Yakṣa, the most important was: What is the way (to reach a decision about *dharma*)? Yudhiṣṭhira's answer satisfied Yakṣa, who then divulged his identity. Although he appeared in the form of a stork there, he said that he was in fact Dharma, Yudhiṣṭhira's real father, and that he had stolen the sacrificial sticks of the brahmin in the form of a deer in order to teach Yudhiṣṭhira a lesson in *dharma*. This story illustrates the ever-elusive nature of *dharma*: one may fail in spite of everything, so no one should take pride in being a moral hero. Let me comment upon the verse cited by Yudhiṣṭhira in reply to Yakṣa's question. Yudhiṣṭhira said:

> There are different Vedas, even the *dharmaśāstras* vary from one another. There is not a single *muni* [teacher-sage] whose view is not different [from that of other teacher]. The truth of *dharma* lies hidden in the [dark] cave. [But] the way [leading to *dharma*] is the one that the *mahājana* had followed.

I have left the crucial term *mahājana* untranslated on purpose. One (comparatively later) meaning of the term is 'a great person', and plurality in such cases is implicit in the grammatically singular expression.

Hence the meaning would be: the path taken by great men is the path in matters of *dharma* conflict. If this interpretation is accepted, then it is simply a reference to 'the conduct of the good people' as an authority on, that is, a determining factor of, *dharma*, which was mentioned in the *Manusaṃhitā*. I believe, however, that the second meaning of the term, 'a great number of people', has a wider significance in the context. This may be a statement of a primitive form of a moral theory: the path is that one wherein lies the good for the maximum number of people. It seems to be a primitive proto-utilitarian view, which need not be surprising; for a sort of primitive proto-utilitarianism seems to be implied by the rational side of any ancient (and well-developed) civilization. Besides, the public rituals in classical India used to be prefixed by a benediction ritual-recitation (*maṇgala*), where the following phrase was commonly used:

bahujana-sukhāya bahujana-hitāya ca.

For the sake of the happiness of many people, and for the sake of the good of many.

The more interesting part of the above *Mahābhārata* verse is, however, the pluralistic ideals that it insists upon. For, the demand for rational decision is always greater when pluralism is admitted. Pluralism has several senses, some of them rather specific or technical in nature. In this context, we may take it in one specific sense in order to make some concluding comments. When pluralism is applied to a moral theory, it may offer the counterpoint to a monistic theory like utilitarianism, which, even in some of its modern versions, tries to resolve all moral issues by relying upon one ultimate, uniform criterion: utility. A theory that refuses to reduce all judgement of (moral) preference to a quantitative form in a single dimension (so that we can calculate), and that allows for diversity of (moral) goods which are sometimes incommensurable, is pluralistic. Pluralism raises several important questions. One is: how are we supposed to combine, in our lives, two or three or more conflicting goals, or virtues or principles, which we feel in our bones that we cannot repudiate? Conflict arises because they seem to demand 'incompatible' actions. If the conflict is only apparent (as it sometimes may be), then rational thinking will help resolve the issue. If, however, the conflict is real, we have cases of genuine dilemma, as I have already noted.

Dharma-morality is pluralistic. Hence we must also face the other questions raised by pluralism, which concern rationality in its formal aspects. The allure of utilitarianism is that, among other things, it offers a neat model of maximization of a single homogeneous magnitude, and hence it is hoped that the formal criterion of consistency and completeness may be achievable here. Thus, compared to pluralistic theories, it seems to be the 'rational' moral theory *par excellence*. Pluralism, however, does not necessarily lead to irrationality. Even consistency seems achievable if we recognize the need to find the consistent ordering of priorities in a pluralistic theory. Two offending principles may be put under strict logical scrutiny with regard to a particular situation, so as to discover whether one can by allowed to override the other. The cases of dilemma have already been discussed, where practical wisdom has to bear the occasional burden of moral emotions such as shame or remorse. They might signal the limits to the formal notion of consistency in a moral theory, without necessarily rendering the theory inconsistent. As far as the requirement of completeness is concerned, I believe this may not be necessary in order to keep a pluralistic theory within the bounds of rationality.[30]

9. CONCLUSION

Dharma does not have a definitive form. It has an ever-elusive nature that has been well illustrated in the story from the *Mahābhārata*. It is also open-ended and rational. *Dharma* does not rule, but (as Robert Lingat once put it), it reigns from above. It is a going concern of the society as well as the individual. It demands the best from our practical wisdom. I have tried to lay down the insights of the ancient writers of India with respect to *dharma*. In many ways, we must admit, their formulation of issues are primitive and dated. But the stories they have told sometimes have far-reaching significance and reveal their wisdom in a new light.

Today's moral philosophy has become increasingly technical. One needs to talk about the decision-theoretic procedures, the Arrow-Sen impossibility theorem, as well as the Pareto optimality. In this background, exploration of the writings of the ancient Indians may not be relevant. I am, however, interested in cultural history, and I believe the historical understanding of the concept of *dharma* has some relevance today. I believe it is a widely misunderstood concept in the modern study of the history of Indian philosophy. I have tried to clear up part of this misunderstanding. Explanation of the traditional ethos of India has always been somewhat controversial among the Indianists of today. The sociologists or social anthropologists propagate one way of looking at it. The development economists favour another way of taking it.[31] Both, however, assume that to understand modern India some basic knowledge of classical

India is absolutely necessary. My exposition of *dharma* and rationality has been partly aimed at this enterprise. Besides—and last of all—what has often attracted me to such a study is that, although the ancients did not always seem right from our modern point of view, what is surprising is that they also often got it right. Today they seem to us to have been mistaken in many ways, but that they did sometimes hit upon the right note is worthy of our notice and praise.

Notes and Referemces

1. B.K. Matilal, 'Kṛṣṇa: In Defence of a Devious Divinity', *Essays in the Mahābhārata*, ed. in A. Sharma (Leider: E.S. Bill, 1991), pp. 401–18.
2. M. Weber, *The Religion of India* (Glencoe: The Free Press, 1958), p. 144.
3. Ibid., p. 121.
4. *Bṛhadāraṇyaka Upaniṣad* 3.1, in *The Principal Upaniṣads with Śaṃkara Bhāṣya* (Delhi: Matilal Banarsidass, 1964).
5. Ibid., 3.2.
6. Ibid., 3.2.13.
7. L. Dumont, *Homo Hierarchicus: The Caste System and Its Implications.* Complete Revised English Edition (Chicago: The University of Chicago Press, 1980).
8. B.K. Matilal, 'Images of India: Problems and Perceptions', in *The Philosophy of N.V. Banerjee*, ed. M. Chatterjee (Delhi: ICPR, 1990).
9. *Chāndogya Upaniṣad* 4.4, in *The Principal Upaniṣads with Śaṃkara Bhāṣya* (Delhi: Motilal Banarsidass, 1964).
10. B.K. Matilal, 'Moral Dilemmas: Insights from the Indian Epics', in *Moral Dilemmas and the Mahābhārata*, ed. B.K. Matilal (Shimla: Indian Institute of Advanced Study, 1989), pp. 1–19.
11. See my 'Images of India', ibid. (note 8).
12. Chapter IV, verse 13.
13. See also B.K. Matilal, 'Caste, Karma and the Gītā', in *Indian Philosophy of Religion*, ed. R.W. Perrett (Dordrecht: Kluwer, 1989), pp. 195–202.
14. *Manusaṃhitā*, with Kullūka's Commentary, ed. Narayana Rama Acarya (Bombay: Nirnay Sagar Press, 1946). For reference to the commentaries of Govindarāja and Medhātithi, see also Kullūka's commentary.
15. *The Mīmāṃsā-Sūtra of Jaimini*, with Śabara's Commentary, ed. M. Nyayaratna (Calcutta: Asiatic Society, 1889).
16. Ibid., note 14.
17. See my 'Moral Dilemmas', ibid. (note 10).
18. Kālidāsa, *Abhjñāna-Śākuntala*, ed. Narayana Rama Acarya (Bombay: Nirnay Sagar Press, 11th Edition, 1947), I, 22.
19. *The Rāmāyaṇa*, Critical Edition (Baroda: Baroda Oriental Institute, 1960–75.

20. *The Ṛg-Veda*, with various commentaries, ed. Vishva Bandhu (Hosiarpur: Vedic Research Institute, 1965).
21. *Collected Dialogues of Plato*, eds E. Hamilton and H. Cairns (New York: Pantheon Books, 2nd printing, with corrections, 1963), *Protagoras*, 352b–356c.
22. *The Basic Works of Aristotle*, ed. R. Mckeon (New York: Random House, 1941), *Ethica Nicomachea*, 7.2.
23. Ibid., 7.3.
24. Ibid.
25. *The Holy Bible, Revised Standard Edition* (New York: Oxford University Press, 1962).
26. *Manusaṃhitā* V. 56, ibid. (note 14).
27. J. Rawls, *A Theory of Justice* (Cambridge: Harvard University Press, 1971).
28. For full details of this episode, see my 'Moral Dilemmas in the Mahābhārata', ibid. (note 10).
29. Bhavabhūti, *Uttara-Rāmacarita*, ed. P.V. Kane (Bombay: Nirnay Sagar Press, 1964.)
30. For a different treatment of pluralism, see my 'Pluralism, Relativism and Confrontation of Cultures', paper for the Plenary Session of the 6th East-West Philosophers' Conference, 1 August 1989, Honolulu.
31. See my 'Images of India', ibid. (note 8).

6

Rationality, *Dharma* and the *Pramāṇa* Theory

What is rationality? I would not dare to answer this question, for experts have pondered over it for a long time. One expression of rationality that is commonly and somewhat uncritically assumed seems to be this. A person *S* acting rationally should decide to do *A* rather than *B* when the two alternatives, *A* and *B*, are such that *A* is more conducive to the self-interest of *S*, or *A* is better (generates more good or has better consequences) or at least less unacceptable than *B* (as is expressed in the 'lesser of the two evils' motto). Another expression of rationality is said to be found in our propensity to reject, or rather, our reluctance to accept, consciously held inconsistent or self-contradictory beliefs. If *p* is believed to be true, then the same person cannot hold *not-p* to be true in the same sense and at the same time, *ceteris paribus*, without being irrational. A third expression is found in our tacit acceptance of the equality of human beings or living creatures in some basic or ontological sense, although empirical evidence shows how inequal they are in respect of intelligence, skills, physique, health, beauty and moral qualities. Such an intuitive grasp of equality is expressed in various ways, the acceptance of the principle of equality before the law, equality of opportunities or other democratic ideals such as justice, freedom and distribution of economic goods. Another, fourth, expression is found in our readiness to believe a conclusion which follows deductively from beliefs which are firmly accepted as true. This may be a special case of the second formulation.

Now all the above expressions are claimed to be typically Western. Are they culture-specific, such that they would not lend any substance to the claim that a principle of rationality is universal? I am hesitant to agree. The first three, it seems to me, can be seen to transcend any cultural boundary or even a temporal boundary. The fourth is an exception, however. The Indian logicians' lack of interest in deduction techniques is noticeable. I cannot be sure whether all four, or at least the first and the third, could be acceptable principles in all cultures or ethnic groups, for I am not a social anthropologist and hence do not have sufficient knowledge of all ethnic groups. However, through my close acquaintance with two or three cultural traditions I can find enough evidence to claim that these three descriptions of rational behaviour would not be restricted to Western society alone but would be honoured in the tradition that classical India represents.

The concept of rational choice has played a very important role in the modern discussion of ethics and economics. Paradoxes are generated and dilemmas arise when, due to our limited knowledge, and non-availability of relevant information, our practical knowledge cannot help us make our decision solely on rational grounds. The case of Buridan's ass (from J. Buridan's *Sophistimata*) is well known. The ass, here a perfectly rational creature, was unable to decide which of two bales of hay he would approach in order to satisfy his hunger—since the bales were placed at exactly equal distances from him. So he chose to starve himself to death! Thank God that we humans are not such perfectly rational creatures, and decision based upon *non-rational* choice is open to us. There are many sophisticated and complicated versions of the general problem of rational choice in the well-discussed '*prisoner's dilemma*' and its variants. When two alternative choices are perfectly balanced, we have a rationally undecidable case where sometimes we are forced to make non-rational or less rational decisions. Such cases are well-known. This mode of rationality can hardly be restricted to Western culture. For certainly in the Indian traditions, we have moral and other types of conflict, as well as moral dilemmas. In a conflict situation, reason (*yukti*) is supposed to lead us to rational choice and so to a decision.

Let us take a classic example—*the Bhagavad-Gītā*. On the eve of the battle of Kurukṣetra, why was Arjuna reluctant to fight? It was due to a moral dilemma—and an almost unresolvable one. On the one hand, he must fight in order to regain the lost kingdom. On the other hand, fighting would mean killing his respected grandfather, his teacher, as well as his cousins and other relatives. What is the use of a kingdom which you can enjoy only after having killed your respected elders and your near and dear ones? Besides, his duty as a *kṣatrīya* urges him to fight, while his responsibility as a family member as well as his duty as a human being requires him to give up the fighting. The arguments on both sides seemed to him equally balanced and hence rationally undecidable. He became, as he said, *dharma-saṃmūḍha-cetāḥ*, 'with mind perplexed about *dharma*' (II, 7).

This will be enough to show that Arjuna was trying to act rationally (in the first sense of the word discussed above), and looking for a way out of this impossible situation. He also talked about freedom, for within the given norms of the society he was at least free to opt out and become a *sanyāsin* or a wandering monk rather than a king, for he said in an unmistakable language. 'I would rather be a monk and earn my livelihood by begging, and not kill these honourable elders, than enjoy wealth and objects of pleasure—all soaked in blood—after having killed these very people' (II, 5).

The usual target of those who think that rationality in the Indian tradition is either non-existent, or takes a very outlandish and hence unrecognizable form, is the hierarchical nature of *dharma* ethics as well as the preponderance of caste-inequality. What is *dharma*? I understand by it a theory of rational behaviour based on a system of moral virtues. In the existing literature, the nature of *dharma* is hotly debated, and no principle was sacred. God was never cited as an authority on *dharma*. Hence the search for a rational basis for *dharma* was on. The scriptures were held as only one of the authorities that were acceptable; and the philosophical stream called *Mīmāṃsā* was developed apparently to examine rationally and reconcile the conflict-ridden scriptural injunctions. It is true that such a search for a rational basis for moral, social and religious behaviours was riddled, in those days, with unconscious bias and inherited prejudice. But this is only to be expected, for even today very few (if any) attempts to formulate social and moral action-guides are free from unconscious bias and prejudice. Even Western culture, which is thought today to represent the paragon of the virtues that constitute rationality, is hardly free from colonial bias in its attempt to deal with the cultures of the third world.

One point, however, stands our. Although the rational resolution of conflicts between action-guides very often degenerated into 'apologia' or 'rationalization' (it still does in modern as well as Western cultures, and that is also taken to be a mark of rationality), the internal and external criticism of *dharma* ethics did not have to wait for an enlightenment. There was a steady tradition of critically examining prevalent religious and moral behaviour. Even the acts of those who are believed to be incarnations of God, Rāma and Kṛṣṇa, did not escape criticism, and their actions were subject to eventual rationalization in later texts, as the different versions of the original epic stories amply illustrate. Whoever retold the story of Rāma, for example, later on (Kṛttibās or Tulsidās or Bhavabhūti) found it absolutely necessary to 'rationalize' various acts of the Lord such as the killing of Vālin and Saṃbuka.

Caste-inequality is seen as ingrained in Indian society. It was thought of as decidedly anti-rational for, as Max Weber said, it denied 'the natural equality of man' (1958, p. 144). We may recall our third expression of rationality in this connection. However, there was a balancing process in the form of the *karma* doctrine, as it was initially understood and explained. Historically I believe that the caste-hierarchy preceded the introduction of the *karma* theodicy (although I cannot prove it conclusively). Caste-inequality upset the balance of the implicit rationality of the Indian mind. The *karma* doctrine was partly invented by those who were trying to search for a rational explanation (= rationalization) of the odd phenomenon of caste-inequality. The *karma* theory may have its own problems. However, its rational underpinnings (which may or may not have an inadequate parallel in the Christian notion of 'just deserts') should not be overlooked. Even Max Weber described it as 'the most consistent theodicy ever produced in history' (1958, p. 121) and regarded it as a pure product of 'rational ethical thought'. The doctrine, at least in theory, allowed that even the lowest of the low in the Hindu caste-hierarchy was at liberty to act in such a way as to climb gradually up the social ladder to reach for the stars (and even become a god in a future life). The point here again is not that it is successful or satisfactory from our modern viewpoint of rationality, but even discounting the Weberian enthusiasm, we can clearly discern the rational undertaking that was at work in developing the *karma* doctrine.

The caste-inequality which has been inherent in Indian society from the very beginning need not and should not be taken to be an indisputable mark of irrationality inherent in the psyche of the Indian people, for inequalities have existed in various forms—slavery, feudalism, the aristocrat versus the common labourer, the class hierarchies of modern societies—in almost every society in the past and it still haunts us even in modern Western democracies. This is not cited as an excuse or an argument in favour of inequality, for many wrongs do not in combination make a right. However, we must note the deeper conflict within the domain of rationality itself. The first form noted above is in conflict with the third at a deeper level. In fact, perpetuation of irrational inequality and lack of freedom is due to this rather irreconcilable conflict: that between the propensity of all to act according to the dictates of their perceived self-interest and the self-interest of the few, fortunate, rich and powerful, being served by the subjection of the rest to servitude, deprivation, torture and exploitation. In this conflict, self-interest of the few often gets the upper hand and inequalities continue.

Rationally guided actions are in conflicts at a much deeper and more subtle level. Recently, this has been much discussed in the literature on the various versions of the *prisoner's dilemma*. To wit: the fishermen's dilemma—when the sea is overfished, it can be better for each if he or she tries to catch more, worse for each if all do; the peasants' dilemma—when the land is overcrowded, it can be better for each if he or she has more children, worse for each if all do. In a country like India, where overpopulation, lack of concern for others and so on, create insuperable difficulties in public and social life, all these are very relevant issues. They are not, however, marks of a lack of rational behaviour (as one may uncritically assume) but indicators of unresolved conflicts (which are admittedly rationally unresolvable), conflicts which get worse because we have not seriously adopted the available ad hoc solutions, the political and the psychological (which includes moral or Kantian and other altruistic) solutions of the dilemmas.

On the other hand, we must note that the classical tradition of *dharma*-ethics, in spite of its endorsement of caste-hierarchy, regarded moral conscience as an important guide to decide what should be done when different *dharma*-duties conflict. Manu, for example, has described *dharma*, as that (1) which is always honoured by the learned, (2) which is followed by those who are above attachment (greed) and aversion (hatred), and (3) which is approved by the hearts of the people (*Manu saṃhitā*, chapter II, verse I). Of the three characteristics mentioned here, the second ensures the impartiality of the *dharma* injunctions and thereby indicates the rational nature of such prescriptive behaviours. The third is interpreted as moral conscience. For later on (chapter II, verses 6 and 12) different authorities on *dharma* are cited, and the heart's approval' or endorsement by the inner faculty of conscience, is emphatically mentioned. The authorities enumerated are as follows: (1) Scriptures, (2) *dharmaśāstras*, (3) Virtues cultivated by the (Vedic) scholars, (4) The good conduct of the honest, and (5) Satisfaction of the heart, or own conscience. Here the intended rational basis of *dharma* is clearly endorsed. The commentator Kullūka quotes the view of Garga, another author of *dharmaśāstra*:

> Satisfaction of the conscience is the only authority in cases of (unresolvable) conflicting alternatives.

This appeal to the satisfaction of the hearts of good and honest persons was very pervasive. Even the poet Kālidāsa insisted that where doubt intervenes, the natural inclinations of the heart of an honest person would be a *pramāṇa* (a decisive evidence): *satāṃ hi sandeha-padeṣu vastuṣu pramāṇam antaḥkaraṇapravṛttayaḥ* (Abhijñāna-Śākuntala I, 22). This switch from the operation of the head (reasoned argument) to the heart (the intuition of good conscience) was not a volte-face but a recognition of the prevalence of dilemmas which are rationally unresolvable.

Sufficient evidence is available from *śāstras* as well as popular (epic) literature to show that *dharma*-ethics was subjected over the centuries to both *internal* and *external* criticism. The *dharmaśāstras*, which achieved notoriety for their support for many irrational (unjust) social institutions, contained paradoxically many passages where dissident voices were heard. Besides, epic and popular literature often told stories in which the nature of *dharma* itself was hotly debated, the existing codes of conduct were criticized, and in particular, institutions like caste were attacked and human values such as freedom and justice were emphasized. These constitute what I have called *internal* criticism of the culture. The external criticism was applied by the *śramaṇa* schools, that is the Buddhists, the Jainas, and the Lokāyatas, where institutions of ritual violence, caste and so on were condemned and rejected. Even in the epics as well as in the *dharmaśāstras*, we hear of the Cārvāka (who is sometimes described as a brahmin, and at other times identified with a Lokāyata *śramaṇa*), who resorted to *hetu-śāstra* or the science of reasoning or *tarka*, that is, *a priori* arguments not based on Vedas in order to attack the *dharma* that was based on the revealed scriptures.[1] This indicates an interesting interface of reason and revelation. Besides, we must note that dissident voices were raised not simply from the lower classes (this would have been unrecorded) but from the higher strata of the society as well, from both *brāhmaṇas* and *śramaṇas*.

To refer very briefly to one or two examples. In the *Rāmāyaṇa*, sage Jābāli, the brahmin advisor of the king Daśaratha, propounded a hedonistic ethics to morally justify his advice to Rāma—that he need not follow the late father's order and spend 14 years in exile, for pleasure was the natural goal of life, and social institutions such as family, filial duties, were man-made and hence could be transgressed whenever necessary.

Manu, or whoever it was who wrote the *Mānavadharmaśāstra*, is supposed to have concluded his discourse (chapter 12, verses 105–11) by reasserting the rational basis of *dharma*, and indicating that in matters of dispute a jury consisting of people from different strata of society should be called upon to adjudicate. He talked about three well-known *pramāṇas*, 'sources of knowledge'—perception, inference and various *śāstras* (testimony)—which must be appealed to for the 'purification' of the *dharma*-ethics (Verse 105). In verses 110 and 111, it was said that 'an assembly of ten or (if ten are not available) three at least, should deliberate and reach a decision', and the jury of ten should be constituted by three scholars versed in the three Vedas, one logician (*haituka*), one dialectician (*tarkin*), one semanticist who also knows etymology (*nirukta*), one versed in the *dharmaśāstras*, and three laymen: that is, one celibate student, one householder and one *retired* person. This clearly was an evidence for the rational-democratic principle, which an author of the *dharmaśāstra* at least implicitly accepted.

Verse 106 here (as well as in many other verses found elsewhere in Manu) underlines the restrictions that were put on the free play of rationality in a *dharma*-discourse. Reason should not be allowed to run wild and contradict the clear and unambiguous injunctions of the scriptures (the Vedas). For our exercise of *tarka*, dialectics, hypothetical reasoning and *a priori* argument cannot establish only one of the alternatives on firm ground, for the counter-thesis can also receive support from such dialectical or *a priori* argument. Besides, as Bhartṛhari has pointed out, if a thesis *A* is established by *tarka* today, tomorrow a greater dialectician or a more intelligent person can prove something that is contrary to *A*. Hence, scriptural authority, with regard to matters where empirical evidence is not available, should be given priority. *Brahmasūtra* II, 1.11 seems to be making a similar point.

This leads us to consider the nature of the rationality as reflected in logical rules as well as in *pramāṇa* theories. I shall conclude by commenting briefly upon the concept of rationality as it was understood in classical schools of Indian philosophy. This concerns the second and the fourth expressions of rationality that I initially mentioned. I shall discuss here what was considered to be a sound, tht is, rationally acceptable, argument by the logicians and philosophers of India. The interesting point to note in this connection is that they were not at all interested in deductive argument or truth-functional tautologies. The so-called *prasaṅga* or *reductio ab absurdum*, which was very close to *tarka*, was looked upon with suspicion, although they were based on the fundamental law of non-contradiction. For their *a priori* nature and lack of empirical data was found unsatisfactory.

The word *nyāya* is used in the early period to denote the concept of a sound and acceptable argument. Vātsyāyana attempted to define *nyāya* as follows: the examination of an object or a fact (*artha* is ambiguous enough to give us both meanings) with the help of the *pramāṇas*, 'instruments of knowledge'. *Nyāya* therefore proves an assumption to be an established fact. The etymological meaning of *nyāya* has, however, a better prospect. It is given as *nīyate prāpyate vivakṣitārthasiddhir anena*: 'It is the method by which the establishment of an intended object or a thesis is obtained.' The *siddhi* or 'establishment' here can be read or interpreted as rational acceptability. Hence, the word *nyāya* (and this must be distinguished from the use of the same term as a proper name of the school or system called the Nyāya) was connected initially with the early vague but intuitively grasped conception of rationality.

The concept of rational acceptability in the early period includes both the given state of affairs, that is, an empirical fact or that which is established by empirical evidence, and what was compatible with, that is, would fit, such facts. In fact, the distinction between actual state of affairs and possible ones was constantly blurred in the early period. States of affair were possibly thought to be actual provided they did not contradict an observed fact or a scriptural ruling. Thus, *nyāya* was contrasted with pseudo-*nyāya* (*nyāyābhāsa*), which Vātsyāyana defined as that which contradicted a perception or a scripture.[2]

The *nyāya* method was a method which was supposed to turn a supposition into a piece of knowledge, on the basis of empirical evidence. It is an inference where certainty about a supposition is reached through comparison and contrast. A known case is cited in support, such that it resembles the supposition in a relevant and essential respect; and in addition, the absence of any counter-example is demonstrated by referring to an actual case which exemplifies the absence of the property to be inferred together with the absence of the evidence in question. This, however, does not make the theory strictly a theory of inference based upon analogy. The idea is that without such empirical support, we cannot turn a supposition into knowledge, in such a way that it would be intelligible and rationally acceptable. The supposition may well be true, but it cannot be certified so unless we follow this method, and unless we do even a true supposition would not be *rationally* acceptable. On the other hand, the method might deliver a rationally acceptable supposition but, due to human limitations, the example cited may be wrongly conceived or misconstrued or misperceived, and the supposition could turn out to be false. That is why it must be checked against the already accepted facts, established through observation, and also against those issues certified by the scriptures.

This requirement for checking against accepted fact, observed or unobserved, can hardly be overestimated. From the general Western point of view, it would seem to be redundant for rationality. However, the Indian concept of rational acceptability, enshrined in the doctrine of *nyāya*, is different in this regard. The constraint imposed upon the concept by the second property of *nyāya* (that it should not contradict the accepted facts) excludes many *a priori* assumptions, as well as thousands of purely rational and conceivable or possible constructions. The intention is to fend off purely rational possibilities from the domain of truths or of actualities.

Vātsyāyana cites one example: 'Fire is cold, because it is a created substance; and all created substances are cold, such as water.' This dramatises the quandary. It is important to realize that on purely 'rational' grounds, if rationality or *nyāya* is defined narrowly without the second restriction, we can prove with our arm-chair method that fire is cold. For the inductive generalization based upon examination of a million cases of created substances could certify that they are cold, provided we fail to encounter a case of fire. It would be foolish to deny such a sceptical possibility, and therefore the argument would be considered valid. This sceptical possibility is of a piece with the 'brain-in-a-vat' type of possibility. However, our acquaintance with a single case of fire (where we have not simply learnt that fire is a designatum of the term 'fire' used by the speaker in such sentences as 'fire is a substance') would falsify the supposition, no matter whether we can prove it by inference.

This also has implications for moral and religious knowledge in the classical Indian context. If the bases of morality and religion are knowable through reason only, if many crucial questions in this domain are deemed to be decidable through reason only, then we are confronted sometimes with irreconcilable choices. The constraints from scriptural or verbal testimony in most such cases can offer a resolution. Consider, for example, the following inference (a modified version of what was cited by Vātsyāyana): 'Telling a lie is a moral duty for it comes naturally to human beings, like eating and drinking.' This dramatizes the fact that it is only by referring to a scriptural statement, or some intuitively grasped moral principle that we show this inference to be wrong. Of course, there may be many other pragmatic reasons or prudential considerations. But then it would not be moral.

Thus we conclude that in this notion of rational acceptability, there are two essential components. First, it must be a warranted inference based upon available evidence. Second, the conclusion should not contradict, that is, should be compatible with, the accepted facts, observed or unobserved.

Notes and References

1. See Manu; there are also frequent references in the *Mahābhārata*.
2. Cf. *pratyakṣāgamaviruddha*; see my *Logic, Language and Reality*, pp. 1–3.

Matilal, B.K. *Logic, Language and Reality* (Delhi: Motilal Banarsidass, 1985).

Manusaṃhitā, with Kullūka's commentary. Edited by R. Rama Acarya (Bombay, 1946).

Weber, M. *The Religion of India* (Glencoe, 1958).

PART II
Epics and Ethics

7

Rāma's Moral Decisions

The story of the *Rāmāyaṇa* extols ethical virtues. These ethical virtues, as I shall argue here, are nothing if not formalistic in character. In fact, some of them were so formalistic, and so much lacking in human material, that they have been controversial over the ages.

I shall call a virtue *formalistic* if it depends upon the fulfilment of a formal promise: of a formal duty of a son to his father, of husband to his wife, of a friend to his friend. Daśaratha had to banish his son, Rāma against his own will and judgement as well as the will of everybody else, the citizens of Ayodhyā, the ministers and the priests, simply because he had to fulfil his formal promise to his once beloved queen, Kaikeyī. Rāma had to go to the forest abandoning his rightful claim to the throne in order simply to fulfil his formal duty as a son. He had to abandon his beloved wife, Sītā, being well aware of her innocence, in order simply to fulfil his formal duty as a ruler, as a king. If the opinion of the citizens was so important that Sītā had to be abandoned in an almost inhuman manner, why did Rāma go to the forest in the first place against the will of all citizens? The answer lies in understanding the same kind of formalistic ethical principles that held the highest authority in the society of which Rāma was a part. It is the most flexible and pervasive Sanskrit term, *dharma*, that is substituted for all such formalistic ethical principles that I am trying to draw attention to here. Even a sage, called Jāmadagnya, in this highly patrilineal society decapitated his own mother at his father's behest, simply because it was his *dharma* to obey his father. And in the same Ikṣvāku family in the past, one thousand sons of King Sagara met their destruction simply at the command of their father. It is the same *dharma, kuladharma* (family honour) to be sure, that Rāma was afraid of, when he decided to abandon Sītā. The same *pitṛpaitāmaha dharma* was invoked by Rāma when he was trying to justify his killing of Vālin:

tvaṃ tu dharmam avijñāva kevalaṃ roṣam āsthitaḥ /
vidūṣayasi māṃ dharme pitṛ-paitāmahe sthitam // 4.8.39

Yet you, who know nothing of *dharma* and simply follow your passions, rebuke me for abiding by my sacred ancestral laws.

The climax of formalism comes at the end of the story, when Rāma has to banish his totally innocent brother, Lakṣmaṇa, because of a formal promise he made. Here is the episode. A sage, who was none but Kāla (Time) himself in disguise, came to hold consultation with Rāma on the condition that no one should disturb them while they would be in the consultation room. Rāma promised to kill the person who would disturb then, and Lakṣmaṇa was asked to guard the door. Meanwhile the great sage, Durvāsas, who, by the way, had already earned a reputation for handing down fatal curses to other people, appeared and demanded an immediate audience with Rāma. Lakṣmaṇa tried to appease him but in vain. The irate sage threatened to curse the whole royal family if Rāma did not come to receive him immediately. Lakṣmaṇa, as anybody with some sense would, under these conditions, chose to enter the consultation room. Rāma came out to receive the sage, who only wanted a good meal at the royal palace on the occasion of his one thousandth birthday! As the sage left, being satisfied with a sumptuous dinner, Rāma had to make the last important moral decision in his life. He would have to kill Lakṣmaṇa in order to fulfil his formal promise. There was a little cheating, at last, in the matter (reminiscent of Yudhiṣṭhira's cheating in his attempt to kill Droṇa). For Rāma said:

tyāgo vadho vā vihitaḥ sādhūnāṃ hy ubhayaṃ samam / 7.106.13cd.

With regard to the good people, abandonment is the same thing as killing.

What does this episode signify? At long last it is clear that factual faults or real crimes do not matter that much. Violation of a formal rule or a stupid promise is all that matters. What wrong did Lakṣmaṇa do? Nothing that was material. He simply wanted to save the family from the terrible curse of Durvāsas. Hence he broke a formal rule. There might have been a shade of doubt, as far as the common citizens were concerned, regarding Sītā's innocence. After all, she lived in Rāvaṇa's place for some time. And we know the nature of the power of gossip. The poet Bhavabhūti rightly observed:

sarvathā vyavahartavyaṃ kuto hy avacanīyatā /
yathā strīṇāṃ tathā vācāṃ sādhutve durjano janaḥ // (*Uttararāmacarita* 1.5)

One should always do one's duty; since bad talk abounds. As regards their purity, a man is as malicious to words as to women.

But what about Lakṣmaṇa? He had not done anything in this context which could be morally questionable. But remember there is that formalistic ethical principle, *dharma*. Violation of a stupid promise would be violation of this formalistic principle. Even Vasiṣṭha declared on this occasion:

tyajainaṃ, balavān kālo, mā pratijñāṃ vṛthā kṛthāḥ /
pratijñāyāṃ hi naṣṭāyāṃ dharmo hi vilayaṃ vrajet // 7. 106. 9

Abandon him, (for) *Kāla*, 'Time', is all powerful, do not fail to keep your promise. For when a promise is not kept, *dharma* is destroyed.

In a man-made legal system, such formalism is not difficult to find. If I promise to pay back my debts before 4.30 p.m. today, but produce the money only at 4.31 p.m., legally this will be actionable. It was the same insistence on formalistic legal system that was invoked by Shylock in *The Merchant of Venice*, when he wanted to have a pound of flesh from Antonio's breast without accepting the money that Antonio borrowed from him. Yudhiṣṭhira's adherence to truthfulness had the same formalistic character. And rightly he is called Dharmarāja.

'To tell a lie is *adharma* no matter what': this is what I am calling here one of the formalistic ethical principles. Thus, to tell a harmless lie so as not to hurt the feelings of an otherwise honest and nice man, would be considered an *adharma*, according to this norm. Yudhiṣṭhira lied only once—the lie that he knew would be sufficient to kill his own guru, Droṇa. But Yudhiṣṭhira deluded himself into believing that he was, after all, making a formally true statement. Here is the story:

It was impossible to defeat and kill Droṇa as long as he was fighting against the Pāṇḍavas with his bow and arrow. So Kṛṣṇa devised a trick. If it were announced that Aśvatthāman, Droṇa's beloved son, was dead, Droṇa was sure to abandon his bow and arrow in grief. And Arjuna would take that opportunity to kill Droṇa. But Droṇa would not trust anyone unless the death news was announced by Yudhiṣṭhira himself. But Yudhiṣṭhira would not listen. He would not lie even if that lie meant his victory and survival. But what a *volte face* in the next moment! It so happened that an elephant of the name of Aśvatthāman was killed in the battle at the moment. Hence, at the request of Kṛṣṇa, Yudhiṣṭhira announced: Aśvatthāman is dead. Droṇa believed his son was dead, and as a result was killed by Arjuna.

One should remember here that Yudhiṣṭhira was aware of the full consequence of this little lie: namely, the death of Droṇa and victory for him. For this heinous little lie Yudhiṣṭhira was only nominally punished view of the sinners in hell at the end of the *Mahābhārata*. Why? Remember that he did not, after all, violate any formalistic ethical law, that is, any *dharma* of uttering formally true statements.

If a man-made law cannot be broken, how can the *dharma*, which is presumably either divinely ordained or traditionally sacred or both, be broken? Dharma was the dehumanized norm of human conduct. Rāma once said, when he was sadly reconciling himself to his hard life in the forest:

eko hy aham Ayodhyāṃ ca pṛthivīṃ cāpi Lakṣmaṇa /
tareyam iṣubhiḥ kruddho, nanu vīryam akāraṇam //
adharma-bhaya-bhītaś ca paralokasya cānagha /
tena Lakṣmaṇa nādyāham ātmānam abhiṣecaye // 2.47.25, 26

If I am angry, O Lakṣmaṇa, I am alone capable of conquering not only Ayodhyā but the whole earth with my arrows. But alas, strength is of no avail here. Being afraid of *adharma* and what others may say, O sinless Lakṣmaṇa, I have not allowed myself to be anointed king this time.

Thus it is that to uphold this dehumanized norm, *dharma*, that is, this body of formalistic ethical laws, Rāma could punish innocent persons like Sītā and Lakṣmaṇa, (and kill an innocent Śūdra, Śambūka, who was only striving for his own salvation.)

To come back to the killing of Vālin. Why was this act regarded as *almost* unpardonable even by the orthodox Sanskrit tradition? I think this was because the method of killing was *apparently* a flagrant violation of the very formalistic ethics of war, of which Rāma was supposed to be the upholder. Thus, the Bengali poet Kṛttivās laments:

Kṛttivās paṇḍiter ghaṭila viṣād/
Vālibadh kari kena karilā pramād//

Krittivās is sad: Why did you blunder and kill Vālin?

But how did Rāma justify his own act when he was confronted by the dying Vālin? He referred to *dharma*, that formalistic ethic. Due to his friendship with Sugrīva, Rāma promised to kill Vālin, provided Sugrīva helped him in recovering Sītā. It was Kabandha, the Rākṣasa, who told Rāma to seek Sugrīva's friendship because he and his four associates would be helpful in recovering Sītā and the *kuladharma* as well, from the clutches of Rāvaṇa. Hence Sugrīva's enemy would be Rāma's enemy too. And the killing of Vālin would mean (a) protecting a friend, and (b) keeping a formal promise and thereby upholding *dharma*. One should add to these the following fact (Rāvaṇa says it in so many words): Killing of an animal from behind is no *adharma* for a Kṣatriya prince, because no formalistic ethical principle would be violated thereby. So what more do we need to persuade Rāma, the supreme upholder of the formalistic ethical laws, to kill Vālin? Protecting a useful friend, recovery of the family honour and prestige by recovering Sītā from Rāvaṇa, and keeping a formal promise — these three should be enough.

Whether one commends or condemns the formalistic ethic which played such an important role in moral decision in the ancient Indian epics, it is important to know what these were. Rāma, by his own admission, feared nobody but *adharma* which, I have pointed out, amounted to violation of some formalistic ethical principle devoid of human interest.

Since between Sugrīva and Vālin, the latter is often thought to be the better of the two, I wish to say a few words in defence of Sugrīva. Sugrīva, it is true, was always attracted to Vālin's wife, Tārā, and he slept with her when Vālin was away, supposedly dead. It might very well be wish-fulfilment on the part of Sugrīva. But remember, wish-fulfilment or dreams do not violate any formalistic ethical principle, any *dharma.* So Sugrīva, at least, was not formally guilty. But what did Vālin do in revenge? He chased Sugrīva away and stole his wife, Rumā. He, unlike Sugrīva had no pretext to delude himself with: namely, that Sugrīva was dead and so there was no harm in stealing his wife. (We should recall that marrying the elder brother's widow was a custom in some Vānara society). Thus, in the eyes of Rāma, Vālin was formally guilty while Sugrīva was not. This Rāma did not forget to remind the dying Vālin:

> *asya tvaṃ dharamāṇasya Sugrīvasya mahātmanaḥ* /
> *Rumāyām vartase kāmāt snuṣāyāṃ pāpakarmakṛt* // 4.18.19

Out of lust you commited a sinful deed: while great Sugrīva is alive, you lived in sin with your daughter-in-law Rumā.

Rāma's considered reply to Vālin's charge was:

> *tad alaṃ paritāpena dharmataḥ parikalpitaḥ* /
> *vadho vānaraśārdūla na vayaṃ svavaśe sthitāḥ* // 4.18.33

O king of Vānaras, do not grieve, (your) killing has been done according to *dharma.* I had (practically) no control over myself (in this matter).

And the *Tilaka* commentary finally says: *daṇḍārtha. adhe darśanānapekṣaṇāt*. The implication is: When killing is meant for punishment, formal war ethics need not be maintained!

Notes and References

The Vālmīki-Rāmāyaṇa. Critically edited by G.H. Bhatt, et al. Seven volumes, University of Baroda, Barodal, 1960–75.

The Rāmāyaṇa of Vālmīki, edited by R.P. Goldman. Volume iv, introduction, translation and annotation by R. Lefeber, Princeton University Press, Princeton, 1994.

Bhavabhūti's Uttararāmacarita, edited by P.V. Kane, Bombay, 1929.

8

Kṛṣṇa: In Defence of a Devious Divinity

1. THE ENIGMA

Kṛṣṇa is an enigma in the *Mahābhārata*. He represents the most confusing kind of moral enigma not only in the epic, but also in the whole of the Hindu ideal of *dharma*. In the icons, he is represented as the Dark Lord, an attractive appearance with a face bearing an enigmatic, mysterious and mischievous smile, the smile, very much unlike the famous smile found in the icons of the Buddha. The Buddha's smile in striking contrast with that of Kṛṣṇa, is straightforward, it radiates with compassion, calmness and peace, it strikes confidence in the minds of the viewers. The ethical doctrine of the Buddha is also straightforward. It is novel, but non-complex. The ethical doctrine of Kṛṣṇa by contrast is different, sometimes it appears to be just the opposite.

Kṛṣṇa is a riddle, a paradox. If anything, he appears to be a devious diplomat. Why should he, as he does, claim to be the Supreme Being, the Ultimate Reality, the Inner Controller of every being? If he is God, then God must be a great diplomat, greatly devious, in whom diplomacy was the other name of duplicity and fraud. Western Indologists, by and large, have been very critical of Kṛṣṇa's ethics and politics. The following may sum up the opinion of the majority of Western Indologists as well as some West-inspired Indian Indologists.

> A bizarre figure! A Yādava chieftain who looks and acts not uncommonly like a mortal—and a very ordinary mortal at that—and who has the incredible effrontery to say that he is a god! A cynic who preaches the highest morality and stoops to practise the lowest tricks, in order to achieve his mean ends! An opportunist who teaches an honest and godfearing man to tell a lie, the only lie he had told in his life! A charlatan who declares himself to be the god of gods, descended

from the highest heaven for establishing righteousness on earth, and advises a hesitating archer to strike down a foe who is defenceless and crying for mercy![1]

Such opinions about Kṛṣṇa are not simply restricted to Western Indology; the Jainas and the Buddhists were also highly critical of the ethics of Kṛṣṇa.

In fact, the author of the *Mahābhārata* himself supplied a strikingly candid list of the misdeeds perpetrated by Kṛṣṇa through the mouth of the dying Duryodhana. When Duryodhana was struck down by Bhīma in an unlawful manner (it was a *de facto* hitting below the belt, breaking the ethical code of the mace-fight), and was dying, he took Kṛṣṇa to task for his questionable part in the battle of Kurukṣetra. In a way Duryodhana was right. According to him, Kṛṣṇa broke the moral code of *dharma* in more ways than one, whenever he found it suitable for ensuring victory for the Pāṇḍavas. Duryodhana called Kṛṣṇa 'son of a slave', for his father Vāsudeva was sort of a slave to King Kaṃsa.

Duryodhana continued to point out that it was Kṛṣṇa who advised Arjuna to place Śikhaṇḍin in front, while attacking Bhīṣma, knowing that the grandsire would not fight Śikhaṇḍin and would let himself be mortally wounded without resistance. It was Kṛṣṇa again who prevailed upon Yudhiṣṭhira to utter that deadly lie which finally led to the killing of the great warrior and revered teacher Droṇācārya. The death of Karṇa was also brought about by Arjuna who attacked him in a cowardly manner when the former was engaged in lifting his chariot-wheel from the mud in which it got stuck. And it was Kṛṣṇa who persuaded Arjuna to kill the invincible Karṇa in this manner. It was Kṛṣṇa again who instigated Sātyaki to butcher Bhūriśravas when his right arm had been cut off. Thus the misdeeds of Kṛṣṇa were well-known and that they cannot be justified on moral grounds was, on the surface, very obvious to any religious believer in traditional India. Can any of these be defended?

The contradictions in Kṛṣṇa's activities as well as in his professed ethical doctrine are self-evident. The Hindu believers were not unaware of them, but still they had been undaunted by such contradictions. The list of contradictions supplied in the above extract stands out, no matter what. But still a tradition that is just about 2000 years old has unconsciously believed that these contradictions must have either some deeper significance, or some plausible explanation. In fact, Kṛṣṇa is not a god, but *the* God for the Hindus, and yet he is very different from the God of Judeo-Christian tradition, or the Allah of Islam. I am not suggesting that there are many gods in the world today, but obviously there are many conceptions of God which have been around and well-entrenched in world religions.[2] So we may ask, what was the Hindu conception of God that was enshrined in the Kṛṣṇa of the *Mahābhārata*?

Let us select a typical case, of almost unpardonable violation of moral principle by Kṛṣṇa, from the story of the *Mahābhārata*. In many cases, Kṛṣṇa unquestionably appears to be the person who 'preaches the highest morality and stoops to practise the lowest tricks to achieve his mean ends'. It is indeed a mystery how a moral hero or a god who should be impartial and whose behaviour should be morally irreprehensible, can perpetrate such acts. However, let us take Kṛṣṇa to be a human being with superior intellect and with a superior sense of justice, fairness and moral responsibility. Then we may begin to understand the puzzle a little.

The battle of Kurukṣetra is the focal point of the *Mahābhārata*, and certainly Kṛṣṇa played a very important role in this battle. He did not fight, but certainly the battle was won by the Pāṇḍavas because of his support and advice. He was the supreme manipulator, who did not shoot a single arrow or use a single weapon to kill anyone, but all the main characters were killed by his superior strategy through behind-the-door manipulation. Kṛṣṇa as we have seen above had something to do with the killing of each of the following heroes: Bhīṣma, Droṇa, Karṇa and Duryodhana. And each time it was through a means that violated the well-known moral codes of any battle between Kṣatriyas. Duryodhana was absolutely right in his accusation of Kṛṣṇa. Even the author of the *Mahābhārata* agreed, and we are told that Duryodhana after his death ascended to heaven before the Pāṇḍavas.

2. THE JUST WAR?

The battle of Kurukṣetra was described as a *dharmayuddha*. But in what sense was it a *dharmayuddha*? How should we translate the expression '*dharmayuddha*'? The word '*dharma*' is an enigmatic term. According to standard interpretation, *dharmayuddha* can be translated as 'the war of righteousness'. It has the resonance of the concept of the 'just war' in Christian tradition. The first verse of the *Bhagavad-Gītā* describes the battle-field as *Dharmakṣetra*—the field where the seeds of moral merit/demerit are sown in order to bring forth the harvest of *karma* or just desert.[3] But what exactly is the point of the imagery? Sometimes a war is described as a case of 'just war' when it is undertaken with a view to protect certain moral and religious values. Was the battle of Kurukṣetra an example of this kind of 'just war'? This has no easy answer. It is a very simplistic assumption that the world can be divided into black and white, that whenever a war, or even a just war breaks out, the two opposite sides would represent unalloyed good and unalloyed evil. In actual cases, it is almost impossible to decide that one side fights for the just cause while the other side represents the absolute evil. Good and evil, right and wrong, are never given in their unalloyed states—a fact, which along with the other well-known questions about whether such values are relative or absolute, situational or universal makes it almost impossible for us to give any uncontroversial verdict of moral judgement. Thus it is that I find it impossible to agree with those who wish to interpret the battle in the Epic as an allegory of the battle between good and evil. All we can say that the Pāṇḍava side was the 'preferred' side, preferred by the author or authors and readers alike, while the Kaurava side was not so. There was greatness on both sides, both tried to maintain a set of moral principles and projects, a set of values and virtues. And there were many evil acts perpetrated by both sides, both stooped to meanness, to devious and devilish strategies, to conquer. But perhaps one side was more abrasive and more arrogant than the other. And if we put the immoral acts and wickedness of both sides, the Pāṇḍavas and the Kauravas, on the weighing scales, it may be that the latter will not be heavier than the former, except perhaps for a couple of greatly grotesque, grossly unjust acts by Duryodhana. The world in fact cannot be divided into black and white, but it contains only innumerable shades of grey. The epic represents the world exactly as such—paradoxically there is more realism in the epic than some of our present-day realistic novels. The situation actually presents us with what Issac Levi has called 'hard choices' under unresolvable moral dilemmas.[4]

If the *Mahābhārata* imparts a moral lesson, it emphasizes again and again, the ever-elusive character, the unresolved ambiguity of the concept of *dharma*. Kṛṣṇa's role was not to resolve the ambiguity but to heighten the mystery, which offered only temporary glimpses of the human and moral realities lying behind the stories, myths, allegories and illustrations.

I believe the battle was called *dharmayuddha* in a technical sense. One technical sense of this many-faceted word *dharma* is this. It means the code of conduct agreed upon and observed by a particular group or community. *Dharma* (in this sense) is what one should or should not do in a particular domain of human behaviour. In the beginning of the battle of Kurukṣetra, in the *Bhīṣma-Parvan*, we get a long list of *dharmas* comprising the code of conduct of each Kṣatriya when they are engaged in a battle with the adversary. Both sides agreed to fight a war on the basis of fairness by observing a number of familiar rules and practices on humanitarian grounds. Nobody, for example, should fight and kill a person who is run-ning away from the battlefield, nobody should attack an unarmed and defenceless person, and so on and so forth—rules that are very similar to that of the war conventions prevalent in any civilized society today. Fighting must be between equals, a charioteer should fight another charioteer, horsemen should fight horsemen. It may be that this battle was called *dharmayuddha* because both sides agreed to observe this *dharma*.[5]

It is of course clear that most of these rules were violated at different crucial moments of the war, and on the Pāṇḍava side Kṛṣṇa undoubtedly was instrumental in the decision to violate the norms. Hence, he seemed to be the devious manipulator, without whose help the battle would not have been won by the Pāṇḍavas.

Suppose Kṛṣṇa was playing the role of omnipotent lord. What could have happened? Was it possible for him to end the battle of Kurukṣetra in one day? An omnipotent lord could have done it. After all, he wanted the Pāṇḍavas to win. At every stage, we see him very unsure and concerned about he outcome of the battle. He knew about the superior strength of the rival side, and hence was afraid that the fight might be lost. Therefore he was planning and plotting all the time to avoid disasters for the Pāṇḍavas. This certainly does not testify to the fact of his being the omnipotent lord. Nor does the trickery which he frequently resorted to on behalf of the Pāṇḍavas prove his God-like moral superiority.

Take the case of Kṛṣṇa's advice to Yudhiṣṭhira to tell a lie—the only lie he had told in his life—the lie that was calculated to kill the great teacher and fighter Droṇa.[6] This was perhaps one of the darkest deeds of our 'dark Lord' Kṛṣṇa. One question that is not often asked is this: Kṛṣṇa was almost as venerable to the author or the story-tellers as he is to us today, but then why did he (or they) not, using the unbounded freedom of any story-teller or narrator, formulate the story in such a way that would have made Kṛṣṇa a patently obvious moral hero without such glaring blemishes in his character? Why this deliberate attempt at mystifying the issues, if this is what it is? I believe the answer is not very obvious, but there are implicit hints scattered all over the text, hints that might be collected and put together in such a way as would dissolve a greater part of the mystery. In fact there may be alternative ways of interpreting the text that we have received in the tradition and hence I would suggest only one such possible alternative which may not seem to be improbable at all.

3. TRUTH AND THE QUESTION OF SURVIVAL

Droṇa was a great hero, venerable teacher of both the Kauravas and the Pāṇḍavas but his behaviour had not always been ideal.[7] He was, to be sure, instrumental in bringing about the inglorious death of the boy warrior Abhimanyu, who was killed by being attacked jointly by seven great warriors including Droṇa. And Droṇa was the ring-leader of the inglorious Seven! So he had already violated *dharma*, that is, the moral code of warfare. It was highly immoral to kill a boy who was fighting most heroically all alone against seven formidable adversaries.

It is interesting to note here another earlier episode in the *Ādiparvan* for it has implications for moral lessons or moral teachings of the Kauravas and the Pāṇḍavas. Droṇa was a brahmin teacher, but he was an expert in archery and the art of warfare. He was appointed by Dhṛtarāṣṭra as the teacher of all the princes, the Kauravas and the Pāṇḍavas. He was apparently appointed to teach the art of warfare, how to fight and kill, but not any moral lessons or war ethics. Once Bhīṣma, the grandfather, wondered: who was taking care of the moral lessons to be imparted to the princes, the Kauravas and the Pāṇḍavas when they were growing up? He first thought it was the duty of Droṇa. So he approached Droṇa and enquired whether the latter was teaching moral lessons to the princes, along with the lessons in archery. Droṇa answered in the negative. When Bhīṣma insisted further, Droṇa went to the paymaster Dhṛtarāṣṭra and asked. Dhṛtarāṣṭra said that Droṇa's appointment was solely for the purpose of teaching archery, and the art of fighting and killing, and he should not bother about teaching any moral lessons. This apparently satisfied Droṇa. This also throws some light upon the character of Dhṛtarāṣṭra—a fact we should recall when we analyse the character of the blind king as well as his characteristic repentance in the *Ādiparvan*.

The episode unveils at least two facts. (a) The princes did not have any formal teaching in morality and ethics. The Pāṇḍavas probably received it from Bhīṣma, to whom the Kauravas did not pay any heed. (b) Droṇa himself did not have much regard for moral lessons. His behaviour was generally within the bounds of morality, but sometimes he transgressed them. One may be reminded here of the story of Ekalavya, in which Droṇa's behaviour was abominable.

Briefly, the story is this. Ekalavya belonged to the lower caste, but he wanted to be one of the best archers of his time. He approached Droṇa, the most well-known teacher of archery at that time, but the latter refused because Ekalavya was born in a lower caste and Droṇa's brahminical background found it undignified. In other words, Droṇa lacked the generosity, open-mindedness and other moral virtues which a proper brahmin (a sage like Gautama in *Chāndogya Upaniṣad*, for example) should have possessed. It is well-known that sage Gautama did not reject Satyakāma (who came to study under him) when the latter said that he was the son of his unwed mother and hence he was unable to tell his father's name or his family name. Gautama embraced the child with affection, accepted him as a student and decided that he must qualify as a brahmin for his exemplary virtues, such as truthfulness. But Droṇa was no Gautama. Rejected, Ekalavya went to a secluded place in the forest, created an image of Droṇa and, accepting that image as his guru for ritualistic initiation as well as inspiration, started learning archery all by himself! He was later discovered by Droṇa and his pupils (the princes) who went to the forest one day on a hunting expedition. Droṇa saw to his utter surprise that Ekalavya's self-taught archery had been so good that he could excel Arjuna, his most favourite pupil. He played one of the dirtiest tricks upon young Ekalvya, who still claimed Droṇa to be his *guru* (in archery) in absentia. Droṇa claimed his *guru-dakṣiṇā* (present for the teacher after the completion of the training) from Ekalavya. He asked the latter to cut off his right thumb and make a present of it to his adopted guru, Droṇa, which Ekalavya did immediately, showing his exemplary courage, integrity and truthfulness. Of course, this meant the end of Ekalavya as an archer. In the background of such admirable self-sacrifice, Droṇa's heartlessness and total absence of any moral sensitivity in his character were thrown in sharp relief. Tradition justly condemned Droṇa and glorified Ekalavya who excelled not only in physical strength or archery but also in moral virtues. Let us now return to the battle of Kurukṣetra.

On the fifteenth day of the battle Droṇa became almost irresistible in his attempt to kill the entire army of the Pāṇḍavas and obtain victory for the Kauravas. Kṛṣṇa saw it in the beginning: If Droṇa could not be stopped that day, the battle would end in another way. What could not have been done by strength apparently, was accomplished through a trick. And it was Kṛṣṇa's trick. Bhīma killed an elephant called Aśvatthāmān and proclaimed that he had killed Aśvatthāmān (which was also the name of Droṇa's only son). Kṛṣṇa saw a chance. He knew about Droṇa's love for his son and realized that the news of his son's death would at least temporarily make him vulnerable. But the son was not dead. Droṇa, ignoring the rumour, continued to fight. He also started killing a number of Pāṇḍava soldiers while they were running away from the battlefield. So the moral code of *dharma* was again broken and the *Dharmayuddha* turned into an *Adharmayuddha*. Some celestial sages, who were watching the battle, approached Droṇa in their subtle bodies and took him to task for stooping to such meanness and violating the ethical code of warfare. Instead of setting an example of greatness, the conduct of the great *ācārya* again became abominable. Being scolded by the celestial sages Droṇa paused for a moment. Kṛṣṇa was looking for this opportunity. Droṇa wanted to know whether the rumour about the death of his son was true. If Yudhiṣṭhira told him he would have believed it. Kṛṣṇa already had convinced Yudhiṣṭhira that since the life of everybody on the Pāṇḍava side was at stake and the dream of final victory would certainly be shattered, Yudhiṣṭhira would have to make a compromise and tell a *tactical* lie. The trick worked and Droṇa was killed.

Why do we feel quite embarrassed and upset about this rather sordid affair? There are plenty of such affairs described in the epic from the beginning to the end, and both sides had their share to contribute. But why is this particularly painful for us? I believe the answer lies in the fact that the two most important and presumably venerable characters are involved—one is Kṛṣṇa, who is supposed to be an incarnation of the Lord and presumably the upholder of justice, morality and *dharma*, and the other is Yudhiṣṭhira, who is also *dharma* incarnate, who is not supposed to deviate from his high and lofty ideal of truthfulness. And yet it is a classic case of backsliding. Yudhiṣṭhira's lie was not even a 'white lie', it was the 'darkest of the dark'—deliberately lying to deceive his teacher and thereby ensuring the opponent's death and victory for his own side. It was a deliberate lie calculated to regain his throne. What can be a more selfish goal than this? And Yudhiṣṭhira was persuaded to take this course! I believe this exposes one of the fatal weaknesses in Yudhiṣṭhira's own character. The author's characterization became more lively by the portrayal of such paradoxicality and conflict of values. Yudhiṣṭhira was not a simple, lifeless, abstract painting of *dharma*. He represented a human prince who had all the virtues but had some serious flaws in his character—he had a vice, he was addicted to gambling. He did his utmost to protect the *dharma*-morality and the ideal of truthfulness, but also failed, like all humans, on one or two crucial occasions. Lying on this occasion was such a case and he lost his moral reward. It was Arjuna who said at that time that this act of lying would be an indelible blemish in Yudhiṣṭhira's noble character.

It would be wrong to construe from this that the ideal of truthfulness should therefore be compromised sometimes in this way. For the ideal had not been compromised at all. The story-teller leaves no doubt in our mind that there had been an almost unpardonable violation of a very noble principle (truth-telling) here. Yudhiṣṭhira had to suffer accordingly. Weakness of the will once more got the better even of Dharmarāja Yudhiṣṭhira.

In fact, Yudhiṣṭhira lacked firmness, which must be an essential characteristic of moral hero. Yudhiṣṭhira suffered from such a weakness. This is also illustrated by his weakness for gambling. On the other hand, he had the stubbornness of a tragic hero. This is shown by his stubbornness in gambling, even when he was losing one stake after another.

4. THE DIVINE ATTRIBUTES

How about Kṛṣṇa? He was the manipulator. To use the terminology of Pāṇini's grammar, he was the *prayojaka kartā*. He had the moral responsibility for almost all the important decisions of the Pāṇḍavas. One may argue that although it was emphasized that *yato dharmas tato jayaḥ*, victory belongs to the party where *dharma* belongs, it was actually the case that *yataḥ Kṛṣṇas tato jayaḥ*, that is, victory belonged to the party where Kṛṣṇa belonged.

Kṛṣṇa Dvaipāyana, during the disaster said 'Where there is *dharma* there is Kṛṣṇa, and where there is Kṛṣṇa there is victory.' (*Mahābhārata* 9.61.30).

Here Kṛṣṇa bears the entire responsibility. But the story-teller does not make Kṛṣṇa, the alleged Lord of the universe, an omnipotent being, and bring about this victory through his magical or supernatural power. Apparently this is the biggest mystery. If we can have a reasonable explanation of this mystery, we can find answers to most of our bewilderment about Kṛṣṇa's doings.

According to the received doctrine, God is supposed to be omnipotent and he should also see that justice is done in the end. But Kṛṣṇa in the *Mahābhārata* did not always claim to be omnipotent. Apart from certain inspired speeches (e.g. in the *Gītā*) he acknowledged his human limitations. He admitted before the hermit Utaṅka how powerless he was to stop the devastating war, and restore friendship between the two warring families. For as he said, the war was inevitable, and he had no power to stop the inevitable.

Kṛṣṇa's own admission that he did not have any power to stop the battle or devastation either of the Kauravas or of the Yādavas (his own race) is an important evidence to show that the Hindu conception of God does not always include the attribute of omnipotence. I believe this constitutes an important difference between Judaeo-Christian theology and Hindu theology. Words such as *Īśvara* or *Bhagavān* are often used to denote what is called 'God' in the Western tradition, but these words do have a number of meanings in the Indian tradition. God in Hindu theology is not always a creator God—that is, he is not a Creator *ex nihilo*. Nor is the Hindu God always a personal being. In the case of Kṛṣṇa or Rāma, he is of course conceived as a personal being, in fact a human being with all possible human virtues and vices. Of course, it has been claimed that Kṛṣṇa (or Rāma) was mightier than anybody else, had intelligence superior to that of anybody else, but this is hardly equivalent to the claim of omnipotence or even omniscience.

Omnipotence is not an important concept in Indian philosophy of religion. It has been generally pointed out the problem of evil was not regarded by the philosophers of India as a serious flaw in the Hindu conception of God. Some Indologists have argued that the problem of evil was not important for Indians because evil was not real but an illusion. In other words this attitude was connected with the transfictioinal approach to the reality of the Indian philosophers in general. This may be so. However, there is another line of explanation. I believe the problem of evil never posed a serious threat to the concept of Theos in India because the attribute of omnipotence was never seriously emphasized. For the problem of evil becomes a serious problem if the problems of the two attributes of God are jointly emphasized in the context: omnipotence and perfect goodness of God. We might also add omniscience to the list. As we have seen, the concept of Kṛṣṇa as God does not include omnipotence. He was mightier than anybody else but he was not omnipotent.

The concept of God however must include a reference to morality and justice. This is even true of the dominant Hindu conception of God. In this respect, as we all know, the character of Kṛṣṇa comes under serious criticism. Examples of Kṛṣṇa's violation of ordinary moral principles are too numerous. Let us see briefly how he defended this move once. At the final stage of the battle, when Bhīma and Duryodhana were locked in a mace-fight, Arjuna asked Kṛṣṇa about the relative strength of the two combatants, and the possible outcome. Kṛṣṇa replied in no uncertain terms that while Bhīma was physically stronger than Duryodhana, the latter was a better mace-fighter than the former and then added:

> If Bhīma fights according to *dharma* (approved ethical code of conduct, he will not win. Hence he should kill Duryodhana by breaking the moral rule (*anyāyena*) (*Mahābhārata*, 9.57.4).

Kṛṣṇa continued to justify this breach of ethical conduct. He said that we had heard that the demons were defeated by the gods in a deceitful fight (*māyayā*). Similarly Virocana was defeated by Indra by unlawful means, and Vṛtra was defeated in a similar manner. Besides, Bhīma had already promised to break the thigh of Duryodhana by the stroke of his mace. Hence there was no other way but to resort to this deceitful means for destroying Duryodhana. For Kṛṣṇa was confident that a fair battle at that time would steal the victory away from the Pāṇḍavas. Kṛṣṇa said that Yudhiṣṭhira 'had done it again'. By agreeing to accept the outcome of the duel between Bhīma and Duryodhana as the final decisive factor of the entire battle of Kurukṣetra, Yudhiṣṭhira had put the prospect of final victory in grave danger; Kṛṣṇa had no illusion about it. He said:

> Having won the battle, he is now throwing it away (*Mahābhārata* 9.57.10).

It is significant to note that Kṛṣṇa gave two different sets of arguments to justify Bhīma's unlawful killing of Duryodhana. To pacify Balarāma he said that Bhīma took a vow of breaking Duryodhana's thigh during the fatal and deceitful gambling match where innocent Draupadī was publicly humiliated for no fault of her own. To the Pāṇḍavas, however, he gave the other reason. In a lawful battle, Bhīma would have been defeated by the superior technique of Duryodhana and hence the whole battle of Kurukṣetra would have been decided in favour of the Kauravas. I shall further expand the nature of Kṛṣṇa's divinity by first referring to the story of Utaṅka.

The Utaṅka episode is interesting in itself.[8] The encounter between Kṛṣṇa and Utaṅka took place after the devastating battle was over. Kṛṣṇa was apparently going back from Hastināpura to Dvārakā. On his way, in the desert of Rajasthan, he met the great hermit Utaṅka and accepted his hospitality for the day. Utaṅka regarded Kṛṣṇa as an *avatāra* of Lord Viṣṇu. He was also unaware that the great battle had already taken place, and everybody had died except a few fortunate warriors. He therefore asked Kṛṣṇa in confidence whether the Lord had been able to settle the quarrel between the two families, and had been successful in avoiding the devastating war. When the good hermit learned what had happened, he was visibly upset and accused Kṛṣṇa of all the evil doings. He insisted that Kṛṣṇa must bear the full responsibility for all the evils of the war, simply by letting it happen when he could have stopped it. Kṛṣṇa then answered that it was unstoppable, even by Kṛṣṇa himself. It was impossible to stop something in the middle. The process of devastation started much earlier, started by both sides through their enmity, greed, jealousy and hatred. It was true that the Kauravas wanted to take over the whole kingdom by getting rid of the Pāṇḍavas by hook or by crook. But it was again the Pāṇḍavas who were abrasive and arrogant enough to insult Duryodhana and the Kauravas in the *Sabhāparvan*. The root of hostility was too deep to be uprooted at a later time, but Kṛṣṇa did whatever he could and tried his best to see that justice was done towards the end. A god does not have to be omnipotent, but he could be noble enough to see that justice is done in the end. It is significant to know that after Duryodhana's fall, Kṛṣṇa greeted King Yudhisthira with a long speech, which was interspersed with the expression '*diṣṭyā-vardhase*' (you have achieved the victory luckily). It was a plain admission that the Pāṇḍavas won against all odds because of luck, not through the omnipotence of Kṛṣṇa.

5. THE FORCE OF EVIL AND HUMAN FREEDOM

Western philosophers and theologians have pondered throughout the ages over the intelligibility of the divine attributes, such as omnipotence, omniscience and perfect goodness. St Thomas and St Augustine are well-known for their formulation of these attributes in a faultless manner. In recent times, Anthony Kenny, Peter Geach, A. Plantinga, Nelson Pike and others of the analytical tradition have discussed these issues to connect them with the contemporary problems of philosophy. Many old issues have been revived but several new dimensions have been added to them. I find some of these issues are strikingly relevant to our discussion of Kṛṣṇa in the *Mahābhārata*.

Recent discussion about the concept of God was triggered off by a paper written in 1955 by J.L. Mackie called 'Evil and Omnipotence'. The discussion rolled on, and Mackie in his posthumous writing, *The Miracle of Theism*, modified his earlier formulation. Instead of calling his formulation of the problem of evil a genuine paradox, he described it as undecidable question. There is no need to rehearse the well-known arguments here. Geach (1973) and Kenny (1970) both have agreed that the strictly philosophical notion of omnipotence is not essential for Western theism.[9] The notion of *Almighty*, in the sense of having power over all things would be enough, according to these philosophers, to be compatible with Western theology. We may follow a similar move in defining Kṛṣṇa's power. In fact, in Kṛṣṇa-theology (or should we say Kṛṣṇalogy?) we need to modify the notion of creator-God, following such Hindu philosophical systems as the Sāṃkhya and the Nyāya-Vaiśeṣika.

According to the Sāṃkhya school, the material world was never created—it evolved out of some unmanifest material form, the abode of all potentialities. Hence there is no Creator God. In fact, in one section of the early the Sāṃkya the category of God was declared as redundant. In Sāṃkya-Yoga system however, God was accepted as one, who was not the creator but the goal of the Yoga practices. In other words one can seek the help of such God and thereby achieve success or *siddhi*. The God of the Yogins (and Kṛṣṇa has sometimes been called Yogeśvara) is supposed to have the highest form of all admirable qualities of humans. He is perfectly good but he does not have to be omnipotent. Hence the conception is free from apparent incoherence. In fact the God of the Yoga system does not do anything on his own, but it is said that we can get something done or accomplished and proceed towards our ultimate goal if we resort to him through meditation or other practices.

The Nyāya-Vaiśeṣika conception of God is different. He can be called the Creator God but in a different sense. Since the material atoms are eternal entities and so are the human souls, we cannot say that God has created them. However, it is at God's will that the atoms come together to create the gross universe where human beings have embodied existence and act freely. Although they act freely, that is, they can choose between what is morally good and bad, they have to act under the constraint of the circumstances in which they are born. Birth and environment are not under their control. This conception of God seems compatible with the Kṛṣṇalogy of the *Mahābhārata*. Bhīṣma at the Rājasūya sacrifice of Yudhiṣṭhira selected Kṛṣṇa as the best of men and hence worthy of worship by all. He listed all the admirable virtues of Kṛṣṇa on that occasion.

There is another important divine attribute which the epic literature ascribes to Kṛṣṇa as the godhead. The *Purāṇa* literature usually speaks of three complementary aspects of the ultimate deity, the creator (personified in Brahmā), the preserver or protector (Viṣṇu) and the destroyer (Rudra-Śiva). This trinity is not relevant for our purpose. What is important to note is that God is also the destroyer and in this aspect he is identified with Kāla or Mahākāla or Time. In the *Gītā*, Kṛṣṇa says, 'I am the Kāla and as Kāla I destroy the world.'

Time or Eternity has often been regarded in Hindu religious literature as the great destroyer of everything, sometimes identified with the supreme deity. In the Vedas, there is an entire hymn devoted to Time where it was emphasized that everything originates in time, persists in time as well as perishes in time. In other words' Time not only creates everything but also destroys everything. In the epic literature, Kṛṣṇa has often been identified with the destructive aspect of Time. As God, he cannot make the world a better place overnight where every being will forget their enmity and hatred towards each other and live in perfect peace and harmony. For every creature is free to perform his own *karma* and thereby creates his own destiny in which God should not intervene. But when the earth is full of hatred and enmity and sin, when Justice is at the risk of being trampled over for ever, when disaster after disaster imperils the very existence of being, then the will of God may intervene in whatever way it can. This is the theory of Hindu God, or Kṛṣṇalogy, as has been expounded in the third and fourth chapters of the *Gītā*.

Kṛṣṇa as Kāla is passionless, free from any human virtues. Here, if not anywhere else, the end justifies the means. He told Arjuna that as Kāla he had already destroyed (was going to destroy) all the kings of the Kauravas and the Pāṇḍavas. Next he would destroy his own Race the Yādavas. All these were needed to release the burden of sin. People with their freedom had acted following their instincts and thereby a 'sad mess' had been created. Hence it was time to let loose the destructive power of the divinity. He, acting as the inner manipulator of every being, would bring about the intended destruction. Therefore he described himself as Kāla. Kāla is also identified sometimes with Yama, the God of Death. We should remember that in the *Rāmāyaṇa* also, the Kālapuruṣa appeared towards the end, to have a secret counsel with Rāma, which marked the beginning of the end of the Rāma story.

6. JUSTICE

In fact, it is an uphill task for anyone who tries to see that justice was done in the end. When the two sides were lined up for battle, it was clear that the Kauravas represented the stronger side by all counts. The Pāṇḍava side was weaker by comparison. On the other hand, it was the Pāṇḍavas who were deprived of their kingdom for thirteen years through trickery and fraud. But above all, the unprovoked insult inflicted upon the defenceless Draupadī in public was the last straw. This particular incident could be regarded as a turning point of the moral balance in the story. This was uncalled for and unprovoked and it was an unparadonable offence on the part of the Kauravas. From that point onwards, as I have already noted, it seems, the balance of justice tilted in favour of the Pāṇḍavas.

It has already been noted that the Pāṇḍava side was comparatively weaker. The weaker side can defeat a stronger side only with the help of a strategy, and strategies cannot always be restricted to fair and just means. There is a touch of realism here. Idealism would have demanded that the good be the victorious over the evil by following the ideally constructed strategies, which should always be fair. But our story-teller preferred realism. Our world is really an imperfect world, and this is all we have. Our story-teller's conception of God was not that of an Almighty Deity. Throughout the Utaṅka episode, our story-teller consciously raised the question of omnipotence but rejected it in favour of realism, contingencies of situation (moral luck) and fatalism. Courses of certain events cannot be stopped. All that Kṛṣṇa was able to do was to salvage justice at the end of the battle. So the paradox became more and more underscored. In order to save justice towards the end, many unjust and immoral acts were perpetrated. But what kind of justice was this? A sense of justice that kills all other senses of justice? A policeman in hot pursuit of a criminal overturns many vehicles and kills many innocent people—a very common sight on modern TV. But is this right? I believe that this is the ultimate puzzle. A puzzle that is realistic enough, for we see it even today all around us, but it is too frustrating to yield a solution.

Apart from the above puzzle there are several intricate problems that can be connected with the incident in the *Mahābhārata*. Let us articulate at least one of them. Yudhiṣṭhira's problem was one of moral integrity. He maintained a very high profile as far as *dharma* or morality was concerned. He never told a lie in his life. So one would expect him to be telling the truth always. But, at Kṛṣṇa's advice, he lied to save his life. Hence there was a visible crack in his otherwise impeccable honesty and moral integrity. But how about Kṛṣṇa? What was his justification for giving this advice to Yudhiṣṭhira? He obviously compromised his moral integrity by choosing to give this advice. Was he acting as an utilitarian consequentialist? Perhaps not. For a consequentialist opts even for a little bit of well-being or happiness (that is, utility) when he violates a well-established moral principle.

For the consequentialist, the consequence must produce more well-being or more happiness. One can obviously produce an argument by which it will be shown that Kṛṣṇa as a moral agent gave up the principle of moral integrity (assuming that moral integrity is an excellence or value) in order to ensure victory for the right side, that was the Pāṇḍavas, or negatively, to avoid disastrous consequences of the defeat of the side which was more *just* than the other. The unpardonable humiliation of the defenceless Draupadī by Duryodhana has already been mentioned. That was also the reason Kṛṣṇa gave to Balarāma, when the latter became extremely angry seeing Bhīma resort to unlawful means to defeat and kill Duryodhana. So one may say that Kṛṣṇa as a moral agent gave up moral integrity to avoid a total miscarriage of justice in the end. But this consequence can hardly be measured in terms of happiness or even well-being. Anybody who has read the *Mahābhārata* can testify to the fact that the conclusion of the war contributed to nobody's happiness in particular. It did not contribute even to the well-being of the Pāṇḍavas. For this, one can simply read the laments of Yudhiṣṭhira after the war. Therefore, the outcome of this apparently deviant behaviour by Kṛṣṇa cannot be explained in consequentialist terms. On the other hand, could we argue that if Kṛṣṇa as well as Yudhiṣṭhira maintained his moral integrity, and did not stoop to this devious means of lying to Droṇa (and thereby leading the great teacher to his own doom), would the world have been a better place or would it have contributed to the general well-being of humanity? We cannot answer affirmatively here, for our inherent sense of justice would have suffered a set-back and our very trust in the moral order of the universe would have been impaired. For the story-teller has made us increasingly aware how far the Kauravas went in their wickedness and immoral actions.

7. GOOD *VS*. THE BEST WORLD

Why do we feel embarrassed and definitely shocked at the conduct of Yudhiṣṭhira and Kṛṣṇa on this occasion? It is because our expectations were high, as far as the Pāṇḍavas and Kṛṣṇa were concerned. Had Duryodhana been involved we would not have thought it to be irregular. But from Kṛṣṇa we expected something better.

There may be another way of looking at this issue. Let us regard Kṛṣṇa as a moral agent here. It was his duty to uphold *dharma* which also included justice, at any cost. The exact nature of *dharma* has remained ever elusive, for it was never spelled out fully. Various stories in the *Mahābhārata* illustrate the point underlying the ever-elusive nature of *dharma*. Of course, *dharma* is mostly represented as a set of rigid moral principles or a rigid moral code of a given society. It was something like the honour code of a given community. It is assumed that to breach the code is to lose one's honour and one's place in the social order, circumscribed by that moral code. But this rigidity can sometimes be challenged by a proper agent who has proven to be superior to others in the community both in talents and intelligence as well as in leadership qualities. This only acknowledges the possibility of what is called today 'a paradigm shift'. Sometimes it is possible for a leader to transcend or breach the rigid code of conduct valued in the society, with the sole idea of creating a new paradigm that will also be acknowledged and esteemed within that order. Our Kṛṣṇa might be looked upon as a leader of that sort. It may be that he created new paradigms for showing limitations of such a generally accepted moral code of truth-telling and promise-keeping. Sometimes situational constraints and the risk of the loss of the greater good might influence a rational agent to transgress certain valued principles. In this case one might say that a threat posed by Duryodhana's victory and the consequential loss of the chance for the restoration of justice, might have influenced Kṛṣṇa's decision to follow the devious course. All these are speculations, but I claim that they are not entirely absent from the moral concerns of the Indian people who have loved the epic for about two millennia. Certainly these speculations are not at all foundationless. The available evidence found in the tradition of the great epics of India lends support to such speculations. I believe the moral consciousness of the people found its expression in such portrayals of dilemmas throughout the epic literature and the different versions of the epic stories at different times.[10]

I shall conclude this discussion by introducing a thought experiment. Suppose there is a divine creator who is also omnipotent and omniscient in some acceptable and coherent sense of these terms. Suppose also that he is about to create a world where pre-existent matter and human souls would be the ingredients. How much choice is left to the creator under these circumstances to create an entirely new world? Suppose there are three possibilities—W_1, W_2 and W_3. W_1 stands for a world as science sometimes is said to conceive it. There is no value, no justice. Things happen mechanically following the scientific rules, properties of matter, and those who suffer and enjoy are only rational beings. There is no standard for good and evil. It is an amoral world.

W_2 stands for a world which is much like that of ours. There is good as well as evil. There is human rationality; sometimes justice is done, sometimes evil forces try to suppress justice. But there is this persistent belief that good will win in the end.

W_3 stands for another world, which we can call the perfect world or the best of all the possible worlds. There is no evil. Or evil has no power over good. Everybody is happy. But in such a way the meaning of happiness is perhaps lost. Or, nobody understands what unhappiness is.

Now, if a divine creator is faced with the choice of creating a world like any one of this, which particular one would He select? For various reasons into which I do not wish to go into here, I suggest that he would select W_2. Whether there is a creator God or not, whether Kṛṣṇa was a devious deity or not, this is the kind of world we have got and hence if justice can be salvaged in the end the creator will fulfil His promise.

Notes and References

1. The extract is from p. 95 of V.S. Sukthankar's posthumous publication, *On the Meaning of the Mahābhārata*, Bombay: Asiatic Society, 1957, where the source was not mentioned.
2. For an earlier comment on the different conceptions of God in the Indian

tradition, see my *Logical and Ethical Issues of Religious Belief*, Calcutta, Calcutta University Press, 1982, pp. 23–41.

3. The first line runs as follows: *dharmakṣetre kurukṣetre samavetā yuyutsavaḥ*. See *Bhagavad-Gītā*, any edition.
4. Issac Levi, *Hard Choices*, Cambridge, Cambridge University: 1986.
5. See the *Bhīṣma-Parvan*, of the *Mahābhārata*, critical edition, Poona. I have discussed this issue in my *Yukti, Niti O Dharma* (in Bengali), Calcutta, 1988, pp. 13–16.
6. *Yadāśrauṣaṃ Droṇam ācāryam ekaṃ*
   Dhṛṣṭadyumnenābhyatikramya dharmam
   Rathopasthe prāyagataṃ viśastam
   tadā nāśaṃse vijayāya Sañjaya.

   verse 1.1.143.

   'I did not hope for victory, O Sañjaya, when I heard that the teacher, Droṇa, was slaughtered by Dhṛṣṭadyumna. *Dharma* was thus violated, for Droṇa at that time was sitting in his chariot unarmed.'
7. See *Droṇa-Parvan*, of the *Mahābhārata*, critical edition, Poona.
8. See *Āśvamedhika-Parvan* of the *Mahābhārata*, critical edition, Poona.
9. Geach, P.T., *Providence and Evil*, Cambridge, 1977; Kenny, A., *The God of the Philosopher*, Oxford: Oxford University Press, 1979; Mackie, J.L., 'Evil and Omnipotence', *Mind*, vol. 6, 1955, pp. 100–212; *The Miracles of Theism*, Oxford: Oxford University Press, 1982.
10. For other ethical issues connected with the moral dilemmas, see my 'Moral Dilemmas: Insights from Indian Epics', in *Moral Dilemmas in the Mahābhārata* (ed. Bimal Krishna Matilal), I.I.A.S., Shimla, and Motilal Banarsidass, Delhi, 1989.

9

The Throne: Was Duryodhana Wrong?

People tell stories, and they love to hear them. Story-telling is a pervasive feature of all civilizations. Stories are told mainly for entertainment, or at least that is how we regard the activity of story-telling. They are meant to entertain others. However, pure entertainment cannot be the sole purpose of creating and re-creating stories, myths, and various other narrative compositions. Stories must have a meaning. In fact, they must have morals, and morals are connected with the domain of morality and ethics. In this sense, there is a very intimate and inherent connection between story-telling and ethical discourse. We may say that since ethical principles are utterly abstract, and the human tendency toward ethical behaviour (presumably in any civilized society) is very nebulous and sometimes unconscious, ethical discourse receives a local habitation and a name through stories and myths. The story-telling activity has thus one important aspect. It is an unconscious concretization of an abstract moral discourse.

The centrepiece of the great epic *Mahābhārata* is the devastating battle of Kurukṣetra. Why did Duryodhana have to fight? For power, for the throne, for pride, for values which were so dear to him. Mostly we regard such mythological battles as the illustrations of the on-going struggle between good and evil, between gods and demons, their moral outcome never forgotten. But I believe when we interpret the *Mahābhārata* battle in this way we take a simplistic and easy way out. Every episode of the epic has a rich variety of significance, it is full of ambiguities, replete with suggestivity.

As far as Duryodhana was concerned, fighting with, or elimination of, the Pāṇḍavas, to secure the throne for the entire kingdom (and not just one half of it) was not at all unethical. He had a firm conviction that he had a natural right to the throne. Hence it was his prime concern to make it safe and secure by the use of any means—fair or foul. For him, it was an end that justified the means.

He was first of all, and last of all, a proud man, and he staked everything to save his pride to the end. Even on his deathbed his proud replies to Kṛṣṇa cannot but evoke admiration for his straightforwardness.

The rivalry between the Kauravas and the Pāṇḍavas was natural. For they were the two lines of succession of the same royal family. The Kauravas were not taught any moral lessons by Droṇa. He taught them only the art of warfare. Even Dhṛtarāṣṭra supported this method of educating the princes. Hence we find that the Kauravas lacked any sensitivity to certain moral issues. But certainly they had other virtues. Duryodhana, for example, was said to be a good monarch—kind and just to his subjects and subordinates, loving to his friends. But the sole purpose of his life was to root out the Pāṇḍavas—that is, he was out to destroy any rival claim to the throne that he held so dear to his life. That he was a good king, benevolent and just, can be easily gathered from an account of his régime when the Pāṇḍavas were in exile. We can refer to poet Bhāravi's *Kirātārjunīya*, Canto. 1, where we get a graphic account of how Duryodhana was ruling the earth. Yudhiṣṭhira apparently sent a spy, a forest-dweller, to find out whether the subjects of Duryodhana were happy under his rule or if they were dissatisfied, and might prefer the Pāṇḍavas to be the rulers. But the report of the spy was different: Duryodhana was behaving like an ideal ruler; as poet Bhāravi pointed out and the spy reported:

> Kind Duryodhana had now conquered all the six so-called 'enemies' [vices] of the prince—this was the ideal that the well-known *dharmaśāstra-kāra* Manu, set forth for any successful king or prince to follow. Besides, Duryodhana had divided each moment of his day and night to devote all his time to do good to his subjects and thereby win their favour. This was how he was trying to change the minds of his subjects.

He wanted to shift the loyalty of his subjects (and the friends of the Pāṇḍavas) from the Pāṇḍavas to the Kauravas. This was possible, as Duryodhana clearly and cleverly understood, when and only when he (Duryodhana) was able to behave in a much better manner than the Pāṇḍavas, and he would show to the world that even he could outshine the Pāṇḍavas by his own virtues and as a ruler.

Manu had set down a number of good policies to be followed by an ideal King who would like to win the favour of his subjects and friends, and thereby obtain their unquestionable support if a war broke out between him and his adversaries. Those policies were to be found in chapter VII of the *Manusaṃhitā*. According to poet Bhāravi, Duryodhana was following the advice of the *Manusaṃhitā* almost to the letter. This was at least a positive merit in favour of King Duryodhana. He could be wicked and evil, but still he was also capable of being an ideal king when the occasion arose.

I have said that Duryodhana had a sort of rightful claim to the throne of Hastināpura. But did he have claim to the entire kingdom? This may be disputed. Succession to the throne is not usually decided by moral or ethical principles. One may ask—what was the law? Or, what was the conventional practice? If we do not want to call it 'the law', we have to ask at least about the conventional practice. How about the claim of the Pāṇḍavas? These are not moral questions, they pertain to the conventional law of succession, but they are in some way pertinent to the domain of morality. I shall try to answer them briefly. The following background to the story is necessary for understanding clearly the issues involved.

Śāntanu was first married to Gaṅgā Devī. They had eight sons, all of whom died (in fact killed by Gaṅgā) except the last one, Devavrata. Gaṅgā Devī left Śāntanu, leaving Devavrata behind. Devavrata was growing up. Meanwhile Śāntanu became infatuated with a beautiful lady Satyavatī, the daughter of the king of a race of fishermen. Śāntanu wanted to marry her but the father of Satyavatī objected. For Śāntanu's throne rightfully belonged to the young prince Devavrata, the practice being that the throne should go to the first-born male child. In fact Devavrata was the crown prince. Satyavatī's father said that unless the son of Satyavatī was given the right to succeed to the throne, the marriage was out of the question. Disappointed, Śāntanu came back with a heavy heart. Devavrata came to learn the cause of his father's sadness and disappointment. He quickly settled the issue by going to Satyavatī's father and making the most remarkable and outstanding promise to remain a bachelor for life, renouncing all claims to the throne. So the marriage took place and they had two sons; one of them died early and the other had two wives but died childless. So the throne was vacant. At Satyavatī's request, the great Sage Vyāsa (and let us remember that Satyavatī was his unwed mother) generated two sons through copulation with the two widowed queens. The son of the first wife was Dhṛtarāṣṭra, who was born blind. The son of the second wife was Pāṇḍu. Although Dhṛtarāṣṭra was the elder of the two there was some traditional hesitation about allowing a born-blind prince to succeed to the throne (see *Manusaṃhitā*, chapter 9). So Pāṇḍu became the crown prince. As a result of an accident, he became impotent.

So the old method of *niyoga* was again sought. *Niyoga* was a practice, acceptable and honoured in higher (royal) societies in those days, by which the wife could, at the request of the husband, or as permitted by the elder member of the family if the husband was dead, copulate either with a brahmin or a member of the family in order to get pregnant and obtain a male child. Thus Pāṇḍu had five sons from his two wives, all through their copulation with various deities such as Dharma, Indra, and so on.

Dhṛtarāṣṭra, however, was the natural father of one hundred sons by his wife, Gāndharī. They are called Kauravas and were headed by Duryodhana. The sons of Pāṇḍu were called Pāṇḍavas, headed by Yudhiṣṭhira. In this way the two lines of successors were created, the Kauravas and the Pāṇḍavas. Yudhiṣṭhira was older than Duryodhana by a few minutes so he might have had a claim over the entire kingdom. But another point to note is the following: Duryodhana was the *natural* son of Dhṛtarāṣṭra, not by proxy as in the case of Yudhiṣṭhira. Hence from the modern point of view Duryodhana might have had a more legitimate claim to the throne.

The throne belonged to the royal family, and from the beginning, Duryodhana clearly understood that he had to fight to fulfil his ambition. So from boyhood days he used to make devilish plans in order to get rid of his arch-rivals, the Pāṇḍavas. It is said that he gave poison to Bhīma. But somehow Bhīma was saved. However his most devilish act was to attempt to burn the Pāṇḍavas alive along with their mother. Such behaviour from Duryodhana can hardly be reconciled with the proud picture of a king as he was depicted in the latter part of the epic. Although the Pāṇḍavas were unharmed, it did not make Duryodhana's character any less villainous. Could we ignore this as a childish game or a sort of foolishness perpetrated due to immaturity? If we do, then Duryodhana's character becomes more realistic in the latter part of the epic. It was a mixture of black and white, of good and evil. Sometimes Duryodhana's character was admirable, and sometimes it was abominable. The devilish treatment of Draupadī in the *Sabhāparvar* was another dark, perhaps the darkest, shade to Duryodhana's character during his adulthood. But even this can somehow be condoned. The insults heaped upon Duryodhana's head at the court of Indraprastha during the Rājasūya sacrifice might have accounted for this rather extreme reaction (see later). But still his actions were beyond any limit of decency. Duryodhana was mad with envy. He had to do something. Hence the gambling match, and hence Draupadī's public humiliation. If we can see how Duryodhana felt at his humiliation by the Pāṇḍavas, we can understand why. But we cannot condone it any further from any point of view, moral or non-moral.

Duryodhana very seldom had to face any moral dilemmas. Perhaps I should be more positive and say that he did not have any, as is evidenced by the epic story. But as I believe that every person, to the extent that she is susceptible to human frailties, entertains some doubts about what is morally good or bad at an unconscious level, I have been less than positive. Duryodhana's main goal was to make the throne completely free from any threat by his rivals, the Pāṇḍavas. This justified to him all his actions against the Pāṇḍavas. The question is how far one may go in such a direction, for there is a limit to everything. For Duryodhana, it seemed that the sky was the limit. He wanted to get rid of them by hook or crook, moral qualms being immaterial to his judgements. He knew the weak spot of his enemy. The enemy was vulnerable and he wanted to take advantage of it. Yudhiṣṭhira's weakness, his vice of gambling was well-known. Uncle Śakuni gave Duryodhana the advice that he needed. The decision to defeat the enemy in gambling was at least a reasonable decision, for the practice was prevalent, and it was approved by the conventional law of that time. The Nala story told in the *Vanaparvan*, which miniaturizes the *Mahābhārata* story in several important respects, twlls of how Nala's wicked brother invited Nala to a game of dice in which the king was forced to gamble away his entire kingdom.

The blind king Dhṛtarāṣṭra was supposedly the alter ego of Duryodhana. The father seemed to have some moral qualms, but they were never very strong. In any case, he had some commitment to the family as a whole. He was virtually the guardian of both the Kauravas and the Pāṇḍavas. He had a responsibility and he was aware of it. That was why after the marriage of Draupadī, he brought back the Pāṇḍavas when he learned that they were not dead, but travelling in exile, hiding themselves from Duryodhana's mischiefs. Besides, the Pāṇḍavas were now married to the daughter of Drupada, and so had an important ally. Dhṛtarāṣṭra acted in good conscience, and divided the kingdom, giving a portion to Yudhiṣṭhira, who built up Indraprastha as his capital city. The Pāṇḍavas flourished and organized a great gathering of all the kings to celebrate at the royal court of Indrapastha. This was called the 'Rājasūya Sacrifice', which would supposedly establish the supremacy of the Pāṇḍavas. The Kauravas were invited to the celebration of this great occasion. The wealth and glory of the Pāṇḍavas dazzled the eyes of Duryodhana. His envy increased a thousandfold. Besides, he was also insulted and went through a period of mild humiliation at the court.

Śakuni at this time became the chief advisor of Duryodhana. According to him, this was the time to strike, not by warfare but by challenging Yudhiṣṭhira to a gambling match. Yudhiṣṭhira might have been a very virtuous person, an incarnation of *dharma* or piety, but he was also an addict. He was addicted to gambling, one of the common vices of a prince, according to Manu. Everybody knew about this great weakness of Yudhiṣṭhira's. This was a fatal flaw in his character. Yudhiṣṭhira himself knew it too. But like all addicts, he was helpless and weak in this regard.

Later in the *Vanaparvan*, Yudhiṣṭhira lamented to himself about this fatal flaw in his character. In reply to Bhīṣma, he said that his weakness for gambling was such that even if he were reduced to a pauper again and again by Duryodhana, he would gamble again when challenged by him or anybody for that matter. It was a strange admission from Yudhiṣṭhira, the Dharmarāja, about a spectacular weakness of his character. How can a moral hero be such a helpless fool? In the *Ṛg-veda*, the gambler's hymn depicts exactly a situation such as this. We know enough about human character to empathize with Yudhiṣṭhira or even the anonymous gambler whose character has been immortalized by the hymns of the *Ṛg-veda*.

Manu in chapter 7 listed eighteen different vices common to a king. Of these ten arise from lust and desire and eight from anger. Gambling is one of these eighteen vices commonly found among the princes. In verse 50 of chapter 7, four vices of the first ten have been singled out as being most disastrous. Reference to gambling as a vice goes back, as we know, to the time of the *Ṛg-veda*. The gambler laments about his fate, his addiction to gambling and the loss of all his worldly belongings, including his wife. In fact this Ṛg-Vedic story cannot but be a precursor to the *Mahābhārata* story of Yudhiṣṭhira. If this is not the realistic picture of a moral hero, with his faults and frailties as well as his strength and fortitude, I do not know what else could be so. It belies the general idea that the epic characters are static, standardized and lifeless.

It is interesting to quote hymn 5 of the *Ṛg-Veda*:

> When I think after my friends have left that I will never go to the gambling match, I hear (all of a sudden) the noises made by the throw of dice. And at the same time like a fallen woman I have to rush for a rendezvous to the gambling house immediately.

The same was also true of Yudhiṣṭhira in the *Mahābhārata*. Besides, in the well-known Sanskrit play, *Mṛcchakaṭikā*, a similar gambling scene has been depicted with great ingenuity (see Act II, verses 5 and 6).

[The Masseur says:]

> The noise '*kattā*' made after the throw of dice steals the mind of even such a man as has lost everything, just as the beat of a drum in the ear upsets the king who has lost his kingdom. I know it, and I am not gambling, and at least trying not to.

In gambling the loss is like the fall from the Sumeru mountain. Still my mind is overwhelmed by this noise, *kattā*, which seems to be as sweet as the cuckoo's song.

Yudhiṣṭhira was invited to gamble. He accepted the invitation and lost everything. Gambling was a very popular sport of the princes at the time of the *Mahābhārata*. In the story of Nala, the hero lost everything in gambling, but he did not stake his wife, although he was challenged to do so by his opponent. The sub-story encapsulates the main story and underlines certain points in it. Nala had the good sense to withdraw at the last moment. However, Yudhiṣṭhira went all the way. The bigger the story, the greater the blunder. He staked and lost not only his four brothers, but also his wife Draupadī, who was then dragged into the court and utterly humiliated by the wretched Duḥsāsana. This was probably the worst form of humiliation that Duryodhana succeeded in inflicting upon the Pāṇḍavas. Not only that, it was a sin against humanity, at least from our modern point of view, and he had to pay dearly for it at the end. From this point onwards, I believe, it was impossible for the *Mahābhārata* story to end in any other way but with the crushing defeat of Duryodhana.

However, Duryodhana's alter ego, his father Dhṛtarāṣṭra, saved the situation for the Pāṇḍavas. This was perhaps the second time when Dhṛtarāṣṭra exhibited exemplary courage and determination, as well as kindness of heart and feeling for family ties. He returned the kingdom that was lost in gambling and set free the brothers and their wife. The Pāṇḍavas were back in their capital. But this was very short-lived. Duryodhana challenged again—this time the stake was not only the loss of the kingdom, but also exile for twelve years with an additional year spent in secret hiding somewhere. Duryodhana thus wanted to perpetuate the exile of the Pāṇḍavas. For, the condition was that if they were found out by the Kauravas during the year of hiding, they would have to go into exile for another twelve years plus one year of hiding. Thus the throne was to be made safe permanently from the Pāṇḍavas, or so it was believed by Duryodhana.

Apparently Duryodhana ruled in an admirable manner, once the threat to the throne from the Pāṇḍavas was out of the way. Although he was still obsessed with the thought of the Pāṇḍavas' claiming their kingdom back at the end of the thirteenth year, it was still an admirable side in Duryodhana's character. The Pāṇḍavas were his enemies, but his friendship with Karṇa was ideal. His generosity with friends knew no bounds. He was an outstanding diplomat. It was through his good diplomacy that a major section of the neutral kings joined him in his battle of Kurukṣetra against the Pāṇḍavas. His army therefore by far outnumbered the army of the Pāṇḍavas.

Duryodhana believed in physical or material force. He made sure that his side was at least physically more powerful than the other side. He dreaded to some extent the non-material forces. He hated magic power, or even moral or spiritual force. His *dharma* (and he also had one, to be sure) was different from that of Yudhiṣṭhira. Yudhiṣṭhira's *dharma* had a spiritual or moral halo around it. Duryodhana's *dharma* was as material as the hard soil. For him, it was the weapon system and the strength of arms that counted, not the spiritual force. Only in the context of such a philosophy can we understand why he chose an army, belonging to Kṛṣṇa, 18,000 strong, to fight for him rather than choosing the 'magician' Kṛṣṇa to be on his side. Duryodhana never accepted the godhood of Kṛṣṇa, hence he ascribed his supernatural powers to his 'black' magic. He never accepted the moral superiority of the Pāṇḍavas, or of Kṛṣṇa himself. He recognized very well that Kṛṣṇa presented a most difficult problem for him. However, he thought that by sheer physical force he would be able to destroy the magic spell that always protected the Pāṇḍavas. His reluctance to accept any negotiated settlement of the dispute was based upon this faith in physical force. When Kṛṣṇa came for the last time for a peaceful settlement, Duryodhana proudly replied that he would not allow the five Pāṇḍavas to enjoy even five villages without war, that is, a real test of strength of both sides, and 'if this calls for total destruction on both sides, so be it'. It takes exemplary boldness to take such a stand. He had the courage of his convictions. This shows that Duryodhana was exceptionally powerful and fearless.

On his deathbed, Duryodhana understood the mistake he made by allowing Kṛṣṇa to be on the side of the Pāṇḍavas. It was a fatal mistake, he admitted. That was why he wanted to imprison Kṛṣṇa when he came as a chief negotiator for the last time. But Kṛṣṇa escaped through magic. Duryodhana recognized his mistake, but never regretted it. He made an exemplary speech justifying his actions throughout, while he was dying. This memorable speech was interspersed with the echo and the re-echo of the following sentence:

ko nu svantataro mayā

Whose end is more admirable than mine?

Whatever extraordinary strength Kṛṣṇa might have possessed, it was occult for Duryodhana, not divine. Unlike Rāvaṇa (at the end of the *Rāmāyana*), Duryodhana never surrendered to Kṛṣṇa even when he was dying. His defiance of Kṛṣṇa persisted when he breathed his last—a fact that Kṛṣṇa himself also admired. Duryodhana lamented to Aśvatthāmān and others that the war was lost in spite of their concerted efforts simply because of the wickedness of Kṛṣṇa as well as due to the frequent exercise of his magic power. We may say that Duryodhana was right. There was another minor incident which lends support to Duryodhana's contention.

At the end of the battle, when Duryodhana was completely vanquished, Kṛṣṇa asked Yudhiṣṭhira to ascend to the throne and requested Arjuna to lay down his weapons and climb down from his famous monkey-bannered chariot. Kṛṣṇa himself also climbed down. Then, as if by a miracle, the famous chariot burnt to ashes. Everybody present was surprised. Kṛṣṇa explained. During the battle of eighteen days, the chariot was attacked and burnt many times by the weapons from such warriors as Bhīṣma, Droṇa and Karṇa. But the chariot did not burn because Lord Kṛṣṇa was in it. Now that the purpose was over, and Kṛṣṇa had climbed down, the chariot was reduced to ashes. It was a 'delayed' action. The incident shows, beyond a shadow of doubt, that the Pāṇḍavas would never have won the war without Kṛṣṇa's help.

Balarāma resisted attacking Bhīma at the request of Kṛṣṇa, but he made a very significant comment in this context. He said that of the three goals of human life, *dharma* (morality, righteousness), *artha* (wealth), and *kāma* (fulfilment of desire), people should never give up the first. Some of them may act in a way so as to combine *dharma* and *artha*, and some may try to combine *dharma* and *kāma* together, while others would attempt for a judicious blending of all the three. But, said Balarāma, Bhīma had destroyed *dharma* in the first place and thereby ruined everything (*Mahābhārata* 9.59.17–19). Kṛṣṇa in reply agreed but said that Kāliyuga was fast approaching and hence the principle of *dharma* would be in great danger. Balarāma, however said that the Pāṇḍavas in any case should attain the notoriety of being the *jihmayodhin* (those who fight with deceitful means), while Duryodhana fought like a hero and would be famous as *ṛjuyodhin* (he who fought a straightforward and lawful battle).

Bhīma, however, committed one unpardonable offence against Duryodhana. He kicked at the head of the dying King Duryodhana, while the latter was lying in his deathbed on the ground with a broken thigh, and was indeed in a very pitiable condition. This action of Bhīma could never be justified and it infuriated everybody including Kṛṣṇa and Yudhiṣṭhira. This probably showed that Bhīma was capable of stooping as low as his obnoxious opponents, the Kauravas. He gave vent to his life-long hatred and anger as well as the urgent desire for revenge. However, we still feel that this behaviour should have been expected from a Kaurava, not from a Pāṇḍava. This was entirely uncalled for, and even Kṛṣṇa did not think it was strategically (or even morally) necessary at all. This, however, corroborates the point I have been making here. In doing evil things to each other, both sides, the Pāṇḍavas and Kauravas, were more or less equal to each other. That is why there is always a touch of irony when a moderner describes the Kurukṣetra as an instance of *dharmayuddha*. For moral codes were broken more often than not in this battle, and both sides were to be blamed.

It would be important to review the hot exchange of words between Duryodhana and Kṛṣṇa at the end of the *Gadā-yudhaparvan*, when the former was dying. When Kṛṣṇa said to the Pāṇḍavas that by luck, the wicked Duryodhana had been defeated, along with all his followers, Duryodhana retorted with a spirited speech. Although he was suffering from excruciating pain, because he was mortally wounded by Bhīma, and his end was coming nearer every moment, he managed to sit up with great difficulty, supported by his weak elbows. Then he spoke, ignoring the pain that was almost killing him. He called Kṛṣṇa a slave of King Kaṃsa, and said that he should be ashamed of himself for what he had done. He said that Kṛṣṇa was neither ashamed nor repentent, although he always used false and treacherous means to defeat and kill the great warriors on the Kaurava side. For example, Grandfather Bhīṣma was killed by Arjuna, who hid himself behind Śikhandin. Second, Droṇa was killed by the wretched son of Drupada when Yudhiṣṭhira was persuaded by Kṛṣṇa to tell a lie before Droṇa. Poor Droṇa believed Yudhiṣṭhira and thought that his son was dead, and therefore gave up his weapons. Then Drupada's son killed the defenceless Droṇa. Third, Bhūriśravas was killed when his hands were cut off. This was also done on the advice of Kṛṣṇa. Fourth, Karṇa was killed by Arjuna in an utterly unfair battle. One of Karṇa's chariot-wheels got stuck in the mud. Hence he begged Arjuna to give him time to pull it out. But at Kṛṣṇa's instigation, Arjuna killed Karṇa right at that moment when he was defenceless. Karṇa would have been invincible at any other time. And last, but not least, Bhīma killed Duryodhana by hitting below the belt—which was utterly unethical and violated the explicitly acknowledged code of a mace-fight. Duryodhana summed up his speech as follows:

> If the Pāṇḍavas fought the Kauravas by following the *Ṛjumarga* (the straightforward and ethical code of conduct in warfare), it was certain that the Pāṇḍavas would not have won. But it is only through deceitful and wretched means that the Pāṇḍavas were able to defeat the Kauravas.

There was much truth in Duryodhana's accusation. Kṛṣṇa's reply was that Duryodhana was killed in the battle, along with his friends, followers and relatives because of his sinful acts. Great warriors such as Bhīṣma, Droṇa and Karṇa were defeated because they were fighting for Duryodhana. It was the indomitable greed of Duryodhana which prompted him to deprive the Pāṇḍavas unlawfully of their half of the kingdom. Kṛṣṇa himself had requested Duryodhana in great earnestness to let the Pāṇḍavas have their share.

Kṛṣṇa then gave a brief list of the misdeeds perpetrated by Duryodhana against the Pāṇḍavas. Long ago, when they were young in age, Duryodhana poisoned Bhīma. Bhīma almost died, but he was saved by a miracle. Second, Duryodhana tried to kill all the five Pāṇḍavas along with their mother Kuntī, by burning them alive when they were asleep in their own house. Third, on the advice of Śakuni, he cheated Yudhiṣṭhira in the game of dice and won everything from him, turning the five brothers into slaves. Then to crown it all, Duryodhana committed the most serious offence by humiliating Draupadī. Draupadī was used as a stake in the gamble by Yudhiṣṭhira and he lost. Duryodhana ordered her to dragged out of the ladies' quarters of the Royal palace and be publicly humiliated at the royal court in front of everybody, including her five husbands, who were rendered powerless by Yudhiṣṭhira's oath. This was the most despicable act for which I believe Duryodhana had to meet his final fate. Kṛṣṇa reminded Duryodhana that in the matter of doing evil deeds he himself did not lag behind. Moreover it was Duryodhana who sent Jayadratha to the forest in order not only to torture Draupadī but also steal her away from the Pāṇḍavas. Last of all, the boy Abhimanyu was killed in the most unlawful battle: seven great warriors against one boy who was in his teens.

Here we see that both sides were blameworthy on many counts. We cannot decide whether it was more sinful on the part of Duryodhana to humiliate Draupadī than Bhīma's breaking the thigh of Duryodhana in an unlawful battle. There was also the moral question of promise-keeping, for Bhīma, on the spur of the moment when Draupadī was being humiliated and Duryodhana showed his thigh to Draupadī in a vulgar gesture, made a promise to break that very thigh of Duryodhana. Perhaps, as I have indicated earlier, the Draupadī incident tilted the balance of fate in favour of the Pāṇḍavas, for otherwise justice would not have been maintained. One may also add Abhimanyu's death to the list of serious and evil doings of the Kauravas. Duryodhana, in reply to Kṛṣṇa, did not repent at all but boastfully claimed that he was dying a glorious death. It was an end, he said, which would be covetable by many (*ko nu svantataro mayā*). And he also repeated that in a straightforward battle Pāṇḍavas would have never been victorious.

Yudhiṣṭhira finally occupied the throne and Duryodhana lost. However, what kind of victory was it on the part of Yudhiṣṭhira? He lamented over his sad lot, over the fact that he had become the king and there was practically no one left, none of those whom he had admired, loved and respected. The devastating battle had taken its toll. Almost all the able male members of the family had died, leaving behind windows and children, the deceased and the maimed. This was certainly not an ideal kingdom. No king would be happy to rule over a kingdom after such a total devastation. After the war, it was the victors who were in tears, which in a way implied that the vanquished ruler Duryodhana was ultimately the victor. This was no joyous outcome of victory. The entire story of the *Mahābhārata* imparted a great lesson in tragedy in this way. And herein lies the religious and moral significance of the story. It generates an ultimate indifference and disgust in us for all sorts of worldly pleasures, joys, victories, competition, challenge, love of power, love of wealth and so on. Total war is one where everything ends in this type of tragic nothingness.

The victorious King Yudhiṣṭhira suffered from a supreme depression after the war. Finally, when he decided to give up the throne, and to go on his last journey, called the Mahāprasthāna, it was even difficult to find a successor to the throne. For even the five sons of the five Pāṇḍavas had been killed. Abhimanyu, son of Arjuna, had been killed much earlier. Uttarā, the widow of Abhimanyu, gave birth to a dead son (for he was already killed by Aśvatthāmān's fatal arrow, which by its magic power entered the womb of Uttarā) but Kṛṣṇa revived him. He was called Parīkṣita. Thus he was the chosen successor to the throne which Yudhiṣṭhira left behind. And thus ended the great rivalry between the two sides of the royal family, the Kauravas and the Pāṇḍavas.

The Throne, the symbol of pride and power was finally proven to be utterly insignificant. The blind king Dhṛtarāṣṭra is one of the most tragic figures in the story. He was, as I have described, the alter ego of Kind Duryodhana. One may say that he was a good father, because he was very affectionate to his sons. However, an over-indulgent father can hardly be called a 'good' father. He was well aware that his sons did not have any moral qualms about anything, and they were always eager to get rid of the Pāṇḍavas by hook or crook. Dhṛtarāṣṭra always felt within himself that he was doing something wrong by allowing his sons to deprive the Pāṇḍavas of their lawful kingdom. When his mind was perturbed, he used to ask Vidura or Vyāsa to impart to him *dharma* lessons, but he never had the moral courage to follow any of their moral advice. He was completely under the influence of his son Duryodhana. Thus his laments for the throne were most genuine near the end. His was an interesting case for our study of weakness of the will. He was in this respect similar to Yudhiṣṭhira. He was often overwhelmed by the moral emotions, regret and remorse. That was why he frequently asked Vidura for advice. I believe, however, that in his case it was more regret than remorse. And even such regrets were short-lived. For seldom had he the courage to alter the course of the events. Unlike Yudhiṣṭhira, who wanted to live up to the high ideals of the *dharmaputra*, Dhṛtarāṣṭra had no ideal before him. His occasional regrets might have been caused by the fear of the consequences that might follow due to the evils perpetuated by his sons.

Twice, he did something good to the Pāṇḍavas perhaps in defiance of his son's will. First, he gave to them a share of the kingdom, Pāṇḍu's share after the marriage of Draupadī. We could take it to be a good moral gesture, or, if we turn our critical eye to the fact of the matter, we might say that he did it to save his family pride, or even to save his own skin. On the whole, it did not produce any good result. For the hostility between the Kauravas and the Pāṇḍavas started with redoubled force when the Pāṇḍavas became both prosperous and popular enough to arouse envy in the mind of Duryodhana.

Second, Dhṛtarāṣṭra showed his humane behaviour after the first gambling match. He returned everything that was lost in the gambling match and King Yudhiṣṭhira was reinstated in his own kingdom. Here again one may doubt whether it was an act of kindness on the part of the blind king, or whether it was provoked by an utter fear for disaster. This may be a very uncharitable assessment of the blind king's character but, as I have indicated, he did not seem to have set a great deal of importance by moral virtues. However, he was concerned for the well-being of his sons. So he might have been genuinely afraid. Draupadī's public insult at the court of the Kauravas went beyond all imagination. The story-teller pointed out that everybody present was dumb-founded and afraid that something terrible would happen when an innocent woman was tortured in this manner. It was also noted that some evil omens started happening, foreboding impeding doom. People reported to Dhṛtarāṣṭra about such evil omens said to be appearing on the horizon. The blind King was afraid beyond measure. There is a statement repeated in the *dharmaśāstra* which runs as follows:

> Where women are honoured and worshipped, all gods become pleased; if women are unnecessarily insulted, a great disaster must be on the way.

Dhṛtarāṣṭra finally decided to act if only to save everybody from the disastrous consequences that might have immediately followed.

The story of the *Mahābhārata* is the story of the royal throne. It is a story of power, pride, and prejudice. It is a story of hatred and deception. There was heroism, strength of arms, moral courage, great wisdom (such as that of Bhīṣma and Vidura), and great diplomacy (such as that of Kṛṣṇa). It is a story of lust and love, a story of jealousy and rivalry, which finally led to a great disaster—the greatest of all—the loss of the royal throne itself. It is one of the most tragic stories of the ancient world. It is a story where some sort of justice was salvaged towards the end. However, the main lesson that one may finally derive after reading the entire story is just the opposite. It is supposed to generate in readers a sort of profound wisdom, a sense of hollowness in everything that a self-centred and self-interested human being considers valuable and desirable, a total lack of interest in worldly pleasures, for it is shown in the end that all the foam and fury for the sake of power, pride and prejudice came to a big nothing. All the three main characters, Dhṛtarāṣṭra, Duryodhana, and Yudhiṣṭhira, who were connected with the throne, came to realize the hollowness of everything. Victory or defeat did not have any effect on the total outcome—a total anti-climax to a great and absorbing story promising a great climactic finish.

10

Karma and Renunciation

1. KARMA

What happened at the beginning of the battle of Kurukṣetra? A decision had to be made before striking the enemy. On the part of the Kauravas the decision had long been reached by Duryodhana. There was not a shadow of doubt about what had to be done: fight and kill. The Pāṇḍava side, however, had always been tormented with doubts, expressed at various junctures of the epic episode. The problems were discussed by Yudhiṣṭhira and by Arjuna. The culmination of the expression of classic doubt and indecision came on the eve of the battle, which was documented in the *Bhagavad-Gītā* episode.

The *karma* doctrine of Hinduism is well-known. It has many facets. The doctrine of *karma* that is primarily ascribed to the *Gītā* is one such facet. But it is unique in many ways. For it tries to resolve a well-known paradox about the interconnection of beliefs, actions and desires. I shall discuss this paradox in bare outlines and try to show how we think Kṛṣṇa, at least, tried to resolve it. There is no doubt that this is one of the philosophically important sections of the *Gītā*.

The simplest connection between beliefs, desires and action is this. Beliefs generate desire and desire generates action to obtain results. However, most desires are such that they are seldom satisfied, even when the results are obtained. For they only generate further desires. This creates a vicious circle, and forces us to be in a perpetual state of bondage through our pursuit of action and the 'rat race'.

2. ŚRAMAṆAS AND BRĀHAMAṆAS

Professor Sukumar Sen, in a private discussion, and Peter Della Santina, in a recent paper, make the point that the *karma* doctrine of the *Gītā* was entirely directed against the śramaṇa, particularly the Buddhist tradition.

Although there was undoubtedly, in the *Gītā*, a sustained indirect criticism of the non-Hindu—the Buddhist and the Jaina—strands of Indian thought, it took me some time to convince myself that Kṛṣṇa's doctrine of *karma* could be a viable alternative to the Śramaṇa prescription of asceticism and withdrawal into a state of actionlessness (*akarma*). The anti-ritualistic doctrine of the śramaṇas is well-known. In fact this is spelled out as anti-brahminism. The opposition between the *brāhmaṇa* and *śramaṇa* is proverbial. But here we are focusing on a particular point which is of radical importance. I venture to add that the problem is ethico-religious and hence falls squarely within the domain of morality.

There is a defence of the brahminical religion of ritual and sacrifice against the onslaught of the śramaṇas or 'free thinkers'. '*Karma*' in the older literature generally meant ritual acts, as the Vedic literature is divided into two parts, *Karma-kāṇḍa* and *Jñānakāṇḍa*, the former dealing with the intricacies of rituals and animal sacrifices and the latter with the wisdom of the Upaniṣads. However, by extension, the word *karma* meant also any action which has moral significance or any other type of consequence. In the *Gītā*, therefore, the word *karma* had a double significance, ritual acts and ethical duties. I shall concentrate on the second type of *karma* which will be directly relevant to our main issue here, moral dilemmas.

3. THE THREE WAYS

The conflict of desires, and the conflict of duties, commitments and so on are well-known facts of life. Whether or not moral dilemmas are finally eliminable through the exercise of the super-intelligence of a 'Harean *archangel*' (see R.M. Hare's *Moral Thinking*), one thing is crystal clear. Such conflicts are ineliminable in life. We can at best hope for temporary resolutions through ad hoc means and situational constraints. A rational agent who acknowledges the overwhelming presence of such conflicts has at most three ways of dealing with the situation. When we adopt any of these ways for the sake of choosing a life-plan, we can regard them as three different moral principles. I can introduce these three different ways of life through a discussion of the significance of a famous and oft-quoted verse of the *Gītā*. I refer to verse 47, chapter 2. Kṛṣṇa says here to Arjuna:

> You have entitlement to your actions only and never to the fruits of those actions. Do not be the causal agent of the fruits of actions; nor should you be attached to the state of non-action.

The state of 'non-action' here undoubtedly refers not only to a sort of moral indifference, but also obliquely to the state of renunciation taught by the Śramaṇa school. There is here an implicit formulation of three alternative action-guides. Let us discuss the last-mentioned first.

4. RENUNCIATION

The *Gītā* frequently refers to renunciation by the word *a-karma*. This is sometimes called the doctrine of non-action. I often wonder whether 'non-action' is a suitable translation. Arjuna had already put forward, though indirectly, a strong argument in favour of this doctrine. He was, as he said, confronted with the most baffling moral dilemma of his life, at a very critical moment. He can do either *x* or *y*, but not both. That is, he can either fight, in order to recover the kingdom as well as the life of luxury that goes along with it, or give up all claims to the kingdom and accept the life of a beggar or a monk: (cf. *bhaikṣyamapīha loke*, *Gītā* the chap 1, v. 5). The suggestivity (*dhvani*) of the word *bhaikṣya* should not be lightly dismissed. It has a connection with the word *bhikṣu*; hence the life of a śramaṇa is hinted at.

5. THIRST

The śramaṇas rejected the Vedic way of life, denounced the practice of rituals and chose the life of renunciation as the only way to achieve the goal of freedom. Not only were ritual acts to be given up by a śramaṇa, but also the aim was to achieve the state of complete non-action. The central ethical doctrine of early Buddhism was renunciation of all kinds of *tṛṣṇā* (*tanhā*), thirst, drive for action to perpetuate life (called 'becoming'). The root cause of 'becoming' is desire or motivation to act to gain some results. In their twelve-membered causal chain, *tanhā* occupies a central position. The chain starts with *avidyā*, that is, misconception, or false opinions, or false beliefs, and *saṁskāra*, that is, the residual *karma* from one's previous birth. But in the present birth, as soon as psychosomatic existence is obtained with sense faculties and mind functioning, *tanhā* (thirst) is generated in beings through the *contact* (*sparśa*) of the faculties with their objects. Desire generates action to bring about the enjoyment of the fruits, which generates further desire, that is, thirst. And from thirst to bondage again, that is, the cycle of birth and rebirth. In this way, according to Buddhism, the vicious circle of birth and rebirth (also called 'recurrence of death and death again') continues until one takes the right step of acquiring the right view, that is, proper knowledge (of the meaning of existence) and thereby gives up desire altogether to achieve the state of non-action. On this interpretation, the Buddhist or the śramaṇa position may be described as one of abandonment of all desire and action.

It is not very difficult to understand that one might well give up all sorts of actions (ritual, religious or moral) in order to avoid all moral conflicts or moral dilemmas. If one chooses the path of renunciation, one is also saved from moral lapses. But there can hardly be complete non-action. The moral consciousness of a person, as well as his or her religious awareness, is such that the person would be inclined to perform good and prescribed acts which will bring happiness and avoid evil. There is a natural expectation in a rational man that it is always possible through the exercise of reason to decide not only what is good and what is bad—but also to plan a strategy of life in such a way that one can always avoid evil and do the best. Further, the expectation is that it is possible to discover or devise a moral system which would be complete, consistent and adequate. The problem is that our search for such a moral or ethico-religious system has never been successful.

6. LUCK

Contingency or moral luck plays an important role in our lives. My remark in the last sentence of the last section is due to the fact that we often find it impossible to avoid genuine moral dilemmas, for which there is not rationally satisfactory solution. We are forced to resolve them, since act we must in situations, by using ad hoc means, but since by acting in one way we violate another deeply regarded moral principle we feel the pressure of moral emotions such as regret and remorse. Why did Arjuna have to choose between the two irreconcilable alternatives? One easy answer is that he should not have put himself in such a situation in the first place. The situation of a moral dilemma that a rational agent finds herself in is partly, if not fully, her own making. Under such circumstances one may feel that it is possible to have a life-plan which would be completely free from dilemmas and conflicts.

If we accept the argument so far, then we can see that the life-plan of 'non-action', or the śramaṇa life-plan, would be a recommendable option. It is true that we can avoid conflicts in action by not acting at all! In other words, if we follow the principle of 'non-action' thoroughly we will be able to follow a life which will not be morally reprehensible. But is it the final answer? Is 'non-action' possible? Even the śramaṇa life-plan is hardly one of total non-action.

7. ASCETICISM

This way of putting matters might unfairly trivialize an important alternative life-style—that of asceticism. However, my intention is far from such trivialization. Some of the noblest and finest human beings (the Buddha, the Jina included) have not only practised but also preached this way of life, and thereby brought peace and happiness to a considerably large section of agonized and suffering humanity. Hence, although it sounds like getting rid of one's head when you want to get rid of the headache, it is not a trivial and easy way out. If I never touch water, I will, of course, successfully avoid getting wet. Thus, the path of non-action may make me avoid the kind of dilemma where both alternatives are equally bad. Arjuna, or the young man in Sartre's well-known example, or Agamemnon in the familiar Greek tragedy—all found themselves with a genuine moral dilemma. Anybody following the *life of action* would undoubtedly face such dilemmas on thousands of occasions. For such conflicts are ineliminable in any active life in as much as contingencies as such are also ineliminable. This is one of the reasons, among others, for giving credence to the doctrine of moral scepticism or even to some other forms of scepticism. One should also note that this type of attitude towards life or asceticism should be distinguished from moral indifference, which is a totally amoral attitude.

It is significant to note that a modern philosopher, Bernard Williams, has identified this attitude of non-action (abandonment of both desires and actions) as one of the viable alternatives that one may choose when faced with the problem of the ineliminability of moral dilemmas. Williams, however rejects it, since according to him, it is hardly compatible with the notion of any moral claim (*Problems of the Self*, p. 178). However, if we reach a conclusion that there is no perfect way of organizing our desires in life to avoid conflict and dilemmas, we may think of two other alternatives: 1) Avoid all beliefs as false (scepticism); or 2) Avoid all possible desires and attendant beliefs (mysticism).

8. SCEPTICISM AND MYSTICISM

Now we may come back to the *Gītā*. The śramaṇa type of asceticism has been indirectly condemned here as *a-karma*—non-action. It was feared that Arjuna's sudden reluctance to fight and his decision to run away from the battlefield was due to an attachment to *a-karma*. However, the philosophy of non-action, which the śramaṇa schools propounded, was in direct opposition to, and as a justifiable protest against, the dry-as-dust ritual activities of brahminism, which involved animal sacrifice and other forms of violence. Thus, there was an attempt made in the post-Śramaṇa period to revive Vedic religion and morality in a much modified form, meeting indirectly the criticism of the śramaṇas. The śramaṇa ideal rejected not only the ritual *karma* but also other acts of moral significance that were pervasive in a caste-oriented society and approved by the householder's work-ethic. The law of *karma* dictated that all such activities were creating as well as contributing further to the bondage of the moral agent. As an agent you have desires and have to act accordingly. You act and obtain the fruits of your actions; these fruits create bondage for you, and in bondage you are forced to act again to create further bondage. This is the implication of the older *karma* doctrine, and the śramaṇas preached a way to break the vicious circle by their philosophy of 'non-action'. The older *karma* doctrine is what I have called the second alternative, and what has been referred to in the *Gītā* as *karmaphalahetu*, the 'agent who also enjoys the fruits of the action'. This alternative is usually followed by ordinary people, who are consequently tormented again and again by conflicts of duties and moral dilemmas. For, as I have already emphasized, there cannot be any perfect organization of one's life-plan in such a way that no conflict will arise.

9. KṚṢṆA'S ALTERNATIVE

The *Gītā* argued against the philosophy of non-action, and developed a new theory of action, which I shall call the third alternative or Kṛṣṇa's alternative: *niṣkāmakarma* or 'desireless' action. I shall discuss this theory after I have made some comments about the *Gītā's* position on ritual activities.

The performance of Vedic rituals was in a way supported by the *Gītā*, for it was argued that the entire society was held together by the performance of the prescribed Vedic sacrifices. The primitive factual belief was that the earth yields its produce with the help of rain from the sky above, on which depends the economic prosperity of the community. The gods control rainfall and so on hence to please gods, humans should perform rituals. Thus, the good of the society is sustained by the ritual acts, and there is a mutual give-and-take relationship between gods and humans. This is a very simplified version of the old Vedic religion of rituals and sacrifices.

10. ACTION VS. DESIRE

However, the life of action (even if we exclude rituals acts from it) is what is preferred by Kṛṣṇa. The later ritualists divided ritual acts into three groups: *nitya* (compulsory and daily), *naimittika* (compulsory, but on certain occasions only), and *kāmya* (with a desired reward). Of these, the first two formed a class by themselves. The agent must perform them but no result or reward could be expected out of them, for such results would not be forthcoming. They are reminiscent of the notion of a categorical imperative in Kantian moral theory. It may be that the 'desireless' action of the *Gītā* was derived indirectly from such notions of the *nitya*-type of action. The third type of action is in a way a pervasive factor where desire motivates the agent to act, and the results of the action in the form of rewards, pleasures and so on create further desire and further motivation for action. The group that I have called, following the *Gītā*, chapter 2, verse 47, *karmaphalahetu* would belong here. But Kṛṣṇa's advice to Arjuna was to avoid also this second path. He suggested a third alternative, the idea of *niṣkāmakarma*, to which I shall now turn.

In chapter 4, verse 16, Kṛṣṇa says: *kiṃ karma kim akarmeti kavayo 'py atra mohitāḥ* (Even the wise are confused as regards what should be done and what should not be done). This is in my opinion a clear recognition of the realities of moral dilemmas in a life of action, as opposed to a life of renunciation. The word *karma* here does not obviously mean simply the Vedic sacrifices or rituals. In the *Gītā*, the following pairs have often been used as representing two opposite positions (they are used presumably in special senses):

sāṃkhya	*yoga*
jñāna	*karma*
buddhiyoga	*karmayoga*
karma-sannyāsa	*karma-yoga*

The words in the first column have often been treated as denotative of the same meaning. The same is true of the second column. If we keep this in mind we can resolve some of the puzzling statements of the *Gītā*.

The word *sāṃkhya* ordinarily meant the metaphysical system called Sāṃkhya. But Kṛṣṇa used it in the general sense of knowledge, knowledge of the metaphysics of a permanent soul. One may also find a resonance here of the critique of the no-soul doctrine of Buddhism. Be that as it may, what is notable here is that pure knowledge or knowledge of 'thatness' or truth (*tattva-jñāna*) is not enough for achieving the final good of mankind. Kṛṣṇa emphasized three things among others, in this chapter:

permanence of the soul, impermanence of everything else including ordinary pleasures and happiness, and the obligation to act in a 'life of action' (including the performance of prescribed duties—scriptural as well as moral), but not to cling to the desire for the fruits of such actions.

11. ACTION WITHOUT DESIRE

It is the last-mentioned that should occupy our attention. For, as far as we can see it is a novel alternative opposed to the other two. Faced with the problem about what should or should not be done, which sometimes becomes almost rationally undecidable, one may decide not to act at all (and choose the life of non-action), or one may act and accept the consequences with regret, remorse and sadness (described as 'tragic cases' by modern philosophers in connection with the Greek tragedies), or, one may act but abandon all desire for the outcome or fruits or anything else. This is the most difficult alternative, as Kṛṣṇa himself acknowledged. It must be preceded by a prolonged practice of Yoga and other virtues. Very few succeed in attaining this kind of a *desireless* state of mind. Kṛṣṇa says that *humans in this state approach the divine stage.* This is a very significant statement. Just as the Creator God is supposed to have created the universe although he has had no unfulfilled desire from which he should have acted, the person in a desireless state of mind should act (for act she must) similarly, and thereby action would not create any bondage for her. She would be free.

The real *karmayogin*, according to Kṛṣṇa, gets the best of the both worlds. He must possess perfect knowledge of the nature of things and persons, but this knowledge would not lead him to non-action. He would do whatever is expected of him by society and he would exercise unbiased reason to decide conflicting alternatives, but he would be completely free from any selfish desires, motives or preferences. If he acts for no selfish desire of his own, such acts will not produce any result that may cling to the agent and create further bondage. Thus he would achieve the goal which the śramaṇas also aim at through their philosophy of non-action.

12. COMPLETE NON-ACTION IS IMPOSSIBLE

In chapter 3, Arjuna asked Kṛṣṇa the crucial question: if you think the path of knowledge is better than the path of action why then do you ask me to fight this terrible battle and confuse me as regards my duty? (chapter 3, verse 13). Kṛṣṇa answered as follows. Abandonment of all actions (*sannyāsa*) by itself does not get you immediate success. Nor can the goal of proper non-action (approved by Kṛṣṇa) be achieved without starting to act in some way or other (ibid., verse 4). In fact, Kṛṣṇa argued that no one can stay even for a moment without acting, for everybody is forced to act according to their inner nature. In fact there are two ways of following the path of non-action. According to one, a person tries to control his faculties of activities, spends time in mental cultivation (meditation) and thereby controls the senses and thereby their objects. But this person is utterly confused. According to what Kṛṣṇa was preaching, it is the false philosophy of non-action (ibid., verse 6). According to the other, a person, having first controlled his senses, starts such actions as are proper and as are expected of him by the scriptures, society and family. He is a proper *karmayogin* if he can remain completely unattached through the control of mind and senses (ibid., verse 7). It is the latter path which is preferred by Kṛṣṇa in the *Gītā*, not complete non-action.

To act, but not to have a desire for any result at the same time, is a very difficult way of life. It is more easily said than done. It needs life-long practice to control the mind and the senses in order to achieve a state where all mundane desires will appear to be devoid of any meaning and purpose and hence undesirable. As people think of the objects or pay attention to them, attachment (as a natural attraction) towards them is generated, and from attachment comes desire (*Gītā*, chapter 2, verse 62). Frustration of desire leads to anger and other passions, and thus the person becomes overwhelmed with passion, with disastrous loss of intellect, and self-destructive tendencies.

So far I have indiscriminately mixed rather different notions from two entirely different philosophical traditions. One is the notion of the *karmayoga* in the *Gītā* and the other is the notion of a moral act. I plead guilty to this charge. I shall try to establish a connection to the end. There are, however, many different ways of distinguishing between moral and non-moral acts. And it is not uncommon to find the same act moral from one point of view but not moral or even neutral from another point of view.

It has been repeatedly emphasized by Lord Kṛṣṇa that human beings can never remain without performing any action. Even the monks, the śramaṇas, and the renouncers may follow the path of no action, but in order to maintain their physical existence in this world they would have to resort to some action or other. Using such arguments, some have developed a pseudo-paradox which is supposed to weaken, if not falsify the theory of desireless action. To perform any action, we need to have determination, called *saṃkalpa*, and the root of such *saṃkalpa* is desire.

This is now the *Manusaṃhitā* has put the matter (see Manu, chapter 2, verses 2–5). The simplest way one may put the paradox is this. One may start an action without having any desire for the fruits of such an action, but one must have to have some desire to start an action. Hence the concept of desireless action is a myth.

13. OBJECTIONS TO 'DESIRELESSNESS'

The above objection can, however, easily be circumvented. We have already referred to the concept *nitya-karma* ('compulsory' action). The idea behind such actions is this. Nothing is gained by the performance of such acts, but it is the incumbent duty of human beings to perform them. The notion of desireless action can be seen as an extension of this type of *nitya* action. Thus the concept of desireless action can be a genuine possibility. The Kantian notion of the categorical imperative in the moral domain is a kindred notion, which shows that the concept is not simply an idealist's fantasy.

There is, however, another objection to the concept of desireless action. This objection is more serious. In fact, this objection confounds any other philosophy of life where total renunciation is regarded as a goal. The paradoxicality of the situation can be explained as follows. We give up all our desires for the fruits of our actions, because only by doing so will we not be entangled in life any further. But this goal of freedom or non-entanglement must also be regarded as another good, and an ardent desire to achieve this goal must be the motivating desire of our desireless action. In other words we practise renunciation in order to achieve the goal of freedom and autonomy, but the very desire for freedom would render the practice of desireless action useless. For renunciation is an act and renunciation with a desire for freedom is certainly not an instance of desireless action. Thus it is that Kṛṣṇa's advice to practise desireless action becomes thereby almost impracticable. The goal of freedom through *karma* becomes ever elusive.

14. POSSIBLE SOLUTIONS

Is there a way out? One solution is, of course, derivable from Kant. I shall not, however, go into the Kantian solution here. Is renunciation a positive act? The concept of renunciation has a negative element in it. Hence, should we not regard it as a negative act (in the sense of *not* doing something rather than doing something)? The traditional philosophers of India had confronted such questions themselves and suggested some good and some not-so-good answers. One solution that is often referred to is this. We have to make a distinction between categories of desires. Desire for food to satisfy my hunger cannot belong to the same category of desires as when I jump into the river (even if I didn't know how to swim) to protect a little child belonging to someone I did not know. In the second case, I may be motivated by my moral concern or one may argue that I was probably motivated also by the glory or praise that I may receive afterwards. It is emphasized by the Indian philosophers that the desire for the ultimate freedom or *mokṣa*, or the *arthatship* desire or compassion to save humanity from suffering, cannot be called desire in the ordinary sense of the term. If the point of this argument is accepted, as I believe it could be, then the above-mentioned paradox might be dissolved. The desire for ultimate freedom cannot create any further bondage. An inadequate analogy is this: if there is a war which will end all wars or hostilities, then such a war cannot create any further war. On the other hand, can there be any such war?

There is another way by which we can reinforce this argument. It has been mentioned several times in the *Gītā*. It is believed in the Indian tradition that God has created the universe, although he had neither any *desire* to be satisfied, nor any *want* to be fulfilled. Philosophers of the medieval period in India cited an analogy to explain the problem. Why should God create the Universe? The answer is that he is like a prince whose father has satisfied all his desires and wants, but still the prince is engaged in creating things for play with his playmates. He is full of joy and delight. But he continues his sport, he remains active and indulges in such activities. It is difficult to ascribe motivations or desires to God in his act of creating the universe, just as we cannot ascribe a motive to the happy prince. The desireless action of a human being should be an imitation of this situation. It is therefore not an impossible feat.

Kṛṣṇa has said to Arjuna in the *Gītā* that people describe God as the creator of the Universe. For a person with perfect equipoise and mental balance, for a person who has nothing to wish for in this universe, how can there be any desire to create? However, the universe has still been created. For God acted in spite of his being totally desireless. Hence it is the duty of those human beings who want ultimate freedom to emulate the so-called Creator God in their activities. God is said to be the Creator, but at the same time he should be called the non-Creator (*Gītā*, chapter 4, verse 13). A human being should in the same manner be considered the agent of the action he or she does, but at the same time if the person has practised the method of desireless action, he or she should be considered the *non-agent* of the action. For an essential constituent of agency must be the presence of desire in the agent for the fruit of the action. If such desire is absent, there cannot be any agency.

Some philosophers might argue that the reward for desireless action (if there has to be a reward at all) is comparable to the so-called reward of what might be called a Kantian version of morality. Very roughly speaking, it is believed that people do not behave morally in the hope of some moral reward. This is often asserted as being a fundamental distinction between moral and non-moral actions. But it is still believed by some that moral actions should have some form of moral reward, although the moral agent, it is true, must not look for such reward. The theory of desireless action can be explained in a similar manner. The agent, according to Kṛṣṇa, must not look for any reward. But towards the end, it is not impossible that some good things will happen to the agent. Here also the paradox ultimately dissolves itself, and the notion of morality is brought closer to the notion of desireless action.

We might take a lesson here from the sphere of Sanskrit and Greek dramas. For a long time, Indologists have argued that the absence of tragedy in Sanskrit drama was due to a profound influence which the doctrine of *karma* exercised on the Indian mind. The Greek dramas are full of tragedies as they are products of the Greek world view. This was at least the argument of the Indologists. I am personally not very sure of this thesis. According to the Indologists, the Greek world was governed by forces which were superhuman in power and uncontrollable. Greek dramas were full of human tragedies which underlined the powerlessness of human will, intellect and fate against the gods. But the later Indian thought was dominated by the law of *karma*. Unlike fate, *karma* was not a blind force which dealt with individuals capriciously or unreasonably. The law of *karma* carefully distinguishes between the qualities of two different actions and judges the individuals by the results they produce. Thus, as I have emphasized elsewhere, Max Weber was right in seeing the law of *karma* as the ground for the germination of a rational system of justice. In this way, throughout the narrative literature in India we have a recurrence of the theme, that is, the law of *karma*, much in the same way as we have repetitions of the theme of *mokṣa* or ultimate freedom as the final goal. Here, however, the concepts *karma* and *mokṣa* converge in a peculiar way. The *Mahābhārata* is the classic text for such a convergence. *Karma* ordinarily leads to bondage; but desireless action leads to *mokṣa*.

Much later in the history, Sureśvara, a direct disciple of Śaṃkara, wrote a book called *Naiṣkarmya-siddhi*. There, he examined many alternatives that were supposed to lead to *mokṣa*, ultimate freedom. One view was that pure *jñāna*, or knowledge of the ultimate reality, leads to *mokṣa*. Another view was that it was a combination of pure knowledge and action or *karma* (ritual, non-ritual and moral) which leads to *mokṣa*. Various other similar views were propounded at that time in India. But the theory of desireless action or *niṣkāma-karma* became the most popular one, and perhaps it was because it was more rationally argued than the others.

Notes and References

Hare, R.M., *Moral Thinking*, Oxford, Clarendon Press, 1981.
Williams, B., *Problems of the Self*, Cambridge, Publisher?, 1976.

11

Caste, *Karma* and the *Gītā*

I

In chapter 4, verse 13 of the *Bhagavad-Gītā*, Lord Kṛṣṇa says:

The assembly of four *varṇas* (castes) has been created by me in accordance with the division of 'qualities' and actions. But although I am its creator, know me as a non-creator and imperishable (undiminished).

The context is rather odd for talking about the origin of the four *varṇas* or the caste-system of Hinduism. And yet the first line of this verse has often been quoted by modern apologists to show that the hierarchy prevalent from time immemorial in the Indian Vedic (Hindu) society, known as the caste-system, was actually based upon merits and capabilities rather than on heredity. But, paradoxically, heredity seems to have been the general practice throughout. For caste is usually determined by birth, and birth is something over which the person does not have any control. If hierarchies are determined by birth, then there is something about which a human being (a rational being, that is) has a right to feel uneasy. For it is somewhat unfair. Hence there is an apocryphal (but also very ancient) line attributed to the well-known *Mahābhārata* character, Karṇa, which says:

daivāyattam kule jamma madāyattam tu pauruṣam.

I translate:

My birth in a family is under the control of the 'book of Fate'[1]
but I myself control my qualities as a human being.[2]

The significance of this line is obvious in the context. A person may be born in a lowly family, but through effort, determination and cultivation of virtues she or he may rise in life and be *somebody*. Karṇa became a great hero, and a king; in fact in the *Mahābhārata* he was the only match for the invincible Arjuna, although he was supposed to be the son of an ordinary charioteer. It can match a modern story where a cabbie's son becomes a prince or a general.

That the heredity-determined hierarchy in a society is somewhat unfair and even irrational was felt much earlier in the tradition. Karṇa's assertion quoted above (apocryphal though it may be) expresses the protest of the dissident groups in the society. A human being's worth must be judged by her actions, virtues and merits, by what she makes of herself, not by her birth. Support of this point comes from another source, which is by no means apocryphal in any sense. Poet Bhavabhūti writing in the eighth century AD, said in his *Uttararāmacarita*:

> *Gunaḥ pujāsthānaṃ guṇiṣu na liṅgaṃ na ca vayaḥ* (act IV, verse 11)

This has been said about Sītā, the abandoned wife of Rāma. The argument of the verse was that Sītā excelled all others by her virtue and merit, hence her abandonment was entirely unjust. I translate the above line:

> Qualities of the qualified persons are worthy of our adoration,
> not their sex, nor age.

This was a remarkable assertion in the predominantly sexist society of so-called traditional India. It is no doubt charged with sexist reflexes, as are, alas, many statements heard in modern society today. I believe our language is *given* to us and as such it always suffers from the defects of the Orwellian Newspeak. Anything you say in it does not really sound right in the light of the newly gained consciousness of injustice, domination and tacit discrimination. Hence it seems to me that the concept of *muting*, developed by the sociologist E. Ardener, is a very suitable one in this context. The subdued group is often the *muted* group.[3]

But let us go back to the *Gītā*. I had read the *Bhagavad-Gītā* many times in my youth. And I must admit that I did not understand many things because I did not know much Sanskrit at that time. At that time its appeal was more in the form of an inspired 'song' sung by Lord Kṛṣṇa to persuade reluctant Arjuna to do his duty. So the crude message was: we must do our duty no matter what. We have been taught to treat the book with reverence. It is regarded (mostly by European scholars) as one of the 'Hindu Scriptures'. In the orthodox Indian tradition, the *Gītā* is regarded as part of our *śmṛti*, not *śruti* (in fact, 'scriptures' is a poor translation of the Sanskrit *śruti*, if not totally wrong). In our Vedānta parlance, the *Gītā* is one of three *prasthānas*, the other two being the Upaniṣads (*śruti*) and the *Brahmasūtra*. Hence anybody interested in the Vedānta (both Advaita and non-Advaita) cannot afford to ignore the *Gītā*.

Western scholars generally identify the *Gītā* as a 'Vaiṣṇava text'.[4] But it is not exclusively for the Vaiṣṇavas, although Kṛṣṇa/Viṣṇu is the main speaker here. In fact, this is a text which is accepted as authoritative even outside the Vedāntic circle. Apart from the Advaitin Śaṃkara, Abhinavagupta, the well-known Śaivite author, wrote a commentary on this text. This falsifies the idea that it is exclusively for the Vaiṣṇava. Besides, I believe this sort of 'exclusivism' which tries to discover a clear-cut and sharp line of demarcation between Vaiṣṇavism and Śaivism and other '-isms' in the Indian context is a product of Western *reading* of Indian culture. It is, mildly speaking, a discourse constructed by the perception of the Western Indologists.

If the message of the *Gītā* is to be taken seriously (as we must from the Hindu point of view at least), then certain paradoxical questions do arise regarding the concept of ethics and morality. These issues have been debated over the ages and many *ad hoc* but not very satisfactory solutions have been given. We sometimes do not wish to see the paradoxes but go on acting according to some dictum or other and believe that these are *given* to us. Must we always indulge in rational thinking before acting? We do not like to share Arjuna's doubts and reluctance. For if everything has been decided for us by the supreme intelligence of Kṛsna, who are we to think about the propriety or justification of the moral codes that the *Gītā* presents?

There are philosophers and other people who believe that there cannot arise any moral or ethical dilemmas because there is always some *right* answer to all apparently paradoxical questions. It is our duty to know the right answers. We may not be able to discover these right answers, but persons with superior intellects can conduct the rigorous 'critical level' thinking (as R.M. Hare insists[5]) and discover the right answers for us, and our duty would be to follow them. There are, however, others who believe just the opposite. Dilemmas are realities. They do arise and a totally satisfactory resolution of them through rational means may be simply unavailable to us.

I wish to concentrate upon one particular issue: the paradoxicality of caste and *karma*. This paradoxicality has often gone unnoticed. To uncover the paradoxicality as well as complementarity of the two notions of caste and *karma*, we have to go back to Max Weber. The caste-hierarchy was anti-rational for it was underwritten by the ritual sanction of pollution, as well as by heredity rather than merit. Predominance of hierarchy is found in all civilized societies, including the egalitarian ones, and its usefulness is not in question here. The question is whether it should be heredity-based or merit-based. Rationality supports the second alternative, whereas practice makes the first alternative more acceptable. The doctrine of *karma*, on the other hand, is, or at least seems to be, an example of ethical rationalism. For Weber this doctrine represents a coherent theodicy. He saw in the caste-*dharma* and its tie-in with *karma*, a completely unique concept; the combination of the two produced for Max Weber 'the most consistent theodicy ever formulated'.[6] It produced a persistent social order. From the point of view of an internalist—an orthodox Hindu, for example—the *karma* doctrine must also be complementary to the caste-hierarchy, for it may resolve the tension created by the unaccounted-for inequalities nurtured in a hierarchical society.

The mixture of caste and *karma*, however, was, as J. Heesterman has recently put it, 'volatile'.[7] The two notions are also mutually opposed to each other. *Karma* or ethical rationalism emphasizes the 'merit-based' nature of the social order, while the caste-hierarchy emphasizes its 'heredity-based' nature. The first allows freedom and self-responsibility, the second closes the door to freedom and accentuates the givenness of social duties and responsibilities. But at the same time their combination became feasible. If the heredity-based caste-hierarchy made the social system anti-rational and unfair, the *karma* theodicy was introduced for the rationalization of the existing practice. The social order that resulted therefrom was not a rational, but a rationalized order. However the inner conflict did not disappear completely. For the heredity-based hierarchy presumably received a rational support as well as a ritual sanction, and the merit-based hierarchy was not given the prominence it deserved.

The merit-based nature of a hierarchy, however, seems to be rational. This awareness became more and more a shared feeling among the members belonging to this social order. The feeling found expression in various forms. Those who denounced orthodoxy rejected the hereditary nature of caste-hierarchy. Those who became renouncers went the same way. But within the tradition itself, many asserted that the merit-based nature of the hierarchy is a more acceptable alternative. Thus *brāhman*-hood is not dependent upon birth or family but is constituted by a set of several moral virtues, several duties and responsibilities. Similarly *kṣatriya*-hood or *vaiśya*-hood. It is the echo of this view—the critical view rather than the view of the conformist—that I believe we find in the line of the *Gītā* that I quoted in the opening sentence.

II

The caste duties are talked about in the *Gītā* in at least four different places: chapter 2, 31–7; chapter 3, 35; chapter 4, 13; and chapter 18, 41–8.

The context of chapter 4 is rather odd, as I have already mentioned. Lord Kṛṣṇa is dwelling on the point that although in this world (*iha*) people perform sacrifices desiring success and do obtain such success (verse 12), God (who created the world, divided people into four *varṇas* according to their merit) should not be regarded as an agent. For agency belongs to the humans (who work with desire in their mind), not to the Changeless One, God. The idea is probably that God works without any desire and the fruits do not cling to him (as is made explicit in verse 14). Hence, although there is no emphasis on how the *varṇa*-division came to be, it nevertheless is pointed out that the caste-classification is not really created by the divine will, but by the distribution of merit according to the law of *karma*. The commentators (e.g. Śrīdhara) note that since the inequalities were not created by God but by the law of *karma* which God only administered, the so-called problem of evil is somehow averted.

Chapter 2, 31–7: Here Lord Kṛṣṇa tells Arjuna that it is his duty as a *kṣatriya* to fight this battle to recover his kingdom. This is the action prescribed by the *kṣatriya* code of duty. In fact, it is morally binding by the principle of group-morality. If Arjuna as a *kṣatriya* fails to act in the prescribed manner, he would be disgraced and condemned by all other warriors. The *kṣatriya* code is also the 'death before dishonour' code. The situation is this: As a human being, as a loving member of the royal family, he feels that the killing of a grandfather and other relatives is bad; but as a *kṣatriya* he is told that it is his sacred duty to fight and kill—a classic case of moral conflict, which tends to inspire moral scepticism.

Chapter 3, 35: It emphasizes again that one must follow one's own *dharma*, duties prescribed by the code, even when performance of such duties could be faulty or devoid of any merit. The expression *svadharma* (the key expression in all such contexts) is intriguing, for it is also interchangeable with *svabhāva*, 'own nature' or simply 'nature'.[8] Thus it may be read as the advice to follow one's own nature, natural inclination, in choosing the course of action. One should try always to be one's own self, not somebody else. Arjuna was by nature a warrior, not a forgiving, self-sacrificing recluse. Hence, Kṛṣṇa seemed to be saying, Arjuna's sudden decision to turn back and run away from the battlefield to be a recluse (cf. *bhaiksyam apīha loke*, Arjuna's pious wish: I would rather be a mendicant) would be acting against his nature. That is, against the grid of a natural warrior, a *kṣatriya*, who always fights for his honour. Thus Arjuna's own *dharma* at this stage is just to fight as best as he can. It would be doing what he can do best and to do otherwise would be dangerous and fatal (cf. *bhayāvaha*).

Chapter 18, 41–8: Lord Kṛṣṇa says that the four *varṇas* (*brāhman, kṣatriya, vaiśya* and *śūdra*) have their duties assigned to them according to the 'qualities' arising from their 'own-natures'. Śaṃkara, in his commentary on verse 41, introduces, as he does on many other occasions, the three Sāṃkhya *guṇas: sattva, rajas* and *tamas*. The first is connected with anything that is good and pious. The second is connected with activity: the dynamic qualities, drive, passion and so on which are not always good, but not bad either. They are, however, much needed for a life of action. The third is connected with ignorance, darkness, confusion, the non-intelligent, mechanical labour and so on Śaṃkara connects the origin of the *brāhmans* with *sattva*; the *kṣatriyas* with *rajas* mixed with *tamas*; and the *śūdras* with *tamas* mixed with a bit of *rajas*. This is a neat classification which acknowledges the different natures (*svabhāva*) we witness in various human beings.[9] But it does not explain the origin of this variety. Both Rāmānuja and Śaṃkara add another crucial comment here. According to them, one's caste or birth is predetermined by one's former lives, that is former *karma*. This seems to be an acceptable rationalization of the prevalent caste-hierarchy. Your previous *karma* (in former lives) is responsible for what you are today (what status in the hierarchy you have).

This type of rationalization was enough to fire the imagination of Max Weber, who even quoted from the *Communist Manifesto* to show how much more acceptable the caste-*dharma* system would become:

> '. . . They (the proletariat) have nothing to lose but their chains, they have a world to win', the same holds for the pious Hindu of low caste, he too can gain Heaven and become a god—only not in this life, but in the life of the future after rebirth into the same world pattern (p. 122).

Verses 42–4 give four lists of virtues and assign them to the four *varṇas* respectively. Thus calmness, self-restraint, ascetic practice, purity, tolerance, uprightness, wisdom, knowledge and faith—all constitute *brāhman*-hood. High courage, ardour, endurance, skill, not turning back on the battlefield, charity, majesty—all these constitute *kṣatriya*-hood. Cultivation, cattle-rearing, trade—these are the constitutive properties of *vaiśya*-hood. Finally, service to others is what makes a *śūdra* a *śūdra*.

III

To list the constitutive properties of *brāhman*-hood etc., was in fact a significant development. For if we depend upon the constitutive properties to assign hierarchical status, lower or higher, then birth or family (i.e., heredity) becomes immaterial for such status distinction. I shall conclude after relating a relevant story from another part of the *Mahābhārata*.

In the *Vanaparvan*, Yudhiṣṭhira, the *Dharmarāja*, had an encounter with a huge python, who was in fact King Nahuṣa, one of the forefathers of Yudhiṣṭhira. Nahuṣa, through his good deeds and piety, obtained as his reward the throne of Heaven, but then his downfall started. For he became too proud and forgot the distinction between *dharma* and *a-dharma*. He kicked at the head of sage Agastya and was cursed, which turned him into a python for thousands of years. He had been waiting, in the form of the python, for a long time to be saved by pious Yudhiṣṭhira through a discourse on *dharma*. So he one day got hold of Bhīma and was about to crush him when Yudhiṣṭhira appeared in search of his brother. The fabulous power of Bhīma, who used to kill almost endless numbers of demons, elephants, pythons, and so on was of no avail. Nahuṣa was more powerful for he had a noble mission—a discourse on *dharma*. Nahuṣa said to Yudhiṣṭhira, 'I will let your brother go, if you answer my questions on *dharma*.' So the discourse started. The first question was: What makes a *brāhman* a *brāhman*? Yudhiṣṭhira listed a number of virtues: truthfulness, generosity, forgiveness, goodness, kindness, self-control and compassion—all these qualities together constitute a *brāhman*. The list is not very different from the one found in the *Gītā*, chapter 18, verse 42. The python asked, 'But this goes against the principle of four *varṇas*. For even a *śūdra* may have all these virtues. Virtues cannot be the monopoly of any caste.' Yudhiṣṭhira replied in unambiguous language, 'Indeed, if a *śūdra* is characterized by all these virtues, he is to be "defined" (cf. *lakṣya*) as a *brāhman*. And if a *brāhman* lacks them then he is to be regarded as a *śūdra*.' The python asked again, 'But if *brāhman*-hood is constituted by a number of virtues, then birth (in a *brāhman* family) would be in vain, where such virtues are conspicuous by their absence.' Yudhiṣṭhira replies, 'Indeed. Since through sexual urge (*rāga*) people copulate and produce children (and copulation is not always between husband and wife of the same caste), birth is always a dubious criterion in such matters. Therefore, the old sages depend upon good conduct (*śīla*) as the indicator of a better person. Even one who is a *brāhman* by birth would be a *śūdra* through poor and despicable conduct.' Yudhiṣṭhira even referred to the 'self-originating' Manu as his authority.[10]

I believe this reflects the presence of what I call the 'internal criticism' within the tradition about the prevalence of the heredity-based caste hierarchy. Hence, if one portion of a whole text is to be treated as a commentary on another portion, then this discourse on caste may be regarded as a commentary on the remarks on caste in the *Gītā*, chapter 4, verse 13, or chapter 18, verses 41–8. In the light of the above remarks a comment such as *guṇa-karma-vibhāgaśaḥ* (in accordance with the division of 'qualities' and actions) is to be regarded more as a criticism of the existing heredity-bound caste system, than an assertion of an already existing practice. But Weber's commendation of the caste-*karma* order was a bit premature. The undercurrent of rationality in the tradition no doubt interpreted the *karma* doctrine in such a way as to make it adjustable to the heredity-bound caste-hegemony. But then we are back with the same old quandary. If one's responsibility extends not only to what one does in this life but also to what one is supposed to have done in one's many (hypothetically construed) former lives, then the thin thread of rationality that presumably tied *karma* to the heredity-bound caste hierarchy becomes too elusive to allow freedom and autonomy. And, paradoxically, *karma* becomes almost synonymous with Fate or Destiny.

It may be argued that my interpretation of these passages of the *Gītā* is only an intepretation, a novel or modern one. But that is all we can do with a text like the *Gītā*. The multivalent character of this text (or scriptural texts in general) is wellknown and welldocumented.[11] I believe the history of the ever changing social and religious ethos of Indian society is to be gleaned from the enormous body of the textual material we have at our disposal. Very broadly speaking, hierarchical society was heredity-bound from time immemorial, which was found unsatisfactory because of its 'irrational' nature. The *karma* doctrine was reinterpreted to rationalize it. My point is also very general. There existed (and I believe, still exists) an internal critique of this within the tradition itself. And this was based upon what I must call a form of rationality not very different from what we call rationality today. This form of rationality came into conflict with the form of relativism which the caste-relative set of *dharma*-prescriptions encourages.

Notes and References

1. It is difficult to translate '*daiva*' in English. In the Indian tradition it is usually opposed to *puruṣakāra*, which means what humans can achieve by their own effort. A parallel, though not quite the same, distinction in the West is between freedom of will and determinism. I believe 'The Book of Fate' captures essentially the core sense of the word in the context.
2. '*Pauruṣa*' is derived from '*puruṣa*' = 'man'; hence, heroism, prowess, achievements, etc., could be indicated by the same form.
3. Ardener (1975).

4. A curious anecdote: Once a colleague of mine in Oxford used the expression 'a Vaiṣṇava text' to describe the manuscript of the *Gītā* which was on display at Bodleian Library Manuscript Display Room. It was an exhibition of the Sanskrit manuscripts in the Bodleian. But an Indian who came to Oxford to see the exhibition was upset because he was an Advaitin (not a Vaiṣṇava) and still regarded the *Gītā* as one of his scriptures. He complained. But of course, my colleague did not want to change the description just to please him. For Western Indologists have for a long time identified the *Gītā* as a Vaiṣṇava text; it makes categorization easier.
5. Hare (1981).
6. Weber (1958), p. 121.
7. Heesterman (1985), p. 195.
8. *Sva-dharma*: On this Heesterman writes, 'it is better to perform the duties of one's own caste, one's *svadharma*, indifferently than those of others with outstanding distinction' (p. 196). This clearly identifies *svadharma* with one's caste-duty. Though this is the general understanding of the term, I believe it misses at least one subtlety: '*sva*' refers to the person himself or herself. Besides, if the division of castes is according to natures of human beings, then what is proper for one's own caste is also proper for one's own self or nature. I believe *sva-dharma* can be interpreted in the second way on several occasions, without emphasizing the caste-bound duties. Manu also refers to '*svasya ca priyam*' (verse II/2) as well as to '*ātmanas tuṣṭir eva ca*' (verse II/6), as one of the authorities on *dharma*, over and above the Vedas, etc.
9. Indian society was pluralistic and hence we find ready acceptance of multiple interpretations of the textual tradition. That the *Gītā* has a multivalent character is today well recognized by even the most devout Hindu. See also Sharma (1986), pp. 248–52.
10. It may be that what Yudhiṣṭhira was made to say here was against the prevalent and dominant views of the society. It is undoubtedly a form of social criticism to ridicule the hereditary nature of the social hierarchy. Hence it seems to me that an authority, like that of a Svayambhu Manu, was needed to combat the authority of other *dharmaśāstrakāras*.
11. Sharma (1986), p. 252.

Ardener, Shirley (1975), editor, *Perceiving Women*, London: Malaby Press.
Hare, R.M. (1981), *Moral Thinking*, Oxford: Clarendon Press.
Heesterman, J.C. (1985), *The Inner Conflict of Tradition*, Chicago: University of Chicago.
Sharma, Arvind (1986), *The Hindu Gītā: Ancient and Classical Interpretations of the Bhagavadgītā*, La Salle: Open Court.
Weber, Max (1958), *The Religion of India*, New York: Free Press.

12

Love and Sensuality in the Epics

1. INTRODUCTION: *KĀMA*

We find few words as indispensible in any discussion of human emotion and at the same time as imprecise in its meaning as the word 'love'. Sanskrit has an equally multifacted term, *kāma*. *Kāma* is arguably a more pervasive concept than love. The three concepts, *dharma, artha* and *kāma* have been discussed and elaborated on by scholars over the centuries. Modern studies of Hinduism are invariably associated with the three or four *vargas* (*dharma, artha, kāma* and *mokṣa*). In fact the simplest way to define Hinduism is to talk about these four.

The idea seems to be this. *Dharma* stands for a person's religious and moral duties as a member of a community. *Artha* stands for 'wealth', and *kāma* stands for 'desire' of the flesh and mind, as well as our drive for the satisfaction of such desires. *Mokṣa* is final release, which, according to the doctrine, should be the goal of every Hindu. Hence, a person should pay attention to each of these four. In other words, a person should not devote all his time and energy exclusively to any one of them. He should not only perform his religious and moral duties, but also make honest efforts to acquire wealth and fulfil his desire before he can try to work for his *mokṣa*.

The above is a very simplistic and unsophisticated way of talking about Hinduism. In fact, in spite of the fascination of modern scholars with these four concepts, I believe that it presents a very distorted view of Hinduism. The only lesson than can be learnt from this doctrine of *caturvarga* (four concepts) is that it presents a very balanced view of life and the world, and some Hindus may take some unnecessary pride in this matter. However, what I find to be of some significance is simply this: by according equal status and importance to both *kāma*, desire of flesh, and *artha*, drive to acquire wealth, side by side with *dharma*, religious and moral duties, this doctrine contradicted the religious and mystical aura that is often associated with Hinduism today.

My desire to talk about love and sensuality has been reflected in the epic literature. And I will show that the attitude of the epic characters towards love and sensuality was unique in many ways. The fact that sexual pleasure can be regarded as not only the highest form of acceptable pleasure but also as honourable and prestigious is proven by certain passages in the *Bṛhadāraṇyaka Upaniṣad.* There transcendental delight has been compared with sensual pleasure (*Bṛhadāraṇyaka*, 1.4.3:)

He did not enjoy himself. Therefore, people do not enjoy (are not happy all by themselves, i.e. alone. He wanted a second, a companion. He became as big as a man and a woman embracing each other. He divided this body into two. From that, the body of husband and wife was created. Therefore, said Yajñavalkya, this body is one half of oneself. It is like one of the two halves of a split pea. Therefore, the empty space is indeed filled by the woman. He was united with her. From that, people were born.

According to Śaṃakara, 'He' refers to Manu or Viraja, and the woman was his daughter, Śatarūpa whom he conceived of as his mate. From their union, human beings were born.

2. KĀMA INTERPRETED AS PLEASURE IN THE EPIC

In the *Karṇaparvan* of the *Mahābhārata*, when Yudhiṣṭhira was suffering from utter depression, Śonaka, an expert in Sāṃkhya and Yoga, came to cheer him up. There was an interesting discussion among Yudhiṣṭhira, Bhīma, Śonaka and Draupadī. The discussion centred around the relative merit and mutual complementariness of *dharma, artha* and *kāma.* The definition of *kāma* that was given there may be of some interest to us.

Kāma is that pleasure which in our mind derives from contact of the senses and the object presented. This mental state is experiential. It has no embodied existence.

Kāma is that pleasure which is experienced by our mind and our heart when our sense organs are in contact with their respective objects.

These verses make it clear that *kāma* can be treated in the context as love-making and sensual pleasure. The rather morbid idea that the desire of flesh is always to be frowned upon as something sinful and must be associated with the feeling of guilt is conspicuous by its absence in many epic tales. I do not wish to suggest that the cultural-religious history of Hinduism eventually did not catch up with the idea of guilt and sin when Hindus talked about sensual pleasure and its irreligious nature. Puritanical attitudes towards sex occasionally became dominant in the tradition, and under this pressure there was a great drive to find allegorical and symbolic meanings for unabashed statements of sensuality in the religious context. There was a complete volte face in the latter Bhakti tradition of devotionalism. However, as far as the epic material is concerned, we do not note this attempt.

The following story from the *Mahābhārata* tells of how the pleasures of sex, called *surata*, was looked upon by even the sages as well as chaste and devoted women. It has something valuable to teach us and it cannot be lightly dismissed. Agastya, a great sage well known for many fantastic deeds, felt one day that he should get married, and he wanted to get married to the most beautiful lady of the land. This was Lopāmudrā, the bewitchingly beautiful princess of Vidarbha. Agastya approached the king, who was not really happy with the proposal, but was unable to say no because of fear. For, if Agastya got angry, the whole kingdom would be reduced to ashes. So, Agastya got married and instructed his newlywed wife to lay aside her beautiful garments and ornaments and other objects of pleasure.

Thus, dressed in rags and animal skins, Lopāmudrā followed her husband to his abode in the forest. Agastya, however, did not after marriage go in for the pleasures of sex. Peculiar as it was, he spent a number of years again in the hardest penance, while his wife was leading a religious life. However, one fine morning the glorious sage, Agastya, saw his wife, Lopāmudrā, as if for the first time. She was still exquisitely beautiful, tender, shining with ascetic practice. Agastya, now, invited her to have sex. But Lopāmudrā declined. She said, 'I would be glad to enjoy sensual pleasures with you, as a married woman should with her husband, but I cannot do it while I am dressed in rags and skins. I need all the objects of pleasure, beautiful clothing, a luxurious bed and so froth which I grew up with in my father's place. When such conditions are fulfilled', said Lopāmudrā, 'my dear husband, I will enjoy the pleasures of life with you.' Agastya was in trouble now, for how could he gather all these things to fulfil the legitimate demands of his wife? Lopāmudrā suggested that he use his Yogic power to create these things, but Agastya declined. For Yogic power should not be wasted in this manner. Lopāmudrā agreed. In any case, Lopāmudrā told her husband to find a way out quickly for she would be aging soon and the period of menopause would come.

Agastya asked her to wait and then set out to visit some powerful kings. He went one by one to three kings who were all willing to give Agastya the things he wanted. But Agastya saw also that all these kings had more liabilities than assets. Hence, Agastya felt that it would be unfair to accept their offerings.

What cannot be taken away from good people could perhaps be taken by force from bad people in order to punish them. This suggestion was made by one of the three kings who accompanied Agastya. There was this wicked demon king Daitya Ilvala who had become extremely rich by stealing from and killing other people, especially the brahmins. His method was to magically change his younger brother Vātāpi into a goat, then slaughter him and prepare the dish for the brahmin he would invite. When the brahmin had eaten, Ilvala would call his brother back to life and the laughing monster would come out of the belly of the guest, who would be killed instantaneously. By slaying many guests like this, Ilvala enriched himself. Agastya went to Ilvala.

Ilvala prepared a dish of goat meat, as before, for Agastya. Afterwards, when he was calling his brother back to life, Agastya said with a smile: 'Your brother, Vātāpi, has been consumed by me. So your foul game is over.' Ilvala was thus subdued and he then fulfilled the demands of Agastya. Agastya wanted for each of the three kings ten thousand oxen with an equal number of gold pieces, and for himself twenty thousand oxen, a golden chariot and many other objects of pleasure. Ilvala had to give all these things and now Agastya returned to his hermitage triumphantly to fulfil the desire of Lopāmudrā.

This interesting little story, a sub-tale in the *Mahābhārata*, illustrates many significant points in Indian culture. It not only shows the rather straightforward attitude of the epic characters towards love and sexuality, but also underlines succinctly the importance of the role of women in such matters. Although the continence of man has been emphasized throughout Indian literature and chastity has been regarded as the highest virtue (the embodiment of which was Bhīṣma), such stories as the one above show us the other side of the coin.

The story illuminates several other aspects of Indian culture. It is significant to note that Agastya could have declined his wife's demand and forced her to make love to him under any circumstances. In modern times, there are cases where husbands having sex with their wives can be regarded as performing rape. We even have modern legislation about this matter. Hence, it is noteworthy that the great sage should pay proper respect to his wife's desire and demands.

3. LOVE AND ROMANCE

A very common idea which recurs in the epic literature as well as in other essays is simply this. In the matter of love-making and sexual pleasures women hold superiority. Now, this may be just part of the male fantasy in those days. We have to mention it for what it is worth.[1]

We should note that between love and romance a distinction is made. Romantic tales are frequently found in the main part of the story. In fact, King Śāntanu, grandfather of Dhṛtarāṣṭra and Pāṇḍu, was romantically involved with both of his wives. His first wife was Gaṅgā. Before marriage, however, the wife made a condition that she would destroy all her future male children by Śāntanu and that her husband should not intervene. If he did, she would leave him for good. Śāntanu was so blind with love that he agreed even to this condition. As soon as they were born, the wife destroyed them and Śāntanu, the father, was unable to intervene. However, when the eighth child was born, he did intervene, as a result of which his wife left him. However, the child was safe. After some time Śāntanu again got romantically involved with another beautiful lady. She was the fisherman's daughter, Satyavatī. Again Śāntanu was allowed to marry her when all the conditions laid down by Satyavatī's father were fulfilled. In this story, notice that the male member becomes more romantically involved than the female member. Śāntanu's first wife made certain conditions before marriage and in the case of the second marriage the father-in-law fulfilled that role admirably.

There are other cases where the female member gets more romantically involved. The marriage between Arjuna and Subhadrā was a romantic sort of marriage through elopement. Subhadrā was the sister of Kṛṣṇa and Balarāma. Subhadrā went to the temple with her companions, at which point Arjuna grabbed her and put her in his own chariot and then they eloped. Of course, the army of Kṛṣṇa and Balarāma was then sent to stop Arjuna and to rescue the abducted princess, but when it was reported that Subhadrā was driving the chariot of Arjuna while he was fighting the army, the pursuit was called off. This romantic marriage was very different from the other kind of marriage, that of Draupadī.

That romance or romantic love should develop into a mature kind of true love, was also a theme in the classical tales. The most glaring example of this phenomenon is the well-known Sanskrit play, *Śakuntalā*, by the poet Kālidāsa. The original story was derived from the epic *Mahābhārata*. King Duṣyanta went to the forest to hunt and met this lady Śakuntalā of exquisite beauty. It was love at the first sight on the part of both the king and the heroine. The first three acts of the play show how this romantic love was brought to a climax, and a form of marriage took place called Gandharva. In this type of marriage, accepted as legal in the context of Hindu marriage, the bride and groom make their own decisions without asking their superiors or friends. The king Duṣyanta got married to Śakuntalā and left her to go back to his palace, promising that he would send people to bring his newly-wed wife back to the palace within two or three days. Meanwhile, Śakuntalā was already pregnant, carrying the royal child of King Duṣyanta.

As it happens, particularly in romantic marriages of this type, especially when a king is involved, the king forgets quickly about his responsibility and Śakuntalā was left in the hermitage carrying the child. When the sage Kaṇva returned to hermitage (the whole episode took place when the saga was not present) he saw the problem and decided to send Śakuntalā in the company of two of his disciples to the royal palace. It was clear to the sage that the king had forgotten his romantic episode and it would not be easy for Śakuntalā to prove that she was actually married to him. Some other things intervened. The sage Durvāsas came to the hermitage after the king left but Śakuntalā was so engrossed in thoughts of her love for Duṣyanta that she failed to show proper respect to the sage. The sage cursed her and said that this man in whose thought she had lost herself would never remember her.

In any case, Śakuntalā went to the royal palace. The two disciples of Kaṇva broached the subject with the king and said she was actually his wife and she was carrying the royal child in her womb. Duṣyanta, all of a sudden, became the self-righteous king, having forgotten everything about Śakuntalā. He was still attracted to the beauty of Śakuntalā, but he could not publicly accept her as his lawfully wedded wife since he had forgotten everything about her.

The rejection of Śakuntalā by Duṣyanta was dramatic and tragic. However, in the next four acts it was shown how the memory of the king was restored and how Śakuntalā regretted their marriage because of the way she had been rejected. For Śakuntalā by then had been taken to a different place and Duṣyanta had no access to her. The child was born and grew up and Śakuntalā's romantic love developed into the true mature love between husband and wife which some sections of Indian civilization glorify. It was also captured by the western critic of Sanskrit plays, Goethe, the German poet who wrote in his appreciation of the play the following:

> Wouldst thou the young year's blossom and the fruits of its decline,
> And all by which the soul is charmed, enraptured, feasted, fed,
> Wouldst thou the earth, the heaven itself in one sole name combine?
> I name thee, O Śakuntalā! and all at once is said.
>
> (tr. E.B. Eastwick)

On the whole, mature love and romance were clearly distinguished in the Indian classical texts. I shall conclude with some quotations from the *dharmaśāstras* which supplement the idea of the illusion of love, true love, *kāma* and so on. The second chapter of *Manusaṃhitā*, verse 3, states that new love springs from the idea of the mind (*saṃkalpa*) and sexual excitement is born out of such ideas of the mind as comprise the pleasures of the senses. The idea of romantic love also occurs in the well-known epic poem of Kālidāsa, *Kumāra Saṃbhava*, where Pārvatī, the heroine, was physically attracted to lord Mahādeva. Even lord Mahādeva was physically moved by Pārvatī's beauty and he was about to accept her for sexual pleasure. It is said that the God of Love was working behind this encounter. However, lord Mahādeva withdrew at the last moment and his anger against the God of Love, which made him temporarily forget his own duty, took the form of a fire which reduced the God of Love to ashes. This, however, persuaded the heroine to seek the favour of the lord in a different manner. She went through a programme of austerities and penance and made herself worthy of the favour of the lord Mahādeva. There is also a shadow here of the idea found in the play *Śakuntalā*. Romantic love and sexuality must not be an end in themselves; they must develop into a true, mature love the partners can share and enjoy.

4. LOVE AND INCEST

Love and incest have been found to be associated in every culture although it has different forms of expression according to the cultural context. Incest is not regarded in Indian culture as something sinful. However, as the civilization progressed through various historical experiences in certain subcultures incestuous love was found deplorable and something that should not be encouraged. A major portion of modern Indian culture can rightfully claim that incest is deplorable sinful and it would not be surprising to find passages in the *dharmaśāstras* that count it as a sin and prescribe punishment for it. However, there are some groups or sub-culture communities where incest has not been taken to be a sin. Let us look at our classical myths. The cosmological account mentions that at the creation of men, Manu, from whom the human generation sprang, was given a daughter from his own body. However, the moment Manu set his eyes upon his newly-created daughter he fell in love with her and tried to pursue her all over the world to have sex.

This was in contradiction with the behaviour of other male children whom God created before Manu, who were not interested in procreation and multiplication. But Manu's case was different. Manu pursued the daughter to the end of the world and then had sex with her, and became interested in procreation and multiplication. Now this Indian way of looking at the origin of mankind conveys certain interesting messages.

Sex as such was not the fruit of the forbidden tree. However, to mix it with incest was a novel idea.

The first official (religious) marriage which was approved by the scriptural tradition was supposed to be between two persons who were related to each other as brother and sister. The male partner was Sūrya, the Sun God, and the female partner was Sūryā, the sister of Sūrya. The *Ṛg-Veda* contains a hymn which describes this marriage between Sūrya and Sūryā, and this hymn is still part of the Vedic ritual and it is chanted during a modern orthodox marriage ceremony. It shows a persistence of the reverence which orthodoxy had of this particular hymn and that it was also incestuous was never a deterrent or reason for giving up this hymn in modern rituals. Thus we can say that incest and love were part and parcel of the role which human beings undertook upon themselves for procreation and multiplication, and therefore one can claim that Indians had a tolerant attitude towards incest.

However, this should not be treated as a licence. As I have already claimed, incest is a sin, a criminal act according at least to the dominant culture of Hinduism. In mythological accounts, incest was never condoned, except for the two occasions that I have already talked about: (a) the first marriage was between brother and sister and (b) Manu was in happy pursuit of his own daughter for that is how he became first among the humans who became interested in procreation and multiplication. And so in our approach of generalizing about a culture like that of classical India we should be very cautious.

5. EMPHASIS ON THE TRADITIONAL ROLE OF WOMEN

There are several cases listed in the epics which capture the traditional role of women in our society. Women were associated with cooking and taking care of the household. Draupadī, in the *Vanaparvan* of the *Mahābhārata*, was in charge of the kitchen and preparation of food for all the visitors of her five husbands. Some days it must have been an impossible task, for strangers used to drop in with hundreds or even thousands of their students to visit Yudhiṣṭhira. The problem was resolved by a magic saucepan. This magic saucepan would go on producing food until and unless Draupadī had eaten from it. Draupadī was the last to have food, after all guests were satisfied and had gone back to rest their meal. However, this provided an idea for wicked Duryodhana to win the battle without any problem. He persuaded a notoriously angry saint Durvāsas to approach Yudhiṣṭhira's place in the forest at a time when Draupadī had already eaten. The plan was this: that Durvāsas would appear late with his disciples and students, all of whom needed to be fed by Draupadī. Since it would be impossible for Draupadī to produce more food that day, the sage would definitely get angry and curse the family and might even reduce them to ashes out of his anger and then Duryodhana would not have to fight a battle.

This story, which took a more pleasant shape in the later versions, points out for us women's role in providing food for guests. However, the situation was saved by Kṛṣṇa. Kṛṣṇa made a gesture and the saga Durvāsas and all his disciples mysteriously felt that they had eaten quite a lot for the day. Hence instead of going to the kitchen for food they all went back to their place satisfied that they had eaten to their hearts' content.

Draupadī's character has been presented in the epic as unique in many respects. Sometimes it has bordered on cruelty and heartlessness, for Bhīma had to kill Duḥśāsana by rending his heart open so that Draupadī's insult could be properly avenged. For Draupadī had promised that she would not braid her hair until the blood of Duḥśāsana was brought to her. This cruelty, however, can be justified if we remember the sort of insult which was offered to her by Duḥśāsana in front of all the elders such as Bhīṣma and Droṇa. Hence we need not be harsh in our judgement of Draupadī's character.

NOTES AND REFERENCES

1. There are many poems in classical literature, although most of them are written by men. There are a few pieces of poetry dealing with love and sexuality written by women poets.

13

Violence in the Epics: Satī and Suicide

Satī, or 'Suttee' as *Hobson-Jobson* records it, is an outrage.[1] It is an outrage in India in the year 1987. Satī, for me, is not a discourse. It is not something to be deconstructed. It is a violent and degrading reality. It is difficult not to sensationalize it; however, I shall try, for the problem is in fact deep-rooted. What we see today is actually the tip of an ice-berg.

It is better to begin at the beginning. The word 'satī' means 'chaste woman'. But since when did it become the name of a whole institution, a practice irrevocably associated with Hinduism for several centuries, or even millennia? The question is difficult to answer. A precise answer is, however, not necessary. That it did become institutionalized within the orbit of the religious tradition we loosely call Hinduism is obvious enough. The practice was not pervasive, but not negligible either. Hence there is no need to brush the problem aside today as a mere construction of a discourse under colonial rule.

Satī is an amalgam of two distinct concepts: religious self-immolation, and the burning of widows at their husbands' pyres. These two concepts are certainly distinct. Both religious self-immolation and the burning of widows were common enough among many ancient tribes, and other primitive religious communities. A brief look at the entry of *Hobson-Jobson* under 'suttee' will dispel any doubt. But the Indians, or rather the Hindus, got singled out for understandable reasons. It has been practised in India, sporadically, over a long period of time. Although the latest form of satī is a medieval growth, its sanction in the ancient narrative and epigraphic literature is not unavailable. It might have existed at the time of Alexander's invasion of India. The inscriptional evidence goes as far back as AD 510. It is glorified in Bāṇa's *Harṣacarita* (AD 650), but the earliest textual support for the practice may go as far back as AD 300. (*Viṣṇu-dharmasūtra*).

Yet in all this, the practice was noted in no uncertain terms as voluntary self-immolation, and a religious one at that. Even Mādrī's decision to die in her husband's pyre (in the *Mahābhārata*) was influenced by the guilt she felt in causing the death of her beloved husband.

What is the use of looking for textual evidence in such matters? I believe we can thereby reconstruct the history a little bit. The very fact that such an influential and authoritive Dharmaśāstra text as that of Manu is entirely silent about the problem, shows at least that the practice was never pervasive or widespread. This may not be a matter of small significance when the idea today is described in Non-Hindu societies with such phrases as the 'burning of widows by the Hindus'.[2] Besides, during the time of the Muslim conquest (AD 900–1200), the practice of satī again became a controversial issue among the writers on the Dharmaśāstras. Medhātithi, the well-known commentator on Manu, denounced the practice as immoral, while Vijñāneśvara and Aparārka, commenting on Yājñavalkya, defended it. This indicates, I believe, a sudden 'flaring up' of the practice at that historical juncture for whatever reason. Self-immolation of the Rajput queens when their husbands went to the battlefield to die was, however, a 'death before dishonour' principle. And similar social conditions might have induced self-immolation as well as widow-burning, for in a male-dominated Hindu society, the chastity or purity of widows became a prominent issue. The Dharmaśāstra texts, for me, are not always prescriptive, but in a special sense 'descriptive'. If there was a social tension, it was reflected in the contemporary writings on the Dharmaśāstra. With a little bit of imagination we can transform the Dharmaśāstra into newspaper reports!

The beginning of the British colonial rule saw another flurry of widow-burning as well as a resulting controversy over textual interpretation. The colonial rulers unwittingly contributed to the problem in at least two distinct ways. First, to follow their policy of non-interference in the 'native's' religious practices (lest it would lead to discontent and revolt against the régime), the rulers gave many mixed signals to their regional administrators, which paradoxically rejuvenated activities in religious self-immolation as well as widow-burning. This point was even discussed indirectly in the Parliamentary Papers. The rulers were unaware of the fact that in Hinduism, religious beliefs were controlled more by regional practices than by some pan-Indian textual tradition. Second, by asking the Sanskrit pandits about the laws of property and inheritance, the rulers precipitated, again unintentionally, forced burning of many young widows in Bengal. For Manu prescribed that a childless widow must have a right to the property of her deceased husband, which the Dāyabhāga text reiterated. Although there was a gap between actual practice and the view expressed in the texts, the issue did not create any problem. But the rulers' insistence on texts and reliance on the Sanskrit pandits created a situation where childless young widows were encouraged through 'religious' indoctrination to commit satī, or sometimes subjected to forced burning by greedy brothers and relatives of the deceased (P.V. Kane seemed to have supported this argument[3]).

This succinct history of satī does not touch the real issue. It may be that Lord Bentinck's prohibition of satī by law did not stop the practice completely. The recent outbreak in Rajasthan exposes another side to the problem. The supposed gain of religious merit by the woman committing satī is nowadays translated into fabulous material gain for the family of the deceased. Sometimes millions of rupees are raised in donation for erecting the satī temple, which turns into a substantial annual family income for generations to come. So the allure is sometimes too much to be ignored.

What is the real issue? Satī can claim to have legitimacy when and only when it truly amounts to a case of active religious suicide. I say 'active' because it must be distinguished from the passive acceptance of death by martyrs. Satī is not martyrdom. Besides, most outsiders (and even insiders may not be excluded here) think of satī as virtually forced upon the individual by the norms of Hindu society. This is wrong. The norms of the society never demanded it. And active religious suicide must be distinguished from the forced ending of one's life. It is true that the position of a widow, in Hindu society generally, was and has been so precarious and painful that suicide would have been, or would even today be, preferable. But if one is inspired to end one's life for this reason, then it can hardly be called a satī, for the religious motivation would be lacking. Hence I find it hard to agree with some today who claim that satī is symptomatic only of the extent of torture of women in Hindu society. For the torture of women has been present almost to the same extent (sometimes even more) in many Asian societies, but there has been no satī and no widow-burning.

Nobody in his right mind can dispute the fact that, in a majority of the cases of reported satī, there was inducement, brain-washing, allurement of a very happy after-life (heaven), and so on. Sometimes, physical force and drugs have been used. All these cases would by the same token be disqualified from being cases of satī, or active religious suicide. A pro-satī lobbyist would naturally not base his argument upon such cases.

There are only two types of suicide close to satī: 1) martyrdom for the cause of one's religion; and 2) *sallekhana*, the suicide of the Jaina monks. If satī has any rational justification, it must be one shared by the other two. A pertinent question then, is why and how can one justify Christian martyrdom but condemn satī unequivocally? A simple answer is: most (perhaps all) Christians who condemn satī look upon it, not as an active religious suicide but as a barbaric practice of 'widow-burning' by the heathens! But even if we ignore such prejudices or misrepresentations or what could presumably be called the 'colonial rulers' *reading* of the Indian situation', we must face the following question: can one support without prejudice Christian martyrdom, as well as Jaina monks' *sallekhana* suicide, and at the same time condemn satī? This is a complex question. If religion is regarded as the 'opiate' of the people then, of course, all three would be in the same boat. But if religion is something more than that, then I have a short but definitive answer: yes, we can. Let me explain briefly.

The three types of suicide noted here would fall under the category that E. Durkheim called 'altruistic', or even 'acute altruistic suicide'. In a way any suicide is a form of egoism, despite the Durkheimian contrast between 'egoistic' and 'altruistic suicide'. But still religious martyrs die to keep a faith alive, and death is usually forced upon them by the circumstances (there were 400 martyrs during the reign of Bloody Mary). Their choice is thus limited, for the alternative is even more demeaning. But satī is by definition voluntary in Hinduism.

A Jaina monk must first live long enough to be old and must devote his entire life to his *sādhanā* to achieve his *nirvāṇa* and it is only at the end, in order not to be a burden to others, that he decides to quietly end his life by retiring to a forest and not getting up or making any effort to procure food. Under such ideal conditions, this seems to be the least violent way of ending one's life, and if there is egoism, it is here the least reprehensible, morally. A satī by contrast is usually the case of a young woman and her resolution has every chance of being the result of a temporary depression, which would certainly pass away with time. Besides, satī is usually described as a short-cut passport to heaven by the texts that approve of it, and there is something morally degrading about such a short cut to the ultimate bliss. Some pro-satī texts even say that an unchaste wife should perform satī in order to have clear entry to heaven!

Satī is, after all, a suicide exhibiting an extreme form of violence and cruelty. We do not know how many genuine satī cases there have been in history, where genuineness consists in their being on par with the Jaina monks in terms of their lifelong commitment to religiosity. It may be that there were none. But despite the proliferation of satī temples, I believe it is wrong to put the majority of modern satīs on a high pedestal along with the Jaina or Hindu monks. For surely, the resolution for suicide at the death of her husband may simply be, even if it is not induced by anybody or anything, a trauma, or the result of a sense of maladjustment to the new situation, where life seems to be losing its meaning—a case that Durkheim rightly called 'anomic' suicide. And this type of suicide cannot be allowed, either legally or morally.

Notes and References

1. *Hobson-Jobson: A Glossary of Colloquial Anglo-Indian Words and Phrases*, H. Yale and A.C. Burnell, 1902 (2nd edn.).
2. For a recent and irresponsible comment, see Allan Bloom's best-seller, *The Closing of the American Mind*, Harmondsworth: Penguin, 1987, p. 2.
3. See P.V. Kane, *History of Dharmaśāstra*, Government Oriental Series, class B, no. 6, Poona: Bhandarkar Oriental Research Institute, vol. II, part I, 1941, pp. 624–36.

PART III

Pluralism, Relativism and Interaction Between Cultures

14

The Problem of Inter-faith Studies

The late Professor Zaehner, my predecessor at Oxford, had expressed grave doubts, in his Inaugural Address in 1953, about the aim and purpose of the Spalding Professorship at Oxford. In founding the Chair, the late Mr H.N. Spalding defined the purpose as follows:

> The purpose of the Professorship shall be to build up in the University of Oxford a permanent interest in the great religions and ethical systems . . . of the East . . ., to interpret them by comparison and contrast with each other and with the religions and ethics of the West . . . with the aim of bringing together the world's great religions in closer understanding, harmony and friendship . . .

In Jansenistic protest, Professor Zaehner said, 'Nor do I think that it can be a legitimate function of a university professor to attempt to induce harmony among elements as disparate as the great religions of mankind appear to be . . . Such a procedure may well be commendable in a statesman. In a profession that concerns itself with the pursuit of truth it is damnable.'

He summed up his view about the study of comparative religion as follows:

> The only common ground is that the function of religion is to provide release. There is no agreement at all as to what it is that man must be released from. The great religions are talking at cross purposes.

About sixteen years later, in his Gifford lectures, Zaehner softened his view about 'comparative religion' and accordingly chose the title *Concordant Discord* (1970) for the lectures. He admitted that he had stressed the discord rather than the concord of religions. 'This was in principle right; for it is the duty of the scholar, even on the popular level, first to analyse the differences and only then to look for a possible synthesis . . .' (p. 8). He even remarked that he might have chosen as the subtitle of these lectures, *A Symphony of Faiths*.

I cannot help feeling at this stage that what Professor Zaehner said sounds strangely familiar to a person who has studied the philosophical doctrines of the Jainas of India. 'Strangely' because he did not seem to have studied Jainism at all. If the problem of the divergence of the world's great religions is presented to a Jaina, he will probably comment as follows: One can overstate the divergence and thereby undermine their common ground. This will incite further antagonism and probable violence. Or, one can overstate the similarity and thereby blur the vital distinction which will result in intellectual dishonesty and barrenness. But we need not be caught between these *two* extremes.

Is inter-faith dialogue really possible? It is awkward to put the question in this manner. For it appears to be only a rhetorical question, and the obvious answer would be no. Let me try to formulate the thesis of those who disbelieve in the possibility of inter-faith dialogue. The word 'dialogue' has been very popular in ecumenical circles. But I myself am not very clear about its exact meaning. So let me put the proposition in the following way. The basic principles of great religions of the world, that is, of Eastern and Western religions, are so different from each other that it is practically impossible for one who understands and *believes* one even to understand the other. Each religion is a whole new world, and it is impossible to move between such worlds. One may, of course, try, so the argument goes, to read the texts and scriptures of another religion, with an academic interest, but he will never be able to 'catch its inner spirit' (whatever the phrase means).

Two different propositions seem to be implied by this position. One, in order to understand (and 'catch the inner spirit', if you like) a particular religion one has to believe in its ultimacy or in the truth that it advocates. Two, one who has no religious experience of, or does not practise, a particular religion, is incompetent to study or understand that religion. In support of the second proposition it is often asserted that it is impossible to understand what 'drunkenness' is unless you have yourself been drunk. I shall leave aside the second proposition and concentrate on the first.

The first proposition, along with the main thesis, seems to imply a sort of religious solipsism. Some time ago, when it was noticed by the linguists and anthropologists that certain American Indians obviously lacked many thoughtways of 'civilized' Europe, B.L. Whorf, a noted linguist, propounded a thesis that claimed that different language-communities have different conceptual schemes. Thus, it is claimed that there are English sentences which are untranslatable into Hopi and that there are ways in which the Hopi conceive things but English-speakers cannot, and vice versa. The strongest philosophical support of Whorf's thesis comes from W.V. Quine who has developed his thesis of indeterminacy of translation. This has been built around the theme that a linguist who is trying to learn a new (hitherto unknown) language, cannot, short of imposing the grammatical structure and conventions of his own language, go very far in translating successfully from the new language into his own language. The remoter the culture or the language is, Quine thinks, the less sense there is in saying what is good translation and what is bad.

There are many philosophical implications of Quine's thesis about translatability. But I have heard one striking interpretation, and therefore, I have brought the scepticism about the possibility of inter-religious dialogue in line with the scepticism about inter-cultural dialogue. The above scepticism might be interpreted to have a bearing on inter-cultural dialogue, since language is, after all, the most important component of a culture. Language is also an important vehicle of culture. There have been critics, in the philosophical circles, of the thesis of indeterminacy of translation. And thus scepticism in this regard can somehow be answered, provided our demand for accuracy and exactness is not too high or too fastidious. One is reminded that scepticism about the possibility of knowledge is also answered in a similar *way*, that is, by lowering our expectations about the standard concept of knowledge.

I have said enough about the possibility or impossibility of inter-religious dialogue. To transform two monologues into a dialogue we need a common ground; some common thought patterns between the participants, as well as a willingness to listen to each other. And such common factors (which include both comparable and contrasting features) are, fortunately, not far to seek in the great religions of the world. (Even Professor Zaehner conceded that 'the variety of religions is indeed a scandal and an offence'.) Fortunately also, it is possible, though difficult, to study and understand even one's own religious tradition from an academic point of view with a fair amount of objectivity.

One of the common factors in all the world's great religions is the Socratic belief that the unexamined life is not worth living. In this sense, then Socrates was a religious philosopher. All great religions, it seems to me, contain a belief that a certain control of the instincts is necessary for our civilized living—a belief that the cultivation of certain positive emotions, for example, compassion and concern for other people or other beings, is a necessary concomitant of any search for personal *nirvāṇa*, freedom or salvation. In this sense, Yudhiṣṭhira was, as the *Mahābhārata* story informs us, an incarnation of *dharma*, 'religious duty'. For, he lived a truly religious life and refused to enter heaven, the so-called highest prize of his religious life, without the animal, a dog, that loyally followed him to the gate of heaven. Thus the dog-incident at the end of the *Mahābhārata* story was perhaps the highest expression of the religiosity that Yudhiṣṭhira had in him.

All world religions seem to include a belief that purely external circumstances cannot constitute the be-all and end-all of human existence, a belief that the world we see with our senses is not all that there can possibly be. Thus, to me, to be religious means to have a humility about what else there is. Moreover, all great religions contain a belief that people can be better than they are as well as a belief that people can experience more than they do.

Human beings' religious urge is invariably characterized by a quest for what may be called a higher or better mode of existence. Sometimes it is called a 'deathless' and a 'painless' state, sometimes an unconditioned *nirvāṇa*. This concept is sharply contrasted with the existing conditions of life, the mechanical, the existential, the trivial, the non-final or the non-essential world. It is thus a contrast between *paramārtha* and *vyavahāra, nirvāṇa* and *saṃsāra*, between the fragile and the immortal, between the finite and the infinite. Some historians of religion call it a distinction between the sacred and the profane. There are many sociological and psychoanalytic explanations of why humans must find the sensible and understandable world not entirely satisfactory, and hence pine for something else that is supposed to be beyond. For a philosopher, however, it is difficult to assert whether such a transcendent state or transcendence exists or does not exist. It is, therefore, equally difficult for him to decide whether man should attach ultimate value to this mode of existence. He can only notice that most people do attach ultimate value to their religious urge.

It is said that Buridan's ass was given a choice to eat from two equal bales of hay situated at equal distance from it. Being unable to decide between the two equally balanced alternatives, and in the absence of any further evidence, it chose to starve itself to death. The ass was most probably a philosopher, certainly a logician. But no person is a *pure* philosopher, and hence he or she is forced to make a choice. For starvation and death may not be a good alternative for most of us. Therefore, we have either the sceptics or the believers. And the philosopher is one who stays on the borderline and observes both sides. To conclude with an old Vedic imagery:

> In a tree there are two birds, of which one tastes the juicy fruits while the other simply looks on.

The one who simply looks on is certainly a pure philosopher and the one who acts is either a sceptic or a believer.

Notes and References

Zaehner, R.C. (1953), *Foolishness to the Greeks*, University of Oxford Inaugural Lecture (Oxford: Clarendon Press).

———. (1970), *Concordant Discord: The Interdependence of Faiths*, Gifford Lectures on National Religion, 1967–69 (Oxford: Clarendon Press).

15

Towards Defining Religion in the Indian Context

Aristotle and the Greeks have defined man as a class of rational animal. Since that time, definition has been practised and discussed by logicians as well as by ordinary men as a very useful procedure in many areas of our life. People often insist on definition as a guarantee for clarity of thought and as a safeguard against intellectual confusions and fallacies. The usefulness of definition, however, has sometimes been doubted. Some, notably A.N. Whitehead, question the goal of definition, that is, clarity: 'Insistence on clarity at all costs is based on sheer superstition as to the mode in which human intelligence functions.'[1] Others feel that by defining a term we may unnecessarily narrow down the sphere of its application.

A well-known controversy as regards the theory of definition is usually framed in the form of a question: what do we actually attempts to define? Things? Or words? If the first, then it is called a real definition. If the second, it is a nominal definition. A third alternative is added by asserting that we define concepts, neither things nor words. There is a strong philosophical tradition, initiated by Socrates, Plato and Aristotle, which regards real definition as part of an important style of philosophizing. Thus, when Socrates asked 'What is knowledge?' or 'What is the soul?' he was, it is assumed, asking for a real definition. Thus, when we raise the question, 'What is religion?' we may be presumed to be raising the question about a thing, not about a *word.* The purpose of nominal definition, on the other hand, is roughly to establish or convey the meaning of a word or symbol. Recent developments in philosophy have focused our attention more and more on nominal definition. Instead of asking 'what is *x*?' we tend to ask 'What is meant by "*x*"?' and the person giving an answer is supposed to formulate a nominal definition, lexical or otherwise. Thus, if we wish to raise the question 'what is religion in the Indian context?' in a way that will find favour with modern philosophers, it is better, to re-phrase the question as 'What is meant by the word "religion" in the Indian context?'

What is the reason for discrediting such a well-established philosophical practice as real definition? One main reason is that a real definition is, in many cases, regarded as a search for the *essence* of things. Aristotle in the *Topics* 1, 5, explained definition as 'the account of the essence of the thing'. But most philosophers now realize that it is difficult, if not impossible, to make sense of the notion of essence. The doctrine of essence, as a metaphysical reality, has very few proponents today. The basic philosophical problem survives in the doctrine of necessity as well as in the modal logic. But it is increasingly questioned why it is *essential* for man to be a rational animal, and quite accidental for him to be a featherless biped (Carnap and Quine), or why it is the essence of a triangle to be bounded by three sides and only accidental that the sum of its interior angles are equal to the sum of two right angles. Essence under these criticisms levels down to our own stipulations, that is, what meaning we choose to assign to a word as its primary or principal meaning. When the doctrine of essence is thus discredited, the theory of real definition based on such essence goes overboard. But there are other styles of real definition which are often free from the problem of essentialism.[2] I shall come back to this presently.

So far, I have not said anything about the Indian theory of definition. It is no wonder that the logical tradition of India regarded definition as an important part of the philosophical activity. But definition, alas, was supposed by these ancient thinkers to be definition of *things*, rather than of words or terms. Awareness of the fact that nominal definition is a more useful and clearer logical procedure was visible only vaguely much later in the tradition. Some Navya-Naiyāyikas of fifteenth to sixteenth centuries AD thus explained that when they were formulating a definition of, for example, *pakṣa*, they were actually trying to explain the *meaning* of the term.[3]

I accept here, tentatively, that 'definition' is a proper translation of the Sanskrit term *lakṣaṇa.* A brief outline of the theory of *lakṣaṇa* is therefore in order. Vatsyāyana defined the *lakṣaṇa* of something *x* as the property that delimits or demarcates the *thatness* of *x*.[4] This is more or less equivalent to Aristotle's notion of definition in terms of *essence*. For the suffix *-tva* which is added to *tat* (*tattva* = thatness) is said to express *bhāva*, 'being.' So the *bhāva* of *x* is the being of *x* or the essence of *x*. But the later philosophers explained that our attempt to define or find the *lakṣaṇa* of a thing need not be a search for the essence of that thing. For any property that is unique to the thing or things in question, can be used to formulate the *lakṣaṇa*.[5] The formulation of a *lakṣaṇa* means the singling out of any unique property which is present in all and only these things we are trying to bring into our definition. It is also admitted that such unique properties may be more than one and thus alternative formulations of definitions with each such unique property is permissible. The purpose of *lakṣaṇa* is to distinguish the class of things to be defined (as denoted by the term to be defined) from the rest of the universe (cf. *itaravyāvartakatva*), and this purpose is well served if the definition mentions some unique property of these things.

It has been argued by Richard Robinson in his excellent book *Definition* (1954) that many practitioners of real definition in the philosophical tradition beginning with Plato, unknowingly formulated nominal definitions, or what he calls word-thing definitions. Thus, he feels, while the real definition as a search for essence should be discarded, many other forms of so-called real definition practised by eminent philosophers should be retained not only as part of our philosophical heritage, but also as a method to be followed in our future attempts to understand the nature of a thing or a phenomenon.[6] Thus, when we raise the question of the definition of religion in the Indian context, we actually try to initiate a discussion on what the term 'religion' means in the Indian context, to see whether it is possible to point out or describe that a certain character (or a set of characteristics) exists, which is nameable by the word religion.

I wish to include two cautionary notes at this stage. First, such words as 'religion', 'mysticism' and 'philosophy' are very common words of wide application. They are attached to realities by various people in various ways. Thus, it is not unusual that these words should cover heterogeneous fields and express a variety of senses. If such ambiguity of the word 'religion' goes unnoticed, it will never be possible for us to define it properly. For we will only try to give a single definition of the word, thinking that it is univocal. But such a definition can easily be refuted by producing a counter-example, that is, an example to which the word is applied in a slightly different sense. Under the circumstances, it is necessary for us to be clear about the definite cases or examples we wish to cover by our definition. While it is not impossible to find a general definition which would, fortunately for us, generate all types of cases actually covered by the common usage of the word, it is at the same time highly unlikely that such a definition could be formulated. Thus we need some stipulation, some inspection of the field, or of the cases we wish to include under the term we are trying to define. To use the Indian terminology we need an acquaintance with the *lakṣya* (examples to be covered by the *lakṣaṇa* or definition) and then make a choice or stipulation that only such and such clear cases be included in our definition and others be excluded. This procedure is recommended in the interest of the success of our programme, although it sounds a bit arbitrary. We can, in other words, decide beforehand whether we would call Marxism, or Humanism, or early Buddhism, a religion before we embark on the project of defining religion. This also explains my qualifying phrase 'in the Indian context', in the above question.

The above condition is not really as arbitrary as it sounds. It is true that Humpty Dumpty insisted that words were to mean what he chose that they should mean. We have sympathy with Alice at her puzzlement as to the feasibility or desirability of such a programme. But our suggested stipulation is not arbitrary in the same sense. We do not insist that 'religion' should mean whatever under the sun we wish it to mean. As a step towards the solution of a very complex problem, we make a deliberate and self-conscious choice of the subset of examples belonging to the set of all examples to which the term 'religion' is applied, one way or other. Mathematicians use such commonly used words as 'point' or 'line' and not only sharpen their use, but also stipulate their meaning. In fact, such a stipulative method can hardly be called unscientific, for scientists commonly use it.

The second cautionary note is that the word 'religion' is one of the words which is surcharged with a high personal emotion. Thus, this word has within its meaning an emotional component which may vary from person to person. This emotional component of the meaning of the word 'religion' has to be separated from its other meanings. This does not mean, however, that the emotional meaning of the word cannot be described or characterized. In fact, the emotional force of a word can often be accurately described, for there are expressions which express such emotions. What I suggest is this. In our attempt to define 'religion' we should be able to distinguish its ordinary meaning from its emotional component. Ideally we would need to account for each component of the meaning of 'religion' as a separate definition of the same term. If we fail to recognize clearly the emotive force of the word we will confuse and intermix the emotional component with the descriptive meaning. Thus, our definition would be highly inadequate.

Sometimes defining a term is used as a means of recommending an ideal. Thus, some existing definitions of 'religion' can be regarded as only recommendations with an evaluative tone. Some philosophers (e.g., F.H. Bradley) would recommend morality as the essence of religion. Others would like to exclude morality from 'religion'. Some would recommend belief in God, in a Divine Mind and Will ruling the universe, as the core of religion. Others would look to the rituals and sacraments (and their inner significance, if any) as giving us what constitutes religion. While I do not wish to dispute the propriety of such recommendations, I still prefer a stipulative redefinition of religion from a practical point of view. Our stipulative condition has a pragmatic value for the success of the programme on hand, while the recommendation of ideals is usually made to persuade others to think of religion in the recommended way. To a great extent the modern dispute over whether Communism and Humanism are religions, reflects a confusion of the latter kind of activity with an actual definition of religion. We recommend knowingly or unknowingly, an idea which every religion should conform to and mistakenly call it the essence of religion. Obviously there are some similarities between a clear case of religion on the one hand, and Communism or Humanism on the other. But similarities provide good grounds for similies and metaphorical uses, but poor reasons for extending the definition of a term.

This brings us to another problem about the definition of religion, the problem connected with Wittgenstein's notion of 'family resemblance'. Wittgenstein has argued that even the resemblances within a group of things to which the same general term applies (e.g., 'game') are nothing but vague and overlapping likenesses which one sees amongst different members of a family. There is nothing common to all such examples, but we see only 'similarities overlapping and criss-crossing, sometimes overall similarities, sometimes similarities of detail'. (*Philosophical Investigations*, I, 66). If 'religion' is such a term where we can only have family resemblances, then an adequate definition of religion will be evermore elusive. To tackle this problem it would probably be advisable to delimit our enquiry to a limited number of examples where one can be confident of covering general resemblances and common attributes.

Although the term 'religion' does not have a proper equivalent in Sanskrit, in most modern languages of India, the word *dharma* is usually offered as a translation of 'religion'. The term *dharma*, however, is a highly ambiguous term in Sanskrit. It has a variety of meanings that are sometimes incompatible with each other. Without quarrelling about the meaning of *dharma* in Sanskrit, let us assume that there is general agreement among people to apply the English term 'religion' to such cases as Hinduism, Buddhism and Jainism.

One may argue that when the word 'religion' is applied to Christianity, or Roman Catholicism, it carries a sense which is not identical with that which the word will have when it is applied to Hinduism and Buddhism. While I concede the point about the uniqueness of Roman Catholicism as a religion, because the uniqueness of every other example of religion has to be conceded, I do not accept the above argument as a whole. For it refuses to admit that there may be some general feature or features which justify our application of the term 'religion' to such examples. The main thrust of the above argument belies even the spirit behind the doctrine of family resemblances.

Of the Indian examples of religion, Hinduism seems to lack a uniform character and should better be regarded as a family of several religious traditions. Buddhism is also partly heterogeneous in character, but still is less intractable than Hinduism. Jainism has a relatively uniform character. Of other religions of Indian origin, I omit Sikhism for the sake of simplicity and not for any parochial reason.

In fact, our task should be to deal not with Buddhist and Hinduism as such, but with the many sub-varieties of these. As soon as we focus our attention on such Indian religions, one striking factor immediately presents itself to us. Belief in an ever-living God, that is, a Divine Mind and Will ruling the universe, is no longer a necessary character of religion as far as its Indian varieties are concerned. While at the popular levels of Hinduism and Buddhism, a belief in supernatural beings or gods is visible, at the higher or philosophical levels, such a belief is as inessential as window-dressing and it is regarded more as a part of the cultural heritage of India than anything else. In view of this fact, we can further delimit the scope of our definition by excluding from our consideration some popular beliefs as well as the rituals and sacraments that go along with such beliefs.

Some may argue that if we omit the 'ritual' part of religion from our consideration, we may be throwing away the baby itself with the bathwater. This may be true, if we think particularly that religion consists only in rituals and sacraments that members of a religious group perform. But certainly there are other senses of the word 'religion'. For example, Communism is thought, rightly or wrongly, to be a religion, not because religion is mainly rituals or sacraments, but for some other character embedded in the notion of religion.

The concept of an everliving God is present only in some sub-varieties of Hinduism, namely, Nyāya-Vaiśeṣika, and some forms of Vaiṣṇavism and Śaivism. The Nyāya-Vaiśeṣika concept of God comes very close to the Christian notion of God, although the two concepts are not identical, The Vedāntic concept of God is very different, and it is perhaps better not to use the word 'God' in such contexts. Even in Mahāyāna Buddhism, Buddha-hood does not come any closer to Godhead. Early Buddhism, Jainism, Sāṃkhya and Mīmāṃsā explicitly reject the idea of a Divine Creator, Divine Mind or a Divine will. In these religious traditions it is believed that each person can attain, through his personal endeavours and actions, a higher (religious and spiritual) status, which will enable him to help others to cope with the problems of life in a better way, just as a good mathematician can help others in understanding and solving mathematical problems. This belief does not exactly amount to a belief in supernatural beings (gods).

The second interesting feature that strikes us in the context of Indian religions is this: morality has been more or less thought of as part and parcel of religion. In fact, although a universal belief in a personal God is absent in India, we can find an almost (Cārvākas and Lokāyatas being excepted) universal belief in a moral order. The old Vedic hymns describe *Ṛta*, a moral order which is regarded as similar to the physical order of the universe. There was, thus, the concept of a moral order pervading the universe, even in the absence of the concept of the great Moralist, God. The word *dharma* replaced the word *Rta* in later literatures. Thus *dharma* came to mean, among other things, a moral order or morality.

Nowadays, a great debate in the West centres around the controversy whether morality is wholly dependent on religion or whether morality should be independent and 'autonomous'. Part of the practical reason for discrediting religion as the basis of morality is this. Faith in traditional religion seems to be dwindling in modern society. Thus some enlightened people feel that religious faith is expendable but morality is not. Historically morality and religion have been closely interwined, and religion in any society has a strong influence on its moral character. But the view that morality is based on religion is hardly tenable. For one thing, while religious rites, beliefs, and practices are dissimilar and different all over the world, there is a striking similarity of general moral codes sanctioned by different religions. Prohibitions against injury to others, stealing, cheating and adultery, with some understandable exceptions, are found more or less everywhere.

In the above contrast between the words 'religion' and 'morality' obviously a definite sense of the word 'religion' is assumed. This sense can be spelled out roughly in two broad sets of belief: (1) Belief in God as the supernatural, (2) Belief in an after-life and concern for this stage after death. Religion also means a set of rites and ceremonies based upon a world-view that includes either or both of the above beliefs and a theory of tackling the problem of what happens after death in relation to God or the world-view in question.

In the Indian context, religion has come to denote a further belief in what may be called the thesis of universal suffering (*duḥkha*). This thesis means that our mundane life-experience is such that it has a lower set of values compared to a separate mode of experience that is characterized by the cessation of suffering (*duḥkha*). Life-experience, including the pleasures and pains of life is, believed to be *duḥkha*, that is, unacceptable as the final end. The goal of religion is, therefore to bring about freedom from this *duḥkha*, cessation of suffering. *Duḥkha*, in my opinion, is best interpreted as the utter conditionedness of human existence. Indian religions believe that an escape from this state is possible. And, paradoxically, it is further believed that the practice of morality is an essential step towards this good. Moral laws are to be obeyed not in order to please any God or fulfil or follow the scriptures, but to follow the *Ṛta* or *dharma*. Violation of this moral order is regarded as akin to acting against nature (remember that the moral order is similar to physical order).

If to be religious means to act so as to proceed towards the goal of freedom, then it means, first and foremost, to lead a moral life. By leading only a moral life, and acting accordingly, one can hope to transcend or surpass this world of conditioning, the world of *duḥkha* and *karma*, and thereby reach the goal of freedom, the unconditioned. Thus morality is like a ladder, very valuable, as a means for achieving a religious goal. This is admittedly a novel use of morality by Indian religious traditions.

There is a logical difficulty in admitting for morality an external basis such as religion. Since the time of Immanuel Kant, most moral philosophers in the West have argued that morality should be autonomous, for otherwise we may be involved in a circularity. For, any set of factual beliefs, religious or otherwise, that is offered as a probable basis of morality, would have to commend itself to our judgement, but if they themselves are evaluative judgements, they cannot constitute a valid basis. Thus, to base morality on such a set of judgements is to argue in a circle.

The above circularity obtains as long as we wish to base morality on religion or on something else external to morality. But it is possible to regard an autonomous morality as the basis of religion. If we can locate an autonomous moral system which is commonly shared by the dominant religions of India, we can explain different religious systems as only different combinations of this moral system with different world-views.

Different world-views, incidentally, call for different goals as the end. Thus, the posited *nirvāṇa* for each system (such as Buddhism, Vedānta or Vaiṣṇavism) is different. Unlike many modern Indian religious teachers, I do not say that different Indian religions simply talk about the same thing in different languages and idioms, just as all roads lead to Rome. Rather, I would say that they talk about different things while standing on a common ground, the moral base.

Notes and References

1. *Advertures of Ideas*, Cambridge, 1942, p. 91.
2. See R. Robinson, *Definition* (Oxford: Clarendon Press, 1954), pp. 156 ff.
3. Thus, Jagadīśa: *pakṣa-pada-pravṛttinimittam ity uktam.*
4. Cf. *tattva-vyavacchedako dharmaḥ*; See B.K. Matilal, 'The Intensional Character of *lakṣaṇa* and *saṁskar*', *Indo-Iranian Journal*, 8, 1964, pp. 85–95.
5. Cf. Udayana, *itara-vyāvartakatvam.*
6. *Op. cit.*, p. 156.

16

Religion and Value

. . . the analysis of a foreign culture principally reveals what was sought in it or what the seeker was already prepared to discover.

(Eliade, 1958, p. xiii)

A purely rational man is an abstraction, he is never found in real life. Every human being is made up at once of his conscious activity and his irrational experiences.

(Eliade, 1961, pp. 203–4)

Professor Mircea Eliade has added an entirely new dimension to the study of 'comparative religion' in modern Western universities. He has chosen to call this new branch of knowledge the 'History of Religion'. Drawing his examples extensively from the rich resources of the religious traditions of China, India, the Near East, from the primitive religions of the world as well as from Christianity, he has unfolded the nature of religion in a novel way: religion is discovery of *the sacred*, that both transcends and manifests itself in this presumably profane, irreligious world of science and commonsense. According to Eliade, this is the discovery which *homo religiousus* has made again and again from the most primitive days onwards. Each religion, even the most elementary one, is, in Eliade's vision, 'an ontology' for *homo religiousus* founds this secular world upon his experience of the sacred, and the secular world of the non-religious is achieved through a process of desacrelization. Eliade's conception of religion is so pervasive that even the modern non-religious man does not, in fact cannot, completely 'free' himself from it.

It is not proper to call Eliade's historico-religious studies a piece of sociology or anthropology. Nor is it entirely satisfactory to call his approach simply psychological or phenomological, for he has brought, to be sure, philosophical orientation to the comparative study of religions. He concludes his *The Sacred and the Profane*:

At present, historians of religions are divided between two divergent, but complementary, methodological orientations. One group concentrate primarily on the characteristic *structures* of religious phenomena, the other choose to investigate their *historical context*. The former seek to understand the *essence of religion*, the latter to discover and communicate its *history* (1961, p. 232).

Professor Eliade, it seems to me, has sought to understand the *essence* or religion and all religions, in the context of their historical development, mythological richness and their 'ritualization' of human existential problems and their attempted resolutions of those problems. His viewpoint has undoubtedly a lasting charm. For, in the midst of a situation where 'comparative religion' is either mistrusted as a piece of clever statesmanship and hence not a proper subject for a dedicated academic (R.C. Zaehner, 1953), or branded as a fashionable mark of some (pseudo-) liberalism which allows believers to see how other believers believe but *wrongly*, Eliade has argued in favour of what Ninian Smart has called an 'empathy-laden' understanding not only of all living religions but even of the religions of the most primitive societies. The subject which we sometimes call, perhaps mistakenly, 'comparative religion' may have a better chance of success if we follow such a procedure. 'Empathy-laden' understanding may be utterly misleading unless philological scholarship supplies a sound grounding to it. Similarly, an exclusively philological understanding of an alien's scriptures may be faultless in itself, but still barren or counter-productive if it is not tempered with impartiality, openness, empathy and lack of personal or culturally-conditioned prejudices. At the risk of sounding obvious, it needs to be said that Eliade would recommend a necessary combination of both, philological competence and the 'empathy-laden' attitude, an openness symbolized by 'what else is there?', in studying foreign religions.

The study of comparative religion sometimes provokes a philosophical or logical question: what do we *mean* by 'religion'? Or, simply, 'what is religion?' Each scholar, to be sure, approaches the problem from his own viewpoint and thereby projects, overtly or covertly, a particular conception of religion. Such projections may both enrich and enlighten the ambiguity that is already there in the word 'religion'. The definition of a concept like 'religion' is, however, a notoriously difficult task. According to some, the task is impossible, either practically (it is like a wild goose chase), or logically (it is like squaring a circle). Notwithstanding such notes of despair, I shall dwell upon the problem a little, in order to see whether some common denominator of those phenomena we call 'religion' in different cultures can be found and articulated.

William P. Alston, having first considered some typical examples of the definition of religion formulated by several philosophers, notes the following 'religion-making characteristics' and then concedes that not all of them need to be satisfied to mark a phenomenon as a religion, but only just 'enough' (1963, p. 7) of them:

1. Belief in supernatural beings (gods).
2. A distinction between sacred and profane acts and objects.
3. Ritual acts focused around sacred objects.
4. A moral code believed to be sanctioned by the gods.
5. Characteristically religious feelings (awe, sense of mystery, sense of guilt, adoration, etc.), which tend to be aroused in the presence of sacred objects and during the practice of ritual, and which are associated with the gods.
6. Prayer and other forms of communication with gods.
7. A worldview, [. . .].
8. A more or less total organization of one's life based on the worldview.
9. A social group bound together by the first eight factors. (p. 5)

The list is rather long. Some of these characteristics are in fact ad hoc generalizations from the examination of a paradigm case, a religion like Roman Catholicism. It is not difficult to cite counter examples to several of the above characteristics, if not all. At the other end of the scale, we might put a tribal religion where moral codes are not believed to be sanctioned by the deity. In fact, even among some civilized people, morality is found independently of religion. One has to recognize, and reconcile oneself with, the fact that Jainism is a religion which definitely rejects the notion of a deity, God or Providence, and Theravāda Buddhism is called a religion but rejects not only God but also the notion of any soul that survive death or obtains freedom in salvation. (Some modern scholars argue that Theravāda Buddhism should not be called a religion for the above mentioned reason. But this is partly an attempt to avoid the issue at hand. Besides, it becomes a questionable move for it envisions a prescriptive definition about the use of a term in our natural language. In any case, this point will raise issues which I must forbear to enter here.)

Ernest Jones, in a paper entitled 'The Psychology of Religion', gave a tentative analysis of the meaning of 'religion', which one may consider along with Alston's list for the sake of comparison and contrast:

1. Other-worldiness, the relation to the supernatural. This has been described as 'the consciousness of our practical relation to an invisible spiritual order'. The spiritual order is invested with the attributes of power and sacredness. The emotional attitudes towards

it vary, those of dependence, fear, love and reverence being the most characteristic . . .

2. The effort to cope with the various problems surrounding death, both emotionally and intellectually.
3. The pursuit and conservation of values, especially those felt to be the highest and most permanent.
4. A constant association with the ideals of ethics and morality [. . .].
5. The connection between religion and the sense of inadequacy in coping with the difficulties of life . . . (1926, p. 265)

It is instructive to compare the two lists—one coming from a philosopher and the other from a psychoanalyst. Various other lists of 'religion-making' characteristics are no doubt available, but we need not go into them here. I would like to focus my attention upon two items only: 1) Religion as a world-view, and 2) Religion as a pursuit of ultimate value. We apply the term religion to an odd assortment of phenomena found in various cultures or culture-groups. Our linguistic practice needs to be explained. The anthropologist might look upon religion as a particular and important component of a given culture and may use any or all of the above characteristics to distinguish it from other components of that culture. A philosopher, however, is, in search of a common denominator, or, if he is an old-fashioned one, for an 'essence' that makes anything we call 'religion' a religion. This leads us to the heart of a philosophical problem that has currency in the modern analytic tradition.

We can face again our old question: can we define religion? And if we cannot, can we claim to have understood religion as a phenomenon? The Buddha once said that certain questions can be answered by counter questions. We may follow the Buddha's way here and ask: do we need a definitive definition of religion after all? A.N. Whitehead, for example, raised a similar objection against the demand for definition and clarity in his *Adventures of Ideas*:

> Insistence on clarity at all costs is based on sheer superstition as to the mode in which human intelligence functions. Insistence on hardheaded clarity issues from sentimental feeling, as it were, a mist cloaking the perplexities of fact (1961, p. 90).

Literary critics sometimes argue that by defining a term we may unnecessarily narrow down the sphere of its application; we cut down or weaken its expressive power in our attempt to relieve it of all its ambiguities. Ambiguities are sometimes powerful tools in expressing our honest thoughts which are not easily expressible in ordinary language. The point of all this is that it is not necessarily the case that we do not understand what religion is, or what religions are, even if we cannot formulate an acceptable definition of it. We can talk about the families of religion, and it may be more promising to look for some essential feature or features within a particular family. Moreover, even if we do not discover what we are looking for, our effort will hardly go unrewarded, for we will then understand, at least, the nature of religion a little better than we did before. By formulating a critique, by searching for a counter example, to expose the suggested, inadequate, and hence unacceptable, definitions, we may make the idea of religion a bit clearer.

The search for the 'essence' underlying all religions is, however, not easily given up. Some believe that a religion must be based upon some notion of transcendence. Others find the explanation of religious phenomenon in what they call the 'numinous' experience. Psychological origin of religious sentiments has also gained some currency. Psychologists attempt to translate religious manifestations in terms of the primary emotions and insights. Theories of psychological origin of religious sentiments may be useful and illuminating, even true, but they are hardly helpful in our philosophical worries about religion as a phenomenon or about the existence of different religions in human society. For instance, even if we try to understand and explain adult love or adult sexuality, it does not help much to answer the philosophical, practical and social issues raised by the notion of human love. More promising, it seems to me, are some other attempts which see each religion as a hypothesis to render the universe as well as the meaning of our life in it comprehensible or as the pursuit and conservation of values, including those thought to be the highest and the ultimate. The first I regard as an interpretation of the Socratic pronouncement: the unexamined life is not worth living. The second I argue to be the implicit trend of such religions which project the notion of the highest truth or an ultimate reality, God, Brahman, *Nirvāṇa* or the Buddha-Nature, for such a truth, if it can be called truth at all, seems also to be identical and indistinguishable from the highest and the ultimate value set up by the believers of that particular religion.

To see different world religions as alternative hypotheses intended to render the universe comprehensible and our life in it meaningful may be taken to be either a counsel of tolerance or a counsel of despair, but it need not be, as we shall see, either. The counsel of tolerance is very widespread today in religious matters. A common, but philosophically uninteresting, way of counselling toleration is to ask us to regard all the other religions as abrogations (sometimes very wild and misguided) of the norm (which is the correct or *true* religion) and the *true* religion is obviously *ours*, not *theirs*. Toleration is advised on the ground that non-interference is thought morally superior to interference in the affairs of others. I call this counsel philosophically uninteresting because (a) it is more a counsel of diplomacy, prudence or caution (e.g. "Don't interfere with the Arab way of life as long as they provide us with oil and attune with our political ambitions"), and (b) it hides an arrogance that comes along with the dogmatic conviction about the rightness of one's own belief-system.

Modern social anthropologists who study other cultures talk increasingly about cultural relativism. Faced with an unfamiliar belief system, they attempt to understand it in the context of the whole culture of which it is a part. If this is done for every religion then religious beliefs become culture-relative and culture-dependent. This holistic approach in the study of a foreign religion is, of course, welcome and salutary, for it definitely helps our understanding. When isolated parts of a culture appear puzzling (like jigsaw puzzles) the overview of the whole may make them intelligible. The counsel of toleration from this point of view is philosophically interesting. But let us examine the position closely.

The above stance of holism actually shades off into relativism. Cultural relativism of this kind runs into many logical problems. For instance, pursuit of this type of relativism will ultimately require us to give up or change the ordinary meanings of such words as 'true-false' and 'right-wrong'. This is a stance which concedes that 'true' is to be understood as 'true for some (a group of) people' and 'right' means 'right for a given society'. Such a view has a long history going back to the *Sophist* and its implication for morality and religion is the claim that it would be wrong for people in one society to condemn or interfere with the values and religious beliefs of another. Such a consequence might have its uses to the liberal colonialists, who refrained from interfering with the natives 'internal affairs', their social ethics, moral code and religious practices. But whether this was more a policy (or politics) of expediency (in which case, it was pseudo-liberalism) or motivated by a genuine belief in the pluralism of human aims, desires, ambitions and goals, is difficult to say.

The view of cultural relativism is admittedly repugnant to many. It is specially unacceptable to those who believe that there is (or there should be) some absolute, that is, universal and objective standard for deciding what is right or wrong morally and what is true or false with reference to our religious beliefs. I shall return to this point later. But first let us note that cultural relativism in its extreme version is philosophically indefensible, if not internally inconsistent.

There is obviously an equivocation in the use of the word 'right' or 'true' when the cultural relativist states his position. He uses such words in the functionalist sense when he says that cannibalism is *right* for some tribe or belief in transmigration is *true* for the Hindus. This is, however, not the sense in which we ordinarily use these words. Ordinarily we use them in a non-relative way. What is right and what is true should be so for everybody, not simply for any particular society or only a group of people. And certainly this is the way we use these words when we derive the familiar consequence of relativism. For we claim that it is not *right* for one belonging to another society to condemn cannibalism, or that belief in transmigration is not a *true* belief for a non-Hindu. Obviously, what is *true* (in a non-relative sense) for the rest of humanity must also be true for a Hindu, and what is *wrong* for the rest of humanity must be wrong for a particular tribe (unless by 'tribe' we mean a group of sub-human beings). We cannot play fast and loose with the meanings of these words in the same logical discourse. The relativist uses them in the functionalist sense in his premises, but in drawing consequences from such premises he uses them in the non-functionalist sense.

It may be said that the relativist does not use these words in the 'absolutist' sense even when he states the consequences of his position. He simply claims that it is not *right for people* in one culture to judge the values of the people in another culture, and what is *truly believed* by a Hindu is not true for a non-Hindu. In other words, he means exactly what he says by such expressions: 'true for society *x*' and 'right for society *y*'. This caveat may exonerate the relativist from the charge or equivocation, but it reduces such terms as 'true-false' or 'right-wrong' to empty words. 'Something is *right* for some African tribe' would simply state that that thing is part of the lifestyle of some African tribe. And similarly, 'belief in transmigration is true for a Hindu' would state that such a belief is part of the Hindu belief-system. The relativist, in this way, seems to fall between two stools, for the consequence is either a logical inconsistency when the equivocation is exposed, or else a vacuity of the meanings of such terms 'true-false' and 'right-wrong'.

The relativist will no doubt face many other problems. For example, identification or proper demarcation of a particular group or cultural unit for which something is true or right would be notoriously difficult. (What if a particular Hindu does not share the belief in transmigration? The Cārvāka Hindu did not.) But we need not go into such problems here.

The value of a form of cultural relativism is, however, determined from a different consideration. It is easy to see that some sort of relativism or holism is a good practical principle for beginners to follow. It turns out to be a piece of good advice to those who begin their study of an alien culture, and obtain acquaintance with an alien religion. It calls for the suspension of value-judgements for the time being until the whole has been properly understood and studied. The pitfalls of quick judgements (value or even factual judgements) based upon insufficient and partial knowledge or acquaintance are only too well known to be emphasized here. A Sanskrit example of a factual pseudo-question based upon insufficient knowledge or rather based upon ignorance, is the following. Someone who never saw and heard of a camel before asked, when he first saw the animal, 'Tell me, is it an elephant that has *shrunk* or a rat that has grown in size?' (cf. *gaja-kṣaya* or *moṣa-vṛddhi*). In any case, it seems very easy to impute false and outrageous beliefs to a member of a foreign tribe than to one belonging to one's culture. Relativism, therefore, should be better understood as a counsel of initial caution.

In the above, I have deliberately mixed moral and ethical issues with religious ones. For as far as relativism goes, the situation does not seem to be very different. Just as the existence of various moral codes for various societies and differences in moral beliefs between different groups and classes within a complex community are well-known factors in favour of ethical relativity and subjectivity of moral values, similarly the presence of different fully developed religious traditions among the civilized human community and divergent religious goals are the premises from which the relativity of religious values may be derived. We may rightly feel repugnant at moral relativism, for agreement in some basic moral codes among all members of our human community seems to be a requirement for the successful survival of human kind. Moral philosophers today have suggested various ways by which it is possible to avoid the pitfalls of moral relativism, but this is not my concern here. The point is rather the following question: do we need, in the same way as morality, one universally acceptable religion, that is, an identical set of religious beliefs for all of us? My inclination is to answer it in the negative, and here I think a significant difference between the two domains, that of morality and religion, emerges. Religion and morality weave and entwine together in all great traditions, but it is possible to disentangle them. If we can successfully do so, we would eventually reach almost the basic moral codes we have been searching for universal acceptance. Besides, we need some agreed-upon principle or set of principles for moral thinking and moral reasoning. But in the matter of religious belief it may not be necessary for all of us to fall in line with one particular set of religious beliefs. For I am arguing in favour of a thesis that looks upon different well-established religious traditions as the pursuit and conservation of certain 'religious' values and sees divergent sets of religious beliefs as alternative hypotheses to render this universe and our life in it comprehensible and meaningful. If there is any plausibility in this thesis, then pluralism, though not necessarily relativism, will be seen more as a factual truth than as a 'scandal' or an enigma.

A fundamental objection to this thesis may be stated as follows: a truly religious man will find it highly unsatisfactory if his religious beliefs are thought to be merely a set of hypotheses. For religious issues are something over which people are prepared to fight and kill one another, and such a commitment cannot be to something that is only 'hypothetically' accepted. Besides, the objection continues, what lurks behind the above thesis is the spectre of subjectivism, and a 'truly religious man' can never accept that his religious beliefs are only subjective. This way of interpreting the present thesis is what I have called above the counsel of despair. A religious person may throw his hands in out of despair and say, 'If your point is not simply a counsel of tolerance, we have no use for it, for it will then be like throwing the baby out with the bathwater.'

This objection is certainly mistaken and it misrepresents the above thesis. In answering it, we may say several things. Let me begin by asking, what is exactly meant by the glib phrase 'a truly religious man'? Obviously, it means a person who has a firm conviction about, and commitment to, a particular religion, and given the fact of the plurality of religious beliefs, such a person must be prepared to allow in theory at least that he might be wrong or mistaken in believing certain *particular* religious propositions—propositions which he in fact firmly believes for whatever reasons. We should concede this much, even if we wish to sidestep, at this stage, the issue whether religious beliefs have factual content or not. A 'truly' religious man in this sense needs to be carefully distinguished from a 'truly' religious bigot. Much of the force of the above objection is derived from the ambiguity of the crucial phrase 'a truly religious man'. All the points in the above argument hang together very well and perhaps more so if we replace the phrase by 'a truly religious bigot'. But the said objection in that case no longer continues to be an objection to, but becomes a vindication, instead, of the thesis in question. It becomes a *bhūṣaṇa*, not a *dūṣaṇa*. For who else except the religious bigots would be honestly prepared to kill one another for the sake of their so-called religion?

By 'a truly religious man' we mean that sort of person as has a firm belief in a particular religion and at the same time is not so bigoted or fanatical as to be cocksure about the falsity or wrongness of any other alternatives. His faith in a particular religion gives him, not arrogance, but humility, from which comes his wonder about 'what else is there?' A truly religious person, then, is well aware of the limitation of his own knowledge as well as the limits and scope of human knowledge. Things which cause him puzzlement are not dismissed by him as being illusory. If we have such a notion of a truly religious man, then the above objection against the thesis I am defending would not hold, for such a person need not find the statement that different religions are like alternative hypotheses particularly unsatisfactory or repulsive.

A truly religious man should also be a truly moral man. I think this is important, for otherwise it may be believed that a truly religious man may ignore his moral duties. I wish to quote an Arabian story to illustrate the point. A highly religious man, who never had his dinner without saying his prayers and thanking God, had a guest one evening, a penniless, starving beggar. The guest unfortunately did not say his prayers when dinner was being served. To his surprise and indignation, the Arab found out that his guest was a worshipper of Fire (A Zoroastrian), and upon this discovery, he was immediately turned away from the house. Thereupon a voice from the sky (presumably of God) said, 'Shame on you, wretched creature, you take pride in being religious, but you were not able to tolerate this man even for one evening—a man whom I have tolerated, fed, protected, etc. for a long time, day after day.' One moral of the story is meant obviously for our cocksure religious man who might feel self-righteous enough to neglect his moral duty. The point is also to teach our religious man probably the humility to acknowledge that there may be other things about religion which he does not know. (The above story brings us closer to the consideration of the case for the religious moralist. I shall examine his case below in connection with our observations on the second defensible characteristic of religion—religion as a pursuit and preservation of values including the ultimate value.)

The subjectivity of religious beliefs is not a necessary consequence of the position I am trying to defend. The above objection is therefore wrong in deriving such a consequence. This can be seen more clearly when we refer to the prevalence of a plurality of theories in other branches in philosophy: phenomenalism, idealism and realism in epitemology, Platonism, conceptualism and nominalism in the philosophy of logic, idealism and materialism in metaphysics. Rival theories are like rival hypotheses for which arguments are given by their proponents; the strength and weakness of each position is thereby exposed. But as long as the hypothetical character of a theory is retained, it would be wrong to say, for example, the realist's belief in the external world is subjective, that is, lacks factual content. For such a claim would imply that we already know and are cocksure about which theory embodies Gospel truth.

I have two alternative proposals at this metaphilosophical or metareligious level. One would presumably be favoured by the believer, the other probably have a sceptical resonance. The first says that truth is a many-faceted gem. This is partly derived from the philosophic insight of the Jaina doctrine of *anekānta*, which claims that truth is like a many-faceted gem, having a manifold sparkling appearance, and each facet might have a completeness and coherence of its own. Using another piece of Jaina imagery we can say that truth is like a huge mountain not all of whose parts can be grasped by anybody at one time, except by a 'noetic synthesis' or what the Jainas call omniscience. Different views are in this way to be regarded as results of different *viewpoints* from which the 'total truth,' that many-faceted gem, has been observed.

If this seems to be too simplistic or poetic, we can use a different imagery. This alternate imagery is derived from the modern philosophy of language. What I have in mind is Quine's thesis about the indeterminacy of 'radical translation' as well as its philosophical consequences. The thesis states that a linguist who tries to translate a new (and hitherto unknown) language cannot, short of imposing the grammatical structures and conventions of his own language, go very far in translating successfully from the new language into his own. From this it is agreed that translations of sentences that are at any considerable remove from what are called 'observation sentences' would be indeterminate. Moreover, it is possible, according to his thesis, for two translators to develop independent manuals of translation using conflicting analytical hypotheses, and both such manuals could be compatible with all speech behaviour and dispositions to speech behaviour, while yet one manual may offer translations that the other would reject. Quine's own position is that either manual could be useful, but as to which was right and which wrong there is 'no fact of the matter'. Quine, however, speaks as a physicalist here and claims that 'both manuals are compatible with the fulfillment of just the same elementary physical states by space-time regions' (1979, p. 167).

If this thesis is plausible and acceptable, then what we mean by a sentence of our language would, relative to some other linguistic scheme, be indeterminate, in the sense that two sentences (not equivalent in that language) may equally serve as translations of our own sentence; and, what is worse, the choice between them would be undetermined by everything we do or say. Similarly what the natives mean may be indeterminate relative to our language. I cite this as an analogy in order to derive support for our own thesis about different religious systems that I am trying to defend. Different religious systems, enriched by diverse historical and environmental concomitants, are like different 'translation manuals'—all of them may be compatible with the totality of 'religious behaviour' of man. As translation manuals, different world religions are only ways of interpreting that kind of experience of man which is called 'religious' as well as his 'religious' yearnings and aspirations. To be sure, and to continue the analogy, we must say that there may be no fact of the matter as regards which one is more true than others, as long as all or most of them match well with the total religious behaviour and religious disposition of man.

The indeterminacy thesis regarding religions requires that if different religions of the world are like different interpretation-manuals for what Professor Eliade, borrowing a term from Rudolf Otto, has described as the 'numinous experience,' then there is little point, *a la* Quine, in claiming that one among these interpretation manuals must be right while the others are wrong. In other words, it would be a travesty of the truth if our understanding of one particular religion rather than any other is a correct interpretation of the 'numinous' experience of man, for there is no fact of the matter about it, no hidden fact, no objective constraint, except the subjective feeling of the particular believer, to decide the matter. Such an argument, I believe, should exercise a sobering influence in a mad situation where a variety of religious faiths among men, each claiming absolute monopoly over 'truth' would fight bloody battles and threaten finally the extinction of the human species.

The sceptical resonance of this indeterminacy thesis may not be fatal to the religious believer. For a religious believer is after all a believer in a particular religion. His faith therefore concerns what we may call the first-order religious beliefs, whereas the indeterminacy thesis is concerned with second-order questions. J.L. Mackie, in his discussion of the subjectivity of morality, has proposed a similar separation of first-order questions from second-order questions (1977, pp. 15–20). It is possible to introduce a similar distinction here. In the present case, using, say, R.N. Hare's 'blik' terminology, we can conceive of a person who may have a 'blik' for a particular religious faith and, at the same time, be totally unaware or unconcerned about second order questions, such as what is the nature of religion, and what is the status of religious beliefs. Alternatively, if such a person, while being a believer at the first level, is concerned at all about the second-order questions, he may be a mild relativist or say that each person's religious belief or even the lack of it, should be a matter of his own choice, and this choice may be guided by his inclinations and dispositions. This assumption may be questioned. But I am only suggesting its possibility. For, as I have already noted, even Quine speaks 'as a physicalist' when he defends his indeterminacy thesis. In our extrapolated version of the indeterminacy thesis we can diffuse the air of scepticism, while allowing its possibility by pointing out that the religious man, like the physicalist, can posit, or believe in, a transcendental reality or the sacred which, according to Eliade, expresses itself through the 'numinous experience'. Besides, our indeterminacy thesis is already committed to the possibility of what we have called the 'numinous' experience.

For a radical sort of ontological relativism developed by a modern analytical philosopher, we have to go to N. Goodman. In his relativistic mood, Goodman has said that, for scientists, truth, far from being a solemn and severe master, is a 'docile and obedient servant'. A similar sort of relativity of truth emerges from T.S. Kuhn's view about the status of scientific theories. In fact, Kuhn's theory of scientific paradigms applies *mutatis mutandis* to religious paradigms. Kuhn describes the scientist's transfer to allegiance from paradigm to paradigm as a 'conversion experience', a decision which the scientist makes 'on faith'.

On the face of it, such a position would presumably make no significant distinction between our trust in physics, and someone's belief in oracles (Wittgenstein), and this would eventually invoke anarchy in our thought. But this way of taking Kuhn's thesis of scientific paradigms would probably be wrong, as he himself has warned in reply to his critics. We need not, however, go into Kuhn's thesis here. I wish to consider instead Goodman's arguments for his 'radical relativism', for they have some direct bearing upon the philosophical point under discussion here. Goodman envisions *a pluralistic universe* (cf. his reference to William James' book having the same title), which must consist of 'many actual worlds, if any'. Faced with the fact that two presumably *true* statements, 'The sun always moves' and 'The sun never moves', conflict with each other, we are naturally inclined to reconcile them by regarding the two strings of words not as complete statements with truth-values of their own but as elliptical for two other statements. We may express them as 'Under frame of reference A, the sun always moves' and 'Under frame of reference B, the sun never moves', whereupon we have two statements, both of which would be true of the same world. Goodman says,

If I ask about the world, you can offer to tell me how it is under one or more frames of reference; but if I insist that you tell me how it is apart from all frames, what can you say? We are confined to ways of describing whatever is described. (1978, pp. 2–3).

Goodman's talk of the frames of reference may be reminiscent of the Jaina doctrine of *anekānta* and *syādvāda*, which I have referred to already in the above discussion. But that is not the important point here. Goodman's relativism is diffused enough to avoid the pitfalls of subjectivism. The important point here, of course, is to see how Goodman tackles his 'trouble with truth'. For him, a statement is true and a description or representation right for a world it fits. He thinks we would be better off if we subsume the truth of a statement or rightness of a description into 'the general notion of fit' (p. 132). He recommends that we regard truth and rightness as ultimate acceptability much as permanence could be ultimate durability, though he warns that both may be inaccessible to us.

Goodman's thesis is directly damaging to an absolutist, who would claim that there is some absolute, independent and neutral reality out there, for that is, he may argue, implicit in our very conception of knowledge. Knowledge, understood as distinct from errors and so on is presumably knowledge of a reality that may exist independently. An absolute conception of reality is not only presupposed by our traditional natural science but also forced upon us by our very conception of knowledge. We seem to have a determinate picture of the world, what it is like, independent of any knowledge, any representation of it in thought, any conceptualizations, beliefs, assumptions or experience. But that picture is ever receding or ever elusive to us, we have only different, endless representations of it. To use Mādhyamika Buddhist imagery, that reality, if it exists, must always slip through our endless nets of representation, and there is no vantage point from which we could have an absolute conception of reality. Goodman's trouble with truth is in fact his trouble with knowledge at the bottom. For he has argued that facts are fabricated for the world in the making and knowledge is no more a matter of *finding* than of *making*.

The above digression into natural philosophy and ontology is meant only to argue the point against the fairly pervasive confusion between a truly religious man and a truly religious bigot. Enough has been said to make pluralism plausible and to show how illogical would be the claim that there is one particular religion which embodies the ultimate truth, and hence that must be right for everybody. Readers will note that what has been said here applies equally well to the non-religious bigot too. For nothing that has been said would decide the issue between a believer and a non-believer. Even if we allow with the believers that a religion is, after all, a world-view set in a transcendental framework, it does not follow that a particular religion has the infallible and absolute grasp of that framework. Nor can a non-believer, who rightly believes that a religious man is guided more by his instincts, emotions and attitudes, or, maybe, by the forces of his 'unconscious' than by his 'vision of truth', feel to be better off in his scientific vision of the world for his believing would no less be dependent upon his attitude, inclinations, and so on. I am not talking of a religious man who ignores completely the world of science and thinks only in terms of the sacred or transcendence, but one who accepts in practice almost everything that a 'non-believer' ordinarily accepts, and then adds a little extra. In a sense, the non-believer seems to be poorer from the believer's point of view. For he sees and accepts this world but sees it, to use Eliade's phrase, as a continuous expression of the sacred. When, for instance, the farmer is rewarded with good harvest due to good rainfall, the non-believer sees it as a natural phenomenon, but the believer not only sees it as a natural phenomenon (with a full causal explanation), but also experiences, let us say, 'God's hand in it'. The addition of this 'little extra' changes, no doubt, the resulting world of the believer, but this is not a complete replacement of one by the other (where the former is destroyed or rejected). In fact, both the believer's world-making and the non-believer's world-making should be accommodated, *à la* Goodman, in our pluralistic universe.

The matter can be put in another way following Eliade's terminology. The non-religious, secular man achieves his world by a progressive process of desacralization, both of himself and of the world he has inherited from his ancestors. For the modern, secular man inherits from his ancestors a world replete with 'religious meaning' and tries to acquire a world of his own by desacralization whereupon the previous world is emptied of its religious meaning. This is what Eliade claims by saying that 'this non-religious man descends from *homo religiousness*' (1961, p. 103). Eliade comments further that some vestiges of the behaviour of the religious man, that of the ancestors, are 'still emotionally present to' the modern secular man, in one form or another, ready 'to be re-actualized in his deepest being'. Whether this last point of Eliade can be defended or not is beside the point here. If it is a fact that the modern, secular man is the inheritor of the religious man of the past, his ancestor, then our study of religion and religions can hardly be ignored, much as the study of history or the study of what our ancestors did cannot be ignored. That a modern, secular and rational man cannot entirely free himself from the engulfing influence of 'religion'—an aquisition of our ancestors by their, let us say, misguided genius—can be seen even in the conception of 'free man's worship' of the Russellian type.

I now wish to revert, after the above diversion, to the second defensible characteristic of religion: each developed religion can be seen as an alternate value-system which incorporates into it not only the not-easily-specifiable common core of human morality but also a final goal (presumably different for each religion) as the ultimate aim of human life. This will bring us to our old friend, the religious moralist, and his position may now be briefly reviewed. Traditionally, the question between religion and morality is discussed in terms of the famous dilemma found in Plato's *Euthyphro*. Is something God's command because it is morally good or right, or is it morally good or right because God commands it? Most religious philosophers opt for the first alternative although some (notably Wittgenstein) have opted for the second. But either way we choose, the consequences remain unwelcome to a theist. The usual criticism is that either ethics is autonomous and the introduction of God or divine intervention is redundant and hence useless, or morality would be reduced to the commands of one who may be a capricious tyrant, threatening people with hellfire, and hence moral motivations would simply be prudential. There is a traditional theistic resolution of this problem to which I will come back later.

The dilemma is usually presented in the relevant literature in the context of a monotheistic religion. We can re-state it without much difficulty for non-theistic religions like Mimāṃsā, Buddhism or Jainism. We can ask, for example: is an act a religious act because it is morally good, or is it a morally good or right act because it is a religious prescription? We may recall that, in Plato's version, the problem was stated, not in monotheistic terms, but in terms of *many* gods. Here it is stated simply in non-theistic terms. One consequence is obvious. We do not have to deal with a personal God who may be a despot, whether tyrannical or benevolent or neutral. But the problem remains. In the first alternative, every moral (i.e., morally good) act becomes a religious act by the same token; in the second, every religious act becomes morally good by the same token. We subsume, at the risk of oversimplification, either morality under religion and allow the possibility of some acts being purely religious, or religion under morality and allow the possibility of some acts being purely moral. It may be that we have transformed the old dilemma into something entirely different but, perhaps, so much the better. It could be argued that a purely religious act is one which is conducive only to one's own *nirvāṇa* or salvation, and hence lacks the 'non-self regarding' character essential to morality. (It may lack the essential *purity* of moral motivation in the Kantian sense, but all this may be debatable—and I will not go into it here.) What could be a purely moral act, not religious at all? Presumably, all such moral acts as we do ourselves and recommend to others, for which there is no overt or covert sanction in the scriptures or in whatever we take for God's command on earth, or such moral acts which cannot be conceivably connected with one's goal of salvation or *nirvāṇa*, that is, one's religious goal. One may feel uneasy here, for religious duties in this case are narrowed down to the overt or covert scriptural injunctions or God's commands, and whatever will be rationally derivable from them. (In fact such a conception closely approximates, in the Indian tradition, the Mimāṃsā concept of *dharma*, which may thence be translated as 'religious duties'.) Our present uneasiness simply reflects the fact that the first model would be more acceptable to some of us. In some wider sense, religion, according to religious persons, would tend to engulf much of morality, if not all.

The first model has other advantages too. A non-believer but a fully moral man under this model cannot go against religion or become irreligious. For his fault is only that of omission, not commission of anything irreligious. He omits the religious activities, but thereby he certainly does not become an inconoclast or an 'outcast'. He might indirectly and unwittingly fulfil some religious goal! Under the second model, however, such a person would not be able to meet his moral responsibilities fully, for if he omits all such religious acts which are interwoven with morality, he would be condemned as a moral agent. Here is, perhaps, an important distinction between morality and religion, that we have assumed already. Omission of a religious act does not make a man irreligious in the same way that the omission of a moral act becomes morally condemnable. A fully religious man, who performs all the religious duties required of him, may not be a properly moral man under the first model, he is also a fully moral man if, that is, he is a fully religious man. In this way, preference for the first model may be shown—the model that is, as I have shown above, derivative of the first horn of the Platonic dilemma.

In the above, I have assumed that the motivation behind an act may not always be *vitally* important for classifying it as moral or religious. Of course, it will have some importance. But because of the prevalence of the interweaving of morality and religion in all great traditions, it may be argued that for an act to be considered as both religious and moral, it is not necessary that it be performed with both motivations. Even if such an act is performed for religious motives, it will not lose its moral quality entirely. A man, for example, may give to charity from either a religious motivation or a moral motivation, for example, concern for others and so on. But in neither case does the act will lose its dual character. It will not be counter-intuitive to call this man a moral agent in either case.

Traditionally, philosophers have distinguished the moral motivation from the prudential one. Usually actions and policies which minister to the gratification or safety of the agent at the expense of others should be deemed as stemming from a prudential motivation. A 'non-self regarding' action, or action taking the interest of others into account, is morally motivated. It could be said that, in a relevant sense, religious acts are 'prudentially' motivated. But this may shatter entirely our exalted picture of a 'truly religious' man. For who can be impressed by a man who performs all his religious duties out of fear of hellfire? To save religion from being degenerated to the virtue of necessity, one must say that the religious motivation must be distinguished from both the moral and the prudential. Religious duties are not always performed out of the fear of hellfire. How else could we characterize what I am calling here the purely religious motivation? This question we will do better to leave out for the present. We might take it to be *sui generis*.

I suggest that we make a distinction between those who are motivated to perform religious acts out of the fear of hellfire and those who are motivated by their salvational goal, or *mokṣa*, or *nirvāṇa*, or love of God. In Indian religious tradition, it has been argued whether motivation for *mokṣa* or *nirvāṇa* is motivation at all. For it is like a desire to end all desires, and calling such a thing a desire may appear to be paradoxical. Alternatively, we can have a war to end all wars (in which eventually the entire warring humanity could be destroyed!). Hence the salvational *nirvāṇic* (i.e., religious) motivation must be a motivation, though of a special kind. But this kind of motivation could be akin to the moral motivation in respect of its *purity*.

We can now consider a possible way by which a religious moralist who believes in a personal God would try to resolve the Platonic dilemma. Let us suppose that there is one kind of life that is most appropriate for humans, for only by that way will they fully develop their natural capacity and achieve deepest satisfaction. Further suppose that it is not open to human investigation, that is, we, being imperfect creatures, would in no way be able to find out that such a life is possible, through our observation, inference and experiment. Now God, being omniscient, would know about it and, being benevolent, would reveal it to his creatures so that they may live what would be for them the ultimately satisfying life. This supposition will no doubt make the first horn of the Platonic dilemma at least acceptable on the face of it. But a non-theist may point out that the conception of an omniscient, omnipotent and benevolent deity hardly seems plausible.

We may formulate and examine another version of the above resolution for non-theistic religions. We need not concern ourselves with the notion of a personal God. But still we need to presuppose that there is such a life which human beings can live but it is not accessible to human knowledge which has its limitations. We have to further suppose that knowledge of such a life is revealed to man through scriptures in *a mysterious way*. A human being, through superhuman effort and endeavour, may raise himself to the stage of a superman, or a Buddha, or a Jina, or a seer, to whom the hidden truth, knowledge of *that life* would be revealed, and through him to the rest of humanity.

This picture seems coherent except for some obvious loose ends. It is no doubt possible, under such a picture, to talk about a common invariant moral code most appropriate to all human beings, and thereby it may allow us to avoid the dangers of subjectivism or moral relativism. But this picture must also allow pluralism of the *purely* religious components of that life. It may not assume, if our previous arguments for religious pluralism have been cogent, that there is only one type of religious fulfillment for all men, so that there should be only one religion for everybody. For it should not destroy the picture of a pluralistic universe which would accommodate not only the believers in diverse religious goals and values but also the non-believers who are morally good. One particular loose end, however, is this: how would such a form of life be accessible to human knowledge. If it is presupposed to be inaccessible in the normal way, we have to depend on either a God, or on a Buddha (or a Jina) who has presumably attained omniscience, or on a Mimāṃsā type of scripture that is absolutely revealed to us, that is impersonal (cf. *a-pauruṣeya*) and absolutely infallible.

I shall conclude with an old *Mahābhārata* story, which brings into sharp focus the human ambivalence between religious and moral duties. A sage, Kauśika by name, had a 'religious' vow always to tell the truth, which would presumably bring him near to his religious goal (*mokṣa* or heaven). One day, a man was running for his life, being chased by a gang of robbers. The gang approached Kauśika, who apparently had seen which way the man had fled, to ask him about the man's whereabouts. Kauśika told the truth and thereby helped the robbers in killing the poor man. Kṛṣṇa, after relating this story to Arjuna, added that Kauśika by this act was finally condemned to hell after death. In order to avoid the Kantian controversy over whether or not truth-telling is the most overriding moral consideration, let us argue in abstraction. Kauśika had the choice of doing *x* or *y*, but not both, and *x* was undoubtedly a moral act (in this probably both the Kantian and the non-Kantian would agree) while *y* was only dubiously a religious act. One can even think of *y*'s being also prudentially motivated. But even without conceding this point, we can see that the moral consideration, for Kauśika, should have been the overriding one, not the dubiously religious one. As far as this is concerned, even a truly religious person would, I think, agree with Kṛṣṇa.

In conclusion, I wish to emphasize two related points. First, it is undeniable that there are acts which are considered moral, and at the same time such that the major religious traditions of the world would be inclined to call them also religious. This is sometimes put as the 'interweaving' of religious and moral codes 'in the great traditions'. Second, even in the face of the diversity of religious beliefs, one has to accept the empirical evidence that there is a surprising agreement regarding certain basic moral principles, such as protection of a member of the same species, universal condemnation of aggression, injustice and deceit, among widely divergent religious traditions. Admittedly, this similarity or agreement concerns only the broadest moral principles, but this is consistent with the wide divergence in the ways in which these basic principles are applied in practice. This, I think, should be a good antidote to general moral scepticism or cultural relativism. For, if intersubjectivity is considered to be a mark of non-subjectivity, the inter-cultural or inter-religious approval of certain very broad moral principles would certainly be an argument against their subjectivity. Further, if one of the major arguments for moral scepticism is the variability of moral codes in different societies (Mackie, 1977, p. 36), then agreement about certain moral principles, if it exists, would be a good argument in favour of their non-relativity. Some moral principles at least would not be patently relative.

NOTES AND REFERENCES

Alston, William P. ed. (1963), *Religious Belief and Philosophical Thought: Readings in the Philosophy of Religion*. New York: Harcourt Brace Jovanovich, inc.

Eliade, Mircea. (1958), *Yoga: Immortality and Freedom.* Translated by W.R. Trask. Princeton: Princeton University Press.

———. (1961), *The Sacred and the Profane.* New York: Harper.

Goodman, Nelson (1978), *Ways of Worldmaking.* Hassocks: Harvester.

Jones, Ernest (1926), 'The Psychology or Religion', *British Journal of Medical Psychology*, vol. 6, 1926, pp. 264–9. Reprinted in his *Psycho-Myth Psycho-History: Essays in Applied Psychoanalysis*, 1974, vol. 2, pp. 190–7. New York: Hillstone.

Mackie, J.L. (1977), *Ethics: Inventing Right and Wrong.* London: Penguin.

Quine, V.W. (1979), 'Facts of the Matter', in Robert W. Shahan and Chris Swoyer (eds), *Essays on the Philosophy of W.V. Quine*. Norman: University of Oklahoma Press, pp. 155–69.

Whitehead, A.N. (1961), *Adventures of Ideas.* Cambridge.

Zaehner, R.C. (1953), *Foolishness to the Greeks*, University of Oxford Inaugural Lecture, Oxford: Clarendon Press.

17

Between Peace and Deterrence

As the title of this piece indicates, I shall be dealing with neither the history of Peace Studies in the West nor the state of *inward* peace or *śānti*, which the Gospels and other religious scriptures talk about. Both are admittedly important, perhaps necessary, for a clear understanding of our present predicament. But I shall address myself directly to the nuclear argument, the question of nuclear defence and deterrence that has confronted us with the prospect of total annihilation of whatever is valuable today on the one hand and the most excruciating moral dilemma of our time on the other.

Between the pacifist's ethic and the consequentialist's verbosity, between the grim experts on the temple of final doom and the complacent, know-all, 'we-know-better', public figures, the issues of war, nuclear weapons and peace get obfuscated, and ordinary citizens get bewildered and lost. The pacifist moral philosophers (absolutist, deontological or Kantian) quote moral scriptures and appeal to our moral intuition to show that since a man is not a thing, but an end in himself, murder of millions of innocent humans, no matter what or how good the consequences may be, is immoral for it is, after all is said and done, the most serious offence against our own humanity. It is, as the Master of Balliol has recently put it, better to *be* wronged, than to *do* wrong.[1] The consequentialists on the other hand go on loudly proclaiming, with untiring repetition, the utilitarian-consequentialist slogans—for the greatest good of the greatest number of people, killing of even a few millions of innocent people, women and children, by nuclear bomb, is justified *morally*, for, in plain words, it is the end that justifies the means. Of course, the utilitarian-consequentialists are greatly divided on many related issues. Many technical and hair-splitting discussions have ensued. Moral philosophers today have discussed a whole array of very pertinent questions such as: how to gauge the utility or the 'good' or 'maximality'? What standards to apply? What yardstick, metre rod or barometer to use? Is the simple numerical consideration enough or adequate? Should we depend on cardinality or originality when comparing utilities? Should consideration for quality override that of quantity? Can quality be measured? Is the excellence of one quality over another always decidable or intelligible? Moral philosophers have for long engaged themselves to analyse minutely such and other questions and exhibited their technical skill and sophistication to enlighten their colleagues. Perhaps, a sort of *felicific calculus* is constructible to measure the *good* that will come about from some important moral decision that we have to make. And perhaps, the problem posed by 'interpersonal commensurability of utilities' are soluble. But these technicalities may be left aside for the present. The nuclear issue is already loaded, overloaded, with technicalities of a different nature. We would do better if we stick to some well-understood general moral principles. For, as the Provost of King's College, Cambridge, who doubts explicitly whether 'the issue of the possession or non-possession of nuclear weapons is in itself a moral issue' or not, frankly admits, it is difficult to think *rationally* about the nuclear strategy because the scenario is so absurdly complex.[2]

Discussion of the morality of an act is no doubt enlightening and sometimes unavoidable but it does not seem to get us very far in practical matters of decision-making. It is a well-recognized problem in today's moral philosophy that we as agents in real life face decision-making with *incomplete* valuation structure. Decision-making with a complete ordering or ranking, which was probably the goal of Buridan's Ass, is all very nice, but this is seldom, if at all, available to us in the present case. Hence if rationality is to guide our actions then even our incomplete valuation structures would be and must be used to eliminate some alternatives, permitting others. However, in the matter of life and death (as it is in the case of nuclear war), we cannot afford to be in the 'shoes' of Buridan's Ass who starved to death, being unable to rank the two haystacks! In fact today's nuclear issue is hardly decidable by some academically oriented moral debate. What is called for is critical and rational thinking impregnated with *sound* prudential arguments. I say this is consonance with the view of Bernard Williams, who once said of the nuclear issue:[3]

> The right concepts with which to think about this subject are broadly those of rationality, not of morality. I believe that this subject has been bedevilled by too much more argument.

There is, of course, a moral or ethical dimension of this issue. However moral philosophical arguments about war and peace have shown a tendency to get more and more entangled in technicalities and enmeshed with issues that are more 'academic' and less practical, where the opposing sides would seem to be both equally right and equally wrong—a real 'Buridan Ass' situation. So there has been, as Williams points out, 'too much moral argument'. But Buridan's Ass was after all an ass, and lacked the ability to decide, which was not surprising. We humans have to decide. Rational discussion may indeed lead to a successful resolution of all our moral dilemmas including this one about the nuclear issue, as R.M. Hare has optimistically argued, provided we, with the help of an Archangel, engage in what he calls 'critical moral thinking' and separate it from *intuitive* moral thinking.[4] But being terribly handicapped by the absence of such advice of the Archangel in the *moral* debate about war and peace we are indeed being led into a situation where the debate degenerates into what is called in Indian logical (Nyāya) terminology a *satpratipakṣa*, a debate-situation where both sides seem to be equally balanced and the debate comes to a standstill, for the available reasons and information (*hetu*) favour equally both, the thesis and the counter-thesis.[5] Further information can, of course, tilt the balance, but alas, in this imperfect world of ours, we do meet very often in moral, legal or ethical debate this type of 'no winner' situation, just as an actual nuclear war would be in today's context—a situation where there will be neither victor nor vanquished in any real sense.

An escape from this *impasse* in the debate must be found by emphasizing the practical and the prudential side of the problem. The practical-prudential side of the problem is by now obvious to any sane person. To put it crudely, it is no longer a matter of teaching the 'bloody' Russians a lesson nor to save the so-called Socialist revolution. The real situation is this. We, the entire humanity on the face of this globe, are sitting upon the mouth of a live volcano and can be blown off at any moment, but we just hope (a sort of hoping against hope) that this will never happen. It is nothing short of sheer madness. The MAD thesis of mutual assured destruction is a fact of life which is supposed to give us stability in today's nuclear age. The paradox is that this fear of mutual wholesale destruction is what keeps us alive, gives us hope, even faith. But faith is, as E.M. Forster once said, a reluctance to look at the evidence. The faith is that our survival depends paradoxically upon this fear of MAD. But it seems dangerously close to the faith of the kind Forster defined.

The world is divided into two opposing camps, we call them Superpowers. They parallel the mythical duo, the Pāṇḍavas and the Kauravas, or the historical Romans and Barbarians. For our own satisfaction and boosting of morale, we may designate these opposing camps as 'we' and 'they', or 'friends' and 'enemies', as 'good' and 'bad'. But hostility among humans is as old as civilization. The world has been divided into opposing camps as it ever was in every age or period of the known human history. There have been fights, battles and wars, there have been destruction, bloodshed and indiscriminate killing, since the birth of civilization. So has been our search for peace. There have been peace-makers in all ages.

The word 'peace' has unfortunately acquired a bad connotation in our Western society today. A pacifist today is usually regarded as a fanatic, even a moral fanatic. This is not simply the verdict of a right-wing politician. Even a rational philosopher like R.M. Hare, while arguing to downgrade and reject intuition in moral philosophy, has said that pacifism is a species of fanaticism for it is a product of 'unthinking subservience' to the 'extreme' form of an ordinarily 'good to have' moral intuition (the *prima-facie* moral principle is that which condemns killing of the innocent and other forms of violence).[6] Since extremism of any sort is censurable (and was it not the very substance of the teaching of the Middle Way by the Buddha?), the pacifist's subservience is censured as fanaticism, and fanaticism even for the noblest cause is not commendable for it closes the door to (Harean) critical thinking. While some rational philosophers censure pacifism as extremism, the politician thinks pacifism to be a menace for a different reason. He believes it to be a sinister outcome of the enemy's secret propaganda. A pacifist for him is either a muddle-headed man brainwashed by counter-espionage and communist ideologies or himself a secret enemy-agent.

I concede that both the above characterizations of pacifism contain some grain of truth. But they are nevertheless mostly untrue, extremely one-sided and narrow, if not dogmatic. When an odd assortment of people like a devout Catholic priest, or somebody like Henry Kissinger or Robert McNamara, talk about peace, nuclear disarmament and nuclear arms limitation, the above portrait of a neurotic pacifist seems to be fading away. I think our today's pacifist may occasionally be a bit naive and non-realist, but not always a neurotic or a fanatic. Given the present situation, Dr Kenny's principle, 'it is better to be wronged than to do wrong in nuclear strategy', may be rather impractical but it is hardly fanatic.[7] Hence we must regrettably note and disapprove of the fact that our common language is being developed into a sort of Orwellian Newspeak where a descriptive term is losing its descriptive force and being endowed with only a negative value (where pacifism = communism = enemy within) much in the same way words like 'Negro' cannot any longer be descriptively used in the southern United States without the extreme negative evaluation that goes along with the word. We should either rescue the word 'pacifism' or invent a new word to take its place to save our OldSpeak. However, this does not mean that some of our present demonstrators for peace have not been brainwashed or can never be enemy-agents.

The word 'peace' itself has many shades of meaning. A digression into India's traditional, classical scholarship may be in order. Baffled by the external behaviour of man and frustrated by everything in the outer world, some would like to search and find 'peace' inwardly in the depth of their souls, or in the serenity of nature. Sometimes we call these people mystics or deeply religious people. But we should be careful in differentiating from this venerable, mystical, blissful notion of peace the kind of peace that we seek to establish between warring nations, opposing ideologies and fighting parties. It is this inner peace that is glorified by the Sanskrit word *śānti*. Admittedly there may be a very well-defined (remote or proximate) connection between the inner peace and the other kind of peace, and in an idealized state of affairs (in an *ideal* world) this connection may even be seen to be directly 'causal' (realization of one leading eventually to the realization of the other). But in our *realistic* assessment of today's world this connection is so remote that even to mention the word *śānti* is to reveal an incorrigible *naiveté* and impractical idealism. The kind of 'peace' that we should be talking about in the present context is not *śānti* but the Kauṭilyan policy of *sāma*, one of the four policies of Kauṭilya's statecraft.[8] It is described as a policy to live together with the enemy, to live together with the adversary conceding to him an equality of status. This is not moral advice, but practical, prudential, Machiavellian-Kauṭilyan advice. Translated into our present day terminology, it is a proposal to talk about politics rather than ethics, about principles of prudence rather than principles of morals. It is not that the two, prudence and morality, do not mix; in fact very often they do. Hare even thinks that it is possible to reconcile morality with prudence 'in the world as we have it' though they may be at odds 'in some logically possible (non-actual) world'.[9] But common sense dictates us to keep them separate if we wish to make any progress in the present debate. Even prudence dictates us to do so. For otherwise, if *per impossible* one finds a decidedly better or preferred *moral* alternative or at least thinks that one has found one, it tends to foster an illegitimate sense of self-righteousness and 'holier than thou' attitude which will infect all one's desires, actions and preferences. And one could be either a pacifist or a pro-nuclear strategist. That is more likely to provoke a dangerous course in today's situation, that is, the confrontation between superpowers for all-out nuclear exchange. Most conflicts start with such moral or religious convictions. Going into a devastating war has always been a decision with conviction. The entire history of war from the beginning of civilization can be cited as our evidence. But in today's world when we are talking about nuclear conflicts, it would be fatal even to think about taking such risks. Risk-taking is inhibited today at all levels by the fear of fatal retaliation. But even so, a phoney self-righteousness induced only by misguided moral thinking may forebode ill. Fools, we are told, rush where angels or even archangels fear to tread. It is at least for this compelling reason, I wish to play down the role of moral thinking from this present debate, while I acknowledge that in an ideal situation moral thinking should take precedence over other considerations.

However one can hardly be indifferent to the discussion of morality and religion in the case of war and peace. It is a moral issue to decide whether we should or should not kill or threaten (and be prepared should the occasion demand) to kill millions of innocent people. It is also a moral issue to decide whether we should own nuclear weapons for the deterrence of a nuclear attack upon us. But too often moral or philosophical discussion in this matter degenerates into logic-chopping and personal preferences while technical analysis of the moral principles involved gets more and more remote from common understanding and common sense. As I have already noted, the Archangel is not available to us for consultation, for helping us to do the critical thinking. Besides, how are we to tell the difference between a true archangel and a Miltonic *fallen* archangel? Beyond a certain point, those in charge of framing public policy usually have developed a 'couldn't care less' attitude for the persuasive power of such critical or philosophical arguments. Instead, a discussion of prudential values and pragmatism would bring us back to the home base and might allow us the privilege of the attention of the policy-makers. Appeal to the Machiavellian-Kauṭilyan principle of *sāma* or the *broader* and *enlightened self-interest* could be more fruitful and may contribute more towards the staving off of the all-out nuclear holocaust. For it is realism. And it is realism, neither blind faith nor pseudo-idealism, that holds more promise in this matter.

Sāma, by which I mean a policy of living together with opposing interests, conflicting ideologies and aspirations, is a state of *neutralized* hostility, not the Utopian goal of peace where all hostilities are supposedly obliterated. Hostility or aggressiveness is a basic human trait. It is derived from the instinctual self-preservation of any form of life. It is both bad and benign, but perhaps in the human context it is more evil than benign. But it cannot be wiped out. It can only be tamed. This is what I call the state of neutralized hostility. It holds at the interpersonal level, and that is how, I believe, civilization has progressed from the days of the cave-man to our modern age. It must also hold at the level of international relations. It should hold between the superpowers, if man is to survive in today's world. It is the product of the counsel of prudence. We may not wish to call it 'peace' and banish the word 'pacifism' altogether. But for neutralizing the hostility we must also banish the concept of world domination by either power.

Stability (or shall I say survival?) in our age is based upon our being able to inflict wholesale destruction and on being vulnerable to such destruction in return. This is the MAD policy of survival, and rightly called MAD, for it does not make any sense. The so-called policy of deterrence is based upon this alleged principle of MAD. Well-known public figures have argued that the acquisition of nuclear weaponry for the purpose of what has been christened as 'deterrence' *does* make sense. It has been repeated in a parrot-like fashion that our nuclear capability is for 'deterrence' which has ensured 'peace'. I shall try to formulate the 'deterrence' argument as strongly as I can in order to see the implications. It will be a difficult task, for the debate on the subject of deterrence has been going on for at least thirty years now.

The greatest deterrent to nuclear war is the assured ability to retaliate causing sure annihilation. The nuclear arms race has functioned increasingly as a way of imposing an effective limit on the actual use of the nuclear warheads stockpiled. To strengthen the point, it is added that there have been no wars involving the superpowers in direct conflict with each other since the nuclear age began. In other words, international stability through nuclear deterrence, though potentially dangerous, has proven durable. Moralists and those who believe in the 'just war' tradition still find some ground for uneasiness here, and they would like to see a shift towards the counterforce targeting of the strategic weapons (as well as more *defensive* weapons) from the threat of all-out counter-population use which at the moment constitutes the essence of the deterrence policy. But this voice of conscience or moral intuition is silenced by others who argue that any attempt for such a shift would weaken the effectiveness of the deterrent and thus increase, rather than decrease, the possibility of nuclear war. It is like saying that since the tug-of-war between two parties is evenly balanced and the rope is at a standstill, any attempt on our part to rearrange the strategic force will be a slack, and will forbode our destruction and the enemy's victory. And this seems to be enough to stifle any criticism, any voice of protest, any moral intuition or any advice of prudence, against the policy of escalation of the nuclear arms race. Many sober and influential writers today (Howard, Williams among them), while they deplore the nuclear arms race and the possibility of an all-out war, nevertheless seem to support the status quo as well as the inevitable drift towards never-ending escalation on the ground that the total nuclear disarmament is not only not achievable but also not desirable because of the extreme unlikelihood of verification being one hundred percent effective. Williams believes that this would be a highly unstable situation and hence we would be better off probably with two sides retaining a nuclear balance at some level.[10]

Of these points in support of the deterrence policy, one can quickly dismiss the argument based upon the 'non-use' so far of the nuclear weapon by either superpowers to settle their disputes. For (a) it does not prove that deterrence has actually prevented war, for no causal or logical connection between the two can be established in this way, and hence (b) there is no absolute guarantee that this state of affairs will continue to obtain in any foreseeable future. A link may however exist between the two, but it is one of the weakest kind and hence it would be suicidal if we rested the most weighty question of security and survival of the human race upon such a weak and insecure link.

The strong argument for deterrence is based not so much upon the threat of assured destruction as on the emphasis that there is no other alternative, no other way than this rather highly immoral posture for an all-out counterpopulation targetting. I consider this argument to be wrong. For mutual threat develops into a psychopathological case like an extreme form of paranoia (between leaders, if not between nations) where reality-perception becomes highly distorted, and that would hardly be an enviable, or even desirable situation. The 'no other alternative' argument despite its strong persuasive power, sounds, on the other hand, too much like fatalism or naive determinism. It is even reminiscent of the partly fatalistic and deterministic advice that Kṛṣṇa gave to Arjuna on the eve of the *Mahābhārata* war (in the *Bhagavad-Gītā*). And we all know what followed: a most devastating war was fought where every creature, everything valuable was destroyed such that even the victor in the sequel decided that life was not worth living any more and in utter depression went away, giving up the very throne for which the bloody war was fought. This should be a sobering lesson. At the level of critical moral thinking, we have to be careful in distinguishing between our archangel and the Miltonic *fallen* archangel.

But lessons from mythology apart, there is a strong reason to believe that this 'no alternative' argument is a counsel of despair and depression. Given the inherent dangers of nuclear deterrence and given the possibility that the *balance* of forces which constitutes the heart of the deterrence policy may be tilted at any inopportune moment to usher in the holocaust, a genuine and sincere search should be undertaken to establish lower and lower levels of balance. These dangers coupled with the monetary costs of escalation should provide the real basis and incentive for our sincere search for an alternative. One can even agree with Bernard Williams's point that we would be better-off with two sides retaining a nuclear balance at some level. But by virtue of his own logic which he spells out as 'the world has eaten the apple of nuclear knowledge—the bomb, having been invented, cannot be disinvented', he should also see the impossibility of retaining nuclear balance at *some* level and the inevitability of escalation. If both sides honestly can agree to maintain a balance, they can very well agree to nuclear disarmament. Due to mutual mistrust the situation would be equally unstable in both cases.

There are several flaws in the 'deterrence' argument even if the whole question is divested of its moral or ethical dimension. For one thing, the argument which promises stability as its end-product, wrongly assumes that we have already the knowledge, not just an opinion, of what in fact we do not and cannot know, that is, good intention and rational behaviour of the enemy leaders. This simplistic assumption can be spelled out as follows. Nobody, not even a mad man, starts a war with the idea of losing it; to prevent war we must convince the enemy that he cannot win. And to do this we need a combination of political will and military capability. And hence the Cruise, the Polaris, Trident I and Trident II. But this version of the argument can hardly be sound for it starts with a wrong first premise. For a mad man *can* start a war without any expectation much less with the expectation to win. Can anybody want to bet? This is precisely the point. The principle of deterrence implicitly makes the illegitimate claim that there will always be good sense and rational deliberation prevailing upon the leadership of the enemy-camp. When it has already been witnessed that leadership may be passed on to such person or persons as become senile or diseased or both, this claims becomes more and more vulnerable and risky. It is more pertinent to ask in this context: was

Hitler entirely rational? Could we look forward to the day when a Hitler-like person becomes the enemy leader? In fact the stakes are too high to allow such risk-taking. Men do grow old and senile, or become irrational, if not senile. Leaders and 'big brothers' are after all men, not gods, and *men alone are capable of acting irrationally*. For only rational beings can, and sometimes do, act irrationally, not the non-rational ones. In short, threat of retaliation is supposed to inhibit the nuclear offensive, but this notion of deterrence is largely dependent upon enemy's perception. But lest such perceptions turn into misperceptions, the threat must not only seem to be real but be *real* and backed by instant readiness to strike. In the present nuclear context, this means that only an irrationally and immorally destructive deterrent force can deter an equally irrational and immoral destructive force. Hence the principle of deterrence is not only highly immoral and imprudent under the present circumstances, it also perpetuates the very uncertain 'balance of terror'. The present 'deterrence' situation is no less unstable than what it would be if both sides (even dishonestly) agree to the policy of disarmament. Hence supposed unstability is no argument against such a policy.

Reverting to moral criticism, some have argued that since the intention to use counterpopulation force is only a *conditional* intention, it should be considered morally neutral. This is however an utterly naive argument. For this so-called conditional intention cannot be an 'apparent' (and hence unreal) intention. Otherwise the policy of deterrence would be a strategy of massive and potentially dangerous bluff. As already insisted upon, the enemy must *perceive* the threat as real and be convinced about preparedness. Otherwise any time the bluff can be blown off. Hence Kenny has argued that in western democracy such a policy requires the individual citizens to be prepared to execute an order to massacre millions of non-combatants.[11]

A more serious and sophisticated version of the argument for deterrence comes from those who pin their faith in what they understand as the moral principle of utilitarian-consequentialism. Intention to use counterpopulation force may of course be judged as evil. But it does not matter, or it matters much less, the consequentialists argue, if a person has an evil intention as long as he never in fact acts on it. The intention, it is conceded, has to be real, for the policy of deterrence to succeed. But if the having of an evil intention succeeds in preventing certain very undesirable, more evil events, such as total destruction, from occurring, then the fact of having such an evil intention may be more than welcome. This is the consequentialists' strategy in the baldest terms. Roughly speaking, the beneficial consequence of retaining offensive and disproportionately destructive nuclear deterrents far outweighs the evil consequences of abandoning or not having them.

This much-used, essentially consequentialist argument, however, loses all its force under a different ethical system, the absolutist, deontological or Kantian system of ethics. For a non-consequentialist the focus of morality is primarily on the act or the agent himself, on the intrinsic character of his intentions, preferences and actions. Roughly speaking, this view regards an act, or an intention to act to inflict violent death upon millions of innocent non-combatants as an unmitigated evil which nothing can wash away. This is so because such an act goes against the absolute prohibition dictated by rationality (Kantian) or an absolute divine prohibition (Christian or Catholic conscience, as stated by Professor Anscombe, the Master of Balliol and many others). The evil nature of such an act, it is argued, can never be condoned or compromised by anything, no matter how much good it may promise or how much evil it may purport to avert. To treat millions of humans as only means to an end is an offence against our own humanity. We have no moral right to destroy the lives of millions as a means even if it is to further the happiness of millions of others. For this is where the essence of morality breaks down, and convenience, opportunism, selfishness and self-righteousness take over. Here the Archangel turns into a Miltonic fallen angel. As against this, intuition of consequentialism is so seductive that even a man like Bertrand Russell once (in 1950) pressed the argument that the West (in 1950) should take advantage of its nuclear superiority and impose the Western-style democracy upon the rest of the world, including the Soviet bloc![12] Was Russell fulfilling the role of the fallen angel? What could have been a more perfect example of blackmail? Perhaps, it would have a good consequence and this is the consequentialist's point which is acceptable, but this good would have generated further evil, perhaps, it would have been more dangerous. The blackmail victim is never conquered but he pounces upon the blackmailer at the slightest opportunity he gets. And we might add, negotiation with a powerful but weakened and humiliated opponent has the same consequence in the end. It does not last.

The above ethical debate cannot be easily resolved. It is by now a well-recognized fact. To get around the posed moral dilemma or to deflect the charge of immorality or evil-doing, it is sometimes suggested that we should either develop more *defensive* strategy, or better still, we should switch gradually from counterpopulation strategic targetting to counterforce strategic targetting or counter-combatant strategy. This is believed to be in accordance with the requirements of the Just War doctrine. The first suggestion is however impracticable, given the present state of tension and 'balance of terror'. Besides, there is in fact no real defensive weapon that is not at the same time an offensive one. Even something like the defensive Chinese wall could be used and was used for offensive purposes; the difference is in the mind of the user. The most recent SDI argument is an improved version of this alternative on which I shall comment presently. The second alternative has more plausibility and perhaps it could be a step towards the right direction to minimize the moral burden. Let us examine it closely.

We may quickly dismiss the rather facile argument that since counterpopulation targetting was normally an accepted policy in the Second World War (used by both the Allied and the Axis), and regarded as a so-called legitimate punitive device, and since threat of such a punitive action is really effective as a deterrent, there is no need to switch to a counterforce strategy. I reject it, for a bad legacy of the past is better given up, otherwise we could even argue for going back to the age of bows and arrows. Surely a counterforce strategy is a better policy, given the circumstances of our wars. However, a more serious question is this: whether counterforce strategy is practicable under the present circumstances. With technological development and introduction of cruise missiles and so on this argument gains some substance and credibility. But the critics will point out that as long as the more devastating thermonuclear warheads are used (as is done currently) it does not get us away from the dilemma of disproportionality and discrimination and we can hardly preserve the non-combatants' immunity. Massive destruction of innocent lives is hardly avoidable under any strategy in the nuclear warfare.

Generally two types of reaction are forthcoming from the above criticism. The first says, 'So why even try to switch?', while the second insists that it is better to improve precision and so forth so that the strategy will by and large work. As Thomas Nagel has ironically put it, 'for the future of freedom, peace and economic prosperity', we can ease our conscience and ignore the responsibility 'for a certain number of charred babies'.[13] Another argument is this: from the policy of all-out thermonuclear exchange (which the counterpopulation strategy may or may not imply) ushering in the doomsday period, we can move to the policy of limited (strategic and tactical) nuclear exchanges in a 'theatre of war' to bring the enemy down to his knees, and in this policy the counterforce strategy would be more useful. Some would go even further to argue that we can replace the high-yield thermonuclear warheads with conventional high explosives in the cruise missile, or even better, we can devise a *decapitation* strategy ('cut the heads off, to subdue the body', 'destroy only the leaders, government and generals') with less and less dependence upon the high-yield nuclear weaponry. All this sounds very nice, if practicable, for it is at least compatible with the moral awareness of the Just War doctrine. But the problem is as old as the question: who is to kill the cat? Besides, the concept of limited nuclear exchange in a theatre of war is very intriguing. Which one is supposed to be the 'theatre'? West Germany? Or western Europe? The late Lord Mountbatten in his famous Strasbourg speech of 11 May 1979 said that the tactical nuclear weapons would not limit the conflict for there could be 'no use for any nuclear weapon which would not end in escalation'.[14]

Further, the critics will readily point out, the counterforce strategy can be 'outfoxed' by the use of many decoys. And the same goes for the new sinister development, the possibility of the Star Wars strategy nicknamed SDI which is just getting off the ground. The SDI alternative has a tremendous popular appeal in its stark simplicity (Star Wars) and the utopian claims that go along with it. Recently several famous scientists have argued why the Star Wars idea is dangerous and would not work.[15] The reasons are briefly as follows: (a) The Star Wars strategy does not defend against low-altitude delivery system, bombers and cruise missiles; (b) the Soviets could keep ahead by building new warheads to shoot down orbiting defensive system; (c) it would be simpler to 'out-fox' the new system by building over time more decoys and other penetration aids; (d) the cost is astronomical; (e) it may provoke a premature Soviet preemptive attack. In other words, it may bring us closer to the brink of all-out exchange and doomsday than taking us away from it even by a bit. The paradox is that the protagonists of SDI welcome this alternative as the effective way to a long-term transition from 'mutual assured destruction' policy to 'mutual assured security'. Even if we ignore such misgivings as expressed by Geoffrey Howe, David Watt and others, the prevailing opinion of the experts is that SDI is dangerously destabilizing and at worst disastrously hostile to European interests. Another argument is that the Russians have already started the experiment secretly, and hence we should not be left behind. It may be true that some well-qualified scientists in the USSR have been experimenting with laser technologies and particle beams. But it would be a bland exaggeration if we claim that the USSR has both the technical and financial ability at the moment to construct ahead of the USA the equivalent of the American SDI (for which Reagan wants billions of dollars and about ten years spent on research). Billions of dollars should work wonders for the free market economy of the USA and its scientific profession. But the fact remains that most well-qualified scientists there are decidedly against this venture and they are not just weak-minded and meek-hearted 'pacifists'.

The ethical dilemma seems insoluble unless we stick to some questionable form of consequentialism or conduct some critical level moral thinking modelled after that of an archangel who has by Hare's definition 'superhuman powers of thought, superhuman knowledge and no human weakness'.[16] Even if we accept some form of 'just war' doctrine, the counterforce strategy cannot completely eliminate killing of thousands of non-combatants and hence cannot remove or lessen the moral burden. Besides, it is also arguable that even the combatants, most of whom are drafted soldiers and may be unwilling fighters, may not deserve to be the victims of massive and disproportionate killing. For example, think of the contrast between a morally pure conscript who is forced to fight with the profoundest regrets and the evil non-combatant hair-dresser in the enemy city who supports his government's policy of war. (The example is due to Nagel.[17]) The decapitation strategy (envisioned also by the SDI strategy) which aims at the total destruction of the generals, government leaders and war-mongering politicians, though acceptable under certain conditions, may not be workable. Besides, it is imperative in any war-situation (in nuclear war it would be more so) to keep the channel of information open in order to preserve some grip on events and salvage what is left. If we 'decapitate' the Russians and destroy the total apparatus of command, control and communication, we would be left with a total blank of response and a fatal blind date. So we are back to square one.

Since moral considerations in the above manner lead us to a dead end, we should try to find a way out through pragmatic and prudential considerations. As I have said earlier, since decision-making is imperative in this matter and inability to eliminate alternative choices typified by the Buridan's Ass situation, is by no means acceptable. Professor Michael Howard's hard questions should be answered by means of only cool rational response and responsible behaviour, not by emotional conviction, blind dogmas and hot-headed rhetoric. It is incumbent upon us that we should negotiate with the enemy, to diffuse, if not to resolve totally, our differences. I shall come back to this point towards the end. It is important to realize that the policy of so-called deterrence is paradoxically blunting all real initiatives for negotiated settlement.

Let me examine the meaning of the word 'deterrence' now, as I have examined the word 'peace'. In a way the word 'deterrence' is somewhat misleading, if not wrong, for its use in the present context is based upon a misleading metaphor. Ordinarily actual punitive action along with a real threat for further such act is regarded as *deterrent* against crimes. This gives the rationale for the existence of the Penal Code in a society. But this model or metaphor does not exactly suit the present context of all-out nuclear exchange. Here the punitive act being almost imponderable as well as unthinkable, the actual threat for such an act loses a lot of its credibility and effectiveness. As we all know so well, the mere existence of a Penal Code is not enough for deterrence actual exemplary punishments are essential to give substance to the concept of deterrence. An example is better than the precept, as it is said. In the context of all-out nuclear exchange, what exists is a threat which inhibits all risk-taking, but it cannot be a *real* deterrent in the same sense, for the threat cannot be substantiated with an actual act of punishment (which will mean total destruction). The point is that the concept of deterrence, as it is ordinarily understood, envisions a much more stable, safe and effective principle tested and testable in many societies, whereas what has been christened as the principle of 'deterrence' here is only a vague threat coupled with highly irrational fear and hence reinforced with inhibition for risk-taking. This spells out a highly psychotic state, not a healthy one as is commonly associated with the concept of ordinary deterrence. This creates a false sense of security.

Proponents of Just War doctrines and friends of the *dharmayuddha* idea of the *Gītā* or the *Mahābhārata* have often posed a question. A limited and strategic nuclear exchange in a chosen 'theatre of war' may be a reasonably acceptable, real option to teach the enemy a lesson and to contain evil (and this punitive act would then contribute to the concept of deterrence). This may be a real option open to the superpowers. But it is potentially far more dangerous than anything else so far suggested. And I can see no reason by the allies of superpowers (whose country would probably be the projected 'theatre of war') would accept it and cooperate. In this context a very queer and slightly different question arises, and coming from a Hindu background I am persuaded by friends to address myself to it. Can we not support the policy of deterrence, if not actual nuclear war, by the argument which the *Mahābhārata* offered for *dharmayuddha*? I believe this to be a wrong question, for it is based upon the assumption that the *Gītā* as well as the *Mahābhārata* promotes violence by supporting the idea of a just war. There is no Just War doctrine in India, as there is in the western tradition. The lesson of the *Mahābhārata* can be differently interpreted. It can very well be, as far as I can see, a very sobering lesson about the final tragic outcome of any devastating all-out war in which there was no real victor. The victor King Yudhiṣṭhira realized that he was as much a victim of the devastating war as was the vanquished. In utter depression he gave up the throne which lost all its significance and went away on his final journey towards the Himalayas. If this is not the lesson for avoiding the all-out war (no matter whether it is waged against the evil party or not) then what else is? Besides, I believe the Kurukṣetra war was called *dharmayuddha* not so much because it was a morally justifiable war against evil but because certain *dharmas*, 'codes of conduct' reminiscent of the Hague and Geneva Conventions, were supposed to have been scrupulously maintained (although they were occasionally broken, which made them more significant). In fact, in India, there is no parallel to the Just War doctrine. The Kurukṣetra war emphasized, if anything, the *ultimate ambiguity of a just war*, the impossibility of making a clear-cut distinction between the good party and the bad party. The so-called good party, that is, the one favoured to win, was guilty of innumerable heinous and morally reprehensible acts, and the 'bad party', the one condemned to defeat, had a number of admirable and morally superior allies, Bhīṣma and Droṇa, who fought valiantly and died for the protection of this so-called evil side. To me this only heightens the practical and the most pervasive dilemma in such all-out wars: *we cannot separate the unmixed good from the unmitigated evil.* This lesson goes against the rather naive assumption of some proponents of the Just War doctrine that one side unambiguously represents unmitigated evil and deserves to be totally annihilated, no matter what. For instance, most pro-arguments for peace in today's context seem convincing and compelling if we speak in terms of the value-neutral and preference-neutral expressions such as 'superpowers'. But it is significant to note that those who support deterrence and envisage the possibility of nuclear war invariably spell out the hostility in the rhetoric of the free world and communism, or alternately the rhetoric of 'socialist revolution' and 'capitalist exploitation'. The rhetoric obfuscates the issue.

In the same vein, it might be urged that even the counsel of Kṛṣṇa to persuade Arjuna to fight, cannot be used to support the present so-called doctrine of deterrence. For apart from a not-too-practical discourse upon a metaphysic of self, Kṛṣṇa's argument was essentially fatalistic and deterministic. Needless to say he did not emphasize that this was a just war against an unmitigated evil. Essentially the argument underlying Kṛṣṇa's counsel, as I wish to read it, was this. The war was inevitable because the die was cast already. It was rather too late for Arjuna to pretend to be a pacifist. For throughout his life, he was preparing himself to conduct a devastating, bloody war like this, and went on acquiring deadly and terrible weapons one after another much as the superpowers have been doing today. The arrow has been shot already towards the target; it cannot simply by Arjuna's sudden, abrupt, and temporary pious wish, stop in the middle. A true pacifist, if there is any, has to purify his own self of all selfish desires, emotions, drives and preferences, and this is a matter of prolonged and painful practice. Arjuna cannot turn into a true pacifist instantaneously just in the battlefield of Kurukṣetra, nor can the leader of a modern superpower. Instant pacifism is as much a mythical concept as the instant *mokṣa* of a modern LSD cult. Hence one can understand the whole point of Kṛṣṇa's counsel to Arjuna merely to 'go through the motions' now, for the decision has long been taken and the action has already begun. (For example, Kṛṣṇa asks Arjuna to consider all these people as already dead, killed in the battle, while he is only an insignificant detail, a *nimitta*, only a factor in the inexorable process of annihilation.)[18] This however does not apply to our modern situation; at least we should be thankful that *we are not yet there!* Potentially, however, it is possible to get into such a situation for the most dangerous development today is the concept of launch-on-warning policy, where a leader, a single individual, will have only a few minutes, sometimes only seconds, to decide whether it was a false alarm due to a mechanical mix-up or whether to push the button to destroy everything on a psychosis of threat for retaliation, which we have been programmed to call 'deterrence'. Hence the lesson of the *Gītā*, if any in the present circumstance, is not to drag ourselves into such a fatalistic situation—a situation into which irrational and uncontrolled preparation for any all-out war tends to lead us. The whole *Mahābhārata* is the story of such a total devastation. This should be the right counsel of Kṛṣṇa as I would like to understand it, not anything else.

This brings us back to the prudential and practical course of action which we must try in order to survive. To repeat what Bernard Williams has said, the nuclear bombs having been invented cannot by any means be disinvented. True, since we cannot disinvent we have to do the best we can, under the circumstances. Since we cannot disinvent the nuclear bomb, and since the concept of deterrence without punitive act plus the real threat for punishment is, as I have argued, fundamentally flawed, and since a controlled nuclear war is the most obnoxious idea ever suggested, and since a truly counterforce or even a decapitation strategy is still unworkable, there is only one option left: a negotiated settlement between superpowers leading to substantial reduction in nuclear arsenals on both sides, and this would be a good beginning, the best we can hope for under the present condition. The advocates of deterrence know that it rests essentially upon the assumed rationality on the part of the enemy or its leader. Without it, there is no *locus standi* for the policy of deterrence. But if this assumption is valid, then one can very well wonder: why can we not put the same assumed rationality of the enemy to a much better use, negotiation on the basis of the *perceived enlightened self-interest of either side*?

Let us then seriously talk about negotiation. Uncontrolled nuclear arms race (in the name of deterrence) heading towards sure destruction must be curbed by gradual negotiation between the superpowers as well as their allies about arms limitations. The progress towards settlement may be slow, hard and rough, but the progress must be steady. It is a healthy sign that there is an expressed consensus nowadays among the superpowers that negotiation is necessary. There are at least three prudential considerations that foster this consensus. First, it is argued that the nature of modern weaponry already in existence makes the further search for more devastating devices completely unnecessary. Second, the number of arsenals possessed by both sides is simply staggering. They have already embarrassingly too many. Third, both sides perceive that maintenance of security is possible at a much lower level and at a much lower cost. Hence if negotiation is possible, it can certainly stop the defence budget from reaching some increasingly astronomical figure. Thus, economy, if not morality, prudence, if not piety, supplies a strong motivation to negotiate. But development in this direction is, as might be expected, constantly being inhibited by mutual distrust and paranoic fear. We should however bear in mind that this almost psychotic fear is not the only reason why all negotiation efforts to control strategic nuclear arsenals are prone to stall. For the mutual perception of the vital importance and desirability of the said negotiation should override the inhibited behaviour that may stand in the way. But what we see today is that the superpowers instead of showing a genuine desire to negotiate are trying to outfox each other or trying to see who can trick the other side into something which will establish the superiority of one over the other. The game of out-foxing each other is a very familiar one.

There are two things very seriously wrong in the present negotiation procedure. First, the argument that 'we must negotiate from the position of strength' (an often repeated argument for acquiring an ever increasing number of the so-called nuclear deterrents) is basically wrong. For if either side wanted to do this, the actual negotiating opportunity will be ever-elusive, and so much the worse for the economic or other pressure which will be ever mounting. The phrase 'position of strength' should therefore be modified as 'the positions of (perceived) *equal* strength'. Second, stable, adequate and appropriate negotiation can only take place between *assumed equals*, and each negotiator must be well aware of this fact. This is what I have called the policy of *sāma*, reconciliation with the adversary, even supposedly evil adversary, conceding his equality, his own self-respect and dignity. The basic fact to be admitted is an old truth: this world should be big enough for both. Paradoxically, no significant treaty or stable and lasting negotiation is possible, given today's situation, with a subdued or humiliated adversary. The greatest illusion today would be to think that one side by some magic trick would be able to bring the other side to its knees and then all will be well. Those who have a life-long conviction that socialism or communism is an unmitigated evil have to slightly change their attitude enough to learn to live with it. And socialism must give space to the other well-established systems.

Two rational agents, meeting for a vital negotiation, may have many disagreements on various 'local' matters: how to run a government, whether and how to legitimize such a government, who should control the means of production, what to do about distributive justice, what to do about civil liberties and so on and doubtless all these are important questions, but these disagreements would seem to be less important in the 'global' context. About individual beliefs and preferences, my next door neighbour and I may be at loggerheads and hold diametrically opposite views, but when the total picture of our webs of beliefs, preferences and motivations are taken into account, such opposition would seem to be neutralized. What is true at the interpersonal level would seem to be true also at the international level. The more our two rational agents, while negotiating, talk about the total perspective, the less disagreement there would seem to be. Negotiation in order to be successful must be increasingly broadbased, multi-faceted and 'global' where sharp 'local' disagreements would not be able to create the stumbling block. The global peace in the present context must take precedence over local issues. For unless we can assure the first, we will never have a chance to resolve the world-wide problems of local injustice, aggression and exploitation. The following quotation comes from no other than a person like Prime Minister Margaret Thatcher during her visit to America in 1985: 'We should have as many talks as possible with the Soviets. If we are to get better results in arms control, we have to have a better dialogue and understanding.'[19] Indeed the dialogue on only a wide range of issues can pave the way for the arms control process.

I have avoided pursuing the moral philosophical arguments in view of the two main considerations. First, without being offensive I think most would agree that moral sensitivity has not been a strong point among our public officials of either block: witness the development and deployment of modern weaponry. Second, and more important, we seem to reach almost a moral blind alley being led into turns by the two forms of moral intuition, the absolutist-deontological and the utilitarian-consequentialist. It may be a good idea to turn once again to the moral dilemma, not in search of some support for self-righteousness which a public figure may need in order to lead the nation towards an all-out war, but to feel the poignancy of one's inner conflict that the dilemma gives rise to. It does not take much argument to show that the absolutist's intuition that certain acts are never to be done, certain measures are never to be taken no matter what, may be right. For otherwise where should we draw the line and resist the most degenerate conclusion that 'anything goes'? There is something very important for us to think about in what Dr Kenny has asserted: for our nations to be reduced to the status of Romania would be far less of a disaster than all cities to be reduced to the condition of Hiroshima and Nagasaki in 1945.[20] On the other hand, given the technology of modern warfare which makes killing or murder of millions of innocent non-combatants almost obligatory, the absolutist ethic leads to a sort of romantic pacifism which may be unrealistic. The consequentialist who rejects this restriction and adopts what yields the most acceptable consequences likewise feels the *bite* of the argument that he has acted on grounds insufficient to justify the action. It has sometimes been suggested that this type of dilemma can be resolved by some coherent moral system based on rationality (R.M. Hare) which will combine the insight of both the absolutist or Kantian and the utilitarian systems. The basic idea is that if we can emulate the Archangel and can distinguish between the intuitive level consisting of prima facie moral principles and the critical level, and then conduct the critical thinking with logic and facts, we will be able to resolve practically all such dilemmas. This will not be very far from the prudential reasonings that I have suggested. If this could be done with regard to this big question, that of modern nuclear warfare, we have at least crossed a major hurdle in our search for a resolution of the impossible situation which the nuclear age has brought us into.

I shall conclude by describing a hypothetical situation. This is however a common ploy in modern moral philosophical argument. I share with Professor Hare the same kind of distaste for some very bizarre examples which are used sometimes to corner an opponent in moral argument. But the following may not be very bizarre and it illustrates the essential points just made. Suppose in an island there are two living persons, Arthur and Robin. They are both suffering from some deadly and infectious disease, but each thinks that it is only the other who has it. Hence, consider the situation 1: each wishes to kill the other in order to save his own life (from infection and death). Then consider situation 2: each one, or just one (it does not matter which one), is told (i.e. it is revealed to him) that the other, has no disease, but that it is he who has the disease which will kill them both. This may provoke the following reactions: (a) He may be a 'noble' saint or a fanatic saint (it does not matter which) and say that he will let himself be killed by the other. This will obviously be the most moral decision by any standard, as far as I can see. But such persons are rare, I am afraid, if they exist at all. (b) He may be a *prudent* person to say that he will not let himself be killed but if he dies within a few months along with the other, it is just too bad for the other which cannot be helped. In my description, this would be prudential though a bit immoral. (c) He may be more self-centred and say that he will kill the other in any case should he get the chance and die if he had to in the process. For if he cannot enjoy life why should the other one? This would be both immoral and imprudent for it is not in his enlightened self-interest which will not give the other a chance, other things remaining the same. Now consider situation 3: after the ordeal of situation 2, it is revealed that the diseases of both have been mysteriously cured. It would be prudent for both Arthur and Robin now to let each other live although they do not have to love each other, in order to be in peace, or I have underlined, in *neutralized hostility*. Now consider situation 4. It is learnt that each has different deadly diseases and their lifespan is equally limited. But it is revealed that if both live together there may be a chance that the two types of viruses may affect each other adversely thus decreasing the risk of their early premature death. Both may live longer if they are friendly enough to be on speaking terms. This I think will lay the solid foundation for neutralized hostility on prudential grounds. With this optimistic note it is better to conclude here after conceding the overwhelming preponderance of pessimism. It is better to have a dream—a dream similar to the dreams of Jean Monnet, or Woodrow Wilson's dream of the League of Nations to end all wars, or Paul Valéry's hope of not only a League of Nations but a League of Minds. For if we do not have even a dream there may not be anything left that is worth fighting for.

Notes and References

1. Anthony Kenny, 'Defence without Deterrence', lecture given at St Antony's College, Wednesday, 29 May, 1985.
2. Bernard Williams, 'A Rational View', Dumais Lecture in the series on The Nuclear Arms Race, Spring, 1981; published in *Resurgence*, no. 90, 1982.
3. Ibid.
4. Richard M. Hare, *Moral Thinking: Its Levels, Method and Point*, Oxford, Clarendon Press, 1981, pp. 44–52.
5. Gaṅgeśa, *Tattvacintāmaṇi*, Anumāna-khaṇḍa, with *Gādādharī*, ed. M.M. V.P. Dvivedi et al, Chowkhamba; Reprint, Varanasi, 1970.
6. Richard M. Hare, op. cit., p. 173. See also his *Freedom and Reason*, Oxford, Oxford University Press, 1963, pp. 157–85.
7. See A. Kenny, op. cit.
8. Kauṭilya, *Arthāsāstra*, ed. R.P. Kangle, Bombay, Bombay University Press, 1960–65, chapter 1.
9. Hare, 1981, p. 194.
10. Williams, op. cit.
11. Kenny, op. cit.
12. Bertrand Russell, 'The Future of Mankind', in *Unpopular Essays*, London, Allen & Unwin, 1950.
13. Thomas Nagel, 'War and Massacre', in *Mortal Questions*, Cambridge, Cambridge University Press, 1979, p. 59.
14. Lord Mountbatten, Strasbourg Speech, 11 May 1979.
15. A letter to *The Wall Street Journal*, 2 January 1985.
16. Hare, 1981, p. 44.
17. Nagel, op. cit., p. 70.
18. *The Bhagavad-Gītā*, ed. R.C. Zaehner, Oxford, Oxford University Press, 1969, chapter 11, verse 33.
19. *International Herald Tribune*, 22 February 1985.
20. Kenny, op. cit.

18

Ethical Relativism and Confrontation of Cultures

1. MORAL RELATIVISM REVISITED

I shall argue that the culture-relativity of moral norms is usually ill-conceived and generally indefensible.[1] Whether there are culture-invariant principles of morality or not is a question that will inevitably arise, but to this I shall give some suggestive answers.

There are various strands in the texture of our controversy over moral relativism. I isolate the following positions:

1. Ethical standards found in different cultures are only in apparent conflict with each other. This plurality exists only at the surface. At some deeper level there is only one set of moral standards to which everybody should conform, and it is possible to discover this singular standard of universal morality through rational means. I shall call it moral monism or singularism.

2. Intercultural plurality of moral standards is reflected also in the intracultural plurality of norms (which is witnessed by the pervasive presence of moral conflicts in persons). 'My country before my family' is a classic example of a practical resolution of such a conflict. The diversity of goods in a single moral domain demands an assessment of their priorities and relative importance leading presumably to a single coherent ordering of goods. This goal may be ever elusive, but a constant effort to order priorities is desirable. I shall call this pluralism.

3. Genuine plurality exists, and some are more right than others, but there is no way to decide or know which ones are better or worse than others. Despite the air of Orwellian cliché, this can be a seriously held position. I shall call it agnosticism. Moral conflicts on this view would be ineliminable.

4. Among the many moral norms available across cultures it is impossible to judge objectively some as better or worse than others, for although they may be mutually comprehensible, there is no transcultural standard of evaluation. Culture-bound norms are neither good nor bad. This is what I shall call soft relativism.

5. Culture-bound moral norms are both incommensurable and mutually incomprehensible, and hence one may say that one norm is just as good or as bad as the other. This I shall call hard relativism.

I believe there are formidable objections to all these positions. Of these, 4 and 5 are clearly relativistic, 3 is in the twilight zone, while 1 and 2 seem to be compatible with realism. I shall try to support a modified version of 2 and argue that while 1 or even 2 may encourage the risk of what is called 'moral jingoism', both 4 and 5 (and to some extent 3) encourage and sustain a sort of moral insouciance that was regarded as a 'virtue' by some liberal colonialists. I further believe that if morality is to be a domain of ultimate importance, then both must be avoided, jingoism and insouciance.

Although we are bound to talk about cultural relativism, our concern here is with ethics. Ethical or moral realism has notoriously been on the firing line, more so than cognitive realism by any reckoning. The controversy about the so-called gap between fact and value is only too familiar. But one can still be an ethical realist while believing the gap to exist. J.L. Mackie has described ethics as 'inventing right and wrong' and categorically denied that there can be any *objective* values (1977). It may be possible to distinguish between two kinds of nonobjectivism: moral relativism and subjectivism. A significant point about subjectivism is what we can call Hamlet's maxim: neither is good or bad, but thinking makes it so. Relativism insists, not on the individual thinking, but on the fact that there are alternative (irreducible) norms embedded in different culture-groups, and hence what is good for one group may not be so for the other. Further it claims that there is no rational basis for choice between such alternative norms. Relativism could be intracultural (as distinct from one derived from cultural relativism), for moral conflicts and moral disagreements are proverbially widespread within a culture or a group, and there seems to be very little scope for rational choice to be made among rival moral theories. Our main target, however, will be intercultural moral relativism.

Some philosophers distinguish between cognitive or metaphysical realism and moral realism and seriously argue in favour of the former while rejecting the latter. There are also those who find it hard to stomach metaphysical realism today (regarding it as a sort of a vestige of bygone ages, a dogma of Western science). These philosophers are also apt to argue willynilly for relativism in ethics. It is a rather curious phenomenon that the metaphysical realist's distrust for moral realism has been rather pervasive. A relevant point has been made by H. Putnam on this issue. He says that the modern tendency to be too realistic about physics and too subjectivist about ethics are in fact 'inter-linked', for both seem to be connected with the not fully examined, but widespread consensus among people about physics furnishing us with one True Theory (truth independent of all observers) and ethics offering us a variety of moral norms, culture-relative or group-relative, and/or a number of irreconcilable (conflicting) moral theories. However, recent discussion on the nature of science or scientific theories as well as on the nature of truth and objectivity has slackened our faith in such a conception of science (that of science providing us with a perfectly 'transparent' description of reality). Thus, it may be contended that the so-called truths of science cannot be entirely 'value-free'' and by the same token the truths of ethics cannot be entirely 'fact-free'.

An uncritical version of ethical relativism is current among people. Bernard Williams has called it 'the anthropologist's heresy', and also 'vulgar relativism', and he has convincingly shown it to be absurd and inconsistent (1981: 132–43). This muddled doctrine was once popular with some 'liberal' colonialists. It asserts that there are ultimate moral disagreements among societies such that moral adjudication of right and wrong is always relative to a given society, and then it goes on to say that we are required to be equally well-disposed to everyone else's ethical beliefs, for it is wrong to condemn the moral values of others. While we might recognize its beneficial effect in the past, during the history of colonization, we need not be blind to the weakness of its theoretical foundation. It is sometimes claimed that we should not upset the essential value-structure of an underdeveloped or developing society by an imposition of the standards or norms of a developed Western society even if such imposition is required for the sake of economic progress, to implement, for example, a speedy transfer of modern technology. Whatever truth there may be in this claim, it seems to be not entirely unrelated to the relativism of the old 'liberal' colonialists. The liberal idea here is connected with the recognition (and fear) of oppression and violence, inflicted usually upon a third-world society in the name of progress, and in view of certain unwelcome results brought about by the modern technocrats in such societies, this may have some *moral* justification. The newly gained ecological consciousness would consider it a good thing not to destroy the environment in thoughtless urgency. But at a theoretical level this kind of ethical relativism has repugnant consequences, for it is not entirely free from the reflexes of colonialism. I shall argue that this is not just true of what Williams has dubbed 'vulgar relativism.' It is in general true of any significant form of ethical relativism. For even if some version of ethical relativism is shown to be coherent or free from inconsistency, it does not establish it as a (non-relatively) true doctrine. Coherence is the first step towards such establishment, but it is not the only step.

It has generally been argued that some version of relativism in ethics is not only coherent but also *true*. For example, we may refer to a version given by Bernard Williams (1981: 132–73). Gilbert Harman has formulated another coherent version (1982). These versions seem to avoid traditional and standard errors of relativism.

For Williams, the truth in relativism lies in the view that there may be two societies with divergent moral systems which will have only what he called 'notional confrontation' between them, one not being a 'real option' for the other, and hence the vocabulary of appraisal ('true-false', 'right-wrong' will have no genuine application. Unlike 'vulgar relativism', this version is free from inconsistency because the concept of 'notional confrontation' allows a form of thought for thinking about the moral concerns of different societies, but disallows any substantive relation of such concerns to our own concerns 'which alone can give any point or substance to the appraisal'. As long as confrontation stops short of being a 'real option', questions of appraisal, according to Williams, 'do not *genuinely* arise' (my emphasis). This seems to be an approximation of what I have called 'soft relativism', which allows incommensurability only as a limiting case. Williams, however, is well aware that there may be some non-standard errors in this view. For example, it is wrong to think today of a culture as completely individuated and self-contained vis-à-vis another comparable culture. In his own words, 'social practices could never come forward with a certificate saying that they belonged to a genuinely different culture, so that they are guaranteed immunity to other judgements and reactions' (1985, p. 158).

In more recent writings Williams (1985, p. 220), having dismissed the anthropologist's point that a non-relativistic doctrine of universal toleration can be based upon the incommensurability of cultural moral codes, has given a heavily qualified account of 'relativism of distance'. This theory envisions notional confrontation between past and present societies, as well as between future and present, and hence can justify the *epoché* of ethical evaluation only in this limited sense. But even this may seem inappropriate, as William concedes, under the historical pressure of a non-relativistic notion of social justice. This 'relativism of distance' seems to be flawless as a theoretical construct, but the non-relativistic notion of justice and equality may over time force an unjust caste-orientated or slave-orientated society to be transformed into a comparatively just one. I wish to comment here on one minor point raised by Williams. This concerns the asymmetrically related options.

It has been pointed out (by Williams) that while some version of modern technological life is a real option for members of surviving traditional societies, their life is not a real option for those belonging to modern technological societies, and this is true 'despite the passionate nostalgia of many'. This asymmetry seems to be simply the asymmetry of time or history, which is usually expressed in such clichés as 'we cannot recreate the past' or 'we can have only one-directional travel through time'. It is certainly true that we cannot live the life of a Greek Bronze Age chief. But it is not clear why Williams thinks that the option to 'go native' culturally is unavailable to modern Western people. Let us pursue this thought a little further. A so-called 'traditional' society today opts for technology along with understandable resistance from many sections, and thus constant readjustment or ongoing reassessment of traditional values (including value-rejection) is called for. When the dust settles down, it would be correct to say that for a member of a 'traditional society' of the third world the modern Western society has been a 'real option' (in Williams' sense). But that does not settle the question why for a member of the latter the former cannot be a real option. For if the member of a third-world traditional society can (if it is possible for him or her to do so) opt for modern Western life, it is as much possible (there is no theoretical barrier *a priori*) for a modern Western man or woman to opt for a life in the traditional society as long as such a society exists somewhere on this globe and knowledge about its value-structure and such is a matter of public knowledge. The 'nostalgia' of a Westerner that Williams refers to needs to be discouraged. For it is undoubtedly a form of neurotic behaviour. But it needs to be emphasized that there is no asymmetry of options here (except, of course, the asymmetry of time). It is also important to realize that when a 'traditional' society develops technology, it becomes a *new* society, not a replica or a blueprint of the so-called 'Western technological' society. It would be, to use Williams' own argument to fortify this point, 'too early or too late' for an Indian to be a westerner and vice versa. It would be too early when the thought of an alternative has not penetrated the consciousness of the Indian, and too late when he is already confronted with the new situation.

Another source of uneasiness in this 'soft' version of relativism is the fact that even a purely notional confrontation of two cultures can give substance to the vocabulary of appraisal. Short of circularity, it is difficult to see why a notional confrontation, which is a situation of confrontation between two cultures without one being a 'real option' for the other, must resolve into rendering the vocabulary of appraisal totally pointless. For we can use *substantially* such vocabulary where there are objective criteria or some other methods, and this possibility cannot be written off in any kind of confrontation.

I shall now examine another version of moral relativism, that which is propounded and defended by Harman. Harman talks about what he calls an 'inner moral judgement' that underlies the agent's motivating reasons to do what he does, and this motivational attitude concerns primarily intuitions of the agent and his peers to keep an agreement. The inner moral judgement is relative to such a tacit agreement. Harman distinguishes moral 'oughts' from other types of 'oughts', and separates the 'right' from the 'good' by focusing upon the agent's moral frame of reference: what he ought or ought not to have done (not what is or would have been a good or desirable act). The argument *seems* impeccable. But one can think of at least two serious flaws that lurk behind it. First, it has a very repugnant consequence. For, it implies that people like Hitler or the Maritians or a member of Murder, Incorporated, can *only* be called *evil* in our vocabulary; they cannot be *judged* to be wrongdoers. This consequence is openly admitted by Harman, and, indeed, he thinks this feature to be partly supportive of the correctness of this position (psychologically speaking, so the argument goes, it is more satisfying for us to call Hitler evil than simply state that what he was doing was wrong!). But what is psychologically satisfying may not be a good evidence for a correct doctrine. How can we separate the concept of evil from that of wrongdoing?

The argument here partly depends upon a sort of (indefensible) dogma about what is actually the correct linguistic intuition. It also lacks a practical content. It becomes necessary to conceive first of all the bizarre creatures coming from outer space and then declare the incomparability of the set of 'morals' or standards accepted in their bizarre society with that of ours. Such an argument seems to be *a priori*, if not circular. As far as the description of Hitler is concerned, what happens to be part of the rhetoric is assigned a literal meaning here. 'Hitler was a monster' becomes 'Hitler belongs to the society of monsters'. First we must be forced to assume that 'their' standards are entirely opposite to 'ours' (the 'alien creatures' must not be like us humans), and then it is an *a priori* argument to show that vocabularies of appraisals, which must get their meaning in relation to such 'agreed' standards, do not make sense across such different sets of standards. The worth of linguistic intuition can be stretched too far. It does not seem too odd to say in English that Hitler, being a rational human being, turned into a madman and committed most serious crimes against humanity, while it would be counter-intuitive to say that Hitler reached an inner 'moral' judgement following his *own* set of 'moral' principles and did those terrible things which he did. The latter part would be an affront to our usual feeling about morality. It is not clear here whether this is 'hard relativism' or 'soft relativism', whether the Martian good is incomprehensible to us or whether our standard simply does not apply there. It seems that Harman would prefer the second alternative. Then the point about psychological satisfaction in Harman's argument can be made to stand on its head. It is because we judge Hitler by our standard that we can condemn him as a wrongdoer (evil).

While Williams is well aware of the difficulties involved in clearly individuating cultures (he gets around this by talking about past and present and future societies), Harman uses science fiction (Martians), common fictions (Murder, Inc.), and 'fictionalized' history (Hitler) to individuate group moralities. Our point is, not that such groups or persons do not exist in our midst (with the exception of the Martians), but that unless we 'fictionalize' or imagine them to be *entirely beyond our pale*, that is, entirely unlike us, the argument loses its substance. These creatures have to share with us only a narrow form of rationality (to make the so-called 'inner moral judgement' possible), but not much else. We may decide to call them monsters (Hitler), mentally deranged or impaired persons (Murder, Inc), or subhumans, but then we have already judged them, that is, excluded them from our moral domain. We cannot expect the 'subhumans' to be moral.

There seems to be an undue assumption that these familiar figures—Hitler, members of Murder, Inc—must be beyond the pale, like the outer-space creatures, and would feel no moral compunction (no inner conflict) in deciding to act in the way they act. This might have led Harman to construe moral relativism in the way he did. It seems that the problem of translation is not the issue here. For we can presumably interpret the Martian activity, or the act of the member of Murder, Inc, by following generally the attribution of beliefs to the Martian and by the Davidsonian hermeneutical triangle of meaning, belief, and action (Davidson, 1980, 1984). But if termination of one's life in a particular way is believed to be *murder* by both the Martians and us, then one cannot stop short of calling the agent a murderer or morally condemning both the agent and the act. If we can attribute other factual beliefs to the Martians, by the same token we would have to attribute to them some of our basic beliefs about values. But on Harmanian theory we simply attribute a sort of rationality (conscious reasoning to reach the inner judgment) to them but not anything else. The point again is not that such persons do not exist but that in the context of moral judgement either we allow them the honour of belonging to the human race and then morally condemn them for their deeds or, as in the case of mentally impaired persons, we may treat them as subhuman, which will be also a (moral) judgement, and relativism will thus lose much of its purchase. Otherwise there seems to be in Harmanian *epoché* an uncanny resonance of the role of the 'tolerant' liberal colonialists or the old confusion of the anthropologists. The 'unconscious' of such liberal colonialists nurtures contempt for the 'savage' practices of the natives, while outwardly there is exemplary unconcern: 'they are not like US!' Once again relativism becomes (mistakenly) a plea for so-called universal tolerance, but in reality one suspects it to be a hedge for a 'put-down' of the alien society.[2]

A classic example of the conflict situation is offered at the beginning of the celebrated Hindu text, the *Bhagavad-Gītā* and the solution therein offers a striking but not entirely unjustified parallelism with Harman's version of moral relativism. Arjuna, the warrior, is torn by conflict on the eve of the battle of Kurukṣetra whether he ought to fight or not, whether he ought to kill his relatives including his honorable grandfather and his teacher in order to recover his kingdom, or quit the battlefield and accept a more modest form of life (a recluse, cf. *bhaikṣyam apīha loke*) to avoid the moral consequences of his impending act of violence. Lord Kṛṣṇa (i.e., somebody like Hare's 'archangel' or even Arjuna's own alter ego) advised to fight. Chief among Kṛṣṇa's arguments was an appeal to the *agreed upon* moral code of the *kṣatriya* caste to which Arjuna belonged. One might say that this was an ideal case (instantiation) of the Harmanian notion of inner moral judgement. For here someone, S, (Kṛṣṇa) says that A (Arjuna) *morally* ought to do D (fighting, killing of relatives), and Kṛṣṇa assumes that Arjuna intends to act in accordance with an agreement (moral code of the Kṣatriya caste or group), and thus Arjuna has reasons to fight (reasons endorsed by Kṛṣṇa and other members of the Kṣatriya caste).

Some critics, both traditional and modern, have repeatedly pointed out that this is a morally dubious position. Arjuna wanted to be a moral hero and not answer the call of his vocation as an actual hero. His vocation was to kill and conquer everybody in the battlefield. He wanted to avoid the morally repugnant consequences of the war by his last-minute decision of withdrawal. In this move he wanted to respond to the pressure of *dharma* of a different kind. As a human being, as a member of the royal family, as a devoted grandson, as a student, and so on he was responding, temporarily at least, to another (different) set of *dharma*, ideals, or standards. Arjuna's dilemma was genuine, for he was both a member of Kṣatriya caste (one *dharma*) and a member of the (royal) family with filial and brotherly duties (another *dharma*). But Kṛṣṇa's advice was that the ethical code of the Kṣatriya caste (which was arguably not very different from that of Murder, Inc., of Harman) must take precedence in this case over other *dharmas*. Within the narrow confines of the caste duties the logic seems impeccable. However, one feels irresistibly that something is morally amiss here. If the story of the *Gītā* were a single episode and the larger background of *Mahābhārata* were forgotten, then Arjuna's dilemma would not seem to be very different from that of the young man in Sartre's much discussed example who, in an occupied country, has to decide whether to join the resistance movement and thereby bring punishment upon his family or remain with the family and protect his parents.

The member of Murder, Inc, in Harman's description does not have to be a mentally deranged person, but some sort of lobotomy should be performed by Murder, Inc, on its designated member to make him immune to any moral compunction towards his decision to kill not only the innocent bank manager but also, say, his father or son or wife or his beloved, simple at 'duty's' call. (Remember that he has to *kill*, not simply terminate the life-motion of a human body.) The Harmanian assumption is that one through rational choice has to be exclusively and solely a member of a group, that is, simply a *kṣatriya* or a Murder, Inc, member, not anything else, not a father, or a son, or a lover. The recent case of Nezar Hindawi sending his unsuspecting pregnant girlfriend to blow up the El-Al plane is also a case in point. Here we meet the familiar 'fanatic' of Hare, who might have had a 'mental' lobotomy through strict indoctrination.

The Harmanian version of relativism shifts our attention from the act to the agent, and in this sense the theory is agent-dependent: we cannot morally condemn the person but only the acts. The argument is sound, but is this plausible? If an alternative explanation of the phenomenon on which Harman's argument essentially depends—the agent's apparently conflict-free conviction about his own moral commitment to which he would not subject others—can be made equally plausible, such an argument for relativism will have very little significance. Harman's argument seems to depend upon an implicit appeal to our *felt* sense of unfairness of morally condemning a person (for doing something) using standards that are not his own or about which he is unaware or to which he is uncommitted. But this may be a 'false' feeling. How can we write off the commitment of a responsible human being to protect life rather than destroy it? Even Arjuna felt that he was committed to a set of norms other than the *dharma* of a *kṣatriya*. Multiple-group membership or multiplicity of commitments is a well-attested phenomenon, but this cannot be a sufficient ground for any significant form of relativism. Pluralism is not relativism. Conflict does not prove relativism.

The case of the *Gītā* may be analysed differently. Although I have disapprovingly referred above to Kṛṣṇa's argument to persuade Arjuna to fight in the *Bhagavad-Gītā*, in order to show my disapproval of the moral relativism that may be implicit in Kṛṣṇa's initial argument, I do not maintain that Kṛṣṇa's final advice to fight would not have any nonrelativistic moral justification. In the larger context of the epic *Mahābhārata*, of which the *Gītā* is only a part, this does have a justification. In the tally of wrongdoings of both sides, the Kauravas and the Pāṇḍavas, Duryodhana (of the Kauravas) certainly exceeded the Pāṇḍavas in malignity by deliberately inflicting unforgivable humiliation upon Draupadī, the rather innocent daughter-in-law of the family. By claiming similarly that what Nezar Hindawi did (even if he did it without any compunction or inner conflict, in which case he is mentally deranged in.our terminology) was morally wrong, I do not claim nor do I imply in any other way that the Palestinian cause is unjust or morally wrong. They are decidedly different issues. But this point is not relevant here.

We may distinguish between the anthropologist's claim of moral relativism across cultures and the sort of (intracultural) relativism forced upon us sometimes due to either the alleged non-cognitive conception of ethical discourse or persistent disagreement (presumably irresoluble) in valuings within a community. One is intimately connected with the other, but we are concerned here directly with intercultural moral relativism. There is a tendency among philosophers to conflate the two. Although sometimes it is harmless, this slide between intercultural variety of norms and intracultural disagreements about moral principles or moral theories (such as Kantian or utilitarian or egoistic) is, to say the least, confusing. Whether different moral theories (or principles) recognized and well-respected within a given culture are reconcilable or not is decidedly a different issue from cultural (ethical) relativism which is arguable on the basis of such notions as incomprehensibility, incommensurability, and untranslatability. It is, however, possible to see intracultural *variation* in valuing as something that is to be explained as reflecting 'ways of life', not as reflecting variable perceptions of objective values. In that case, as we will see in the next section, we have reason to believe that intracultural (moral) relativism is only a special case of cultural relativism.

2. THE ANTHROPOLOGIST'S DILEMMA

Ethical systems are believed to rest on basic axiomatic constructions of reality that are ingrained in different worldviews or cosmologies. Therefore, the anthropologists have argued, relativism is inescapable, for such axiomatic constructions of reality are irreducibly varied, being part and parcel of different cultures.

These culture-relative axiomatic constructions are presumably conditioned by human cognitive abilities, their capacity to synthesize sensory inputs, to process them in order to formulate their informational content and to abstract from them generalities. Our anthropologists argue that they have empirical evidence for showing that these cognitive abilities vary from culture to culture, group to group. The Eskimos, for example, have a large number of words in their vocabulary for 'snow,' for they can certainly perceive more features of the 'snow' phenomenon to which we are presumably blind. Here the premise of the anthropologists is not in dispute; the conclusion is. For the premise does not entail mutual incomprehensibility of cultural constructs, nor even the incommensurability of the standards of valuing across cultures. What it proves is pluralism. There is, however, another component of the anthropologists' argument, a *reductio ad absurdum*, which makes relativism a plausible and attractive hypothesis. Some of the alien's beliefs or his alleged standards of valuings *appear* to be irrational by our own reckoning. Since it would be 'absurd' to attribute irrationality to the alien, we content that these standards (or 'beliefs') are rational when interpreted within the context of his own worldview, which is different from ours. Hence relativism saves the embarrassment of the liberal anthropologist who finds comfort in the thought that of course 'we' are superior beings (rational) while 'they' are not.

There is another way of arguing the same point. Different norms need not be incommensurable. Two systems are incommensurable when they not only have different constitutive rules but are also rivals such that (in the Quinean sense) there is 'no fact of the matter' to decide in favour of either. Thus, different cultural constructs may or may not entail the thesis of incommensurability. But the anthropologist can still argue that even commensurability may not give rise to 'real confrontation' or to a 'real option' in Williams' sense. The core values of a culture, the relativist insists, are immanent in its collective activities, in its myths, rituals, kinship systems, customs, in standard interpersonal behaviour, and they account for our motivation for action. The culture's ethical system is not available externally for real confrontation with another separately. So we have relativism. This seems to be akin to a Quinean indeterminacy thesis where many acceptable but conflicting translations are possible among schemes (there being 'no fact of the matter' to decide in favour of any). To wit: the embeddedness of ethical norms defies piecemeal options. Internally coherent worldviews as wholes are competitors; there is no Archimedian point from which to choose one over the other. Moreover, prospects for any change or option for such embedded norms would necessarily require destruction of the culture as a whole.

This picture is in accord with the social scientist's conception of ethical relativism. It rejects ethical absolutes in a way that is reminiscent of the Athenian sceptics (Sextus), who obtained quietude and abstained from the rashness of dogmatism through consideration of comparative ethnography (Needham, 1985, p. 35). I believe such scepticism cannot be easily dismissed.

Modern ethnographers, however, would allow that a conscious 'individual' belonging to a particular culture may self-consciously be able to articulate explicitly and discursively the ethical norms embedded in his culture. In the process he would have to distance him from his culture or community and develop an internal critique for looking across boundaries in order to have the *real* options derivable from his knowledge and acquaintance of other cultures. But the doings of such an individual cannot seriously affect relativism. The individual who chooses to be 'outcast.' in this way may be regarded as a new community with perhaps only one member, but then his ethical norms would be embedded in his changed, or thoroughly modified, world-view or cosmology. They would be, in other words, part and parcel of his own axiomatic constructions of reality. To cite an example, in a traditional Indian society, the highly Westernized people formed without difficulty and perhaps unconsciously a distinct and distinguishable separate community of their own vis-à-vis the old traditional society, and we can witness the possibility of 'peaceful' coexistence and not real confrontation or conflict between such distinct cultural groups or subgroups.

We may make a further concession in an attempt to vindicate relativism and refuse to accept the 'gap' between cultures, between 'we' and 'they'. Cultures, as indeed we have noted above, are never found completely individuated and self-contained vis-à-vis other cultures. But during contacts and confrontation traits are borrowed freely and then integrated into the borrowing culture's worldview or cosmology. The core of the culture, however, shows resilience and resistance to any radical change. Hence, traits or new values that cannot be integrated with the core are ignored or rejected. A cultural anthropologist observes such resilience and resistance and hence concludes that there is cultural continuity, and therefore the sets of ethical norms ingrained in such cultures, or ways of life, with their priorities among virtues and their dependent moral rules, are also preserved intact, precluding any real option through real confrontation.

This is another powerful argument. It would, if true, uphold the sort of relativism that is not obviously incoherent. It does not depend upon mutual incomprehensibility, or completely on incommensurability. A culture is compared with a language (Wittgensteinian 'language-game'). This analogy, for the relativists, has a deep consequence. A culture, like a natural language, apart from satisfying some common need of the people, has to grow within the constraints of a particular history and geography over a period of time, developing its particular norms and vocabulary. The recognition of the 'particularity' in the study of cultures, as well as awareness of diversity in ideals for a complete life and in standard patterns of admired activity, naturally makes room for a sort of ethical relativism wherein values of different cultures cannot be assessed against each other, moralities cannot be compared or criticized, much in the same way the grammatical peculiarities of one language cannot be evaluated against those in another language. It is a good analogy, but can it be sustained?

I shall now argue that this is not quite right. (1) Noticing that a culture resists drastic changes in norms, we may unconsciously be driven to a belief in the immutability of the norms or the central core of a culture—a belief that may well amount to a sort of 'essentialism'. Arguably, during violent interface between cultures (and it does not matter whether confrontation is real or notional), if there is asymmetry in power and richness, either the central core of the weaker culture is destroyed or it maintains a very precarious and mutilated existence. This empirical fact, however, does not show that the essentialist dogma is well-founded.

Once we give up the 'essentialist's' dogma, we would find it natural to talk not about mutilation or destruction but mutation and change. Violence or aggression would still be present due to alleged asymmetry, but that is a different issue. Any form of oppression is repulsive, and insouciant relativism may be a veil for negative oppression or neglect. In a dynamic world, however, cultural norms cannot remain immutable. In the context of ongoing mutation and change the reinforcement of peculiarities in the pursuit of a distinguishing ideal will have its trade-offs, will entail a sacrifice or suppression of some other dispositions that were previously admired or are now admired in other ways of life. Such value trade-offs are features of any living and growing culture. A culture is like a living organism: it grows and changes and adapts itself to the ever-changing environments. In this process 'sour grapes' are many. But by contrast, if an organism loses this behaviour of *adaptive preference formations* (Elster, 1982a, pp. 219–38), it becomes a piece of dead wood to be preserved in a museum. Everything has a cost, even growth or survival. Therefore, if a culture modifies itself over a period of time vis-à-vis another culture, the ethical norms embedded in it must take the same route.

Particularly during an interface, both sides (weak and strong) go through a 'conversion' procedure, the asymmetry is only in degrees of modification. This fact seems to conflict with the assumption of any significant form of relativism. There may not be any real appraisal by someone standing apart using transcultural standards of evaluation, but internal forces of both cultures, which make interaction possible, would make the possibility of such appraisal at least compatible.

(2) This modified relativism still seems to be open to the Davidsonian objection against conceptual relativism: 'Different points of view make sense, but only if there is a common coordinate system on which to plot them; yet the existence of a common system belies the claim of dramatic incomparability' (Davidson, 1984, p. 67). The phrase 'axiomatic constructions of reality' obviously presupposes the scheme-content duality. This duality is unintelligible, for we cannot find an intelligible basis on which it can be said that schemes are different. However, the 'looseness of fit' (that no doubt exists) between the commonly shared world or the broad base of humanity on the one hand, and the different interesting things people want to do and/or talk about on the other hand, may give some content to the supposition of different conceptual schemes, for this seems to bypass the Davidsonian objection. But even this alleged Davidsonian lack of concern for alternative interests (Hacking, 1982, pp. 61–2) need not frighten the liberalists, for the Davidsonian dismissal of the third dogma (of the duality of scheme and content) is compatible with the

open-endedness of certain types of dialogue or statements which may accommodate alternative interests. But this does not support ethical relativism in any 'exciting' form. Acceptance of plurality of interest does not amount to relativism, as we have noted already. Among music lovers, for example, there will always be those that are for the latest pop music, while others will prefer Mozart.

(3) Stuart Hampshire has argued that there are 'two faces of morality' (1983, pp. 2–3)—the rational side and the less than rational, the historically and geographically conditioned, the less than fully articulate side. This distinction seems to coincide with the intuition which led the Indian ethicists to champion group-relative *dharmas*, on the one hand, and distinguish between, on the other hand, what they called *sādhāraṇa dharma* and *viśeṣa dharma*. These two aspects of morality, the 'universalizing' and the 'particularizing' aspects, underline the distinction between two modes of understanding and explaining—one is more natural in natural sciences and the other in social sciences, in linguistics and historical studies. Social science may emulate natural science, but the gap will always be there as long as it has one foot rooted in humanistic studies, and if this is uprooted, social science would not be social science. What the cultural anthropologists notice, the embeddedness of a certain set of values in a given culture, may indeed be true, but in accepting this we should not overlook another layer of values, another aspect of moral norms, those that relate to the abstract and universal, species-wide requirements derived from basic human necessities. This is sometimes reflected in our talk about a distinction between mores and morality. Our supposition is that there may indeed be some sort of incommensurability, or 'undercommensurability,' and hence a sort of relativism among cultural norms as far as the 'particularizing', the historically conditioned, and therefore in some sense contingent, side of morality, is concerned (cf. *viśeṣa dharma*). This side naturally offers the strongest resistance to change during confrontation and interaction, although in a dynamic world nothing that is a 'particular' or a 'concrete' object is totally immune to mutation. But there is also that more general side of morality, those aspects that respond to man's need as a biological creature, and of which only he himself is aware and capable of doing something about, not the other creatures.

To articulate this culture-neutral side of morality is not an easy task. These values or value-experiences may not be totally immutable across cultures or over time, but there is some sort of constancy in them to make them enduring and invariant. Being pressed further, one may provide a list of (invariant) moral virtues, something like what the Indian ethicists called the set of *sādhāraṇa dharma*. Granted that the exact definition of these virtues would be debatable, moral philosophers, surprisingly, have seldom spent time on the articulation of such basic virtues. Alternatively, one may develop a thesis that pleasure and pain in some basic (but specific) sense provide such reasons for action as is agent-neutral (Nagel) or even culture-neutral. Or one may investigate whether the Rawlsian notion of 'primary goods' which include liberty and opportunity, income and wealth, the bases of wealth, and so on or Sen's notion of 'basic capabilities', need for nutritional requirements, for participation in social life, and so on, which are recognizably culture-dependent, can be sharpened and modified to provide a basis for articulating culture-transcendent (culture-neutral) values.[3] Or, one may develop a viable concept of human need. As Phillipa Foot has said (1982: 164),

> Granted that it is wrong to assume identity of aim between peoples of different cultures: nevertheless there is a great deal that all men have in common. All need affection, the cooperation of others, a place in a community, and help in trouble.

It may be that the Martians, if they exist, are differently constituted. But we are talking of human need and want. It is important to realize that the Martian culture is deemed to be 'alien' in one sense, but a third-world culture or a tribal culture is 'alien' in a different, much less exaggerated sense. To call them 'human' is to attribute to them certain dispositions, certain patterns of beliefs and propensities to desire things, and dispositions to act so as to avoid excessive pain and suffering and to want pleasures. Attribution of beliefs, desires, and want is a 'package deal'; certain modes of valuings cannot be separated from it.

3. DIVERSITY AND REALITY

The lesson from comparative ethnography need not engender universal scepticism about moral values. The problem cases, the irrational beliefs, or bizarre ethical principles of alien cultures may be given alternative explanation without assuming relativism. If we take their apparent bizarreness or irrationality to be coming from the fact that they are judged by the standards of a modern Western world-view, we veer toward relativism. It satisfies the 'liberal conscience, wary of ethnocentrism.' As Charles Taylor (1982, p. 99) has remarked, 'It takes the heat off; we no longer have to judge whose way of life is superior.' But if instead we shift our attention from the property 'apparent bizarreness' to the locus of that property, the principles or moral beliefs, and examine whether they really qualify as moral principles or beliefs in the strict sense that we tend to attach to them, we might be in for a surprise. False starts are many. It may be that what we take to be the moral or factual belief of the alien vis-à-vis our own (contrary) moral or factual belief is simply a (wrong) construal by us of the alien's behaviour from what he apparently says and does, in which case we need not christen it as a moral or factual belief and a *fortiori* need not attribute irrationality or bizarrerie to such mental states. Inferential errors are very common.

The anthropologists usually christen such dubious, unexamined, and hence irrational mental states as full-fledged beliefs and then turn to explain their alleged bizarrerie with recourse to symbolism, metaphors, or non-literal interpretation. But symbolism has its own problems. Relativism becomes a smooth doctrine to get rid of the rough edges of such symbolism (Sperber, 1982).

Alternatively, we may be content with the attribution of beliefs and values to the alien and follow the Davidsonian line (1980) that such beliefs and wants cause action. But irrational human action or behaviour may be furnished with a number of psychological explanations, wishful thinking, adaptive preferences, self-deception, rationalization, and so on. Thus, I believe, a view of human irrationality (rather than a *separate* worldview conceived by the relativist) can offer causal explanation of the genesis of the alien's irrational beliefs and values and the actions prompted by them. Sometimes social historical explanation of bizarre behaviour is in order.

Despite the so-called 'culture shocks', quaintness, and sometimes a bizarre feeling which a member of one culture experiences when confronted with an 'alien' culture (for those interested, I refer to the poem by Craig Rains, *A Martian Sends a Postcard Home*) a cross-cultural assessment of certain central ethical issues is not only possible but also probable.[4] As E. Gellner (1982, pp. 185–6) has pointed out, the anthropologists seldom report complete *failure* coming back from a field trip; they often report success or partial failure.[5] Yet

on the often rather *a priori* reasoning of relativist philosophers, who start out from doctrines such as ultimacy and self-sufficiency of 'forms of life', we might have expected such failure to be much more common. It is *success* in explaining culture A in the language of culture B which is, in the light of such a philosophy, really puzzling.

Admission of diversity resulting from normal, post-enlightenment humility, as well as open-mindedness to learn 'what else' is there, does not amount to any exciting form of relativism which may be objected to by a realist. The enlightened, self-conscious modern citizen thinks (with some justification) that if his own right to recommend a moral norm for another person (his neighbour) is as thorny a question as the justification of morality itself, the more so it must be to recommend a moral norm to a distant culture-group. This may induce humility and tolerance, and perhaps it demands—rightly I believe—patience, care and caution lest we prejudicially judge, when we try to understand and interpret the alien's ethical code. When the so-called code becomes sufficiently *transparent* to us, so that we can also rank it, the 'excitement' of relativism subsides. One may of course decide, despite transparency, to refrain respectfully from ranking or judging it, as, in Harman's example, the pacifist who has conscientious objection to war may, with respect, refuse to judge others who do not have such an objection. But this refusal of the pacifist, *pace* Harman, does not support any interesting kind of relativism. It can be explained in terms of the lack of interest on the part of the pacifist to analyse the situation any further or to make any comparative value judgement. What is politically expeditious may not be ethically relevant. The point is whether recognition of *difference* can always be morally neutral.

Cultural relativism is actually a recommended hypothetical construct, being in fact instrumental to our understanding of a culture from the internalist's viewpoint. In practice, however, cultures and subcultures do *flow* into one another. They are rarely like *dead* watertight compartments. We may reassert the earlier point about the improbability of finding two fully individuable, clearly self-contained and self-sufficient cultures for an effective theoretical contrast. In the interaction both sides get modified, though sometimes subtly and imperceptibly. Side by side there are many cases of irrational formation of mental states, wishful thinking, possible self-deception, and adaptive preferences. People do react and respond under confrontation, and by then it is *too late* for the *epoché* or the relativists. If, however, we talk about the preconfrontation period, ethical relativism then should either remain unformulated or be only an idle hypothetical construct to be formulated in the post-confrontation period.

Much has been made of the Wittgensteinian notion of 'forms of life' or even that of his 'language-game'. But, as Williams has argued, the issue here was not really relativism (1981: 160), for otherwise, if the relativist element is added to the notion, we face 'the gravest difficulty' in the philosophy of social sciences. We have to posit the existence of culturally distinct groups with different worldviews and hold at the same time that our access to them is inescapably and non-trivially conditioned by our own worldview. And this cannot stop short of what Williams calls 'aggregative solipsism' (1981, p. 158). The relativist story about the plurality of 'forms of life' should therefore be taken with a pinch of salt. As Paul Seabright has recently argued (1987, p. 27), the social scientist's explanation of 'forms of life' (even in the Wittgensteinian sense) is not only possible but necessary, and sometimes this explanation will be directly causal in nature. One might similarly argue that transcultural criticism of ethical norms is equally possible. Just as the causal explanation cannot by itself require us to alter our practices, transcultural criticism may similarly not be enough to effect the value-rejection. But it can certainly illuminate our understanding of ethical norms, ours as well as theirs.

4. CONFRONTATION AND CONVERGENCE

Introducing a contrast between nature and convention, some philosophers maintain that ethical norms are based mostly or entirely upon convention or cultural underpinnings and not upon 'the naked man' (as Hampshire once put it, 1983, p. 142). But man is not only a cultural creature; he is also a natural biological creature. It is 'the naked man' whose needs, pleasures, pains and wants would have extreme relevance to many basic issues of ethics. The description of man is not exhausted by a complete enumeration of properties that result from his cultural underpinnings alone. If we strip him or her of all cultural underpinnings, we reach 'the naked man'. It is generally easy to ascertain that the group heritage or the collective personality is sometimes glorified by such expressions as 'national character'. But most of what are presumed to constitute the 'national character' of a group may simply be some persisting peculiarities that distinguish a group of people from their neighbours as well as determine the set of responses they make to various situational questions. An ethical code determined by such contingencies would *ex hypothesi* be culture-relative, and the anthropologists' point about embeddedness would be true of such codes. But this does not affect our argument in favour of a set of basic values concordant with the value-experiences of the 'naked man'. The common dispositions, constitutive of the concept of 'the naked man', may be recognized as numerous simple facts about needs, wants and desires, for example, removal of suffering, love of justice, courage in the face of injustice, pride, shame, love of children, delight, laughter, happiness. In other words, the connotation of our 'naked man' need not be some intractable human essence. The suggested commonness of responses and emotions does not presuppose the essentialist dogma.

There is a substantive ethical insight in the modern discussion of both contractualism and utilitarianism—it is the universal attribution of moral personality. On this assumption we regard that other human agents, including agents in the so-called 'alien' culture which is confronted by us or which confronts us, are, as subjects of practical reasoning, on the same footing as ourselves. Such basic insight into the nature of moral thinking itself is derived as much from Kant as from other ethical philosophers. This insight, when it is properly comprehended, may require us to transcend the practical problems presented by the bewildering variety of ethical codes across cultures and to assess the intercultural valuings. In the ultimate analysis, or as a sequel to a series of confrontations and interactions, one may imagine the possibility in the future of a convergence of certain basic, culturally invariant ethical norms. The question arises whether there is any substance to this thought at all.

We have distinguished, à la Hampshire, between moral norms that are local and culture-relative and those that are culture-invariant. It is not unthinkable that a partial convergence, if not a full one, is possible through proper confrontation and clash between cultures, a convergence, not necessarily of local moral norms, but of course of the basic ethical norms, to the extent these norms and ideals are responses to the needs of the 'naked man'. Some local norms may be more deeply entrenched in a desired and respected way of life in a given society. Preference for this way of life would have to be 'perfectly prudent preference' (to use a phrase from Hare), that is, it has to be what someone would desire if fully informed and unconfused. To exclude the slave-society or the caste-society we have to banish 'anti-social' and 'irrational' preferences from this set of preferences, and then we can justifiably apply the term 'moral' to such norms. Such parochial moral norms may remain non-convergent even when a confrontation of cultures takes place. The internal dynamism (within a culture) looks beyond the cultural boundaries (and unconsciously towards a sort of convergence where singularism may be a guiding principle). Since today's world is not cut up into self-contained bits, this internal dynamism seems to be enhanced, leading to value-rejection or value-acceptance or both, and this need not always be 'sour grapes'.

The claim of the non-relativist is minimal: certain basic moral principles are neither agent-relative nor contingent upon any specific type of social order. These principles are sometimes claimed to flow from the 'nature' of human needs. One may understand this as an attempt to uncover a core of shared rationality that is reached by gradually peeling off or stripping down the overlay of distinctive cultural mores, local customs and individual idiosyncrasies. It may be that the vision of convergence foresees the existence of One World and hence is little more than an idle pipedream. But the non-relativist may say in reply that there is already One World for us to share, although we neither have, nor do we need, *one kind of man* to share that One World. All that the liberalism of post-enlightenment of even the post-Second World War period wants to preserve and maintain as valuable, and for fear of whose loss the liberal philosophers are prone to embrace relativism, would remain unthreatened by our admission of the singularity of the world alongside diversity of peoples. Although the prospect for convergence is necessarily foreseen by one kind of person, one special group perhaps, it is accessible, to be sure, to all kinds of people, without its being the case now (or even in some foreseeable future) that all do accept it. If this position is akin to moral singularism, it is at such a basic level that it does not encourage moral jingoism, or an attitude of 'holier-than-thou' towards an 'alien' culture. Our theory is, however, that an alien culture cannot remain totally 'alien' after confrontation and interaction. In this context we decry the talk of relativism that is often used as a ploy (or a pseudo-philosophical defence) for keeping the culture of a subdued group completely separated in a protected area, as a museum piece or an 'endangered' zoological species. For it becomes a modern version of liberal colonialism caught on the wrong foot. There seems to be an echo of this point in Dan Sperber's not-so-popular comment:

> In pre-relativist anthropology, Westerners thought of themselves as superior to all other people. Relativism replaced this despicable hierarchical gap by a kind of cognitive apartheid (1982, pp. 179-180).

The position which I am defining is sensitive to the liberalist's worries but avoids his blunder of being too sympathetic to relativism. It is mildly optimistic about convergence and mildly predictive of singularism at a certain basic level. But it accommodates pluralism (and regards it as a contingency) with respect to the *viśeṣa dharma* or culture-relative (local or parochial) norms. It may at the same time be compatible with such pluralism as would assume that a single coherent ordering of goods is not only desirable but also possible. Rather it would endorse a sort of agnosticism (though not scepticism) about the possibility of resolving conflicts of (intercultural as well as intracultural) moral principles through only rational means. It only allows that there would be certain contingent factors (alongside reason) which could resolve (causally) many 'practical' ethical conflicts. This position also concedes that while some principles may be objectively better than others, we may recognize only this much without exactly recognizing which ones. (There is a limit to human capacity at any time.) To return to Putnam, 'belief in a pluralistic ideal is not the same thing as belief that every ideal of human flourishing is as good as every other's (1981, p. 148). In recommending clearer understanding among humans for the convergence of certain vital interests and goals, we do not recommend elimination of all different natural languages, or a return to the pre-Tower-of-Babel period. Clearer and unambiguous understanding does not necessarily require use of only *one* natural language by all.

The significant, and perhaps the central, issue in relativism is that the moral principles are culture-relative in a way that we can either apply the predicate 'neither right nor wrong' or 'neither true nor false' to such principles or judgements reached thereby, or we can say 'such questions do not arise'. In this sense this is reminiscent of the last alternative (*koṭi*) of the Buddhist or Nāgārjunian tetralemma: 'Is it? Is it not? Is it both? Is it neither?' I shall therefore conclude with a comment on Nāgārjuna. We should remember that Nāgārjuna rejected all the alternatives including the 'neither-nor'. This will show that the description of Nāgārjuna's Mādhyamika philosophy as relativism is entirely wrong. I believe 'The Middle Way' is not relativism in any significant sense. If the Buddhist tetralemma is not just a puzzle presented to confound our intellect, the lesson to be learnt here may be that the doctrine is closer to nonrelativism than what is ordinarily assumed. By rejecting the previous alternatives Nāgārjuna no doubt rejected the forms of realism that were current during his time. But by rejecting the fourth alternative he did reject relativism too and perhaps hinted by his *upāya-kauśalya* that a return to realism without dogma is not only possible but also advisable. This may bring us back to reality but not to the original *construction* of reality that was refuted already by Nāgārjuna; it is a new open-ended way of dealing with reality without the usual dogmas of empiricism. The Mādhyamikas do not give up the world.

Notes and References

1. I am grateful to R. Needham, G.A. Cohen, J. Lipner, M. Nussbaum, A. Chakrabarti, G. Spivak, M. Kraust, and A.K. Sen for their comments on an earlier draft of this essay. Another version of this essay was presented at the Plenary Session of Extraordinary World Congress of Philosophy held at Cordoba, Argentina, 20–6 September 1987. Some comments on the anthropologist's dilemma were inspired by a letter from F. Marglin.

2. It should be admitted that Harman's defence of relativism is logically faultless. The problems that we have mentioned lie with the assumptions or premises. For example, he insists on the notion of agreement in intuitions and answers a point about a slave-society. There, after insisting that 'this society was to be one in which no aspects of the moral understanding shared by the masters spoke against slavery' (p. 203), he concedes, 'in fact that is unlikely, since there is *some* arbitrariness in the idea that people are to be treated in different ways depending on whether they are both slave or free' (his emphasis). I have simply insisted upon this arbitrariness, once we accept the agents as people.
3. I say this with much trepidation and recognize that neither the protagonists (Rawls and Sen) described these notions as culture-neutral. It is arguable whether these notions will have transcultural validity in any significant sense, for they have developed in a culture-specific manner. But I believe they may be given culture-neutral significance and still retain their substantive moral values to the extent that they respond to the needs of the 'naked man'.
4. Ethnocentrism is, however, a state of mind. The members or some members of an ethnic group could be so ethnocentric, and therefore so blind to anything admirable—even comprehensible—in other peoples' culture, that they can really be identified with the ethnocentric inhabitants of Escher's 'different worlds' in his famous painting *Relativity*. Contacts between these inhabitants of different worlds (though they may make use of the same staircase) are in Escher's conception out of the question. The utterly ethnocentric person cannot even make the first move to comprehend that there are 'other worlds', much like the celebrated frog (in the Indian parable of 'the Frog and the Well') who, living all his life in the well, never comprehended that there was a world outside. There may be a possible paradox here. Relativism is the suggested way to overcome ethnocentrism, while (extreme) ethnocentrism provokes hard relativism. The first significant step to overcome such ethnocentrism is not only to recognize that there are others but also to comprehend that their beliefs and acts may to some extent be incommensurable with ours. But then they may also be, under certain circumstances, real options for us. Thus, even soft relativism may dissolve. The reference to Craig Rains is thankfully received from P. Mitter.
5. A comment made by B. Scharfestein in private correspondence may be relevant here. 'Each of the relativist philosophers seems to have a front door that opens on lonely incommensurables, relatives too distant to be sure they understand anything of one another, but a back door that opens on a common world, in which neighbours talk companionably across their fences.'

Davidson, D. 1980. *Essays on Actions and Events*. Oxford: Clarendon Press.
———. 1984. *Truth and Interpretation*. Oxford: Clarendon Press.
Elster, J. 1982a, 'Sour Grapes—Utilitarianism and the Genesis of Wants.' In *Utilitarianism and Beyond*, ed. A. Sen and B. Williams. Cambridge: Cambridge University Press.

———. 1982b, 'Belief, Bias and Ideology.' In *Rationality and Relativism*, ed. Hollis and Lukes, pp. 123–48.

Foot, P. (1982), 'Moral Relativism'. In *Relativism: Cognitive & Moral*, pp. 152–66. (see Harman, 1982).

Gellner, E. 1982. 'Relativism and Universals.' In *Rationality and Relativism*, pp. 181–200.

Hacking, I. 1982. 'Language, Truth and Reason.' In *Rationality and Relativism*, pp. 48–66.

Hampshire, S. 1983. *Morality and Conflict.* Oxford: Blackwell.

Hare, R.M. 1981. *Moral Thinking.* Oxford: Clarendon Press.

Harman, G. 1982. 'Moral Relativism Defended.' In *Relativism: Cognitive and Moral*, ed. J.W. Meiland and N. Krausz. Notre Dame: University of Notre Dame Press, pp. 189–204.

Hollis, M. and S. Lukes (eds). 1982, *Rationality and Relativism.* Oxford: Blackwell.

Mackie, J.L. 1977. *Ethics: Inverting Right & Wrong*. Middlesex: Pelican Books.

Needham, R. 1985. *Exemplars.* Berkeley: University of California Press.

Putnam, H. 1981. *Reason, Truth and History*. Cambridge: Cambridge University Press.

Quine, W.V. 1960. *Word and Object*. Cambridge, Mass.: M.I.T. Press.

Rawls, J. 1972. *A Theory of Justice.* Oxford: Oxford University Press.

Seabright, P. 1987. 'Explaining Cultural Divergence: A Wittgensteinian Paradox.' *Journal of Philosophy* (January 1987).

Sen, A.K. 1979. 'Equality of What?' Tanner Lectures.

Sperber, D. 1982. 'Apparently Irrational Beliefs.' In *Rationality and Relativism*, pp. 149–80.

Taylor, C. 1982. 'Rationality.' In *Rationality and Relativism*, pp. 87–105.

Williams, B. 1981. *Moral Luck.* Cambridge: Cambridge University Press.

———. 1985. *Ethics and the Limits of Philosophy.* London: Penguin Books.

Wittgenstein, L. 1958. *Philosophical Investigations.* Oxford: Blackwell.

19

Pluralism, Relativism and Interaction Between Cultures

I. PLURALISM *VS.* SINGULARISM

Singularism denies that there can be a variety of conceptions of the common good cherished by different groups of human beings. Pluralism, on the other hand, allows for multiplicity in the concept of the common good, as well as freedom of choice on the part of the individual to choose their own community life. Relativism goes a little further than this and holds that one such conception of the good is as good as any other, there being no overarching standard. Pluralism keeps open the possibility of ranking these different conceptions of the good. The burden on the pluralist, as well as on the relativism, is to devise a judicious blend of social and political institutions, which will accommodate such diversity. The pluralist, therefore, is usually regarded as a liberal, who has the desire to accommodate such diversities. However, even a conservative can be a pluralist. In fact one may claim that a conservative who preaches non-interference with the right of others to pursue their own good is better equipped to be a pluralist. He would demand that the state should be as far as possible neutral on questions of personal morality and common conceptions of the good, and the aims of life. Besides, the state should provide a framework of law, and also other institutions—a framework within which individuals and communities can pursue their own goals. pluralism stipulates that we do not need substantive moral agreement, except for the basic agreement about the indispensability of mutual toleration. Conservatism does not mean authoritarianism. The conscience of a conservative can allow authoritarianism only at the risk of hypocrisy.

One may say that a conservative not only prefers one conception of good to another, but also believes that his own conception is the best one. However, such blindfolded conservatism suffers from a basic inconsistency. A pluralist conservative must first accept the diversity in the notion of the good. In principle, it may be conceded that one particular notion of the good is better than any other, but we really do not know which one. Besides, short of indulging in a dogma, we cannot say that one particular way of life ('form of life', if you like) is best for the whole of humanity. Even if we believe in a pluralist ideal, it does not mean that we have to believe that every ideal of human flourishing is as good as every other. pluralism is not relativism, not quite. What is important politically is to emphasize the following fact: interference with the right of others to pursue their own good should not be allowed or justified under any circumstances, except when such a pursuit causes *harm* to others. However, spelling out what causes '*harm* to others' is a difficult matter in regard to which there is no unanimity. I shall return to this point later.

Our awareness of the diversity of human groups, variety of races, classes, castes and communities, and consequently the presence of a plurality of human goals, desires, aptitudes, abilities and aims, is very ancient. But still it has not fostered the ideals of pluralism. Singularism has always been a seductive ideal. Even the enlightened socio-political thinkers of the nineteenth and twentieth centuries (influenced by their predecessors) talked in terms of a singularistic goal, in terms of a single and unified conception of the good that is valid and desirable for all types of human beings; this was the concept of 'a harmonious universe'. The general pattern of the argument they used in order to reach their anti-pluralistic conclusion can be given as follows. Freedom, or rational self-direction, is inherent in every man and woman. The obvious problem, however, is said to be that this all-important faculty lies dormant in most, and the problem of a diversity of goals arises. Not everybody can judge what is best for him or her. The clearest example would be the case of children. Rationality lies dormant in them, but it can be awakened through training, discipline, force or even coercion. Using such premises and supporting examples (Nyāya's *sādharmya-dṛṣṭānta*) the enlightened European thinkers reached, by a not-too-circuitous road, a paradoxical conclusion which gave unequivocal support to the most abject forms of authoritarianism. It was paradoxical for they were both enlightened and liberal as well.

This type of authoritarianism has been the breeding ground of singularist and anti-pluralistic ideals. It is still important for us to note the steps of this argument. For despite the fact that the fallacies and mistakes of these admirable thinkers (we must remember that they are still our 'heroes' in the field of socio-political thought and this particular case does not detract from their glory have been pointed out by many today, the argument, as well as its conclusion, still holds a spell upon us, and many even today unconsciously become its victims. Hence it will pay to rehearse the steps of this old argument.

Sir Isaiah Berlin, in a slightly different context, has identified the mistakes of these thinkers (whom he has also much admired). I shall quote from his famous essay, for it would be no exaggeration to say that nobody has been able to surpass Sir Isaiah in presenting this argument in its simplicity, elegance and profundity. Sir Isaiah was defending his 'two concepts of liberty' (1969, p. 151):

> Comte put bluntly what had been implicit in the nationalist theory of politics from its ancient Greek beginnings. There can, in principle, be only one correct way of life; the wise lead it spontaneously, that is why they are called wise. The unwise must be dragged towards it by all the social means in the power of the wise; for why should demonstrable error be suffered to survive and breed?

A few pages later, Sir Isaiah sums up (1969, p. 154):

> Let me state then once more: first, that all men have one true purpose, and one only, that of rational self-direction; second, that the ends of all rational beings must of necessity fit into a single universal, harmonious pattern, which some men may be able to discern more clearly than others; third, that all conflict, and consequently all tragedy, is due solely to the clash of reason with the irrational or the insufficiently rational—the immature and undeveloped elements in life—whether individual or communal, and that such clashes are, in principle, avoidable, and for wholly rational beings, impossible; finally, that when all men have been made fully rational, they will obey the rational laws of their own natures, which are one and the same in them all, and so at once wholly law-abiding and wholly free.

Need we add anything more? The premises here unequivocally challenge the ideals of pluralism. Those ideals can be defended, I believe, and without making a concession to a pernicious form of relativism.

In fact, I shall try to do more than that. For I believe that though the excitement about relativism today may force us to reject the dogmas of singularism, some relativists still find the above argument attractive and in this way are inclined to collect ammunition to silence their opponents. The popular form of relativism goes several steps further than accepting the pluralistic ideal. However, I believe it is possible to accept the pluralistic ideal without giving in to this popular form of relativism—that is, without proclaiming loudly, as is often done, that since every truth is relative, there is no such thing as good or bad, right or wrong, true or false; it is all relative.

To return to our quotation from Berlin. The first two premises are obviously identical with the two complementary sides of the singularistic doctrine that defies the pluralistic ideal. They can even be reformulated to support another conclusion: the plurality that we experience all over the world throughout history is only apparent or falsely created; our rational wisdom, which some of us may be fortunate enough to have fully developed, can easily see through this veil of appearance and experience directly the deeper unity of mankind. A so-called deeper insight into the conflict-free, harmonious universe, a new Garden of Eden, as not only the ultimate truth but also the ultimate goal of all of us, is such an attractive and charming idea that many people in different ages have *fallen* for it (if one excuses the Biblical metaphor). Even today we find a considerable number of optimistic followers. Hence the warning is worth repeating.

The third step in the argument is almost patently false. For the historical evidence is that actual clashes and conflicts, and the resulting bloodshed and massacres, are not always due to the disharmony between reason and unreason, but are actually due to the clash of one irrational choice over another by different human communities. It is easy to see why the singularist's contention, that a rational resolution of these conflicts would bring down the kingdom of heaven upon earth, would be too simplistic a solution for an utterly complex situation. Apart from the romantic overtures towards a *unified* garden of Eden, the idea has no substantive base. It is difficult to see how we can promise a 'Rose Garden'.

2. PLURALISM AND RELATIVISM

One may argue that if the pluralistic ideals are conceded, if one denies that there is a common goal and unified good for all human beings, and one denies further that the kingdom of heaven on earth is possible if every human becomes enlightened enough to exercise their rational wisdom and rational self-direction, then are we not giving in to a pernicious form of relativism? Of course, in the field of ethics and morality, relativism has many things going for it. Since the beginning of social anthropology, along with the rise of liberal colonialism, we have learnt to 'respect' the ethical and moral standards of others. Even if we do not understand fully why the native calls a particular act 'good', we have no right to condemn him or force the native to explain himself in the light of reason. It becomes another question of morality to use the language of 'qualitative contrast' (a term taken from Charles Taylor) to describe the native practices which the outsiders do find obnoxious. This is, on the face of it, a kind of tolerance that should be practised, for it also amounts to a value and hence involves a sort of moral obligation. However, *tolerance* ought to be practised with *sincerity* (both being moral virtues). And it is next to impossible for a singularist, one who believes *firmly* in the superiority of his own way of life over all others, to be tolerant and sincere (i.e. unhypocritical) at the same time, as far as *respect* for other's way of life is concerned.

Modern developments in epistemology and philosophy of language have supplied much ammunition to the moral relativists and moral sceptics. W.V. Quine (1960) formulated his celebrated thesis of indeterminacy of translation, which has had far-reaching effects. Some implications of this thesis have been used, rightly or wrongly, by the cultural anthropologists in support of their thesis of cultural relativism. It is often emphasized that transcultural evaluation of norms is not possible. If the language of 'qualitative contrast' is not interculturally valid, the notion of ethical or moral absolutes must be rejected as a dogma of singularism. Comparative ethnography induces moral scepticism. Ethical norms are regarded as being immanent or embedded in the cultural norms, and when these cultural norms vary or are taken to be incommensurate with one another, ethical relativism is the inevitable conclusion. Such relativism, however, has often been criticized for being basically inconsistent and confused, if it is seriously held by anyone as part of his ethical thinking. B. Williams has called it 'vulgar' relativism.

There are several ways is which a defensible, non-vulgar form of (moral) relativism can be formulated. Relativism, in fact, has been formulated and defended by several philosophers today. A few specimens will do. One may start with the following observation. Each culture has its own axiomatic construction of reality which is an integral part of what we call its world-view. The ethical system of each culture is embedded in such an axiomatic construction of reality. We can formulate the thesis of ethical relativism by using such notions as 'real confrontation' and 'real option', and introducing a watertight distinction between 'real' and 'notional' options. Each ethical system is unique to its own culture and there cannot be any real confrontation between one such culture and another, and hence one cannot be a *real* option for the other. The concept of 'notion confrontation' is, however, very important here; it saves the thesis from the already mentioned charge of inconsistency. The concept of the 'notional', it is argued, allows us to think about the moral concerns of the 'alien' culture, so that we can use the language of condemnation and admiration across cultural boundaries, but it does not lead us to think of there being any substantive relation between our moral concerns and theirs. As long as such a *substantive* relation is not thought to exist, the question of appraisal of theirs with ours does not arise. For, as Williams has argued, it is the presence of some substantive relation between moral concerns of different cultures 'which alone can give any *point* or *substance* to the appraisal' (1981, my emphases).

The above is my reconstruction of the thesis, on basis of the formulation of Bernard Williams in his earlier writings. I do not wish to attribute the above entirely to Williams. For he has recently talked about some important 'riders' to his formulation, and patently used it only as a heuristic device to clarify our understanding of relativism. Hence let us call the above the view of some philosophers whom I regard as my *purvapakṣins*, and not hold Williams responsible for the entire argument. However, I believe this 'notional confrontation' somewhat arbitrarily excludes the substantive relation between the moral concerns of different cultures. It is not made clear why and how such thinking of relating the moral concerns must be excluded. In fact, if the member of one culture-group is fully exercising his well-developed rational wisdom (which alone can sustain his practical reasoning) he is bound to raise the question of a substantive relationship between our moral concerns and theirs and this will give *point* to the transcultural evaluation. In fact, the borderline between 'real' and 'notional' confrontation tends to vanish under pressure, unless of course we are talking about two completely individuated cultures, such as a society of a by-gone age on the one hand and a contemporary society on the other.

In short, this type of relativism receives support if the possibility of 'real confrontation' is excluded between cultures. However, such a possibility can be excluded only if the cultures are very remote from each other, either in time or in space. The relativism or incommensurability of the values of society of bygone ages (the Bronze Age, for instance) with those of a modern society is philosophically uninteresting. Hence as long as proper individuation or separation of two contemporary cultures (conceiving them as two 'windowless monads' to use Bernstein's phrase) does not seem possible, we can argue against such relativism. I call this 'the Impossibility of the Individuation of Cultures' (IIC) argument.

Another way is to introduce a sharp distinction between two types of language of appraisal or contrastive choice: one is 'right-and-wrong' and the other is 'good-and-evil'. The former belongs to the agent's own ethics or moral frame of reference while the latter does not. A moral agent is conceived here as belonging to a group or community which has its own special set of ethical principles. The agent reaches his 'inner moral judgement' after considering such principles as he and his peers have consciously or unconsciously agreed to keep. If the agent acts on the basis of such inner moral judgement, it should be considered *right*, no matter whether such an act is in fact good or evil from our point of view. This means that when a member of the society Murder, Incorporated (cf. Harman, 1982) performs his duty, and kills somebody following the 'ethical' code of the society he belongs to, we cannot judge him to be doing something *wrong*, although we can call him an evil human being.

This formulation is derived from the moral relativism of Gilbert Harman. I must say again that my formulation may not exactly represent the view of Harman. The protagonists of the above view would also depend upon the possibility of the proper individuation of group-moralities, and besides, they must make a sharp distinction between what is wrong and what can be called 'evil'. We may insist that each group has its own particular code of ethics which its members must follow, no matter what. Here probably one may suggest that ethics could be distinguished from morality, in the sense that the former is group-related while the latter is not. Ethics on this view is something like the honour-code of a particular group. However, such a distinction does not resolve the basic problem of morality. Elsewhere I have shown that there is a striking resemblance between such a view of 'group-related morality' and some version of the classical *varṇadharmas* of the Hindus. Thus Arjuna was asked to follow his 'inner moral judgement', and thereby decide to fight the Kauravas because that was what a *kṣatrīya* should do (Matilal, 1989a, 1989b).

This type of moral relativism has its own problems, although it is based upon impeccable logic. First it has some *repugnant consequences*, for one has to support the action of someone like Hitler as *right* from the point of view of the agent's own moral frame of reference. We can only call such actions *evil*, that is, not good, from our point of view. But this separation of the concept of evil from that of wrong-doing is highly questionable. I call this 'the Repugnant Consequence' (RC) argument. Besides, why should every code of conduct which is unique to a particular group be honoured as its *moral* code of conduct, or *moral* frame of reference? It seems to defy our linguistic intuitions about the word 'morality' if the code of conduct of Murder, Inc is to be called a 'moral' code. Must every code of conduct in any fanciful club be regarded as an ethical code? Must the diabolical action dictated by some diabolically-minded human beings belonging to a club be glorified as constitutive of the morality of its members? People are different all over the world, but the pertinent question is: How much? Or, to what extent? It is true that they belong to different societies which are historically and geographically conditioned, and hence have developed different faiths, myths, rituals, kinship systems, standards of interpersonal behaviour. The culture's 'ethical' system may be built upon all of these factors, which motivate them to act. But this is not everything. It does not exhaust the domain of morality or what the motivation for some fundamental moral action is all about. Besides, the pervasive presence of moral dilemmas in this world shows, among other things, that the moral agent cannot be exclusively the member of one particular group. Criss-crossing of group-loyalties gives rise to almost unresolvable moral dilemmas, for which the service of rational wisdom is required. In sum, this formulation of relativism suffers from both defects. That is, both arguments, IIC and RC, can be levelled against it.

3. RELATIVISM AND REALISM

Moral relativism has recently been receiving support from the rise of forms of relativism in other fields, such as theoretical science. Quine, who is not himself a relativist, had said (in 1960) that there may be two or more translations of the native's sentence which are sometimes in conflict, and there is no fact of the matter to help us to choose. In 1970 Thomas Kuhn, who is also not strictly a relativist, propounded his thesis according to which we have very little to go upon in choosing among incommensurable theories. In fact, Kuhn has argued that we cannot depend upon the avoidance of error as a criterion without running into the problem of circularity or a question-begging situation. For we cannot specify the truth-condition of one of the rival theories, say T_1, unless we specify it relative to another theory, T_2, in a way that would entail the falsity of T_1 and the truth of T_2. This type of assessment begs the question unabashedly. We may depend upon, Kuhn says, such epistemic issues as simplicity, fruitfulness, accuracy and so on, but here again there may be genuine differences regarding what constitutes, for example, simplicity. Without settling such disputes, we can hardly make a rational choice among incommensurable theories. Simplicity and so on are epistemic or cognitive values. Besides, scientific inquiries are, according to Kuhn, value-laden in many ways. Now, since the disputes regarding such cognitive values are not settleable, the only way to settle disputes regarding value commitments is through persuasion or coercion.

Such well-argued views have given strong impetus to the rise of modern relativism. Conflicts are not to be resolved through further inquiry, disputes concerning values of different kinds, cognitive, moral, political or aesthetic, would be and actually are settled overtly or covertly by persuasion. What we have called one's rational wisdom has not been able to yield (even when used properly) a satisfactory result, for example, agreement as regards the choice. Kuhn has, of course, been criticized for his view. Isaac Levi, for example, rejects the conclusion that avoidance of error cannot be a critical desideratum in any inquiry (pp. 40–1), and perhaps, further inquiry and marshalling of more information may be desirable in some cases. However, moral conflict should be seen in the broader perspective of conflict in values in other areas. Levi insists that there are similarities between decision making unresolved conflict in scientific inquiry and in practical deliberation.

None of these points, however, endorse the rather facile and unacceptable form of relativism. They only require that the singularist's picture of the unified universe, his notion of truth, and of good, needs revision or modification. I believe the pluralist ideals can be better formulated as not necessarily to imply the facile form of relativism. Pluralism and Realism may be made compatible.

Even on the non-objectivist view of ethics, one's ethical reflections do not stop at the boundary of one's own culture but extend beyond to others. No stance of pseudo-liberalism, using the notion of hyper-commensurability as a ploy, can deflect our ethical censure or praise of the *other's* actions. Some sort of universal obligation is implicit in our modern conception of the ethical, such that we are apt to censure someone even in our own culture, if he fails to meet some basic ethical obligation under the pretext of some group-loyalty or loyalty to his own self or his family.

I believe that the notion of incommensurability is what often obfuscates the issue here. For this notion is sometimes claimed to imply material unintelligibility, and therefore mutual uncriticizability. But if incommensurability or undercommensurability of standards (or lack of a common denominator in terms of which we can transcend the problems of intertranslatability) does not stand in the way of mutual appreciation, and respect, it cannot by the same token stand in the way of mutual criticism, intelligibility and understanding.

Realism, that is, hard-headed metaphysical realism, has recently been very much on the firing line, and is criticized as an old legacy of what we used to call 'science'. Putnam has called it the *externalist* perspective, and found it almost indefensible. Some philosophers like Richard Rorty have found the old controversy between Realism and relativism or idealism useless and counterproductive, and suggested that the sooner we give up this style of philosophizing the better. However a sort of popular or vulgar pragmatism or relativism has become widespread today, which has been extended from the field of metaphysics to ethics and morality. It has been hailed as the 'liberating' message and has generated insouciance. From the strictures of a number of academic philosophers against the viability of metaphysical realism, the idea has so spread at the popular level that any belief in the absolutist's conception of truth and good is instantly ridiculed: 'Do you believe in witches and unicorns?' Cultural diversity is often conflated with the relativity of good and bad about almost everything, and it puts on the garb of a pseudo-liberalism where it is further conflated with freedom, openness and equality or other sets of moral virtues. What was regarded as a serious academic discussion or controversy between relativism and realism in the metaphysical and moral field, conducted with sophistication and care for technicalities, has now been vulgarized and regarded by a majority of uninformed students and common people as a useless enterprise, for they all claim to *know* that everything is relative. The situation had become so much worse that it irritated, not without justification, many well-known writers and professors like Allan Bloom, who wrote a best-seller, *The Closing of the American Mind*, rebuking and ridiculing at every step, sometimes unfairly, the new wave of relativism, where, he rightly observed, the extreme left and the extreme right might converge. Bloom, however, displayed, somewhat unwittingly, embarrassing ignorance of any other culture and thereby might have forfeited his claim to be critical of any seriously formulated relativism. To be critical of the popular and uninformed version of relativism, perhaps on just grounds, can be greeted with cheers. However, Bloom went to the other extreme and argued in favour of the old, blindfolded singularism. And this, to be sure, must be regretted.

4. CULTURAL CONFRONTATION

Cultural and ethnic diversity does not lead to the type of relativism that Bloom and others have criticized. Even a plurality of goals may be made compatible with non-relativism. I believe one can argue for a minimal universal moral standard which is claimed to be applicable to all human beings irrespective of race, sex, colour, religion, culture, national or social origins, birth or other status. Given the prevalent mistrust today in any form of abstract totality, universalism or rationalism, it might indeed be going against the current to argue for a minimal universal ethic. Some even having acknowledged that human beings as biological creatures may share some common features, may contend that such a universalism is boring and unexciting. Shylock's claim in *The Merchant of Venice*, for example, was true but uninteresting, on this view. However, the two qualifications 'universal' and 'minimal' should be emphasized. The sense of 'universal' has already been indicated. I shall further amplify it later. I believe our notion of the ethical law demands some sort of universality, as I have already mentioned. The qualification 'minimal' is what makes it non-antagonistic to cultural and moral diversity as well as to partial incommensurability of such diverse values. In fact, the view that I wish to defend seems more defensible, not in spite of, but because of, the fact that it is arguable in full awareness of the pervasive presence of moral and cultural diversity. Besides, the theory of minimal universal morality which is being advanced here, should be distinguished from the view of the protagonists of the 'National Law' doctrine, and certainly from the singularism that people like Allan Bloom prefer. It is important to emphasize the distinction because, in spite of the obvious similarity between them as regards their universality (and probably inalienability), the 'National Law' doctrine lacks the flexibility as well as amenability to contextual interpretation in the background of cultural and social diversity, which the proposed minimal universal morality doctrine enjoys. Plurality of morals, cultural norms, and social obligations are facts that are not in dispute here. Nor is the fact that there are irreducible residues in each cultural norm which are claimed in part to be incommensurate with those from another norm. What is in dispute is whether the following argument holds. If there does not exist any universal, context-neutral rational standard to judge the relative merit or demerit of such different culture-dependent values and practices, or if, *à la* Bernard Williams, there is no *real* confrontation among them such that one cannot be a *real* option to another, then, we are forced into a position of relativism, which, if true, runs counter to the claim of universality of the minimal moral standard that I am inclined to support. I believe the argument does not hold. Even if we concede incommensurability, that is, the argument in favour of relativism of a majority of culture and ethical values (such that a rational choice among them seems not sometimes impossible but in fact unnecessary), it is not contrary to the claim made here about a minimal number of universal, by which I mean culture-neutral or context-neutral, moral values which are and should be constitutive of the ethos of any human society. The qualifier 'human' in 'human society' is important, although we need not appeal to any universal essence of man. I do not believe that this minimal ethics has to be based upon such universal essence. It can be based upon some, empirically given, common concerns of humans.

Elsewhere I have argued that cultural confrontations do take place and have often taken place in the history of mankind, and some of them are *real* even in the sense that Williams wishes to attach to the adjective in his phrase 'real confrontation' (Matilal, 1989a). Cultures and societies, or at least present-day cultures, are not like watertight compartments, which may seldom confront one another in reality or interact. They interact each with the other, sometimes generating violence, sometimes peacefully and almost unconsciously accepting value trade-offs and value-rejections. That is why the IIC argument holds. For the Williamsian kind of *notional* confrontation, we have to imagine two self-contained and totally isolated cultures with guaranteed immunity from external influence and hence with guaranteed immunity from evaluation and criticism from outside. Such cultures are mostly theoretical constructs, which sustain a defensible type of relativism. Williams himself recognizes this and in his later publication (1985) talks about 'the relativism of distance' which exists between past and present societies, or between past and future societies.

But what does this empirical evidence prove? It does not, of course, prove that a coherent construction of the relativistic position on the basis of *notional* confrontation, is impossible. In fact, such construction ideally may help us to understand a culture and most of its values from an internalist's viewpoint, and that is an acceptable device in comparative ethnology or ethnography. But in practice, in today's world, cultures and sub-cultures do flow into each other, interacting both visibly and invisibly, eventually effecting value-rejection and value-modification at every stage. This only shows the vitality of cultures, which are like living organisms, in which internal and external changes are incontrovertible facts. As indicated earlier, a culture as well as its constitutive values, moral and non-moral, basic and non-basic, faces both the internal critique (originating from the insiders through exercise of their rationality) and the external challenge from the confrontation with other cultures, both causing change, development, mutation as well as acceptance of different values within that culture. A culture that does not react and change with time is as good as a dead one, or it is dying or at best it maintains a fossilized form of existence, fit to be turned into a museum piece. A culture is also compared with a language (a reflex of the anthropological discipline); a living culture is like a living language which keeps changing (though slowly) over a period of time, assimilating new idioms and phrases, new structures and forms (which we often call the creative aspect of a language). A dead language does not change, nor does a dead culture.

Here we may make another point about Quine's celebrated thesis of the indeterminacy of translation. It is a coherent theory-construction comparable to some extent to the relativism of distant cultures and it has the same character of being a heuristic device for a better understanding of the nature of meanings as translational constants. Radical translation, however, assumes that the native's language is unchanging and the Gavagai-culture does not interact, through assimilation and modification, when confronted with the linguist's culture over a period of time. But the empirical evidence goes against it, and eventual inter-translatability with negligible traces of indeterminacy is not only possible but actually takes place after a period of time. This is not a criticism of Quine, for we concede the point about the indeterminacy of the mental at a certain level.

Comparative ethnographers have pointed out that there are certain core values unique to each culture which show resilience, resist change, or even possess immutability in the midst of confrontation and interaction with other cultures. The culture's ethical system being immanent, such core values are not available for *real* confrontation or transcultural evaluation. Hence a sort of relativism is still inescapable for the pluralists. My critique of this view is two-fold. First, it assumes an 'essentialist' view of culture: particular cultural essences, constituted by particular core values, are immutable much like the essence of a particular species of animal. (This is not exactly the 'false essentialism' that Bernstein has warned us about. However it is something similar.) Once we give up the essentialist dogma, and admit mutation and change, the analogy does not work. We are after all creatures of history and we must concede our finitude and fallibilism. Second, it assumes too much on the basis of too little evidence. Granted that one experiences 'culture shocks', sometimes very odd and quaint and sometimes very bizarre feelings, when one is getting acquainted with an 'alien' culture, and consequently also with its values and mores, but this does not supply enough evidence for the uniqueness and immutability of the core values. In fact, certain historically conditioned and geographically or environmentally generated values, and practices, sharpened and shaped by local myths, rituals and kinship systems an so on are the hardest to give up for a member of a particular culture, and hence they offer the greatest resistance to change. They are also the hardest for the outsiders to comprehend or to translate in their own culture, for commensurable values and concepts are not often available. It is for this reason we tend to look upon them as *essential* constituents of the uniqueness of a particular culture. But they also yield to slow change almost imperceptibly as the causal factors keep changing and disappearing. Of course, cultural conservatists would like to preserve some of them, and fundamentalists would like to revive a few practices and beliefs, but the preserved, historical relics, and the revived practices, when they are taken out of their contexts, can never be the same. The life of a Bronze Age chief or a medieval Samurai can be real options for us only if they are 'revived' or 'reconstructed', although they would not be the *same* lifestyles of the bygone ages. We cannot go back in history.

5. ON THE IDEA OF THE BASIC MORAL FABRIC

Some sort of relativism (in the sense of absence of any transcultural standard of evaluation or in the sense of incommensurability of cultural and ethical norms) does exist between cultures and correspondingly between their moral codes or values at a certain level. This is not denied here. However there are limits to how much individual moral systems can differ from each other. In order to be recognized as moral systems there must be a common reference point, or system of coordinates, as Davidson demands for alternative conceptual schemes (Davidson, 1974). We can again borrow concepts from the field of linguistics and say that just as there are many context-sensitive rules in the description of any language, there are context-sensitive ethical codes in communities, but this does not preclude the presence of some context-neutral rules. I submit the following thoughts for consideration: the supposition of context-neutral rules assumes that there is a basic moral fabric in all societies, all communities and cultures, which holds their members, human beings, together. This should not be conflated with the old Universalism, nor with some boring commonalities of the species, nor with any objectionable form of essentialism (viz., all humans have the same essence). Since we talk about minimal agreement in norms, this view concedes relativism up to a limit but rejects it when it militates against the basic fabric of the human world.

There are many faces of morality, but at least two main sides of morality deserve our attention here. One can be called the 'rational' side, the general and the necessary constituent of any human society. The other is the less than rational, the historically and environmentally conditioned, hence the contingent side of morality which varies from culture to culture. If we are not too squeamish about the use of certain words, we may call the first the universal or general morality which constitutes the basic fabric or minimal moral standard that I have talked about, and the second, the particular morality, most of which arises from the loyalty of a group to a preferred way of life, such preference being also historically conditioned. A sort of relativism may exist with regard to the latter, but the former seems to be non-relativistic. It is the latter kind that creates the hardest problems for our understanding and for commensurability of the 'alien's' values. Much of the talk about a facile form of relativism that I have alluded to in the previous section is due to a lack of understanding of these problems. It has persuaded most people to take seriously the (illicit) generalisation that all moral standards are relative. Very often the locally conditioned mores of a society may pass for its morality. It may be convenient to call the latter the particular *ethical* code related to a particular society, to distinguish it from the basic minimal moral standard which is or should be, I claim, common to all existing societies today. Here I am drawing from the insights of the traditional ethicists of India, who entangled as they were in the complicated labyrinth of the group- and caste-related ethical duties, made a fundamental distinction between the *sādhāraṇa dharma* (general moral duties) and *viśeṣa dharma* (particular moral codes).

The particular side of morality may be unique to each culture or individual community, for it is connected (causally or otherwise) with the particular community's distinctive way of life, its institutions, membership conditions, and values. Each culture has certain unique rules, virtues and obligations. Family relationship, marriage rules, interpersonal behaviours, some rules of sexual conduct and so on are examples of such particular morality. Religion adds another dimension to the diversity of morals. Each religion has its own particularity as well as its sectarian varieties. Each religion consists of a belief in the superhuman origin of a doctrine embracing norms and ultimate goals as well as a group of people who hold the belief and have an obligation to comply with such norms (e.g. a particular way by which to live and behave with others). In this way diversity in world religious is a major contributory factor to diversity as well as relativity of particular morality.

The general and cultural-invariant side of morality can, on the other hand, be illustrated in very general terms and sometimes left open to contextual interpretation. The contextual interpretation need not, and should not, detract anything from their universality or generality. Formulation of a principle depends upon the contingencies of a particular linguistic convention generating a limited number of expressions and hence the universality of such a formulation may often be open to challenge.

In fact one can use the point made by Bernard Williams about the 'thicker' ethical concepts of some 'hyper-traditional' societies by referring to his main example of a certain school slang (Williams, 1985, pp. 143–5). The ethical concepts of this hyper-traditional society may be such that the external observer (the anthropologist) may be barred from saying what the locals say, but not barred from recognizing that what they say can be true. Even the well-known 'disquotation principle' about truth does not in this case require that what the members of the hyper-traditional society say, involving such 'thicker' ethical concepts, cannot be true.

It may be worthwhile to start with the common elements in the ethico-religious teachings of the three or four Indian religions. (One may inquire whether they are associated with certain 'thicker' ethical concepts or not.) There are at least four moral virtues which they all recommend, and which are also common to other world religions. First, there is what we usually call respect for life, but which I would like to call non-violence (not strictly in the Gandhian sense), thereby slightly broadening its scope. It is presumably derived from the virtue of kindness or compassion for others. One of the fundamental constituents of a common morality entails this principle, and it is also necessary for the adequate maintenance of any worthwhile social life. We do not, however, need a supernatural agency for the imposition of this value (or any other value); human rationality can be the legitimate arbiter. It is significant to note that in Indian traditional religions (such as Buddhism), no supernatural power is invoked as the arbiter of value.

Respect for life or non-violence requires that life should not unnecessarily be endangered, and that wanton killing (of humans as well as animals) must be prohibited. No person should act in such a way as to harm the life of his fellow being. Some qualifications may be necessary, for there may be moral justifications for taking an animal's life, or even a human life. Besides, this justification may vary from person to person, or society to society. Self-preservation or self-defence may be one allowable justification which has universal application. Besides, abortion and euthanasia are examples of wanton killing according to some, not according to others. Hence some sort of contextual interpretation may be necessary here. But I am personally sceptical of such justifications according to the varying contexts. For in most cases such a justification is hardly moral; it is prudential or otherwise. Hence, if from a moral point of view we have to maintain the universality of the said principle, we have to exclude most of such contextual interpretations. Mahatma Gandhi's famous example was that of a snake: whether to allow it to bite a saint or have it killed. And even there he was not sure whether an exception can be made (on this point, see Jaini 1979, p. 315; also, my review of Jaini). Besides, if certain killings (for personal gain, or sadistic pleasure, or because the victim is 'racially inferior') are permitted by certain particular moral codes, if, in other words, there is conflict between universal and particular morality, then according to the view I am defending, the universal morality should override the particular. Otherwise it will go against the basic fabric of human society as a whole. To allow somebody to kill a human being for a reason, justifiably or not, is also to use the person as a means, not an end. This goes against the celebrated Kantian doctrine: 'treat humanity, whether in your own person or in that of another, always as an end withal and never merely as a means.' Kant's own explanation is, of course, that a human being must be treated as an autonomous agent (p. 56, sec. II). But even so, the connection between the respect for life and an interpretation of this Kantian universal principle can possibly be shown, although I shall not go into it here.

Among other moral virtues, claimed to be universal, is truth-telling or the prohibition against lying. Again social life would be impossible without this prohibition. Kant claimed this prohibition to be absolute. Here, the Indian religions, especially Hinduism in its *dharmaśāstras*, make an exception. As against Kant they hold that the obligation to tell the truth to a would-be murderer in search of his intended victim can be violated. There is an interesting *Mahābhārata* episode which illustrates and illuminates various facets of this argument nicely (I have discussed it elsewhere; Matilal, 1989b). The other two moral virtues recommended by the Indian religions may or may not constitute the fabric of universal morality today. But there lies some insight which seems worth exploring. One is the prohibition against stealing, conditional upon the presence of the institution of property. We can take property here not necessarily as personal or private, for there are public and community properties. The simple Buddhist way of formulating the virtue is 'not grabbing or taking what is not yours'. As long as the institution of property remains a common factor of all human societies, the universality of this prohibition would not be unfounded. Besides, 'free-loaders' and 'free-riders' are even today terms of moral reproach in most societies. Excessive greed for money, power or personal gain is condemned, even in today's society.

The universality of the fourth prohibition would perhaps be most debatable. Prohibition of adultery is conditional upon the institution of marriage. But it cannot be universal. However I prefer again the Buddhist way of putting it: 'not to play false, in sexual intimation, with one's partner.' This may not depend upon the institution of marriage. Violation of sexual ethics, when such ethics might be allowed a contextual interpretation depending upon the societies or groups, seems to be morally reprehensible. Rape may be a particular case of this prohibition.

One question lurks behind all this, which I must answer at this stage. By occasionally allowing contextual interpretation, albeit to a limited extent, am I not conceding some sort of relativism, which I have previously denounced? My answer is simple. If this sort of relativism is conceded, it is still very different from the very 'exciting' sort of relativism that I have denounced already. Alternatively, we may rule that the last of the above virtues may not constitute the fabric of a universal morality. Contextual interpretation is needed because the universality of some of these principles suffers (and shrinks) when we deal, as we must, with a particular formulation of them in reference to particular languages or social practices.

There may be other moral virtues or principles or obligations which could form the fabric of the basic universal morality in the same vein. For example, we could add justice, social responsibility, an obligation to choose good (or a lesser evil) rather than evil. Even some notion of justice was not absent from the set of virtues extolled in traditional India. For instance, in the *Sāṃkhya-kārikā*, verse 2, the Vedic religious rituals are denounced, for they supposedly produced results (wealth for some poverty and unhappiness for others), that were unfair, unjust and iniquitous. Besides, a common argument against theism (in Buddhism and Jainism) was that if God created the world, how could he have created inequalities (see also *Vedānta-sūtra*, 2.1.32–4).

I base this moral fabric upon what I take to be the common concerns of all *known* human societies. It may be called *relative to all known reasons*, to all things considered (in a way reminiscent of R. Carnap's notion of total evidence in inductive reasoning). If any human society is discovered by anthropologists where one or more of the above concerns is *proven* to be absent, then this notion of the universal moral fabric should be modified. I concede this possibility.

Proceeding in a different vein, one may develop the notion of general morality by taking the happiness of all creatures, and the alleviation of their pain or suffering, as basic, and then recommend action-guides which must be obeyed by all. Alternatively, one can formulate a defensible concept of *human need* and then talk about such a need-based general ethic which would be culture-invariant and agent-neutral. Human beings as biological creatures need food, clothing and shelter, there is need for nutritional requirements, for participation in social life and so on pluralism, or even an occasional allowance for context-dependence, does not stand in the way of defending the view that there is a basic or minimal moral fabric which is universal and context-transcendent. This does not deny the diversity of human goals, nor does it concede the old singularism nor moral jingoism, nor even the convergence of all human goals through rationality as conceived by the nineteenth century liberals. Philippa Foot has remarked:

> . . . granted that it is wrong to assume identity of aim between people of different cultures; nevertheless there is a great deal that all men have in common. All need affection, the cooperation of others, a place in a community and help in trouble (1982, p. 164).

I concede that the formulation of the above principles may be shown to be inadequate to meet the claim of universality. I have said that their universality seems to shrink when we deal, as we must, with a particular formulation of them in a particular language with a given culture. The fault here, it seems to me, lies more with the contingencies of a given linguistic apparatus, and/or of the cultural condition (in the context of which the particular formulation has been given) than with the principles themselves. Arguably, one may say that the particular formulation captures the principle in the sense of illustrating it, although the formulation itself suffers from lack of generality. This is, I believe, the problem with any notion of universality.

I have touched upon the politics of relativism in my introductory comments. However, there is more to this politics of relativism. It has been noted by some post-modernists on the continent that the traditional non-relativistic (singularistic) self-understanding of the West has thrust itself towards reduction, absorption and appropriation of 'the Other' to itself. The Western conquest of the world, its imperialism and domination (both in the material world and in the thought-world), and the resulting violence (in both thought and action)—all these can be seen as the attempt to avoid and contain the disturbance and ruptures that the strangers, the absolute other, may create. Against this background, a concession to incommensurability of the other and acceptance of a relativistic stance has been, and would certainly be welcome. However, even relativism can be a tool in the hand of the oppressor. For example, a 'liberal' colonialist may follow the policy of benign and not so benign neglect and thereby successfully resist the liberal forces in the native's own tradition and let superstitions, conservatism and fundamentalism take over. The important point is that singularism does not always foster imperialism, nor does relativism necessarily encourage liberalism. It may encourage a pseudo-liberalism and a love of exotic rituals. The latter can easily be a subterfuge for the implicit claim of superiority of one's own cultural practice. Prolonged political domination of the *other* cannot be stopped (even by the politics of relativism) short of a cultural conquest, and consequent cultural bankruptcy of the *other*. However, during confrontation and interaction, both sides, the dominant and the subordinate, are bound to change almost imperceptibly, and there will be, as I have already said, value-change, value-rejection and value-mutation. For (echoing a comment once made by Hegel, we may say) the slave can change or influence the master, much as the master can change the slave.

In conclusion, I wish to point out that in order to sustain any acceptable form of social life, a basic fabric of universal morality is absolutely necessary. And if our talk of human rights in today's world has to receive any significant defence (if, that is, the Declaration of Human Rights of 1948 is to have any point), such rights should be based upon the notion of the basic universal moral fabric that I have tried to explore here (see also Milne, 1986). Imitating our poet-philosopher Tagore, I might add, that 'where knowledge is free' and 'where the clear stream of reason has not lost its way in the dreary desert sand of dead habit', there and then we can make this basic universal moral fabric a little more visible to others than it is in today's mad world of war, bigotry, fundamentalism and power-brokerage.

Notes and References

Berlin, Sir Isaiah, *Four Essays on Liberty*, Oxford, 1969.

Bernstein, Richard, 'Incommensurability and Otherness—Revisited', Paper at the Plenary of the Sixth East-West Philosophers' Conference, Honolulu, 1989.

Bloom, Allan, *The Closing of the American Mind*, New York, 1987.

Davidson, David, 'On the Very Idea of a Conceptual Scheme', 1974, reprinted in *Inquiries into Truth and Interpretation*, Oxford, 1984.

Foot, Philippa, 'Moral Relativism' in J.W. Meiland and M. Krausz (eds), *Relativism: Cognitive and Moral*, Univ. of Notre Dame Press, Notre Dame, 1982, pp. 152–66.

Harman, G., 'Moral Relativism Defended' in Meiland and Krausz (eds), *Relativism* (see Foot), pp. 189–204.

Jaini, P.S., *The Jaina Path of Purification*, University of California Press, Berkeley, 1979. Review of Jaini by B.K. Matilal, *Bulletin of the School of Oriental and African Studies*, London, 1980.

Kant, Immanuel, *Fundamental Principles of the Metaphysic of Ethic* (tr. T.K. Abbott), 10th edn., London.

Kuhn, Thomas, *The Structure of Scientific Revolutions*, Chicago, 1970, 2nd edn.

Levi, Isaac, *Hard Choices*, Cambridge, 1986.

Matilal, Bimal, 'Ethical Relativism and Confrontation of Cultures' in *Relativism: Interpetation and Confrontation* (ed. M. Krausz), Notre Dame, Indiana, 1989a.

———, 'Moral Dilemmas: Heights from Indian Epics' in *Moral Dilemmas and the Mahābhārata* (ed. B.K. Matilal) I.I.A.S., Shimla (Delhi, 1989b).

Milne, A.J.M., *Human Rights and Human Diversity*, London, 1986.

Putnam, Hilary, *Reason, Truth and History*, Cambridge, 1981.

Quine, W.V., *Word and Object*, Cambridge, Mass., 1960.

Rorty, Richard, *The Consequences of Pragmatism*, Brighton, 1982.

Taylor, Charles, 'The Diversity of Goods,' in Sen and Williams (eds), *Utilitarianism and Beyond*, Cambridge, 1982.

Williams, Bernard, *Moral Luck*, Cambridge, 1981.

———, *Ethics and Limits of Knowledge*, Penguin, 1985.

PART IV
Ideas from the East

20

The East, the Other

I. INTRODUCTION

Once a very well-known Oxford philosopher was asked by a young faculty member at Harvard, 'What do you think of Eastern philosophy or even Indian philosophy?' To this came the quick reply, 'Nothing good has come out of the East except the sun.' This exchange took place at the Harvard Faculty Club—and the joke had its desired effect. Everybody burst out laughing. The young faculty member was embarrassed. Several years later this quip was reported to another American professor who was engaged in organizing a course in Eastern thought. The latter replied by a counter-question: 'Is that not enough? What would we have done without the sun?'

Such dinner-table jokes can hardly be substitutes for serious discussion of the rather intriguing issue: apart from social anthropology and Oriental scholarship, are there any ideas in the East that are worth having and might benefit the Western man or woman? This is not a rhetorical question. Apart from the two disciplines that I have already excluded, there is a persistent image of the East in the Western mind—the East that is exotic, mysterious and mischievous. It is the mystique of East. To raise the above question is not to endorse this idea of the East. For the East can hardly be a mystery to an Easterner, not at least in the same way as it appears to the Westerner. The mystique of the East is essentially a Western construction.

The practice of the Europeans to refer to the 'other' by the term 'East' and associate it with the 'sun', is, surprisingly, as ancient as the first century before Christ. The separation of the West from 'the East' or 'the Orient' was officially established during the Roman Empire. Virgil, we are told, called this land 'other' in his *Aeneid*: the people were 'of the dawn', and the land was 'the East'. See for example, Virgil (1995), *Aeneid* VII,

606 (p. 163), and VIII, 686 (p. 187). This original association of the term 'the East' with conquest and imperialism has been strangely resilient.

It may be that Rudyard Kipling was right: 'the East is East and the West is West. Never the twain shall meet'. We are creatures of history, but we try to depict ourselves as ahistorical, that is, ageless. Hence, almost all our pithy remarks are dotted with 'never', 'ever', 'nothing', 'always', and 'everything.' Contingent facts are often mistaken for necessary ones, as omnitemporal. Kipling made the same mistake. Hence we can 'deconstruct' his text, by 'displacing' it from its historical context. The meeting of East and West is an irreversible fact today. It depends now upon both the East and the West—it depends upon how we react and respond to this new reality. Should the West limit itself to *The Jungle Book*, and regard the 'jungles' of the Orient as part of a wonderful imperialistic annexation? Or should it search for something more substantive in the realm of ideas from the East?

2. LIBERAL EDUCATION: THE NEED FOR CHANGE

A couple of years ago, an interesting debate raged in different university campuses of America and reverberated elsewhere over a question that could set new directions for higher education in the West. The debate concerned itself mainly with American higher education, although it had implications also for other western nations. The issue was: should students be required simply to read a fixed core curriculum consisting of works on western civilization; and if so, what should it be?

The heart of the dispute, as it crystalized at Stanford University, was whether to amend or remove from the university's 'Western Culture' courses a roster of fifteen prescribed Western classics. They ranged from Homer and Dante to Darwin and Freud—all part of a sacred canon, as it were, or at least, that is how they were (and still are, and perhaps rightly so) regarded by many scholars and academics in the West. It was not by any means a coincidence that these authors were all white, western, males, or, according to the language of the Police Department all over the United States, 'male, Caucasian'. The dominant group for a pretty long time, it must have its own spokesmen in the field of education, and Orwell's Newspeak is only a metaphor for all such domination—or, at least, that was how it was felt by the protagonists for the new movement, consisting mainly of blacks, Hispanics and women. Liberal white males also joined in.

The demand was for revision of the core curriculum. The idea was to build a new, theme-based programme. It was cleverly called CIV (an acronym for Culture, Ideas and Values) at Stanford. The classical scholars, conservative politicians and educationists, including the then Education Secretary William Bennett, were understandably alarmed. Bennett described the attempt as equivalent to 'trashing Plato and Shakespeare'. In this context, also, it was easy to understand the appeal of such books as the best-selling *The Closing of the American Mind* by Allan Bloom of the University of Chicago (Bloom 1987).

The cry for revision of the core curriculum, and introduction of CIV courses, meant in actual terms a paring down of the existing roster of well-known western classics prescribed for the freshman at the universities. At Stanford, it was resolved that all such students should read from at least one non-European source chosen by the professor, and the professor should give 'substantial attention to the issues of race, gender and class'. This was done apparently in response to the criticism of Eurocentricism, and in recognition of the essential pluralism of Western civilization in literary and social terms. It was made possible by the shift of the power-base resulting from the growing presence of women, blacks and people of colour.

The new eclecticism that had thus a modest beginning in American education raised fears in the minds of some conservative people. In academic circles, it led to a dispute about the definition and nature of the Western culture, for the issue rounded on the question of how young people should be educated to become knowledgeable participants in the culture. Attempts were made to make the supporters of the revision appear as red-eyed revolutionaries and iconoclasts. Allan Bloom's classic caricature of a young freshman's logic for supporting the study of other (non-Western) cultures was a case in point. The extremists denounced the old curriculum as almost exclusively WASP, male and East Coast. The extremists in the opposite camp branded the new movement as a specimen of 'intellectual affirmative action' and roused the rabble by declaring it a project designed 'to alter the nature of civilization itself'.

Not all the classicists, moderate or conservative, were convinced. A culture self-consciously chooses to strike a new course, which marks the vitality of the particular culture itself. Paradoxically, the argument of the conservatives who denounced the revision can be turned on its head and used to herald this new wave of change. It is interesting to notice that the claims of all these conservatives converged on one point: not only is western culture superior to others, but it is the only culture that is rationally based. Nowadays this is boldly proclaimed mostly by those who do not know anything else but Western culture. How can there be any claims of exclusiveness for a particular culture, if it is not based upon knowledge of the other or others? Martha Nussbaum, herself a first-rate classicist and a philosopher, in her trenchant criticism of Bloom, has said, after quoting Bloom:

> This statement shows a startling ignorance of critical and rationalist tradition in classical Indian thought, of the arguments of classical Chinese thinkers, and, beyond this, of countless examples of philosophical and nonphilosophical self-criticism from many parts of the world. . . It shows as well a most un-Socratic unwillingness to suspect one's own ignorance. I have rarely seen such a cogent, though inadvertent, argument for making the study of non-Western civilizations an important part of the university curriculum (1987, p. 22).

Books written by blacks, Jews, Hispanics and women have now been studied and taught, though in most CIV courses, they constitute a tiny part of the reading list. Perhaps, at the freshman level, to expect more would be impractical. The above quotation, however, opens up the horizon much further by referring to the Asian cultures. The otherness of these oriental cultures has the added charm of being ancient, traditionally grounded, and, despite the widespread ideas to the contrary, they are both rationally intelligible and in some areas even 'commensurable'. Some knowledge, instead of distorted ideas or prejudiced opinion, of the vast literature and philosophy of these cultures would tend to make one a bit more humble before claiming the alleged exclusiveness and superiority of Western culture.

It is, it may be claimed, natural and to a considerable extent perhaps desirable, to entertain a feeling of superiority about one's native culture. This is not simply tied to nineteenth-century nationalism. It gives one the dignity and self-esteem that one may need in order to develop one's full potential and to make a contribution to the world culture. The Chinese thought that China was the centre of the world. The idea was not entirely foreign in the Indian subcontinent. Hence the West which has recently seen an unprecedented globalization of Western science, technology, and philosophy as well, can rightly be proud of Eurocentricism. This, however, can be taken too far.

3. TURNING EAST

The Hellenistic heritage of Western civilization is so overwhelming that we tend to go back to the Greeks to trace the origin of many significant concepts and issues. In Greek mythology, different parts of Asia, as well as India as a whole, were supposed to have been conquered by Dionysus. It is strange to note that Dionysus is also credited in Greek myths with the spread of the vine cult which was connected with crude religious/ mystical orgies under the influence of intoxicants. This atavistic picture of the mysterious East has long been sustained in the Western mind.

We may move quickly from myth to history. The contacts between Greece and India in history are in many ways well-documented. Alexander's invasion of the East led to a direct acquaintance with the land and the people of the East, especially of Persia and India. Somewhere around the third century before Christ, a history of India, *Indika*, was written by Megasthenes. This constitutes a substantive body of western 'knowledge' of Indian ideas, Indian religions and the Indian people. Some Greeks settled in the East and became acquainted with Buddhism in particular, which led to the composition of the most famous document, in the domain of religion, of a sort of East–West dialogue in the environment of the ancient world.

The text, which forms part of the Buddhist canonical literature in Pāli (1st or 2nd century AD), is called *The Questions of Milinda*. This was supposedly the record of a dialogue in which the Greek King Milinda (= Melander, Menandros, *c.* 155–130 BC) asked questions, and the Buddhist monk Nāgasena answered and explained the doctrines of Buddhism. It is undoubtedly significant to note that what happened some two millennia ago in north-western India, became a model for the Western search for, and encounter with, Eastern religious ideas, which had been repeated at different periods in history. The basic pattern remained the same. In fact, even in the present century, there have been many who have emulated (or at least tried to emulate) Nāgasena when they have been confronted with modern Milindas from Europe and America.

Even some of the religious issues or philosophical puzzlements discussed in the Milinda-Nāgasena dialogue, typify the questions still asked today by those in the West about Eastern religions, and Eastern gurus (not all Buddhists) are only too willing to oblige in accordance with their own understanding. For example, the following is a citation that tries to answer the question about the notion of soul or personhood:

And the venerable Nāgasena said to Milinda the king, 'You, Sire, have been brought up in a great luxury, as beseems your noble birth. If you were to walk this dry weather on the hot and sandy ground, trampling under foot the gritty, gravely grains of the hard sand, your feet would hurt you. And as your body would be in pain, your mind would be disturbed, and you would experience a sense of bodily suffering. How then did you come: on foot, or in a chariot?'

'I did not come, Sir, on foot. I came in a carriage.'

'Then, if you came, Sir, in a carriage, explain to me what that is. Is it the pole that is the chariot?'

'I did not say that.'

'Is it the axle that is the chariot?'

'Certainly not.'

'Is it the wheels, or the framework, or the ropes, or the yoke, or the spokes of the wheels, or the goad, that are the chariot?'

And, to all these the king still answered no.

'Then is it all these parts of it that are the chariot?'

'No, Sir.'

'But is there anything outside them that is the chariot?'

And still he answered no (Śāstri, 1979, pp. 20–1).

The Buddhist decomposition of ego (or using modern jargon, one may call it the deconstruction of the self) is unfamiliar in Western religious movements. It has been variously received and criticized by moderners. In fact, for some, not only Buddhism but all Eastern religions, by their emphasis on meditation and search for the inner reality and quietitude, appear to be socially inactive, amoral and excessively world-negating. It seems that their aim is to turn humans into inert and insensitive organisms—something that the action-orientated and progress-motivated Western religious ethos finds revolting and wrong. Thus it is that Professor Harvey Cox of Harvard, in his *Turning East*, recognized this Western attitude as an obstacle:

> The obstacle was me. I could not afford to overlook the fact that, ever since my late teens, I have had a standing suspicion of excessively 'inward' and socially passive religion. Especially since my college years, . . . I have steered clear of any religion that seemed to give people an excuse for withdrawing from the pain and confusion of the world (Cox, 1979, p. 11).

However, Cox, in spite of his 'prejudices,' *turned East* and by his own admission filled a previously unnoticed void in his life.

'Turning East' amounts in fact to turning *inward* for many in the West. It is not the case that the 'inward' looking trend has been absent in Western religious history. Pietism has been there, so has there been mysticism, passivity and the idea of total surrender of individuality. However, they were not dominant. These traits were not even exceptions.

They remained in the West, until the new wave of Orientalism took over, largely unnoticed, unemphasized, unsung and unglorified. The 'mainstream' religion has either ignored or rejected them. However the subdued and the suppressed sometimes return under a different garb, as Freud seemed to have taught us. Ideas from the East thus appear to be unfamiliar and striking and exotic, and yet send a seductive and friendly invitation to many in the West.

Turning inward, searching for the inner reality, has been perceived as the dominant trend of the Eastern religious or Eastern cultures. However, this has irreversibly become part of modern Western culture. Meditation, relaxation, 'let go', the holistic approach and so on have become part of the current (Western) vocabulary. Although a tiny minority exhibit explicit enthusiasm for such Eastern ways, certain concepts and practices have been assimilated and integrated in modern Western culture. The East has been annexed by the Western empire, not simply in the domain of politics or economics, but also in the domain of ideas and thoughts. The modern challenge (which reached its peak in the sixties and seventies of this century) of the Oriental guru and religious masters may have persuaded some to become converts, but that is only the luxury of the few. The Western thought-world has plundered other cultures and enriched itself with the booty although the booty has been transformed beyond recognition and assimilated totally.

In fact there is nothing wrong or unfair in this. A living culture always examines and interprets the Other, and in the course of time, it not only confronts the Other but also tries to absorb it as much as it can. Interpretation of the Other gets off the ground by the initial attribution, consciously or unconsciously, of basic home-grown beliefs to the alien and then the construction of an alien culture follows. Even the dominant culture absorbs ideas from the sub-dominant, though unconsciously, much as the master's behaviour is adopted as Hegel once said, from the slave's behaviour.[1] The slave's culture borrows from the master's openly in the market place. The master borrows, if there is something worth borrowing, self-deceptively, in secrecy. And the master annexes it, makes it his own such that it becomes unrecognizable as an adoption.

There are, however, many disclaimers, fortifying the assertion of the article of faith in the ethnic purity, uniqueness and/or superiority of one's own race or one's own national character. But how can one understand or become self-consciously aware of one's own uniqueness without understanding the *Other*? Uniqueness is, of course, there, but in the context of a living culture interacting with others, no uniqueness is static or immutable. The old uniqueness vanishes to make room for new uniqueness, being enriched by adoption and absorption. Thus it is that an Englishman may claim that his world-view is unique in the sense that there is very little scope for religious spirituality, or a mysticism that regards the material world as illusion, but it is informed only with a transfigured morality. G. Lowes Dickinson, in his *An Essay on the Civilisation of India, China, and Japan*, tries to underline this uniqueness of the Englishman's character:

> . . . [A]n Englishman has no conception even of the meaning of a philosophic or religious problem . . . His religion, when he has one, is a transfigured morality, not a mysticism. He is practical, through and through, in spiritual as well as in material things. Between him and the Indian the gulf is impassable (1914, pp. 18–19).

The echo of Rudyard Kipling's famous statement is unmistakable here. Dickinson dismisses Berkeley as an Irishman and Hume as a Scotchman. This construction of an ideal Englishman can in fact be extended to that of 'the Western man' when we wish to contrast him with the Oriental. However, outside the context of the contrast which is meant to help our basic understanding, such abstractions as 'the Western man' and 'the Oriental' do not have any reality. Their status is as good as a still photograph in an ever-changing, dynamic universe.

For example, in antiquity when some intercourse between Greece and the East was a fact, it may be, as some (see M.L. West, 1971, pp. 28–35) have surmised, that the idea of the Time-god or the Pherecydean Chronos as a cosmic progenitor, 'who always existed, began everything by generating progeny from his own seed' (West, 1971, p. 28), was a reflection of the Zoroastrian Zurvan in Zoroastrian cosmology. According to this, in the beginning nothing existed except Zurvan, Time, conceived as a divine agent, who had sexual union with himself and produced the twin brothers Ohrmazd, the creator of heaven and earth and all that is fair, and Ahriman, creator of the demons and all that is evil.[2] This cosmogony is paralleled by the *Kāla*-cosmogony found in the *Atharva-veda* in India, and later elaborated in the *Maitri Upaniṣad*. *Kāla* is Time, which transpires as *Mahākāla* (the Eternal Time) in later (Vaiśeṣika) philosophy and mythology (in the Purāṇas, Lord Śiva = *Mahākāla*). Not only is the similarity between *Kāla* (= Zurvan) and Chronos striking, but also the conjecture about the borrowed nature of the latter receives some support from the fact that the idea lacked any identifiable precedent in the earlier Greek accounts of cosmology. The rudiments of the idea of the Time-god are also found in Egyptian myths. However, if the Western historians start with the idea that no non-Greek culture is anything but barbarian, and borrowing from the barbarians is not to be allowed, then there will be resistance to any such evidence. The master cannot *openly* borrow from the slave.

What I have said about the minor idea of the Time-god may be true of another very complex, but related, idea, that of metempsychosis. The Egyptians probably again had their share. But it would be futile to throw any more light on the primitive origin of the idea of metempsychosis. There might have been many gifts of the Magi to the early, pre-rationalistic, Hellenistic thought-world, which are traceable in numerous Greek cosmogonies. Afterwards, the growth and maturing of the rational approach to philosophy in Greece apparently eliminated all foreign influences or borrowings. However, one can be struck by the similarities that do exist between the later Greek sceptics (Pyrrho, Sextus Empiricus) and some Buddhists and sceptics of India (Nāgārjuna and Sañjaya) as well as between Neo-Platonism and early Vedāntic thought as recorded in the Upaniṣads and so on. Again, there does exist an opinion which depicts Pyrrho travelling to India and having discourses with some Indian monks, '*śramaṇas*'.[3]

The extensive parallels between neo-Platonism and Vedānta have been noted and studied by many. It has been difficult to prove influence one way or other. J.F. Staal, in his *Advaita and Neoplatonism* (1961), concentrates on Śaṃkara, who belonged to the eighth or ninth century AD and underlines the points of similarity and contrast. However, ideas such as that of metempsychosis, of cyclical Time, of the self-luminosity of consciousness, of the illusory nature of evil, of the magical or the deceptive nature of the material world, all go to show that Western man is not always what he is made out to be—a cool, rational, and scientifically-minded person, and that the gulf between the Western person and the Oriental is not always impassable. Mysticism or monism is not the monopoly of the East. However, any idea, even mysticism, has undeniably its local or regional trimmings.

Our travels into the past are always full of surprises. Those who undertake such journeys in ancient Greece and ancient India cannot fail to notice the affinities. The poet A.K. Ramanujan has expressed it beautifully:

> . . . every Plotinus we read
> is what some Alexander looted
> between the material rivers.
>
> ('Small-Scale Reflections on a Great House', 1971, p. 42)

It is not important for my purpose here to determine whether Pythagoras visited India or not, or whether, as Apollonius had claimed, Pythagoras received the Indian ideas indirectly through Egypt. However, it is certainly significant that in a tradition that is presumably noted for its rational-scientific approach, the famous names like Pythagoras, Plato and Plotinus have often been referred to along with their possible association with Eastern mystical ideas. It is as if our Western man is embarrassed to acknowledge anything that is even remotely irrational or mystical as part of his indigenous heritage. This, it seems to me, tells us a lot about not only the West's perception of the East, of India in particular, but also the Western self-perception of the West's own culture. As already noted above, in order to preserve the image of a rational, cool, calculating, pragmatic and moral Westerner, some would dismiss even Berkeley and Hume as aberrations, as exceptions rather than the rule.

The image of the East as the archetype of whatever is covered by the irrational, mystical, emotional and the mystic side of the humans has been sustained in the West, surprisingly, for more than two millennia. There is the *romantic* image as well as the *vulgar* image, particularly of India. We do not know whether Alexander met the ascetics in India and had religious discourse with them. For all we know, it is false. However, the myth has perpetuated for a pretty long time. There may be a grain of truth in the reported discourse between King Milinda and the monk Nāgasena. However the legend, or rather the reference, to Buddhism in India is found in the West as early as *c.*150 in the form of Clement of Alexandria, who lived *c.* AD 150–215 . The rather simplistic contrast between East and West, that is, between the spiritual East and the material West, gathered momentum from the stories of the encounter between the 'gymnosophists' of India and the Greek conqueror or his emissaries—the stories being repeated in many forms throughout the literature. The model provided a curious mixture of history and imagination, fact and fiction, with the Western man conquering the foreign lands, the material, and the Eastern man teaching about the conquest of the inner world, mastery of one's own self instead of mastery over another. The model was not entirely unknown to India, where the *Bṛhadāraṇyaka Upaniṣad* describes the encounter between King Janaka and Yājñavalkya. The theme became popular throughout the Purāṇas. The celebrated Janaka (King of Mithilā) is made to say:

> *anatam bata me vittaṃ yasya me nāsti kiñcana*
> *mithilāyāṃ pradīpatāyāṃ na me dahyat kiñcana.*

> I have endless wealth, although I do not have even a penny.
> If my city of Mithilā is burnt, nothing burns that belongs to me (*Mahābhārata*, 12/17/18 crit. edn.).

Alexander, even the Alexander not of history but of the literary romances, was no Janaka; and yet the Alexander of the romances was gradually Indianized as a Janaka, showing some respect for the Indian gymnosophists or ascetics who scorned the idea of world-conquest and emphasized the conquest of the spirit or the inner world. The asceticism of the Indian monks was well known to the Church Fathers of early and medieval Europe, and even the implementation of the practice of Christian ascesticism might have been in part influenced by an idealization of Indian ascetic life. Modern European scholars have considered the possibility.[4] The point-by-point similarities between Buddhist and Christian monks may not be simply a coincidence. It can at least be safely surmised that an admiration of Indian style ascesticism was used by the medieval writers in the promotion of Christian ascetic practice.

Asceticism, spiritualism, mysticism, the search for the Inner Self, negation of the material world, devaluation of material happiness—all these constituted the hallmark of the East in the mind of the Western man in the ancient world. The medieval period was a period when the East sank almost into oblivion for the Western man, barring occasional revival of the older stories and sporadic references to Buddhist and Indian ascetic life. The situation continued until the studies of the Orient started in Western academic and other institutions. This was the era that was greeted by some as the 'Oriental Renaissance'. In the language of Richard Schwab:

> The effect of oriental studies was to undermine the wall raised between two cultures; such studies fulfilled their real purpose by transforming the exile into companion. However . . . (1950, p. 1).

There is always an 'however' after such a sweeping statement. The study of the East was prompted by a cherished image of the East, and the results of such studies in turn reinforced the original image. Perceptions of the East were for the most part guided by what the perceiver constructed with his own concepts and categories, for there cannot be any perception without conception. Construction always impregnates one's perceptions. To continue with Schwab:

> However, the partition was dismantled in accordance with special interests and controversies, intellectual, spiritual, or political, in the West itself. More and more the concept of the Orient was drawn into polemics, pushed towards the right or the left, the top or the bottom of the map, depending on the disposition and the stakes of those who invoked it (1950, p. 1).

Whether or not there was an Oriental renaissance in the West, in the way Schwab claimed, is not the issue for us today. Schwab was struck by the sudden appearance of the Orient and Indological scholarship in the creative works of some of the European writers of the late eighteenth and nineteenth century. However this is no longer important. Likewise it is not the issue here whether the politics of colonialism or Orientalism (in the way Edward Said intended it) is still a moving factor among Orientalists today. All these may be true within limits. However, since the Beat-generation and the Hip-generation of the sixties another phenomenon has claimed the focus of our attention: the sudden aggression, in a much larger scale than before, of the Oriental (tradition) religions in the modern Western affluent society, and the consequent mushrooming of what Khushwant Singh once called the 'guru business' in the Western world. There have been many sociological and psychological studies of this phenomenon. It is very unlike the mythical Alexandrian search for eastern wisdom, or King Milinda's debate with the Buddhist monk Nāgasena. Even the intellectual interest that Ralph Waldo Emerson and the 'Boston Brahmins' had in India's religion was very different. It is a new phenomenon, although by now it is about thirty years old.

The fad and the fashion will pass away. Gurus will rise and fall. Some like Professor Harvey Cox will claim to become a better Christian by 'turning East'. But when the tide dies out and recedes what, if anything, will it leave behind? This is not easy to answer, although one thing is sure. It will never be the same. Already different Christian Churches have reorganized their priorities. Meditation and mystical thoughts, myths, devotion and rituals are not, and have never been, totally absent in the Occident. It was a question of emphasis for which gradual demythologization and de-ritualization took place in history. Attention has now shifted to capture the imagination of those who were going elsewhere. However, serious interest in Buddhism, in different phases of Hindu thought, in Zen, in Sufism and other oriental religions, still persists in certain circles. Ideas survive like different brands of Oriental cook-books. Some like them while others hate them!

Notes and Referemces

1. See Hegel (1807), pp. 111–19.
2. See Zaehner (1955).
3. See for example Sextus Empiricus (1933), Introduction by R.D. Berry, p. xxxi.
4. See C. Eliot (1921), esp. vol. I, p. xii, and W.Y. Evans-Wentz (1935), esp. p. 36.

Böhtlingk, Otto, ed. (1865), *Indische Sprüche*, vol. III (St Petersburg: Kaiserliche Akademie der Wissenschaften).

Bloom, Allan (1987), *The Closing of the American Mind: How Higher Education Has Failed Democracy and Impoverished the Souls of Today's Students* (Harmondsworth: Penguin).

Cox, Harvey (1979), *Turning East: The Promise and Peril of the New Orientalism* (London: Allen Lane).

Dickinson, G. Lowes (1914), *An Essay on the Civilisations of India, China and Japan* (London: J.M. Dent & Sons Ltd.).

Eliot, Charles (1921), *Hinduism and Buddhism: An Historical Sketch*, vol. I (London: Edward Arnold & Co.).

Evans-Wentz, W.Y., ed. (1935), *Tibetan Yoga and Secret Doctrines* (Oxford: Oxford University Press, paperback ed. 1967).

Hegel, Georg Wilhelm Friedrich (1807), *The Phenomenology of Spirit*, trans. by A.V. Miller, with analysis and foreword by J.N. Findlay (Oxford: Clarendon Press, 1979).

Nussbaum, Martha (1987), 'Undemocratic Vistas', in *New York Review of Books*, vol. 34, no. 17, 5 Nov. 1987, pp. 20–6.

Ramanujan, A.K. (1971), *Relations: Poems* (London: Oxford University Press).

Schwab, Raymond (1950), *The Oriental Renaissance: Europe's Rediscovery of India and the East, 1680–1880*, trans. by G. Patterson-Black and V. Reinking, foreword by E.W. Said (New York: Columbia University Press, 1984).

Sextus Empiricus (1933), *Outlines of Pyrrhonism*, vol. 1, with translation and introduction by R.G. Bury (London: William Heinemann Ltd).

Staal, Frits (1961), *Advaita and Neoplatonism: a Critical Study in Comparative Philosophy* (Madras: University of Madras).

Śāstri, Swami Dwarikadas, ed. (1979), *Milindapañha Pali* (Varanasi: Bauddha Bharati).

Virgil (1995), *Aeneid*, trans. by E. McCrorie (Ann Arbor: University of Michigan Press).

West, M.L. (1971), *Early Greek Philosophy and the Orient* (Oxford: Clarendon Press).

Zaehner, R.C. (1955), *Zurvan: a Zoroastrian Dilemma* (Oxford: Clarendon Press).

21

Salvation in a Bottle: Religion, Psychedelics and Mysticism—A Post-mortem

Give me a button of wild peyote
To munch in my den at night,
That I may set my id afloat
In the country of queer delight.

Give me a flagon of mescalin
to wash o'er my mundane mind
That I may feel like Schizophrene
Of the catatonic kind.

So hey! let me in the visions of light
To banish banality,
Then will I surely catch a sight
Of the Real Reality.

So ho! let all resistance down
For a transcendental glance
Past the superego's frosty frown
At the cosmic underpants.[1]

1. DRUG AND RELIGION

The issues connected with drugs today are varied and extremely complicated. The relevant problems can be classified under various headings: medical, clinical, pharmacological, sociological, anthropological, psychiatric, psychoanalytic, theological, philosophical, ethical, legal and religious. Thousands of books and pamphlets dealing with most of these aspects have been published over the last three decades.

The drug problem, in short, is controversial and highly sensitive.

However, we are not interested, in this context at least, in the kind of problems that the drug barons, the Noriegas and others have created. It is a major issue, but not in the context of Eastern religions.

The controversy over drugs and the use of drugs in religion, is not new. It is almost as old as human civilization. However, with the modern discovery of certain synthetic and very powerful drugs like LSD, and with the rise of such messiahs like Timothy Leary and Richard Alpert, Oriental mysticism and drugs became readily associated with each other.

It would be difficult to go into the details of the various issues raised in connection with the modern psychedelic movement. The drugs that are relevant for the 'psychedelic revolution' are only those that have some effect on the brain and the spinal chord, on which the brain rests. In other words, these drugs affect what is called in medical terms the Central Nervous System. The Central Nervous System is like the control centre of our psychosomatic life. It controls not only our body but also our mind, that is, our sensations, emotions, thoughts and feelings. In medical history, these drugs first appeared as pain-relievers and thus fulfilled a much-needed function in therapeutics. Patients suffered from pain under the influence of various diseases, and it was the doctor's duty to cure the disease. But in most cases, the method of cure, if it existed at all, was gradual and slow. Meanwhile the patient groaned under pain. Thus, the first batch of pain-relievers were welcome additions to the pharmacological list. It was seen that some drugs like opium could reduce the sensation of pain.

Philosophers, over the ages, have worried whether pain has any separate reality apart from the sensation of pain. Some uncompromising realists like the Naiyāyikas of India advocate that pain and the sensation of pain are, at least theoretically, separable entities, while others like the Buddhists and almost all other reputable philosophers of East and West tend to argue that pain is indistinguishable from, and hence identical with, the sensation of pain. The problem of a physician was, however, different. When he saw that he could remove the sensation of pain, at least temporarily, without being able to remove the 'cause' of pain, he welcomed the addition of the group of drugs called 'pain-relievers' to his pharmacy. Following the style of the Book of Genesis, one might say, '. . . and the physician (God) saw that it *was* good', and hence he let it stay. If the physician cannot make the patient better instantly, he can at least make him or her *feel* better in a moment.

2. PAIN AND ALLEVIATION OF PAIN

It is an open question how far pain is somatic and how far it is psychical. It is in fact at the borderline of psyche and somatology. But as long as the patient forgets his pain, the physician need not worry about the problem. The drugs that have created controversy today are not 'pain-relievers', but are usually classified as 'mind influencers'. But their original connection with pain-relievers is obvious. For a pain-reliever is also believed to *manipulate* the 'mind' of the patient by affecting the central nervous system. One thing is, however, clear. It is easy to see why such drugs should be taken to signify religion and the grace of God. Their immediate effects were welcome. Some of these drugs soothe even the agonies of a cancer sufferer. Others can calm the frenzies of a schizophrenic. And there are still others which can twist the mind into experiencing sometimes ecstatic (and occasionally horrible) visions. Thus, it does not take long to realize that the introduction of these drugs in pharmacology will generate, through their uses and abuses, some long-standing effect on society. As some drug-experts have noted: 'their ability to ease the abrasive contact between man and reality has made them coveted and widely used commodities.'[2]

On a very superficial reading, the original aim of some of the important religions on earth (e.g., Buddhism and Jainism) was to remove suffering or pain or anguish of mankind in the form of disease, old age and death. Thus, the Buddha, for example, has been called the 'great physician' (*mahāvaidya*) in the Buddhist scriptures. When a drug can produce instant relief from pain, it is usually looked upon as a miracle or gift of God. More so, when a drug like hashish or modern LSD can produce pleasant visions and hallucinations to make us forgetful of the problems, agonies and cruelties of the 'real' world. A religious doctrine, after all, tries for a similar goal: removal of pain, suffering and the agonies of life.

The other important aspect of a religion is the promise of enlightenment, which is sometimes regarded as a sort of mystical enlightenment or a blissful state of consciousness. Some religions are openly claimed to be pathways to this mystical state while others are, perhaps, less explicitly and less decidedly so. Mahāyāna Buddhism, Zen and some forms of Hinduism belong to the first group. Christianity and Islam fall into the second group. Thus, if a drug can trigger off at least the simulation of such mystical visions (and who can decide what is a real sensation of bliss and what is only a simulation of it?), it can very easily be developed into a religious cult.

The connection between psychedelic drugs and oriental religious movements was something that the Oriental as well as the Orientalist deplored. However, the introduction of some new drugs has often been hailed with religious fervour. The case for alcohol (which is also a kind of drug, to be sure) is well known. When the distillation process was well-established in AD 1300, alcohol was hailed by a French physician, Arnauld de Villeneuve, as really 'a water of immortality'.[3] What can promise 'immortality' except religion?

Even the minor drugs like tea and coffee, and dangerous drugs like tobacco and coca, had their hey-days at the time of their first introduction in civilized society. Dr Sigmund Freud, father of modern psychoanalysis, in his 'pre-psychoanalytic' period had experimented (in fact, self-experimented) with cocaine. In 1886, he wrote a paper 'on Coca,' where he outlined the historical events which led him to his self-experiment. A year later he delivered a lecture before the Psychiatric Union of Austria about the general effects of cocaine.

Both cocaine and opium are now well recognized to be harmful. But it is probably paradoxical that their medical uses have proved to be immensely beneficial to mankind. Opium is refined into morphine, which is a successful and reliable analgesic (the medical term for 'pain-reliever') today. Cocaine, the derivative of the Coca plant, serves as an important anaesthetic agent. It goes without saying that the introduction of anaesthetic drugs has revolutionized modern surgery. What was before a crude and cruel art is now a modern life-saving science.

3. DISCOVERY OF 'MIND DRUGS'

It was the discovery of certain anaesthetic drugs in the nineteenth century that laid the foundation of modern surgery. Some earlier anaesthetic drugs were reputed, before their medical use, to be exhilarating and agents for making people 'high'. Ether, for example, was first known to medical students as a drug that was more highly toned than simple boozing. It generates some euphoric feeling of buoyancy and unconsciousness. And thus, it was fashionable among the medical students. But Dr C.W. Long of Jefferson, Georgia, used it on a patient to remove a tumour painlessly.[4] Similarly, nitrous oxide or laughing gas was used in the nineteenth century for anaesthetic purposes. But philosophers and psychologists of the late nineteenth century were not indifferent to the anaesthetic discovery. William James himself sampled the laughing gas and wrote about his experience in metaphysical terms in a note to an article entitled 'On Some Hegelisms', which appeared in the philosophical journal, *Mind*, in 1882.[5] Even in 1902, James wrote as follows:

Nitrous oxide and ether, especially nitrous oxide, when sufficiently diluted in the air, stimulate the mystical consciousness in an extraordinary degree. Depth beyond depth of truth seems revealed to the inhaler. This truth fades out, however, or escapes, at the moment of coming to; and if any words remain over in which it seemed to clothe itself, they prove to be the veriest nonsense. Nevertheless, the sense of a profound meaning having been there persists; and I know more than one person who is persuaded that in the nitrous oxide trance we have a genuine metaphysical revelation.[6]

In the middle of the twentieth century, medical science witnessed another revolution, with the discovery of what are known as psychotropic agents or 'mind drugs'—drugs that are tranquillizers and those that clinically relieve depressions. This ushered in a new era in the treatment of mental illness. Some physicians thought that at last they could *cure* mental illness with drugs. But this proved to be an illusion. What happened was this: these drugs contributed to the treatment of the mentally ill by making the past crude and cruel methods such as 'straps', 'straight-jackets' and shock-treatments, almost obsolete. Mental hospitals no longer remained horror chambers but became more humane institutions. Just as the anaesthetic drugs have made modern surgery possible, so also the psychotropic drugs have turned mental hospitals into real hospitals and not the torture houses of the past.

Such is the interesting history of drugs and clinical medicine. The controversy over drugs and religion stems from newer discoveries of the 'mind drugs'. Recent controversy centres around the more powerful 'mind' drugs', such as mescalin, psiolocybin and the most potent of all synthetic drugs, LSD (Lysergic Acid Diethylamide). Some call them 'mind distorting' drugs in obvious disapproval of their use. But the proponents call them the 'consciousness-expanding' or 'mind-manifesting', or in short, 'psychedelic' drugs. It is the non-clinical use of such drugs, a use that has been stamped as 'religious' and 'spiritual', which is our main concern here. In fact, these drugs had been claimed by some to be the best religious gift of God to man—a claim that has transformed the 'drug' research into a spiritual revolution and messianism. And so Timothy Leary had renamed the LSD movement as 'the League of Spiritual Discovery' movement.

4. CONSCIOUSNESS-EXPANDING AND MYSTICISM

I have shown earlier that it is natural for persons having an absorbing interest in religion and mystical experience to be involved in and inquisitive about the 'consciousness-expanding' or psychedelic drugs. It cannot be said that the trend of oriental mysticism in the West was always associated with psychedelic drugs. For there is no evidence to show that Emerson, Thoreau and other New England Transcendentalists, or the 'Boston Brahmins', who introduced oriental mysticism in America, experimented with drugs. But there were others who did. William James' self-experiment has already been mentioned, and two other important figures must be mentioned in this connection. One was a poet, who, about a century later, became the poet-prophet of the hip generation, Walt Whitman (1819–92). The other was a Canadian psychiatrist, who was also the superintendent of a mental hospital in London, Ontario: Richard Maurice Bucke (1837–1902). It is significant to note that Bucke became Whitman's official biographer. And James quoted extensively from Whitman and Bucke in his *The Varieties of Religious Experience* (1902).

Whether Walt Whitman experimented with hashish, marijuana or some other psychedelics before he wrote his inspired *Leaves of Grass*, is a matter of conjecture today. It was William Braden, who writing in 1967 asserted that Whitman's *Leaves of Grass* echoed and re-echoed 'with Oriental and psychedelic intuitions'.[7] Braden argued that it was the simplest way to explain the sudden change in Whitman's literary gift. His early writings were dull and tedious while *Leaves of Grass* was inspired. Whitman acknowledged reading the publications of the New England Transcendentalists like Emerson. But mere reading was, perhaps, not the only thing to inspire him to produce such verses as this:

2. Now I absorb immortality and peace,
   I admire death and test propositions.
4. I was thinking the day most splendid, till I saw what the not-day exhibited,
   I was this globe enough, till there tumbled upon me myriads of other globes.
5. Now while the great thoughts of space and eternity fill me, I will measure myself by them

   And now, touched with the lives of other globes, arrived as far along as those of the earth,
   Or waiting to arrive, or passed on farther than those of the earth,
   I henceforth no more ignore them than I ignore my own life,
   Or the lives on the earth arrived as far as mine, or waiting to arrive.[8]

R.M. Bucke was about thirty when he first read Whitman's *Leaves of Grass*, which, by his own admission, had a very profound influence upon his life. Bucke's first major publication, *Man's Moral Nature* (1879) was dedicated to Walt Whitman in the following words:

I Dedicate This Book to the Man Who Inspired It—To the Man Who of All Men Past and Present that I Have Known Has the Most Exalted Moral Nature—to Walt Whitman.[9]

Bucke was not born in Canada. His parents emigrated to Canada from England when he was quite young in age. He graduated from the Faculty of Medicine at McGill University and practised medicine for some time. Eventually Bucke founded the medical school in London, Ontario, and became superintendent of the Ontario Hospital there. In 1901, his magnum opus in mysticism, *Cosmic Consciousness—A Study of the Evolution of the Human Mind*, was published in Philadelphia by Innes & Sons. This book, along with William James, *The Varieties of Religious Experience* (his Gifford Lectures on Natural Religion at the University of Edinburg, 1902) became two important landmarks in the study of mysticism in the West at the beginning of this century.

Bucke wanted to distinguish between self-consciousness and 'cosmic consciousness' as follows. The latter, in his opinion, is an intuitive awareness of the cosmos and of the life and order of things in the universe while the former is simply an awareness of the self's own thoughts. He proposed an analysis in this light of several cases of mystical illumination in history—beginning with the Buddha and Christ and ending with Blake and Whitman. However, he did not have, unlike James, any positive sympathy for the drug-induced state of heightened consciousness. He only noted briefly that a sense of euphoria—'a kind of artificial and bastard cosmic consciousness' (Bucke, 1901, p. 314)—could be induced by such anaesthetic drugs as ether or chloroform.

James, in his Grifford lectures, went a step further. He was not reluctant to concede that chemicals or drugs might produce genuine mystical states. He talked about his own self-experiment and explained how he was led into this experiment by reading Benjamin Paul Blood's *The Anaesthetic Revelation and the Gist of Philosophy*. Referring to Blood's description, he remarked: 'This has the genuine religious mystic ring!'[10] And in this way, I believe, James laid the foundation for Aldous Huxley's self-experiment with mescalin in this century—an experiment that influenced the modern psychedelic controversy to a considerable extent.

Aldous Huxley was not one of the 'Yankee Hindoos'. Huxley arrived in California from England just before the Second World War. His predilection for mysticism (of both Eastern and Western varieties) was evident from his earlier writing, *Time Must Have a Stop* (1945), and *Perennial Philosophy* (1946). Whether or not he was driven to mystical convictions by the horrors of the war, we do not know. The so-called modern explosion of mystical trends took place in North America when the prolonged Vietnam War was going on. Some sort of escape from reality (or, at least, what ordinary people call 'reality') into another world characterizes any form of mysticism. The explosion of 'mystical' religion coincided with a bloody war. But we should not make too much of this point. We do not always have to look for a bloody war in order to be convinced that reality or the *given* or the present situation is bad or undesirable.

The highly influential, and also highly controversial, book of Huxley, *The Doors of Perception* (1954), was written after his own self-experiment with mescalin. It was another English emigré in the New World, Humphrey Osmond, who visited Huxley in 1953 and finally initiated the latter into the mysteries of mushrooms and mescalin. In his book, Huxley stated a thesis, perhaps for the first time, in a significant form—a thesis that was for some time lurking behind the minds of his predecessors in the drug-versus-religion controversy. Huxley's thesis was: drug-induced mystical experience should be viewed at the same level as mystical religious experience. The book evoked strong emotions and criticism from contemporary religious scholars. The implication of Huxley's proposition was fatal to the religious orthodoxy. As it was put by one of Huxley's severest critics, R.C. Zaehner, Professor of Eastern Religions and Ethics at Oxford: 'It must then follow that the vision of God of the mystical saint is "one and the same" as the hallucination of the lunatic.'[11]

5. CRITICISM OF THE DRUG-INDUCED MYSTICISM

Professor Zaehner, who entered the Roman Catholic Church in 1946, was so upset by the religious implication of Huxley's proposition that he himself experimented with mescalin (in December 1955) to disprove Huxley's contention. Zaehner's self-experiment has been reported in Appendix B of his *Mysticism—Sacred and Profane* (1957, pp. 212–26). Zaehner's criticism of Huxley has softened down in his latest book on drugs and mysticism (1972). In fairness to Huxley, however, it must be noted that he was still a bit hesitant to replace religion by chemistry. He only suggested that chemistry may be potentially helpful to religion. To use his own words:

> I am not so foolish as to equate what happens under the influence of mescalin or of any other drug, prepared or in the future preparable, with the realization of the end and the ultimate purpose of human life: Enlightenment, the Beatific Vision.

All I am suggesting is that the mescalin experience is what Catholic theologians call 'a gratuitous grace', not necessary to salvation but potentially helpful and to be accepted thankfully if made available.[12]

In 1945, the synthetic drug LSD was discovered through an accident by Dr Hoffman in the Sandoz laboratory in Switzerland. It was Dr Humphry Osmond who pioneered the clinical use of LSD while he was working in Weyburn, Saskatchewan, between 1951 and 1959. He is also responsible for the coining of the new term 'psychedelic' which replaced the older, rather derogatory, terms like 'hallucinogenic' or 'psychotomimetic'.

To coin a new term actually means to add a new meaning or significance—a new dimension—to the function of these drugs. And this purpose was more than accomplished within a few years with the rise of Timothy Leary and the LSD cult. Psychiatrists sometimes disagree about the clinical value of LSD. It has been useful in the treatment of mental illness especially, and perhaps ironically, alcoholism and even addiction to heroin. Though Dr Osmond seems to be in favour of the use of LSD for the purpose of research and experiment (including self-experiment), he warns also of the potential dangers and has reservations about its indiscriminate use.

Despite James, Bucke and Huxley, the psychedelic movement could never have been a messianic movement as it is today without the arrival on the scene of two Harvard professors, Timothy Leary and Richard Alpert. Both professors had respectable Ph.D.s and research backgrounds in psychology. They became colleagues at Harvard. The transformation of these Harvard professors into the High Priests of the LSD cult is an interesting story and it is too well known to be repeated here. Leary was more messianic about LSD than Alpert. Alpert was for some time the liaison between the flamboyant Leary and the university authority. But in 1963, both Leary and Alpert were dismissed by President Pusey from the Harvard faculty. Leary remained the High Priest of the LSD cult. Alpert changed his 'religion' and became Baba Ram Dass. He found a guru in India and established a spiritual centre of his own in America.

I have shown above the partial English heritage of the modern psychedelic movement in North America. Even Timothy Leary gratefully acknowledges this English heritage. He has written in his *The Politics of Ecstasy* (1970):

It is a curious fact that the American psychedelic movement is almost completely a British import. LSD. Pounds, shillings and pence. Consider the lineage. The key architect of the revolution is a British psychiatrist named Humphrey Osmond. Who? He invented the term *psychedelic*. . . . And thank you, Evans-

Wentz and Arthur Waley, for Aldous Huxley. . . . And thank you, William Blake and A.A. Orage, for Alan Watts, mischievous Zen master, lyric Anglican priest (high church), source, inspiration, and guide (although most of them don't know it) for San Franscisco's flower children. . . . My understanding of marijuana and LSD is mainly due to my listening to and watching Alan.[13]

In a lecture delivered at a meeting of Lutheran psychologists and other interested professionals, at Bellevue Startford Hotel, Philadelphia, on 30 August 1963, Leary described how he was converted to the psychedelic cult:

> Once upon a time many years ago, on a sunny afternoon in the garden of a Cuernavaca villa, I ate seven of the so-called sacred mushrooms which had been given to me by a scientist from the University of Mexico. During the next five hours, I was whirled through an experience which could be described in many extravagant metaphors but which was above all and without question, the deepest religious experience of my life.[14]

This must have been the summer of 1960 when Leary and many other academics spent the vacation on research grants in Mexico. Why Leary's experience was described as 'religious' we will see later.

Mention must be made of the contribution of Alan W. Watts to the psychedelic movement in the sixties. Watts took up the cue where Huxley left it. Watts' *The Joyous Cosmology—Adventures in the Chemistry of Consciousness* is the rightful heir to Huxley's *The Doors of Perception.* If Huxley was a bit hesitant, Watts went all the way. He claimed in unambiguous language that the consciousness-changing drugs when accompanied by sustained philosophical reflection can lead a person, who is in search, not of kicks, but of understanding, to deeper and higher levels of insight (see Watts, 1962, p. xvii). Leary and Alpert, who wrote the foreword for this book, said, 'Watts follows Mr Huxley's lead and pushes beyond' (Watts, 1962, p. xiv). The *foreword* was apparently written by Leary and Alpert just before their dismissal from the Harvard faculty.

Watts apparently knew Buddhism, specially Zen, and connected the psychedelic movement with what may be called the neo-Buddhist movement in North America. Thus his endorsement of the psychedelic movement became significant for the American youth on whose minds some of the tenets of Buddhism had already made an impact. Both Leary and Alpert reported in their *foreword* to Watts' book how since 1960 staff-members of the Centre for Research in Personality at Harvard University had engaged in systematic experiments with three synthetic substances—mescalin, LSD and psiolocybin—a fact which later led to their dismissal from the faculty at Harvard. It was claimed by them, that these synthetic 'drugs' should not be regarded as drugs but as 'sacramental foods'. According to the pharmacologists, they are not narcotics, nor intoxicants, nor energizers, nor anaesthetics, nor tranquillizers. They are, from the ordinary viewpoint, nothing but hallucinogens. But the drug-cultists resented this term, and hence preferred the term 'psychedelics' coined by Dr Osmond.

Leary and Alpert have argued that the conventional models of western psychology—psychoanalytic or behaviouristic—were quite inadequate to map the 'richness and breadth of expanded consciousness' (Watts, 1962, p. xiii) induced by these drugs. Thus, the 'researchers' were forced to take recourse to non-dualistic conceptions of Eastern philosophies. In other words when scientists are ambivalent and sceptical, religion has taken over. What ordinary logic or rationality does not find easy to explain is easily assimilated by 'mysticism'. It was claimed by the cultists that these psychedelic drugs were the solution of all psychological and social ills. Use of these drugs with proper indoctrination and sacraments would transform human society and make this world a better place to live in. Just as a religion is traditionally recognized as something that is supposed to purge human society of evils and make this world more livable, use of psychedelic drugs is also supposed to do the same thing. Thus, Leary claimed his drug cult to be a religion. In fact, the claim was that it is the best form of religion that God (as well as chemistry) has given man so far. The cultist saw himself at the vanguard of a new era when instant ecstasy or instant *nirvāṇa* or mystical consciousness can be 'turned on' and 'turned in' almost with the rapidity of the push-button system of a television set. Leary, perhaps on good grounds, scolded the over-formalistic, television-game oriented North American society. He called it the 'TV stage set defined by mass-media-social-psychology-adjustment-normality'.[15] But ironically and unfortunately he uses the same TV-terminology to propagate his newly founded psychedelic religion: 'Turn on, Tune in, and Drop Out.'

Lest it be assumed that religion (and God) was being replaced by chemistry, or rather by chemicals, the drug cultist was quick to point out that the mystical experience was only 'triggered off' by the drug and not 'created' by it. Thus, Alan Watts explained: '. . . speaking quite strictly, mystical insight is no more in the chemical itself than biological knowledge is in the microscope.'[16] Noting the ambivalence of some people who think that a chemical is too simple a means for our access to the 'much higher and deeper' religious experience or mystical insight, the cultist argues that this is a misconception resulting from a misplaced fear. It may seem to be an insult to human dignity if we can possess a wisdom or insight that can be 'turned on' like the switch of TV set. Are we to be finally regarded as chemical automata? This ambivalence is noticeable even in Huxley (1954). In fact, the 'mind' drugs raised very serious questions for the scientists and psychologists, and particularly for the philosophers. As Dr de Ropp wrote about the relationship between mind and matter:

The mind of man does not exist in a vacuum. It is associated with the chemistry of the brain and this chemistry underlies all our manifestations. Neither thought nor emotion can occur without some chemical change. The cruelty of the tyrant, the compassion of the saint, the ardor of lovers, the hatred of foes all are based on chemical processes. However hard we may try, however earnestly we may wish to do so, we cannot separate mind from matter or isolate what we call man's soul from his body. Were this not so the action of drugs on the mind could never be understood. It is precisely because all mental and emotional processes have a chemical basis that these drugs exert an action. If mind existed in a vacuum apart from matter we would not be able to influence it by drugs.[17]

Religious people were rightly perturbed at the implication of the drug movement. R.C. Zaehner expressed their common feeling adequately:

Huxley could, and should have gone farther. Mescalin is clinically used to produce artificially a state akin to schizophrenia, more specifically the manic phase of the manic-depressive psychosis. It must therefore follow, if we accept the fatal 'platitude', that not only can 'mystical' experience be obtained artificially by the taking of drugs, it is also naturally present in the manic. It must then follow that the vision of God of the mystical saint is 'one and the same' as the hallucination of the lunatic. There would appear to be no way out, unless the original 'platitudinous' premiss is unsound.[18]

In plain language, the criticism is: how can something genuinely spiritual come out of a chemical substance? How can you buy salvation in a bottle? The 'drug' movement becomes *wrongly* associated with dangerous drugs such as heroin as well as with the not-so-spiritual beat generation and the hipster world. And this understandably has raised public alarm.

The drug-cultists also argued that human dignity is not at all at stake if we admit that the psychedelic 'drugs' are only means to gain genuine wisdom or mystical experience just as a microscope is a means to gain genuine knowledge of science. Thus, Alan Watts urged:

If they [psychedelics] are an affront to the dignity of the mind, the microscope is an affront to the dignity of the eye and the telephone to the dignity of the ear.[19]

Similarly, Dr Leary prescribed that taking of LSD should be regarded as a 'religious sacrament', not to be confused with 'kicks' or entertainment.

It is further argued that it is not the privilege of only certain organized religious disciplines of the world to enjoy the *sole agency* of providing mystical insight. Huxley might have had doubts, Zaehner might have been too much involved with the concepts of sacredness and profanity of existing religions, but Alan Watts was predictably sure, and announced:[20]

[. . .] I can find no essential difference between the experiences induced, under favorable conditions, by these chemicals and the states of 'cosmic consciousness' recorded by R.M. Bucke, William James, Evelyn Underhill, Raynor Johnson, and other investigators of mysticism.[20]

6. THE 'SOMA' CONTROVERSY AND ITS IMPLICATION

I will fail in my duty here if I do not report on the contribution of the mycologists (specialists in the study of mushrooms) to the psychedelic movement. It was a type of mushroom, after all—the 'flesh of God' (*Iteonanactl*) of the Aztecs—that 'turned on' Leary in the summer of 1960 and finally converted him into the psychedelic religion. By a remarkable coincidence, at the same time, two well-known mycologists, Gordon and Valentian Wasson (husband and wife) were pursuing their own research in Mexico on sacred mushrooms and their relation to the origin of religious ideas among primitive peoples. The Wassons took part also in the ceremonies of the cult of the Mexican Indians. In other words, both husband and wife were initiated by their Indian friends into the tremendous Mystery of the mushroom. To use the phrase of Gordon Wasson, they were 'bemushroomed'.

The Wassons propounded a theory about the origin of religion among the primitive people—a striking surmise which gave a 'booster' shot, as it were, to the already emerging psychedelic religion. In the language of Gordon Wasson:[21]

I do not recall which of us, my wife or I, first dared to put into words, back in the '40's, the surmise that our own remote ancestors, perhaps 4000 years ago, worshipped a divine mushroom. It seemed to us that this might explain the phenomenon of mycophilia *vs.* mycophobia, for which we found an abundance of supporting evidence in philology and folklore.[21]

Wasson's conjecture is based upon folklore and some archaeological evidence which shows the Middle American cult of a divine mushroom—the cult of 'God's flesh' among the Indians of pre-Columbian times—can be traced back to about 1500 BC.

Wasson was highly imaginative in his so-called scientific surmise. He compared the mushroom cult of the Mexican Indians with the Eleusinian Mystery of the Greeks. He was apparently over-excited to be on the brink of uncovering the secret of the Mysteries with the help of mushrooms or some hallucinogenic plants. On the whole, he clearly endorsed a regeneration of the mushroom cult in the modern age.

The Wasson couple preferred to describe their branch of research as Ethnomycology. They derived their inspiration from their teacher and guide, Professor Roger Heim of Paris, director of the *Laboratoire de Cryptogamie*, and editor of the *Revue de Mycologie*. While mycology is a recognized branch of botany or biology, 'ethnomycology' is a creation of the Wasson couple. The main thesis of this new branch of 'science' was what I have already quoted above: 'Our remote ancestors, perhaps, 4000 years ago, worshipped a divine mushroom.'[22] The important psychedelic agent in the sacred mushroom of Mexico has been isolated by the scientists (biological chemists), and it is known as psilocybin.

Gordon Wasson has claimed that the mystical or ecstatic visions enjoyed by countless prophets, mystics and ascetics in the past clearly duplicate the mushroom agapé of Mexico. Although he has conceded that St John did not eat mushrooms before he wrote the Book of the Revelation, nor did William Blake eat mushroom in order to write about the 'vision', he nevertheless has argued that mushrooms had the advantage of permitting many 'to see, more clearly than our perishing mortal eye can see, vistas beyond the horizons of this life, to travel backwards and forwards in time, to enter other planes of existence, even (as the Indians say) to know God'.[23] Even Plato, who wrote about an 'Ideal World of Archetypes beyond this imperfect mundane existence' had drunk, according to Wasson, of the potion in the temple of Eleusis and had spent the night seeing the great vision. This, Wasson considers, is the solution of the Eleusinian Mystery.

Wasson has actually reinforced the psychedelic religion of today with his poetic and prophetic pronouncements about the primitive religions of Mexico, Greece and Siberia (and finally of India, for which see below). His argument seems to be based on the following plea: if, in the forgotten past, the religions of man started with the help of a mushroom, why not revive it again? If we want to be religious, let us be 'bemushroomed'. This is how he expresses his poetic vision of the origin of religion:

> As man emerged from his brutish past, thousands of years ago, there was a stage in the evolution of his awareness when the discovery of a mushroom (or was it a higher plant?) with miraculous properties was a revelation to him, a veritable detonator to his soul, arousing in him sentiments of awe and reverence, and gentleness and love, to the highest pitch of which mankind is capable, all those sentiments and virtues that mankind has ever since regarded as the highest attribute of his kind. . . . Some are shocked that the key even to religion might be

reduced to mere drug. On the other hand, the drug is as mysterious as it ever was: 'like the wind it cometh we know not whence, nor why.' Out of a mere drug comes the ineffable, comes ecstasy. It is not the only instance in the history of human kind where the lowly has given birth to the divine.[24]

Wasson has continued to make contributions to his twin projects: (a) his newly-found subject Ethnomycology and (b) fostering the belief that all important religions around the world started with the discovery of psychedelic mushrooms. It was William Braden who suggested that Wasson's 'mushroom' theory of the origin of religion should be applied to the enquiry into the origin of the Vedic religion of India (1967, p. 42). As early as 1968, Wasson fulfilled this expectation. His magnum opus, *Soma: Divine Mushroom of Immorality* came out in 1968, where he startled the Orientalists and Indological scholars by putting forward his 'identification' of the Soma plant. Soma, in his opinion, was fly-agaric *Amanita Muscaria*—the mushroom of the Siberian shaman.

It was Wasson's first major publication in his *Ethnomycological Studies*, study no. 1 (promised in his earlier article on 'The Hallucinogenic Fungi of Mexico', 1962) with twenty-four colour plates and three maps. The work was sumptuously produced, printed on handmade paper specially water-marked. The price at its publication was $200. Wasson said in the beginning: 'This is the first time that a mushroom has been proposed in the Soma quest.'[25]

I have already mentioned Wasson's prepossession with the hallucinogenic mushroom and its religious significance. With such preconceived ideas, when he read poetic descriptions of Soma in translation—in fact, translations of some *Ṛg-veda* hymns by K.F. Geldner and L. Renon—he felt that the hymns of *Ṛg-veda* fit the fly-agaric like a glove. That Soma was nothing but *Amanita Muscaria* was a sudden revelation to him, which he describes as follows:[26]

> True, one must possess some awareness of the psychotropic plants of the world and their role in primitive religion. Given that familiarity, a reading of Geldner, Renou and Bhawe leads straight to the fly-agaric.[26]

We can notice the significant role of a sudden *flash* or intuition (or, is it the mystical intuition of the 'bemushroomed'?) in Wasson's discovery throughout. It was a sudden flash or intuition that led him and his wife to surmise that our remote ancestors discovered religion by eating a psychedelic mushroom. Again, another 'straight' intuition. His argument consists mainly in drawing parallels of Soma ritual with the fly-agaric cult of Siberia. He had also produced beautiful colour plates of fly-agaric plants along with fragmentary quotations from the translation of the *Ṛg-vedic* hymns, which, he thought, reinforced his thesis.

Indologists of Europe and America were understandably surprised by Wasson's thesis. Some well-known scholars like Professor D.H.H. Ingalls of Harvard University and Professor F.B.J. Kuiper of Leiden have endorsed Wasson's identification of Soma with the fly-agaric. This has been done almost with a sigh of relief! For the Indologists, the identification of Soma was an ancient puzzle created by the Indologists themselves through conflicting suggestions regarding the identification. Soma was previously identified as *Sacrostemma, Ephedra*, rhubarb hops, *Cannabis Indica*, or others. In short, the identification of Soma was a hopeless puzzle which Gordon Wasson's thesis seemed to have solved.

Wasson was invited to read a paper on Soma at the annual meeting of the American Oriental Society at Baltimore in April 1970. Professor Norman Brown of Pennsylvania chaired the occasion and D.H.H. Ingalls and J.A.B. van Buitenen of Chicago commented on Wasson's thesis. Both accepted the identification as valid, on the whole, and hailed it as a new discovery. They differed from Wasson only on some minor details. Wasson presented a modified version of the same paper with some colour slides at the International Congress of Orientalists, Canberra, Australia, in January 1971. Later on, this paper along with Ingalls' comment was published as an essay of the American Oriental Society (Essay No. 7) in memory of Louis Renou (see Bender, 1971).

That Wasson's thesis should be provocative and challenging to the Indologists was only to be expected. But that the well-known Indologists would accept it without much criticism of a serious nature was a bit surprising even to Wasson. Ingalls, however, has disagreed with one of the major details of the Wasson thesis: his theory of the urinated Soma. Seeing that the Siberian tribesman not only used to chew the fly-agaric but also drink the urine of a person who had eaten fly-agaric, Wasson has tried to find evidence of this practice in the *Ṛg-Veda*. Ingalls has shown that Wasson failed to prove this point—prevalence of this practice among the Vedic Indians. The texts cited by Wasson in support of his point admit of a different interpretation. Not only that, Ingalls believes that the practice, in all probabilities, did not exist in Vedic India. For Ingalls argues, the Vedic Aryan community was quite open about bodily functions. Thus, if the practice existed at all, the Vedic poets would not have shied away from describing it in unmistakable language.

The kind of analytic insight which Ingalls had shown in repudiating

Wasson's contention about the existence of the practice of the urinated Soma among Vedic Indians could have been carried further. I think that if the detailed arguments of Wasson in support of his main thesis, identification of Soma with the fly-agaric, were subjected to criticism in the same way, one would have hesitated to accept the identification as valid beyond any shadow of doubt. The welcome criticism of Wasson's thesis came from Professor John Brough of Cambridge University, England. In his scholarly article, 'Soma and *Amanita Mascaria*' (1971), Brough argued that Wasson's thesis should be very cautiously examined before acceptance. A major part of Wasson's book had been devoted to drawing parallels with European folklore and the fly-agaric cult of Siberia. Brough summed up his opinion as follows:

> These sections of the book are full of interest as an aspect of cultural history; but as a matter of simple logic, such parallels have no probative value.[27]

Brough's scepticism was well founded in logic as well as in the interpretation technique of the Vedic hymns. Wasson's arguments based upon the poetic epithets and tropes of Soma found in the Vedic hymns can easily be discredited. Even Ingalls admitted that part of Wasson's argument was weak. He remarked: 'Not all the epithets remarked on by Wasson need be taken just as he takes them.'[28] But there are many other insuperable problems, if Wasson's identification is accepted as correct. If Soma were the hallucinogenic fly-agaric, it is difficult to explain certain facts. First, the Vedic Aryans were an extremely warlike nation and in mythology Indra frequently went to fight the demon, Vṛtra, with vigour and energy after drinking Soma. To the Vedic Aryans or Indo-Iranians, bloody battles were real in life. True, man can use psychedelic drugs or other tranquillizers to escape from the horrors and realities of war. But whoever has heard of a victorious hero going out to fight to win and destroy the opponent under the influence of some psychedelic mushroom? The peaceful Aztec tribesmen of Mexico were a very different sort of people compared to the warlike Vedic Aryans. For an inebriant these Aryans would have tried anything (even a mushroom), but it is doubtful whether they would have cared much for a hallucinogen.

Second, there is no clear case of an unambiguous description of a psychedelic experience in connection with the Soma hymns. It would be an insult to the poetic genius of the Vedic *ṛṣis* if we contend that they were unable to record an experience which they frequently had presumably under the influence of Soma. Third, Soma was primarily the name of the drink rather than the plant. In this connection, one observation of Brough (which, according to Brough, was first suggested by Mrs Brough) is quite pertinent:

> . . . if the Soma-plant had been a mushroom, it would be strange that the elaborate Vedic process of pounding out and filtering the juice should have been necessary. Why should the plant not have been simply eaten? (1971, p. 338).

This is a valid point since it contrasts with the fact that the Siberian fly-agaric was usually eaten in Siberia. Drinking was practised among the Siberian tribesmen only in connection with the 'urinated' material of a person who had eaten fly-agaric. That was why, I think, Wasson was very much intent on finding evidence of the 'urinated' Soma in the Vedic hymns. But Ingalls has successfully rejected this part of Wasson's theory, and thereby, I think, the original thesis about the identification of Soma with the fly-agaric has been sufficiently weakened.

Brough's further point is that the fly-agaric, when consumed, may cause nausea, vomiting, convulsions, stupor and even coma. Thus, he observes, '[h]ere it would seem, is a plant whose effects are totally unsuitable to stimulate Indra and human warriors for battle'.[29] There is also a lack of any description of this property of Soma in the Vedic hymns. Did the Vedic poets, who were so eloquent in praise of Soma, forget to mention it? I do not think this was only an omission on the part of the Vedic poets. It is only probable that they were simply not describing the red mushroom, the fly-agaric, but something different from it.

Commenting on the puzzle as to why British botanists in India never considered mushrooms in their Soma quest, Wasson has said: 'The English people, mycophobes to the core, ignored the "toadstools" of India.'[30] Wasson's answer to Brough's criticism, I believe, would follow this line. In other words, Brough's objection might be ascribed by Wasson to his supposed mycophobia. Wasson himself being of Anglo-Saxon origin, was a 'mycophobe' until he came to adopt a new religion—a religion which led him into his 'research' on the connection of mushrooms with the origin of important world religions. But, as far as I can judge, it is not a question of such subjective factors as mycophobia or mycophilia, but of relevant facts which Wasson, in my opinion, has not been able to supply sufficiently to justify his thesis about the identification of Soma. Thus, Brough might have been right in his criticism that in Wasson's arguments imagination plays the 'all-important' role, not the relevant facts.

Wasson's thesis had considerable influence upon the psychedelic movement. One major attempt of Leary and other drug cultists was to convert the psychedelic movement into a respectable religion and a spiritual movement. LSD, for Leary, stands for the League for Spiritual Discovery. What better way was there to argue in favour of this movement than to claim that not only the Mexican Indian religion of the Aztecs, or the Peyote religion of the Siberian tribe, but also the Vedic religion of India originated from the use of psychedelic mushrooms? Thus, Wasson's thesis which also implied that the psychedelic fly-agaric of the Siberian Taiga was, in prehistory, 'the divine inebriant of all Eurasia', was more than welcome to the drug-cultists who preach psychedelic religion to the young people.[31]

I have no objection to believing in the psychedelic origin of the Vedic religion, provided it can be shown conclusively that this was the case. But such a thesis has not so far been proven conclusively. What Brough said in the conclusion of his paper on Soma seems to be very reasonable:

> It would seem that much work remains to be done in botany, chemistry and pharmacology before it will be sensible to make a further attack on the problem of the botanical identity of the Soma-plant (1971, p. 361).

Let me make it clear also that I do not think that Soma was a fermented drink. Thus, on this point Wasson is right.[32] Max Müller and other Indologists were wrong when they thought that Soma was an alcoholic drink, and hence Wasson's criticism of such a theory is valid. The second point I agree on with Wasson is that Soma was undoubtedly an inebriant, and hence a drug. But my objection lies in identifying Soma as a hallucinogen or a psychedelic drug. The spirit of Vedic ritualism (and certainly we are talking about Vedic ritualism when we talk about the early phase of Vedic or Indo-Iranian religion) does not seem very suitable for the psychedelic character of its origin. These ritualists were matter-of-fact people with many down-to-the-earth goals in their mind. They had, so to say, different axes to grind than taking psychedelic drugs in order to transform or 'alter' their awareness of so-called reality. Thus it is that the drug cultists understandably appealed to the speculative religion and philosophy of Upaniṣads rather than to the Vedic ritualism. But the Upaniṣads were certainly later in history. It is significant that the Upaniṣadic teachers talk about a philosophy according to which *Brahman* or the universal consciousness is the ultimate reality in which all individual consciousness merges just as all rivers merges into the blue ocean. But nobody has so far suggested (as Wasson did suggest about Plato[33]) that Śāṇḍilya or Yājñavalkya taught the doctrine of *Brahman* as the ultimate truth under the influence of some psychedelic mushrooms. The drug-cultists had also claimed that it was this Upaniṣadic monism or the Mahāyāna

Buddhism (see Alan Watts, 1962) that was more in accord with their psychedelic religion of spiritualism than the God-oriented systems of Christianity, Judaism or sectarian Hinduism.

7. PSYCHEDELICS AND EASTERN MYSTICISM

In the sixties, along with the hippie scene in the West, a lot of research activities and publications were centred around the psychedelic movement and the effect of LSD on human personality. The first important book was the pioneering work by Robert E.L. Masters and Jean Houston, *The Varieties of Psychedelic Experience* (the title being reminiscent of James' *The Varieties of Religion Experience*). This was published in 1967. The authors (husband and wife) claimed to have spent a combined fifteen years in 'closely controlled and thoroughly documented research' with psychedelic drugs. They observed 206 drug sessions and interviewed another 214 persons who had ingested psychedelic drugs under various conditions. Although the authors deplore the messianic approach to the psychedelic movement, they remain optimistic and hopeful about the outcome of this movement in any case. Thus, they write:

> To be hopeful and optimistic about the psychedelic drugs and their potential is one thing; to be messianic is another. Both the present and the future of psychedelic research already have been generously injured by a messianism that is as unwarranted as it has proved undesirable.[34]

Their approach was no doubt research-oriented. But they were not so much concerned with the use of these drugs in the treatment of mental patients or alcoholics as they were with what they called the 'phenomenology' of the psychedelic experience of otherwise normal individuals.

According to their report, only eleven of their 206 psychedelic subjects were able to reach what they called 'the deep integral level' attended with 'illumination' and 'positive self-transformation'.[35] But in spite of this, the book nevertheless veered towards the justification of the psychedelic cult as a spiritual movement. There is a chapter called 'The Guide', which describes the role of the 'guide' in a psychedelic session comparable to the role of the priest over guru or shaman in religious cults. To quote the authors:

> It should be one of the chief tasks of the guide to assume the role of Virgil in this chemically-induced Divine Comedy and to help the subject select out of the wealth of phenomena among which he finds himself some of the more promising opportunities for heightened insight, awareness and integral understanding that the guide knows to be available in the psychedelic experience.[36]

They charted a training programme for the guide and insisted that he must himself be the subject of at least two psychedelic sessions and have actual psychedelic mystical experience before he could pass as a guide. The same point had been more forcefully made by Alan Watts.[37] One may say contrariwise that the role of a guide in psychedelics and the role of a guru in a religious movement are 'phenomenologically' indistinguishable and hence identical. Thus, messianism has, in fact, been endorsed by Masters and Houston. Besides, once the religious significance of the LSD experience is accepted, it is difficult to draw a line between messianism and non-messianism. For it is difficult to see in such an inquiry where the spirit of scientific research goes out of the window and religious conviction takes over. In the last chapter of the book, various charts, statistics and case histories were provided to show that ingestion of LSD, even in 'non-religious' settings, might produce an experience which was deeply 'religious' and 'mystical', eventually introducing a personality change in the subject. Thus, the authors vindicated the claim that the kind of experience that was 'the goal of many difficult-to-follow religious disciplines'—experience that was variously known as 'confrontation with God or even union with God' or as 'feeling of Oneness and ultimate bliss'—would easily and within a short period of time, be brought about by psychedelic sessions. If this is so, what more is left to stop short of a messianism about psychedelics?

It is significant to note that the authors were heavily influenced by Wasson's theory about the psychedelic origin of religion and God-consciousness in mankind. They were also influenced by the writings of a reputable philosopher, W.T. Stace (1961). Masters and Houston further surmised about the connection of psychedelics with the origin of Hatha Yoga in India. Using some not so reputable sources like the book of Phillipe de Felice (1936), it was argued that the development of Hatha Yoga in India must have been due to the scarcity or unavailability of the Soma plant! Obviously such a wild conjecture can be meaningful only to those who are looking for the psychedelic origin of all religions and mysticism. It is to be noted that while the fly-agaric was never available in India (and even Wasson admitted this fact), there were plenty of other psychedelic agents available to these Aryan people. Besides, it can be shown that while the Soma was the property of the Vedic Aryans, the Yoga techniques were probably known to pre-Vedic India. On this matter one can consult the archaeological evidence of the Indus Valley civilization.

Besides, all these wild conjectures about the psychedelic origin of Indian religions do not, and cannot, answer certain common questions like these: if Soma were a psychedelic substance that became scare in Vedic India, why were not some of the hemp plants, so common in India and the Middle East, accepted as its substitute? Why, when the Vedic priests came to use surrogates, did they not choose another mushroom or another psychedelic plant? While Wasson recognized that these questions were very natural, he had no answer for them. He *felt* that his identification of Soma was as sure as anything and that such questions did not matter much. He said, 'it is not incumbent on me to face the problems of post-Vedic history, an area where botany has only a minor role to play.'[38]

In the late sixties, certain conferences were held on the problem of psychedelic drugs, where concerned medical doctors, psychiatrists, sociologists and theologians used to meet and discuss the problem to get their ideas across. In March 1967, a public symposium was held in the Wesleyan University Chapel on the impact of LSD on man and society. All the papers presented were later published by Wesleyan University Press under the title, *LSD, Man and Society*, edited by Richard C. DeBold and Russell C. Leaf. In October 1967, the R.M. Bucke Memorial Society of Montreal convened another conference on a similar subject. These papers were published by the Society later under the title, *Do Psychedelics Have Religious Implications?*, edited by D.H. Salman and R.H. Prince. Both conferences reflected many interesting aspects of the drug movement.

The clinical psycho-therapeutic use of LSD was advocated and started early in the fifties by a number of physicians such as Charles Savage (1952), R.A. Sandison (1954), H.A. Abramson (1955), and H. Osmond (1957). Dr A.A. Kurland reported in the Wesleyan University conference about the results of LSD treatment on patients mainly at Spring Grove State Hospital at Baltimore. The therapeutic effects of LSD on narcotic and alcoholic patients have generally been good. But a timely warning has been given by Dr Kurland. These drugs affect the brain of man in some unusual ways, many of which are not relevant to their therapeutic use. For example, the production of 'visions' is not essential for clinical purposes.[39] Kurland further concludes:

> The analogy that we have sometimes used to try to convey the role of LSD in therapy is that of a scalpel in surgical intervention: the scalpel is helpful, but without the skilled surgeon it is merely a dangerous instrument.[40]

Dr Savage takes a similar cautious approach. He along with Dr Raymond Prince has compared the psychedelic experience to the state of elation found in mysticism and has used B.D. Lewin's thesis that these states are regressions to an infantile state of fusion with the breast.[41] (This important point will be discussed by me later in the general context of mysticism.) Savage (1967) has argued that psychedelic therapy is useful because it leads to what he calls personality maturation more rapidly than conventional psychotherapy. But he too has admitted that psychedelic therapy has not always been successful.[42] Thus, he stops short of recommending psychedelic therapy as the easiest substitute for psychotherapy.

8. DRY AND PSYCHIATRY

Dr Walter N. Pahnke had conducted research and exploration of the possible religious and mystical components of psychedelic experience. He was present in both conferences mentioned above. He was both a theologian and a psychiatrist. His Ph.D. thesis at Harvard was on *Drugs and Mysticism* (1963). Thus, his research brought a new tone to the psychedelic movement. But unfortunately, he was more concerned with psychedelic experiments on otherwise normal human beings for exploring the religious and mystical component of their experience. But as other physicians warned, the method was potentially dangerous.

The following question arose in this connection: why should we use otherwise normal human beings as 'guinea pigs' for exploring an area whose scientific value is dubious? I think Dr Pahnke's theological background has induced him to overestimate the value of whatever is stamped as religious or mystical or transcendental experience. It is not that he was not aware of the risk involved. Such comments as, 'First, there is a definite risk, which is certainly greater in uncontrolled than in controlled conditions,'[43] and 'it is a misconception to imagine that LSD is the magic answer to anything,'[44] bear witness to his ambivalence. But apparently due to his predilection for religion and mysticism, he found the connection between LSD and religious experience a 'fascinating area of research' (1969, p. 81).

In fact, Dr Pahnke was more in sympathy with the messianic fervour of Timothy Leary. He describes Leary's 'Turn-on, Tune-in, Drop-out' advice as an attempt to 'criticize modern American culture'. 'Drop out' for him meant withdrawal, not from everything, but 'from the meaningless games in which we are involved, to allow full-time commitment to spiritual exploration'.[45] Thus, his conviction of the value of religion and spirituality played an important role in his 'scientific' research. He even interpreted 'dropping out' as dropping into a 'worthwhile and interesting career, one that may be full of great satisfaction and a sense of accomplishment'.[46] Interesting certainly it is, but I have grave doubts whether it is worthwhile at all. Without being 'uptight' about drugs, one can seriously doubt the value of such psychedelic experiments.

Dr Raymond Prince of Montreal was another psychiatrist whose overt interest was in the realm cf spirit and what he called the anthropology of religion. He argued that 'there exists a spirit realm which may exert a potent influence over the world of men'.[47] His argument derives strength and support from Wasson's thesis about the psychedelic origin of religion. Prince pointed out that a belief in the spirit realm was based upon 'the world view of most cultures'.[48] And it was this belief that was essential to the theory that Prince propounds about psychedelic drugs, deliriums and divination. He argued that man's contact with the supernatural and the spirit realm happened in the past not only through psychedelic drugs but also during deliriums associated with infectious diseases, psychosis and exhaustion. The advantage with psychedelic substances is that 'they permit entry into the spirit realm at will'.[49] In another publication (1968b), Dr Prince established some basic similarity between mystical or 'trance' states and what are called 'possession' states induced generally by orgiastic dance in tribal communities (e.g., a voodoo service in the Haitian capital) (1968b, pp. vi–vii). But as I have indicated earlier, the theses of Dr Prince cannot be taken seriously. We not only find his 'spirit' realm unintelligible, he also talks about some hierarchical levels in the 'spirit' realm. For we have to say that those who are in the 'possession' states are in touch with lower spirits while those who are in trance states are in gradually higher realms. But so far I have not seen any convincing argument to prove the reality of different 'spirit worlds'. The 'spirit-worlds' are connected with witch craft and black-magic and hence of dubious value.

An interesting piece was contributed by Arthur J. Deikman in the 1967 conference in Quebec. Deikman, having noted that mystical experience could be induced through psychedelics even in a non-theological setting, has put forward the following theory:

> Mystical experience achieved through meditation and psychedelic drugs is basically a process I call 'deautomatization'—the undoing of autonomic processes of perception and cognition resulting in, temporarily, a capacity for perception and cognition that is less efficient but potentially of wider range.[50]

But Deikman's scepticism has proven to be right. While conceding that one could use psychedelic drugs to maintain or increase faith in a particular religion, he questioned the ethics of such use. He noted in parenthesis:

. . . the image of a church administering drugs that drastically alter the state of consciousness in order to promote its own perpetuity is one that makes me quite uneasy and smacks too much of '1984'. Pahnke's experiment, if expanded in scope, would be uncomfortably close to such a picture.[51]

The reference here is to the type of experiments Pahnke conducted a couple of times in 1962, on the basis of which he wrote his Harvard Ph.D. dissertation. These experiments are reported in Pahnke (1966 and 1969).

There are two important issues. The first is concerned with the origin of religion or religious inspiration within mankind. While I disagree with Wasson's theory of the psychedelic origin of religion, I concede that a weaker form of the thesis may not be far from the truth: the origin of most primitive religions was associated in some way or other with some drugs or medicinal herbs or with the mysteries of some plants or vegetables. Some of these plants inebriate, some are poisonous, some cure pains and soothe griefs. They are seen to heal wounds, relieve sufferings and induce ecstasy. Some of them generate pleasant visions and hallucinations.

Our primitive ancestors learnt the mysterious properties of these plants the hard way. Robert S. De Ropp (1958, p. 6) commented:

Impelled by hunger, they ate what they could find, root or berry, leaf, flower, or fungus. . . . They purged, they vomitted, they convulsed, they collapsed, and the sum of their writhings and spewings, accumulated through the ages, provided the basis for the science of pharmacology.

The knowledge of these drugs naturally became the carefully guarded secrets for a privileged class. Members of these classes were the forefathers of the priests, shamans and witch-doctors in a religious community. Thus, the Vedic Soma, the Ambrosia of the Greeks, the *amṛta* of epic India, Nepenthe of Homer, Peyote of the Aztecs and the Coca of the Incas—all were endowed with a halo of sacredness and divinity. But not all of them were necessarily hallucinogenic or psychedelic.

The second issue relates to the use of psychedelic drugs for therapeutic purposes. Psychedelic drugs are no panacea for all human ills. While messianism with LSD had been admonished, some thought that the use of psychedelics under 'controlled conditions' to foster our religious and mystical awareness could be all right. Not only Huxley and Watts, but also Masters, Houston, Pahnke and many others argued that to satisfy a sort of 'metaphysical hunger' one might recommend the taking of psychedelic drugs.[52] This is also wrong. Part of the reason for its falsity lies in the fact that these new messiahs held a different view about the value of religious and mystical consciousness in human society. But the more compelling reason for giving up the drug-cult was the gradual awareness of the effects of these psycho-chemicals upon the constitution of the human mind. Even the experts were quite wary about these effects. Dr Kurland, for example, said, as mentioned before, that a psychedelic drug was like a scalpel, which was 'a dangerous instrument' when it is not in the hand of a skilled surgeon.

The exalted consciousness or elation that may happen as a result of the ingestion of the drugs should not be taken at its face value and should not be used as convenient grounds for justifying one's religious faith or mystical yearnings. People should be told in unambiguous language that they cannot buy salvation in a bottle. Those who are just looking for 'mental peace and ultimate bliss' will have to find them the hard way. To quote a facetious remark:

> One can, after all, give a man peace of a sort simply by hitting him over the head with a club. If this is the only sort of peace that drugs can offer we might prefer to do without it.[53]

This position may seem to be very conservative. However, conservatism in defence of human dignity and human life is no crime.

9. ZAEHNER ON MYSTICISM

Professor R.C. Zaehner was a severe critic of the psychedelic movement. After presenting descriptions of a number of classical records of religious and mystical experience (of both East and West), Zaehner argued that drug-induced mysticism (the virtue of which Huxley and others have extolled) falls far short of the 'genuine' mystical experience of saints and holymen (see Zaehner, 1957). According to him, it is extremely misleading to call the drug-induced experience an 'authentic' religious/mystical experience. The subtitle of Zaehner's book was *An Inquiry into some Varieties of Praeternatural Experience*. The term 'praeternatural' needs some explanation. The dictionary meaning of 'praeternatural' or 'preternatural' is something that is out of the ordinary course of nature, hence something that is unusual or non-natural. The professed intention of Zaehner was to improve upon James' theory of religious experience, and by using his own improved version, Zaehner wanted to distinguish clearly sacredness from profaneness, authentic religious experience from make-belief. He defines 'praeternatural experience' as that in which

> sense-perception and discursive thought are transcended in an immediate apperception of a unity or union which is apprehended as lying beyond and transcending the multiplicity of the world as we know it.[54]

Zaehner took James to task mildly for not maintaining a sharp distinction between (as well as for not making an evaluative judgement about) the 'diabolical' mysticism and 'authentic' religious or mystical experience. On the other hand, James' approach to the question of religion and mysticism was more pragmatic and non-partisan, while Zaehner's approach has unfortunately been somewhat dogmatic. Zaehner's conclusion implied, for example, that to have *authentic* religious experience, one has to believe in either the Catholic Church or some similar religious system. An experience that is mystical, but non-theistic in nature, is not sacred, it is profane, or to use a different expression, it is merely a 'praeternatural' experience, not a genuine religious experience.

To categorize a mystical experience as authentically religious, one has to depend upon the verbal report of such experience. Even to decide otherwise, one has to depend upon the verbal report. But in the verbal report of such an experience one uses a frame of reference that one believes in and is most acquainted with. Thus, only an authentic believer or a practitioner of an authentic religion can have an authentic religious experience because only such a person can describe his experience in such a way which will not be in conflict with that authentic religion he believes in. Thus, for Zaehner, and many others, a drug-induced state can never be an *authentic* religious experience.

Zaehner established his major thesis in *Mysticism—Sacred and Profane* (1957), that while drug-induced experience might sometimes (with proper set and settings) simulate religious (mystical) experience, it was not 'the real thing'. This is somewhat close to R.M. Bucke's view that drugs may produce a 'kind of artificial and bastard consciousness'. In fact, this position of Zaehner against the psychedelic movement had been shared in some way or other by almost all churchmen, theologians, Indian Swamis and modern Zen masters. The general contention is that the drug-induced state is, at its worst, a kind of psychotic state, or madness or delusion, and, at its best, a kind of 'preternatural' experience equivalent to those of some poets, nature-mystics and monist philosophers.

The inherent weakness of this position, however, lies in making the Christian God the central part of any (religious) mystical experience and thereby unconsciously rejecting such god-less religions like Buddhism, Zen or Vedānta. Masters and Houston pointed out another obvious counter-example to Zaehner's contention.[55] The Peyote rituals of the Native American Church induced a theistic mysticism with the help of a psychedelic drug.[56] In fact, the Native American Church believes in God and Jesus Christ, and thus Zaehner's thesis about the connection between God and religion, between good and bad forms of mysticism too was a sweeping generalization.

For such reasons among other things, Professor Houston Smith of Syracuse University, whose admiration for all types of mysticism and particular sympathy for the psychedelic movement were well-known, attacked Zaehner's dogmatism and criticized him for his lack of openness of heart. Professor Smith compared Zaehner's refusal to admit drug-induced mysticism as authentic with the seventeenth-century theologician's refusal to look through Galileo's telescope and accept what they saw.[57] Smith's analogy may be valid, but Zaehner's argument against 'profane' mysticism still stands scrutiny. I would stop short of construing Smith's analogy of Galileo's telescope as a sound and 'scientific' justification of psychedelic drugs. Smith is, however, liberal enough to accept the drug-induced experience as incontrovertibly religious and mystical. And one can admire such liberalism. The same position about drug-mysticism has been taken by W.T. Stace, as has been reported by Masters and Houston.[58] Smith, however, puzzled over another problem which seemed to him to be more pertinent. This is the question of how this new fact about drugs, mysticism and religion is to be interpreted and incorporated into our common religious philosophy. I consider this question pertinent and have tried above partly to tackle it. More penetrating analysis may not seem that urgent today.

The drug-cult is dead today. At least it is no longer a serious issue in religion. But the movement raised certain important issues about religion and mysticism. It underlined modern man's 'metaphysical hunger' for a sort of altered state of consciousness, for an 'otherworldly' experience. There have been other substitutes for answering this need for the Western man's and the Western woman's search for something tangible in his or her religious pursuit.

Notes and References

1. The quotation is from a mediverse called 'Psychedelics' by Dr F.W. Hanley, Calgary, Alberta.
2. Modell and Lansing, p. 51.
3. Modell and Lansing, ibid.
4. Modell and Lansing, p. 52.
5. Vol. 7, pp. 186–208.
6. James 1902, p. 387.
7. Braden (1967), p. 96.
8. Bowers, 1955, p. 175.
9. Bucke, 1879, p. v.
10. James, 1902, p. 390.
11. Zaehner, 1957, p. xiii.
12. Huxley, 1954, p. 58.
13. Leary, 1970, pp. 87–9.

14. Leary, 1970, p. 13.
15. Leary, 1970, p. 30.
16. Watts, 1962, p. 20.
17. de Ropp, 1958, p. 7.
18. Zaehner, 1957, pp. xii–xiii.
19. Watts, 1962, p. 20.
20. Watts, 1962, p. 17.
21. Wasson, 1961, p. 26.
22. Ibid., p. 26.
23. Ibid., p. 35.
24. This is from the Annual lecture of the Mycological Society of America, Stillwater, Oklahoma, 1960, published in *Botanical Museum Leaflets*, Harvard University, 1961, 19 (7).
25. Wasson, 1968, p. 10.
26. Ibid., p. 67.
27. Brough, 1971, p. 332.
28. Ingalls, 1971, p. 20.
29. Brough, 1971, p. 360.
30. Wasson, 1971, p. 12.
31. Ibid., p. 13.
32. Wasson, 1968.
33. See Wasson, 1961, p. 36.
34. Masters & Houston, 1967, pp. 4–5.
35. Ibid., p. 148.
36. Ibid., p. 131.
37. Watts, 1962.
38. Wasson, 1971, p. 13.
39. Kurland, 1969, p. 34.
40. Ibid., p. 34.
41. Lewin, 1950.
42. Sava, 1967, p. 71.
43. 1969, p. 80.
44. Ibid., p. 81.
45. Ibid., p. 74.
46. Ibid., p. 82.
47. Prince, 1967, p. 11.
48. Ibid.
49. Ibid., p. 11.
50. Deikman, 1967, p. 58.
51. Ibid., p. 59.
52. Jean Houston, 1967, p. 32.
53. De Ropp, p. 5.
54. Zaehner, 1957, pp. 198–9.
55. 1967, p. 257.
56. See Slotkin, 1956.
57. H. Smith, 1964, p. 524.
58. 1967, p. 312.

Abramson, Harold A. (1955), 'Lysergic Acid Diethylamide (LSD-25): III. As an Adjunct to Psychotherapy', *Journal of Psychology*, vol. 39, pp. 127–55.

Bender, Ernest (1971), *R. Gordon Wasson on Soma and Daniel H.H. Ingall's Response: An Essay of the American Oriental Society*, no. 7 (New Haven, CT: American Oriental Society).

Blood, Benjamin Paul (1874), *The Anaesthetic Revelation and the Gist of Philosophy* (Amsterdam, NY).

Bowers, Fredson, ed. (1955), *Whitman's Manuscripts: Leaves of Grass, 1860* (Chicago: University of Chicago Press).

Braden, William (1967), *The Private Sea—LSD and the Search for God* (London: Pall Mall Press).

Brough, John (1971), 'Soma and *Amanita Muscaria*', *Bulletin of the School of Oriental and African Studies*, vol. 34, no. 2, pp. 331–62.

Bucke, Richard Maurice (1879), *Man's Moral Nature: An Essay* (New York: G.P. Putnam's).

———. (1901), *Cosmic Consciousness: A Study in the Evolution of the Human Mind* (Philadelphia: Innes & Sons).

DeBold, Richard C. & Leaf, Russell C., eds (1969), *LSD, Man and Society* (London: Faber and Faber).

De Félice, Philippe (1936), *Poisons Sacrés, Ivresses Divines: Essai sur Quelques Formes Inférieures de la Mystique* (Paris: Éditions Albin Michel).

Deikman, Arthur J. (1967), 'The Overestimation of Mystical Experience', in Salman and Prince (1967), pp. 57–61.

De Ropp, Robert S. (1958), *Drugs and the Mind* (London: Victor Gollancz).

Huxley, Aldous (1945), *Time Must Have a Stop* (London: Chatto & Windus).

———. (1946), *The Perennial Philosophy* (London: Chatto & Windus).

———. (1954), *The Doors of Perception* (London: Chatto & Windus).

Ingalls, Daniel H.H. (1971), 'Remarks on Wasson's *Soma*', in Bender (1971), pp. 20–3.

James, William (1882), 'On Some Hegelisms', *Mind*, vol. 7, pp. 186–208.

———. (1902), *The Varieties of Religious Experience—A Study in Human Nature* (London: Longmans, Green, and Co.)

Kurland, Albert A. (1969), 'The Therapeutic Potential of LSD in Medicine', in DeBold and Leaf (1969), pp. 20–35.

Leary, Timothy (1970), *The Politics of Ecstacy* (London: MacGibbon & Kee).

Lewin, B.D. (1950), *The Psychoanalysis of Elation* (London: Hogarth Press).

Masters, Roberts E.L. & Houston, Jean (1967), *The Varieties of Psychedelic Experience* (London: Anthony Blond).

Osmond, Humphry (1957), 'A Review of the Clinical Effects of Psychotomimetic Agents', *Annals of the New York Academy of Science*, vol. 66, art. 3, 14 March 1957, pp. 418–34.

Pahnke, Walter N. (1963), *Drugs and Mysticism: An Analysis of the Relationship between Psychedelic Drugs and the Mystical Consciousness*, unpublished Ph.D. thesis presented to the Committee on Higher Degrees in History and Philosophy of Religion, Harvard University, June 1963.

———. (1969), 'LSD and Religious Experience', in DeBold and Leaf (1969), pp. 60–84.

Pahnke, Walter N. & Richards, W.A. (1966), 'Implications of LSD and Experimental Mysticism', *Journal of Religion and Health*, vol. 5, no. 3, pp. 175–208.

Prince, Raymond H., ed. (1968a), *Trance and Possession States, Proceedings of the Second Annual Conference of the R.M. Bucke Memorial Society, 4–6 March 1966* (Montreal: R.M. Bucke Memorial Society).

Prince, Raymond H. (1968b), 'Preface', in Prince (1968a), pp. v–vii.

Salman, D.M. and Prince, Raymond H., eds. (1967), *Do Psychedelics Have Religious Implications?, Proceedings of the Third Annual R.M. Bucke Memorial Society* (Montreal: R.M. Bucke Memorial Society).

Sandison, R.A. (1954), 'Psychological Aspects of the LSD Treatment of the Neuroses', *Journal of Mental Science*, vol. 100, pp. 508–15.

Savage, Charles (1967), 'Lysergic Acid Diethylamide (LSD-25): A Clinical-Psychological Study', *American Journal of Psychiatry*, vol. 108, pp. 896–900.

Slotkin, J.S. (1956), *The Peyote Religion: A Study in Indian-White Relations* (New York: Octagon Books, repr. 1975).

Smith, Huston (1964), 'Do Drugs Have Religious Import?' *Journal of Philosophy*, vol. LXI, no. 18, 1 October 1964, pp. 517–30.

Stace, W.T. (1961), *Mysticism and Philosophy* (London: Macmillan).

Wasson, R. Gordon (1961), 'The Hallucinogenic Fungi of Mexico: An Inquiry into the Origins of the Religious Idea Among Primitive Peoples', *Harvard Botanical Museum Leaflets*, vol. 19, no. 7, pp. 137–62.

———. (1968), *Soma: Divine Mushroom of Immortality* (New York: Harcourt Brace Jovanovich).

———. (1971), 'The Soma of the Rig Veda: What Was It?', in Bender (1971), pp. 1–19, repr. from *Journal of the Oriental Society*, vol. 91, no. 2, April–June 1971, pp. 169–87.

———. (1972), *Soma and the Fly-Agaric: Mr Wasson's Rejoinder to Professor Brough*, with an Introduction by Richard Evans Schultes (Cambridge, MA: Botanical Museum of Harvard University, Ethno-Mycological Studies, no. 2, November 1972).

Watts, Alan W. (1962), *The Joyous Cosmology: Adventures in the Chemistry of Consciousness* (New York: Pantheon Books).

Zaehner, R.C. (1957), *Mysticism—Sacred and Profane: An Inquiry into Some Varieties of Praeternatural Experience* (Oxford, Clarendon Press).

———. (1972), *Drugs, Mysticism and Make-believe* (London: Collins).

22

Yoga, Mediation and Mantras: The Oceanic Feeling

1. POPULAR NOTIONS ABOUT YOGA

Various Yoga techniques and methods of meditation have gained renewed momentum in the present century. 'India is a land of yogis, snake-charmers and beggars'—this is the picture that most Westerners still cherish in their heart. In the beginning of this century any educated Indian who went to America (since he did not look like a snake-charmer) was very often taken for a *potential* Yogi. A few lines from the *Memoirs* of M.N. Roy, a well-known political leader of India in the twenties and thirties, describe his experience during his stay in Mexico as follows:

> Theosophists, particularly those who had never set their foot on the sacred soil of India, held a very dogmatic view about ancient Indian culture. In private conversations with some leading theosophists of Mexico, I disagreed with the view and maintained that even in the remote past India was not populated by Rishis and Munis in constant communication with the mystic Mahatmas perching on the Tibetan plateau beyond the crests of the Himalayas. My sacreligous view scandalised the adopted children of Mother India. [. . .] It was a curious experience, to be confronted with learned academicians whose palpable ignorance of the history of their adopted motherland was concealed by the blind faith that it was the home of divine spirits (Roy, 1964, p. 549).

With the growing concern and enthusiasm for Yoga, meditation and spiritualism, some Westerners today still take trips to India or to Japan or to Sri Lanka, just to find a guru of their own choice.

Why has Yoga been so popular in the West? The reasons are manifold. Only some of them can be noted here:

(a) Yoga is supposed to be a *spiritual* system, so it must be an answer to what is commonly expressed as 'Western materialism'.

(b) Yoga is connected with psychic phenomena, which sympathizers designate as parapsychology. So it is a way of getting away from the 'suffocating' behaviourism and materialistic metaphysics which are in conflict with the religious sentiment of common people. Yoga is believed to have proven that extra-sensory mental powers, ESP, clairvoyance and telepathy are all possible. Thus, one can be satisfied that there is a soul apart from the material body. For without a soul, how can one possibly think of spirituality?

(c) Yoga is said to be the gateway to a healthy life. One feels that Hatha Yoga does something for one's body. One becomes more joyful and energetic. Being healthy means for most of us being more happy and more holy! Witness the 3HO Foundation of Yogi Bhajkan—the Healthy, Happy and Holy Organization. Maybe the 'Yogic' physical contortions appear to be a bit weird to the Western mind, but then that is why they do 'all those good things' to your body and mind.

(d) Yoga system is an Oriental occultism—an esoteric system, and therefore, if we know about it we might be in possession of all those 'powers' we always wanted to have—levitation, thought-reading, clairvoyance, and so on.

(e) Yoga is also an aphrodisiac. Many writers of Yoga exploit the theme of Yoga and sexuality. In this respect, Yoga is joined by its counterpart, Tantra. Thus, the two extremes of Indian spirituality, asceticism and eroticism, meet here in making Yoga a marketable commodity in the West. In Kundalini Yoga, the 'serpent power' (which is also interpreted as sexual power or sexuality) is harnessed and therefore you can do impossible things!

(f) Yoga is relaxing. Yoga releases tensions. Yoga buys mental peace and calmness of mind.

Apart from all these commonly emphasized aspects, which may account for the popularity of Yoga in the West one way or another, there is the further point that certain respectable scientists and psychologists in the West have shown great interest in 'Yoga' research. And some of them have expressed hope in the future potential of Yoga research. But besides all this, the significant fact is that some of the above hyperbolic claims about Yoga do contain the tiniest grains of truth—a fact that tends to perpetuate all these illusions about Yoga. We might quietly pass over the parapsychological aspects of Yoga, leaving the matter to Dr Joseph

Bank Rhine of Duke University and critics to decide (*New Frontiers of the Mind*, 1938). We can also discount all those stories about Yoga working like a miracle medicine on the body and mind of a Yogi. But the following facts still remain:

1. Some Hatha Yoga exercises do contribute to physical fitness. And hence they can be conveniently adopted in modern physiotherapy.
2. Meditation practice prescribed by the *classical* Yoga system of India is nevertheless based upon a still viable theory of mind, and as a result, serious followers of this prescription may achieve some kind of mental peace where obvious tensions are released and inhibitions partially overcome.

I have mentioned the stories of enchantment and disillusionment. One may find such a story in Arthur Koestler's book, *The Lotus and the Robot* (1960). The story of Koestler's disillusionment with Yoga as well as with Oriental mysticism in general is a moving one. And he was not the only one. To quote Koestler:

> Among Westerners who have tried to enter the spirit of Yoga the hard way, Dr Bernard was probably the most persistent, modest and sincere. He wrote his last work on Hatha Yoga after many years of devoted practice, and in the index to that short book there are two moving headings:
>
> *Miracles*, none transpired.
> *Supernatural*, not revealed (1960, p. 132).

Koestler's account cannot be brushed aside by the Yoga proponents today as a piece of cheap journalism. On the other hand, the modern interest in Yoga among intellectuals is not just another fad. It has persisted for a considerable period. It is a phenomenon. We may pass over a fad probably with an indulgent smile. But it is a different story with a phenomenon. There are nowadays severe critics as well as enthusiastic supporters of this phenomenon. Both sides have been able to put forward good arguments. But according to Jeffrey Masson:

> What we see in an ancient Indian ascetic is not so very different from what we an observe in our own lives, if we have the patience and the internal courage to seek for it. If we do not, then we can turn to the society around us, and find expression for these derivatives there. How else can we explain to ourselves the current obsession with meditation? To some it seems self-evidently true. To some it seems silly. To the analyst, it is neither: it is an expression of something much deeper, and it requires to be understood. The same is true of the interest in health-foods. Here too is an area that extends back into India's past: hardly an early text

exists that does not have something quite revealing to say about diet and its relation to sexual life. . . . Or can we ignore the fact that so many Yoga centres find themselves next door to the increasingly popular interest in Karate? Can we dismiss this seemingly accidental co-location of contemplation and violence? (Masson, 1974, p. 315).

The above questions are suggestive of further problems. They may need as much serious consideration from the psychologists as they do from the sociologists. When we look deeply into the history of some Indian varieties or religious cults, we can discover a paradoxical situation—a 'tug of war' between asceticism and eroticism. One has to be the reflex of the other. Otherwise, how can we explain the eroticism of Kṛṣṇa and the asceticism of the Vaiṣṇavas? Is it not a fact that an ascetic Yogi looks forward to his goal which is an ecstatic enjoyment often compared to (sexual) pleasure multiplied a million times? One can quote the authority of the Upaniṣads in this matter. To illustrate the point let me describe here a very strong and popular movement in the Western world—a movement that began in the sixties. Its proponents call it the International Spiritual Regeneration Movement.

2. TRANSCENDENTAL MEDITATION

At the centre of this movement is one guru who is called a Maharishi (a great sage). His main doctrine is the doctrine of transcendental meditation. The promise is that of the advent of the Kingdom of Heaven on Earth, or a Utopia. To quote from one of the pamphlets of Maharishi, in which a programme for world peace is described (*World Peace and Deep Meditation*):

Even if only one-tenth of the adult population of the world were regularly to meditate for short periods everyday, and so produce these infinitely peaceful influences that arise at the deepest level of consciousness, it would take not more than a few months to remove the entire accumulation of tension in the world. War would be impossible for centuries to come.

It is good to see that Maharishi and his followers are concerned about such important problems as world peace.

Maharishi Mahesh Yogi was born in India probably in 1910 or 1911. His father was a government revenue inspector. Maharishi obtained his graduate degree in Science from Allahabad University. After graduation, he started working in a factory in the town of Jubbulpore (or Jabalpur) in Madhya Pradesh, India. It is said that at some time while he was working in Jubbulpore, he came under the influence of Śaṃkarācārya.

Śaṃkara or Śaṃkarācārya (*c.* AD 788–820), the great protagonist of Advaita Vedānta, established four *āśramas* at four corners of India. Each *āśrama* continues to exist even today, and the head of each of these four *āśramas* assumes the title Jagadguru Śaṃkarācārya. The position is comparable to that of the Pope in the Catholic Church. A method is followed to choose a successor each time the head dies. But unlike the Catholic Church, these *āśramas* do not hold any direct control over the religious life of all Hindus. Anybody who joins the monastic order is supposed to practise Advaita Vedānta philosophy in his life through asceticism and meditation. Anyway, our Maharishi once met the Śamkarācārya of Śringeri *āśrama* in South India. It is said that his encounter with His Holiness Śamkarācārya was the turning point of his life. He decided to join the order.

He is supposed to have spent thirteen long years at the Himalayan *āśrama* (called Badrikasrama in Northern India) studying, meditating and practicising Vedānta. Then he finally came down to the plains (Madras in the south) from the mountains to become the chief guru.

It was in Madras, in 1959, that Maharishi reached the resolution to 'dedicate his life to the limitless goal of the spiritual regeneration of the world'. And the 'world' obviously meant in this context the materialistic West, Europe and North America. Probably the idea was that if there had to be a spiritual 'regeneration', it better be at the heart-centre of materialism—the West. Maharishi is supposed to have spent thirteen years of his life acquiring ancient wisdom at the feet of Jagadguru Śaṃkarācārya Swāmi Brahmānanda Saraswati Mahāraj—the wisdom that he 'now gives *freely* to the world'.

Charles F. Lutes, once World Governor of the International Spiritual Regeneration Movement, gave a dramatic description of Maharishi's announcement to spread his doctrine of meditation all over the world:

> On a warm and dusty afternoon, high in the Sequoia National Forest, Maharishi sat at the foot of one of nature's largest trees, surrounded by a handful of people. These were the devotees who had gathered to hear the plans unfold—of how Maharishi was to bring his message of Transcendental Meditation to a world groping in darkness that had long yearned for such a message.
>
> The question in everyone's mind that day was—how could one lone saint, no matter how greatly endowed or ever so dedicated to his insuperable task, accomplish such an impossible dream? (Preface to Maharishi, 1968).

The 'plan' was to establish in every country in the Free World a centre of meditation and thus to initiate the untold thousands to allow them to enjoy the benefit of Transcendental Meditation. In fact, it was the blueprint of the Spiritual Regeneration Movement. In the ancient pilgrimage town of Rishikesh on the Ganges River at the foot of the Himalayas, there is now Maharishi's Academy of Meditation and the World Headquarters for the Spiritual Regeneration Movement. At this centre, each spring Maharishi used to give courses, for three months, on meditation techniques. He trained people from the West to be teachers of his system of meditation. These people, after the training period, went out into all parts of the world to spread his teachings. Maharishi himself has travelled around the world, going mainly to Europe and North America, to speak and teach the wisdom of the 'Twentieth Century'. All this was only a 'dream' in 1958, according to Mr Lutes. But now the Spiritual Regeneration Movement is a reality according to the followers of Transcendental Meditation.

Within a brief period, Maharishi became a celebrity. He was also the guru of the celebrities. The well-known case of the Beatles may be recalled. The newspaper reporters used to refer to Maharishi as the 'Beatle Yogi'. Of the Beatles, George Harrison was reportedly the first convert. And then he persuaded the others—Paul McCartney, Ringo Starr and John Lennon. They all became his disciples. They also attended his Meditation Course at Rishikesh, India.

It has been critically remarked that Maharishi's appeal was mainly designed for affluent westerners. Whether he himself was responsible for this slant, we cannot tell. It is trite to observe that most of his disciples were those affluent people who were seeking some kind of relaxation and 'spiritual peace' which their money could not buy. Maharishi himself publicly denounced this slant which his movement had supposedly been accused of. Faced with such questions about his movement, he used to answer them wittily. To quote from one of his lectures:

> A few months ago I was in America. People are so tense in that country. They began to meditate and they began to say this meditation is a non-medical tranquillizer. The best attributes that they could say of the meditation was that it helped them to sleep well in the night. Without tablets. I told them sleeping well is the result of keeping awake well in the wakeful stage. (1968, p. 85).

But in spite of Maharishi's disclaimer, the fact remains that primarily affluent Western society responded to his call for Spiritual Regeneration. Besides the Beatles, Hollywood celebrities like Shirley MacLaine and Mia Farrow became his disciples and began studying Yoga under him. Maharishi's own observation of this fact was as follows: these enormously affluent people realize that they lack something in their lives, but they cannot pinpoint it. There are certain things that cannot be gained from the outer sphere of living. And it is supposed to be delivered by Transcendental Meditation.

Unlike some other Indian swamis, Maharishi did not want his disciples to take vows of abstinence and poverty. This was one of the attractive sides of his doctrine. For spiritual regeneration in the material world, you do not have to give up your affluence, your wealth or your materialism. It may sound a bit contradictory to the teachings of Yājñavalkya, imparted to his wife in the *Bṛhadāranyaka Upaniṣad*:

> Then spake Maitreyī: 'If now, sir, this whole earth filled with wealth were mine, would I now thereby be immortal?'
>
> 'No, no!' said Yājñavalkya. 'As the life of the rich, even so would your life be. Of immortality, however, there is no hope through wealth.'
>
> Then spake Maitreyī: 'What should I do with that through which I may not be immortal?' (IV, v. 3–4, p. 145).

Paradoxically, Maharishi referred to the Upaniṣads (in his words, 'to the Vedas') as the source of his wisdom and his doctrine. Maharishi said that his doctrine of Transcendental Meditation does not reject the material world but helps to acquire 'greater happiness' within it. This is the fruit of modernity. Hence Maharishi claimed that he discovered a new path. Although he was in the disciple-tradition of Śaṃkarācārya, his doctrine was very different from the ideal of asceticism and withdrawal from sensual life that Śaṃkara apparently preached.

One need not surmise from the above that Maharishi lives a luxurious life which is against the ascetic ideal. For I believe he can rightly claim that he himself is a celibate, a monk and does not have 'any pockets' to carry money. Our concern, however, is with what he preaches and teaches others to do. A particular example is in order here. Maharishi says:

> You might have been hearing or reading in the philosophical books that it is the desires which are responsible for the suffering of man. It is the *inability* to fulfil the desires that is responsible. Every man must aspire for more in life. . . . All that ideology to kill the desire, to kill the ego, to annihilate the mind, all that does not belong to the man in the world. It belongs to the monk's way of life. . . . It is not necessary to go for a monk's life. It is not necessary to have any sense of detachment, or renunciation, or any such abstainment from life, or ignoring the responsibilities of life. . . . The only one thing to be done is meditation, to be added as a part of the daily routine. That is all. (1968, pp. 80–3).

Meditation is supposed to improve your power to enjoy life. I believe that if the sense of guilt is absent as the above teaching implies, one would be less inhibited in one's enjoyment. Thus, it is probably psychologically true to say that meditation improves your power to enjoy life. Meditation can do a lot of things to one's mind. There are untapped sources of energy and power in our minds. We seldom know about this side of the mind. Hence meditation can truly help one to relax, to feel happy, to enjoy bliss. Maharishi has taught that the rich should not be inhibited by a sense of guilt.

Let us now see briefly what this 'transcendental meditation is'. It is not a Sanskrit or Indian expression, nor is it a direct translation of any convenient Sanskrit phrase. The word 'meditation' is the usual translation of the Sanskrit term *dhyāna*, a method of concentration and mental culture recommended primarily by the Pātañjala Yoga system as well as various branches of Buddhism. The Buddha himself is said to have realized the doctrine of 'four noble truths' through meditation. But that was a different sort of meditation. Buddhism talks about two types of meditation: *samatha* and *vipasyana*. Meditation offers the practitioner analytic insight or *prajñā*. Transcendental Meditation is, however, different. The word 'transcendental' is added here, I believe, in order to distinguish Maharishi's *unique* teaching from other methods of meditation. In Maharishi's own words, his meditation is 'a very simple, very direct technique of attaining that state of life where neither the mental plane decays nor the physical plane decays, mental and physical planes come to the level of the spiritual plane which has eternal life and knows no change' (see Maharishi, 1968).

Maharishi says that the Kingdom of Heaven lies within man, and his meditation is supposed to unlock the door of this Kingdom of Heaven, to the Ultimate Bliss, to 'transcendental consciousness'. Maharishi, curiously enough, has claimed that the message of Christ has for long been misunderstood! In fact, his claim is much greater than this; accordingly to him, all religions for many centuries have missed one essential point: the Kingdom of Heaven is within us. It has been said that because of this fundamental (mis-)understanding there has been so much suffering, so much distress, so much disharmony. Maharishi has asserted that the other essential point missed by most religious people throughout the ages is this: one can be good only after one has realized God, and thus God-realization should be our primary concern, and being good, secondary. Most religions have, according to Maharishi, so far wrongly put the cart before the horse by emphasizing that one has to be good and do good in order to realize God. But it is supposed to be the other way around. He quotes from Christ to support his novel theory about religion:

But seek ye first the Kingdom of God and his righteousness; and all these things shall be added unto you (Mathew 6.330).

Without much hesitation, Maharishi has pronounced that all religious scriptures or religions themselves—Islam, Buddhism, the Bible, the *Gītā*, the Vedas, the Upaniṣads—all teach merely this, that we should not worry about being morally good or bad at all, but try to find the Kingdom of God which is within us. And we find this Kingdom of Heaven which is within us through Transcendental Meditation.

If religion has done anything in the civilized world that is good and valuable, it is in the area of ethics and morality. Roughly, one can say that religion has told man to be good and helpful to others, to try to forget hatred and cultivate love of others, not to kill others, to be honest and conscientious. Religion prescribes such admittedly difficult-to-follow moral codes of conduct. And man tries apparently to abide by these rules because otherwise he thinks that he will violate the order of God, or disturb the *dharma*. Whatever may be the reason, it is undeniable that each good and respectable religion upholds certain moral principles which have proven good for humanity. However, if it is stressed here that being good is difficult, but seeing God (or, being God, if you like) is unbelievably easy, then the doctrine may be easily misunderstood.

3. RELIGIOSITY AND MORALITY

Let us turn to a related issue. There are religious persons all over the world, and specially in the Orient, who think that to be good is more important than seeing God or being God. To illustrate this point, I shall relate an interesting and profound story found in the *Mahābhārata*. The story also reveals the ambivalent nature of Indian mysticism—a point which modern Western intellectuals have unfortunately either missed or ignored completely. It is the story of Tulādhāra (12, 252–4):

A certain sage was so holy that he sat immobile in the forest for one whole year. Birds nested in his hair, and he did not move a muscle until the baby bird had hatched, grown up and flown away from the nest. He was a yogī, and thought to himself: there is none so holy as me. 'Oh, yes,' said a disembodied voice, 'there is, indeed, one far more holy than you; and his name is Tulādhāra.'

'Where can I find him?' asked the proud ascetic.
'Search.'

So the great and yogī travelled. One day, tired in his travels, he stopped on the outskirts of the city of Benares, in a small spice shop, one of many thousands that dot the entrance to the holy city. The owner of this little shop sells honey, cloves, cinnamon and other household spices. Looking into the sage's eyes, the owner suddenly tells him: 'I am Tulādhāra, so-called because my scales are always equally balanced. I charge no more to the wealthy merchant than I do to the poor maid.' The sage was thunderstruck, that here in this ordinary spice shop was to be found the one man in India more holy than he was. He asked him many questions, philosophical and theological. But alas, Tulādhāra could tell him only very little: he knew but one rule of conduct, that he should not deliberately harm any man, and this he tried to do as best as he could.

What morals should we derive from this story? One of them must be what I have stated above: being good and honest is more important and desirable even from a religious point of view than being God or being holy, practising meditation and yoga. There are many other lessons to be drawn from this little piece. But, for the present, the above one will suffice.

A brief description of the process of Transcendental Mediation may be in order here. Usually a 'proper' thought (represented, to be sure, by a *mantram* or sound vibration, to be given by the guru at the time of initiation) is selected and one has to go on experiencing in meditation the 'subtle states' of that thought until 'its subtlest state is experienced and transcended'. Maharishi explained this process in his much publicized book, *The Science of Being and the Art of Living.* An analogy is used to express this abstract thought. The mind is like an ocean and thoughts are like bubbles starting at the bottom of the mind-ocean and rising up to the surface-mind. When a thought surfaces, it is cognized at the *conscious* level. Maharishi says that a particular thought passes through many stages of development before it comes to the surface, and that those stages or levels of consciousness are not usually appreciated by us:

> If there were a way to consciously appreciate all the states of the bubble of thought prior to its reaching the surface level, that would be the way to transcend thought and experience the transcendental Being. (1963, p. 48).

After outlining this theory, Maharishi asserts that his technique of 'transcendental deep meditation' is the way, and perhaps the easiest way, if not the only way, to appreciate the whole depth of the mind, and thus to arrive at the state of transcendental Being, the state of pure consciousness, self-awareness.

In the worldwide meditation centres established by Maharishi, there are usually two thirty-minute meditation sessions in a day. The followers of Maharishi meditate upon a *mantram* given by the guru. It is again and again emphasized by Maharishi that the practice of transcendental deep meditation cannot be imparted through a book but only by 'personal guidance' (1963, p. 58).

4. TRADITIONAL YOGA

Each religious leader who professes to preach a new religion has to face today certain typical questions. It is interesting to see how the protagonists of Transcendental Meditation have tried to answer such questions. While in the classical Yoga system (the one expounded by Patañjali with its eight 'limbs'), concentration (*dhāraṇa*) is considered an aid to meditation; that is rejected here. According to Maharishi, 'concentration is a strenuous process' and hence it cannot be accepted as a preparation for the 'non-strenuous' technique of meditation (1968, p. 112). Thus, it is clear that the Yoga meditation that Maharishi is talking about is not the classical Yoga meditation that Patañjali described. The classical Yoga system, to be sure, was an ascetic liberation. The eight stages are:

(1) restraints (such as 'not to steal' and 'not to lie'),
(2) psychic discipline,
(3) physical postures,
(4) breathing control and exercise,
(5) withdrawal from senses,
(6) concentration,
(7) meditation, and
(8) trance or stasis.

But, Maharishi admits that this would be a very strenuous procedure for today's world. And unlike an orthodox Indian Yogi, he claims that he has devised an easy way, a simple technique, which will lead to the same goal.

5. PEACE AND MEDITATION

Transcendental Meditation, it is claimed, may provide not only refreshment and vigour but also *peace*. Let us ponder over this intriguing concept, 'peace'. The word 'peace' is frequently uttered today and is conveniently used for various purposes. But there is a problem of equivocation involved, which is often misleading. 'Peace' is sometimes used as a translation of the well-known religiously surcharged Sanskrit word *śānti*. This word is as old as the Vedas and often associated with the mystic-magic sound *Om*. Even in Buddhism, Nirvāṇa is said to be *śānta*—complete cessation of all discords, conflicts and disturbances. Similarly, 'peace is used in a religious context in the Christian tradition. The same word is also used in a secular or mundane sense to denote simply 'tranquillity' or just 'stillness', 'lack of sound' (as in the expression 'peace and quiet'). There is a third use of the term in a technical sense. When it is used along with 'war' (as in 'war and peace') it means 'a ratification' or 'treaty of no-war' between two powers previously at war. The expression 'a peace' means a truce. Although the Sanskrit term *śānti* is sometimes used to denote this last meaning of 'peace', the more common Sanskrit word for it is *saṃdhi*. In Sanskrit books on polity, *vigraha* and *saṃdhi* are equivalents for English 'war' and 'peace'.

Now, the point of the above banal exercise is simple. When Maharishi started his Spiritual Regeneration movement in North America and Europe, the Vietnam War was on. Thus, the most important thing in the mind of conscientious people, especially of the younger generation, was the horror of war. And as their main concern was war, people turned inward for relief. Maharishi, at that moment, preached that his system of meditation was the harbinger of 'peace' on earth. The abhorrence of war and its horrors, and the realization of its hollowness as a principle, led people to look forward to anything that would offer the prospect of 'peace'. A booklet by Maharishi, *World Peace and Deep Meditation*, was published at this time by the Spiritual Regeneration Movement Foundation.

'Peace' in the context of hostility and war means an end of the war, a 'cease-fire', a negotiation and an end to the bloodbath. Nobody, except those with a highly romantic outlook, expects this 'peace' to mean a sort of 'spiritual' peace in the religious sense—a sort of Kingdom of Heaven on Earth. But partly because of the equivocation that I have pointed out above, most people wanted to believe that the goal of all these new religious movements was the end of all war and bloodshed. But it is one thing to achieve a sort of tranquillity internally through meditation or even external stillness (which has its own charm) by retiring in a quiet place; it is an entirely different situation when one wants to achieve a 'peace' (a truce, a *saṃdhi*) in Vietnam or in the Middle East. War or bloodbath is a reality for which we need a *real* substitute, not just a transcendental experience.

Maharishi has, however, offered a programme for 'world peace' with the help of Transcendental Meditation in his booklet. First, he has given a very simple view about how and why wars take place in the world. Wars break out, he says, because of anger, lies and hostility at the individual level between one man and another. 'For the forest to be green, all the trees that make it up must first be green themselves.' War is thus the integration of all individual hostilities and tensions. If this state of affairs is to be changed, Maharishi says, the individual must change, and there is no other way but the Deep Meditation of Maharishi, which can give a man peace within himself. After such arguments, it is claimed that if about one-tenth of the world's population try to practise the Deep Meditation of Maharishi for only short periods (30 minutes) every day, then world-peace will be possible. In other words, only with Deep Meditation can we ensure the Kingdom of Heaven on Earth.

As a theory, the above has its attraction and a romantic charm. The analogy of green trees and green forest is beautiful, but, to revert to another common idiom, we cannot see the forest for the trees. Wars break out, to be sure, for many complicated reasons in which personal friction between one individual and another is of little concern. Economics is one of the main reasons for world tension, which had in the past led to bloody wars. Among other reasons, there are, of course, religious bigotry, national bigotry, threat for destruction, desperation, and above all, the ambition of the strong to take over the rest of the world. There is little chance of remedying all these evils by any known means at our disposal. However, a Deep Meditation session may give one a sort of personal peace, and this is not a small achievement.

The psychedelic movement had attracted many qualified psychologists and scientists to conduct 'phenomenological' research in the exploration of the 'new frontiers' of the mind. Maharishi's movement for Transcendental Mediatioin similarly created great enthusiasm among certain psychologists and scientists. In fact, interest in parapsychological phenomena received a new impetus in the sixties. The exploration of mystical consciousness has led to the establishment of a whole new branch of psychology—a new 'science' of human consciousness or the psychology of consciousness. The paranormal states are now called by a less eulogistic and a much broader term 'altered states of consciousness', which includes not only mystical experience but also hypnotic states, ESP and dreams (see, e.g. Ludwig 1968, Tart 1969).

6. MEDITATION AND STATES OF CONSCIOUSNESS

The Experience of Being produced by Maharishi's Deep Meditation is classifiable as an altered state of consciousness, according to the new psychology of consciousness. A number of psychiatrists have been engaged recently in the study of electroencephalograms and electrocardiograms of different altered states of consciousness including the alleged mystical states. Quite in keeping with this trend, R.K. Wallace recently studied the physiological effects of transcendental deep meditation. In 1970, he wrote an article in *Science*, 167, on the 'Physiological Effects of Transcendental Meditation' (pp. 1751–4). In 1972, in collaboration with H. Benson, Wallace published another article in *Scientific American* under the title 'The Physiology of Meditation' (226, no. 2; pp. 84–90). Wallace argued that it is possible to demonstrate that states of consciousness reached through this meditation are different from the states of waking, sleeping and dreaming. He further argued that they are different even from the states induced by hypnosis and auto-suggestion. Wallace showed himself to be a great enthusiast of Maharishi's Transcendental Deep Meditation Movement. Thus, if the physiological manifestations of transcendental meditation can be shown to be different from that of auto-suggestion or hypnosis, that will certainly be welcome to Maharishi and his followers. For Maharishi has, time and again, argued that his meditation system has nothing to do with auto-hypnosis or auto-suggestion (1968, p. 113).

Critics may try to compare Transcendental Meditation with auto-hypnosis, not just hypnosis. Auto-hypnosis is described as a self-induced hypnoid states which may be induced by the subject either consciously or unconsciously. Charles T. Tart of the University of California at Davis conducted research on hypnosis. He was one of the modern protagonists of researches in altered states of consciousness. He suggested a redefining of the term 'hypnosis' (he speaks of Deep Hypnosis), which would induce a more humanistic sort of experience and 'a *more transcendental* kind of experience'. In fact, Tart described the experience of his subject (who is, according to Tart, 'particularly gifted' and has also 'done some meditation on his own and had some psychedelic drug trips in the past') under *deep* hypnosis in such a manner that it becomes 'phenomenologically' indistinguishable from mystical experience. Even such terms like 'a feeling of oneness with the universe' has been used in this description. To quote Tart (p. 350):

> And I think what we have here is a transition to a new state of consciousness. In many ways, it sounds like what has traditionally been called Void. I am a little leery of using that word because the Void is a great thing to be in, and you get a lot of prestige and all that sort of spiritual one-upmanship. But it kind of sounds like the Void.

Thus, I think, when *hypnosis* is defined or described in this less pejorative sense, Wallace' objection to the comparison between deep meditation and deep hypnosis seems to disappear. One may note that both hypnosis and meditation have been mentioned here as being 'transcendental'.

Critics pointed to another difficulty. Wallace agreed that the physiological manifestation of Deep Meditation was comparable to that of Yoga or Zen meditation. But he argued that transcendental meditation was a 'simpler' technique and hence much more desirable. Transcendental meditation was conducive to 'rest and relaxation', to developing 'creative intelligence' of the subject, and to making use of his 'full potential in studies, career and recreation'. It is to be noted that Maharishi himself was not very happy about some of these characterizations such as 'conducive to rest and relaxation' and 'non-medical tranquillizer'. Thus, let me quote his comments again:

> A few months ago I was in America. People are so tense in that country. They began to meditate and they began to say this meditation is a non-medical tranquilizer. The best attributes that they could say of the meditation was that it helped them to sleep well in the night. Without tablets (1968, p. 85).

Maharishi openly denounced such an interpretation of transcendental meditation. Wallace's interpretation also conflicts with the professed aim of the Spiritual Regeneration Movement. It is one thing to claim for promotional reasons that something or some technique is relaxing and conducive to restful sleep (a point that can be demonstrated by experiments), but it is another thing to say that the same technique is conducive to the spiritual regeneration of mankind. In sum, nobody can dispute the fact that the practice of meditation can do us a lot of good—a restful sleep by releasing tensions, among other things as well as the spiritual regeneration of the spirit of mankind, for that only can save us from the storm. But how that can be done must remain an open question.

Notes and References

Hume, Robert Ernest (1921), *The Thirteen Principal Upanishads*, trans. by R.E. Hume, (Delhi: Oxford University Press, 2nd revised ed. 1995).

Koestler, Arthur (1960), *The Lotus and the Robot* (London: Hutchinson).

Ludwig, Arnold M. (1969), 'Altered States of Consciousness', in Tart (1969), pp. 9–22, reprinted from *Archives of General Psychiatry*, 1966, vol. 15, pp. 225–34.

Maharishi Mahesh Yogi (1963), *The Science of Being and the Art of Living* (London: International SRM Publications, revised ed. 1966).

Maharishi Mahesh Yogi (1968), *Meditations of Maharishi Mahesh Yogi* (London: Bantam Books).

Masson, J.M. (1974), 'Sex and Yoga', *Journal of Indian Philosophy*, vol. 2, pp. 307–20.

Rhine, J.B. (1938), *New Frontiers of the Mind* (London: Faber & Faber).

Roy, M.N. (1964), *M.N. Roy's Memoirs* (Bombay: Allied Publishers).

Tart, Charles T. (1969), *Altered States of Consciousness: A Book of Readings* (New York: John Wiley & Sons).

Wallace, Robert Keith (1970), 'Physiological Effects of Transcendental Meditation', *Science*, vol. 167, no. 3926, 27 March 1970, pp. 1751–4.

Wallace, Robert Keith and Benson, Herbert (1972), 'The Physiology of Meditation', *Scienfitic American*, vol. 226, no. 2, pp. 84–90.

23

Back to Godhead: The Hare Kṛṣṇa Movement

While Hari roamed in the forest
Making love to all the women,
Rādhā's hold on him loosened,
And envy drove her away.

(Miller, 1977, p. 78) (Pt II, 1).

1. APPEARANCE OF CHANTING IN THE STREETS OF A WESTERN CITY

In 1969, I was walking along the streets of Philadelphia near the University of Pennsylvania campus, when I heard a musical noise and looked around to see something which dumbfounded me for a few seconds. Clad in saffron robes (*dhooti*), and with shaven heads, some Vaiṣṇava monks were chanting, accompanied by the beating of special drums and cymbals (*mṛdaṅga* and *kartals*):

Hare Kṛṣṇa Hare Kṛṣṇa Kṛṣṇa Hare Hare
Hare Rāma Hare Rāma Rāma Rāma Rāma Hare Hare

They were also asking for a donation in exchange for incense packets. For a moment I thought I was dreaming of my childhood days in rural Bengal. But no. These people were in the streets of Philadelphia. I was dumbfounded.

My reaction to that Philadelphia street scene in 1969 was not how a Westerner would react if he were to see a UFO or a Martian. Professor Harvey Cox described a similar experience, which, he said, turned him 'eastward' (*Turning East*, 1977).

To return to Philadelphia in 1969. I approached the chanting group and was greeted with 'Hare Kṛṣṇa', to which I murmured back 'Hare Kṛṣṇa'.

As I donated some money in exchange for an incense packet, one of the group informed me with great enthusiasm about the great movement, 'the greatest of all' (to use his own words), that had begun universally only two or three years ago in New York—the Hare Kṛṣṇa Movement. I bought one issue of their magazine: *Back to Godhead*. Inside I found an article by Howard Wheeler (*alias* Hayagrīva): 'The Hare Kṛṣṇa Explosion—the Joyful History of a Dynamic Transcendental Movement.'

Personally I have always been intrigued and puzzled by the word 'transcendental'. A religious movement today in the West is usually described as 'transcendental'. Religious teachers use this expression very effectively to make an impact on people's minds. Only a hundred years ago, the New Englanders, the 'Yankee Hindoos', were called the New England Transcendentalists. More recently Maharishi Mahesh Yogi initiated his worldwide movement with the doctrine of Transcendental Meditation. Thus, there is little wonder that the Hare Kṛṣṇa movement should also be stamped as a 'transcendental movement'. Words are powerful weapons, and sometimes, apparently meaningless words serve as effective instruments. (Witness some political campaigns, TV commercials and *mantra* recitation in some esoteric religions.) What the word 'transcendental' means precisely in all of these religious contexts, except for the general sense of 'surpassing' or 'excelling other' (hence 'extraordinary'), is difficult to say. Immanuel Kant christened the term by using it to denote the *a priori*, that is, that which is not derived from experience but concerned with the *presuppositions* of experience. Kantian philosophy for this reason is sometimes called Transcendentalism. But I do not intend to enter into a diatribe here with regard to the meaning of the word 'transcendental'. For that was the job of the positivists, who long ago lost their battle.

The Hare Kṛṣṇa movement in the West has expanded very rapidly. It was one of the ex-Beatles, George Harrison, who has been perhaps the largest single contributor to the movement, both financially and spiritually. He alone donated $20,000 to facilitate the publication of the Guru's (Prabhupāda's) book: *Kṛṣṇa*: *The Supreme Personality of Godhead*. He was also the chief patron of the London Hare Kṛṣṇa temple, which was strategically located only a few steps away from the gates of the British Museum.

The Guru of the Hare Kṛṣṇa movement in the West is called Prabhupāda His Divine Grace Śrīmad A.C. Bhaktivedānta Swami. We will call him Prabhupāda. Two other ex-Beatles, John Lennon and Paul McCartney, about this time announced in their New York Press Conference that they were disillusioned with Maharishi and TM. But George Harrison had found a new 'Yoga'. He described his new Guru as a 'Bhakti Yogi' following the path of Devotion. He wrote in 1970 (in his '*Words from George Harrison*' in the beginning of the *Kṛṣṇa* book):

> If there's God, I want to see Him. It's pointless to believe in something without proof, and Kṛṣṇa Consciousness and meditation are methods where you can actually obtain GOD perception. You can actually see God, and hear Him, play with Him. It might sound crazy, but He is actually there, actually with you. (Prabhupāda 1986, p. vii).

Then, a few lines below, he continues:

> By chanting:
>
> Hare Kṛṣṇa, Hare Kṛṣṇa
> Kṛṣṇa Kṛṣṇa, Hare Hare
> Hare Rāma, Hare Rāma
> Rāma, Rāma Hare Hare.
>
> one inevitably arrives at KṚṢṆA Consciousness. (The proof of the pudding is in the eating!) (Prabhupāda, 1986, p. vii).

Harrison concludes his sermon as follows:

> I also request that you make an appointment to meet your God now, through the self-liberating process of YOGA (UNION) and GIVE PEACE A CHANCE.
>
> ALL YOU NEED IS LOVE (KRISHNA) HARI-BOL.

Thus the Beatles' reported repudiation of TM did not stop the wave of Eastern religious movements in the West. Nor did it slow down the progress of TM. George Harrison's appeal was heard by millions of willing Americans, Canadians and Europeans. The wave gradually reached its peak.

2. SIKHISM AND YOGA

Spiritual movements of many varieties—Indian, Tibetan and new American Yogas, Taoism, Buddhism and Zen, Scientology and Sufism—are visible on the Western scene. By a conservative estimate, more than a hundred spiritual masters, mostly Oriental, have established their spiritual centres in California and in many other Western cities. Let me digress a little with the very interesting story of a Sikh master from India, Yogi Bhajan, who became another international guru. Yogi Bhajan was a Sikh with a beard and white Sikh turban, married with three children. He taught Sikh *dharma* as well as Kundalini and Tantric Yoga.

Yogi Bhajan came to America from New Delhi. In September of 1968, he was asked to leave an important post for a mission to Canada and the United States to teach the secrets of the ancient and evolved Science of Yoga to all capable of receiving them. He was aware that the Science of Yoga has been obstructed and polluted in the Western world hence came to cleanse people of their negativity and to train teachers.

The Western followers of Yogi Bhajan wear white turbans and robes and are advised to grow beards if they can. The women disciples have to remain satisfied with simply covering their heads with a white scarf and with a sari. For Yogi Bhajan, to be sure, was against the recent Women's Liberation Movement in the West. He had said in one of his spirited speeches delivered from his Los Angeles Ashram: 'Neither have they (women) grown beards like men, nor will they ever.' Thus the guru had argued that women can never be equal to men no matter how much the advocates of Women's Liberation may try. It should be noted also that Yogi Bhajan remained a married man. And Bibiji, as his wife was called by his disciples, lived with him and helped him in organizing various spiritual centres. It is claimed by Yogi Bhajan's disciples that his humility and power as a Yogi and his worldly experience as a married man and career man (he held a Government of India post before he came to North America) eminently qualify him to train teachers in the techniques for a Healthy-Happy-Holy life.

In 1969, Yogi Bhajan organized what is now called 3HO Foundation (Healthy-Happy-Holy Organization). It was a federally tax-exempt, 'not-profit' California Corporation with affiliates in six states and with International Headquarters in Los Angeles. It was established, according to the Founders, for the advancement of education, science and religion, for charitable and educational purposes and for training individuals to develop and expand their capabilities. The Foundation at one time claimed to have more than one hundred centres all over the world—in countries like the USA, Canada, Mexico, Puerto Rico, Israel, Great Britain, Belgium, the Netherlands, France and Japan. The disciples of Yogi Bhajan had not only gone out to open 3HO centres, but since earning one's own living is part of the master's teaching, they created a business to support themselves: a chain of vegetarian restaurants, a brass bed factory, construction companies and so forth.

The 3HO Foundation published a quarterly magazine called *Beads of Truth*. It contained transcriptions of Yogi Bhajan's lectures and some physical exercises called Yogic exercises. The magazine contained pictures and news of the 3HO movement. A look at this magazine will readily remind one of the *Back to Godhead* magazine of the Hare Kṛṣṇa movement. Instead of containing pictures of shaven heads and saffron robes, it contained chanting scenes and congregations of persons with white robes and white turbans or headcovers. 'God' and 'Guru' were printed on almost every page of the magazine. For Yogi Bhajan, '*God is vibration; the Divinity in You is in the control of the breath.*' Chanting and breathing exercises are central to his teaching. Like the Hare Kṛṣṇa people, the 3HO people chanted the mantra. Their mantra was, however, called 'the ĀDI Mantra,' the *first* mantra which runs as 'Om namo Guru Dev Namo.'

The movement of Yogi Bhajan and his 3HO Foundation has many parallels with the Hare Kṛṣṇa movement. Both are of Indian origin. And it seems both have come to stay. It is claimed (somewhat rightly I believe) that both the Hare Kṛṣṇa movement and the 3HO movement (as well as many movements of similar kind) have made it possible for millions of young people today to leave drugs. 3HO publicly offered a controlled rehabilitation programme for heroin and methadone addicts. The Hare Kṛṣṇa movement does not announce its drug rehabilitation programme, but it has been said that a considerable number of ex-drug addicts did join the movement and have remained out of trouble with success.

If one spiritual movement is described in some detail, patterns of many other similar modern spiritual movements may thereby be understood. The idea is not to suggest the slang 'if you have seen one, you have seen them all'. Being a Sanskritist myself, I am only following a well-known and time-honoured style of the Sanskrit writers expressed as *iti dik*. To wit: describe one type and leave the rest to the imagination of the readers.

Both the Hare Kṛṣṇa movement and the Yogi Bhajan movement are claimed to be based upon two well-known and well-established Indian religious traditions, Vaiṣṇavism and Sikhism. The former's spiritual master, Prabhupāda, translated a number of ancient Sanskrit texts, and Yogi Bhajan preached materials from Guru Nanak, the founder of Sikhism.

3. THE KṚṢṆA CONSCIOUSNESS MOVEMENT

The story of the rise of Kṛṣṇa as the supreme personality of Godhead in the Western hemisphere is not without its interest. It was told by Mr Howard Wheeler, alias Hayagrīva, in pages of the *Back to Godhead* magazine.

But who was this Guru, His Divine Grace Śrīmad A.C. Bhaktivedānta

Swami Prabhupāda? Hayagrīva's answer: he came as a 'nearly penniless stranger' to America in 1965 to spread 'the transcendental message of *The Bhagvad-Gītā*'. What was he doing before he took upon himself this laudable task? To answer to this question, we have to go to India. The account of his background given in the next paragraph is gleaned from a book by Faye Levine.

His Divine Grace was born on 1 September 1896, in Calcutta, India. His name was Abhay Charan De (which, I believe, accounts for the initials, 'A.C.'), and his father's name was Gaur Mohan De. His family, like millions of other families in Bengal, belongs to the Vaiṣṇava faith or to the Sakta faith. This is, as far as my experience goes, the general pattern. Thus, the De family was Vaiṣṇava in this sense. Abhay Charan De graduated from the University of Calcutta with economics and philosophy as two minor subjects. He married in his twenties and had five children. He ran a drug store (owned by the De family) at this time. When his father died in 1930, he became the full-time manager of this pharmaceutical business. At about this time he was officially initiated into the Gauḍīya Vaiṣṇava Society, one of the many Caitanya sects (followers of Srī Kṛṣṇa Caitanya of sixteenth-century Bengal) of Vaiṣṇava Hindus. His guru was then head of the North Calcutta centre of the Gauḍīya Vaiṣṇava Society, Prabhupāda Bhaktisiddhānta Saraswati. Since A.C. De knew English, his official guru asked him to explain Vaiṣṇavism in English for Westerners. In 1936 the guru died.

How far the above account is true, I do not know. The background story, however, sounds reasonably straightforward. For the idea of transmitting and propagating Vaiṣṇavism, especially preaching the message of Lord Gaurāṇga (alias Srī Kṛṣṇa Caitanya) in the West was not really new in 1930 in Bengal, nor certainly in North Calcutta, where the Gauḍīya Vaiṣṇava Society had the Radhakrishna Temple.

Mr Shishir Kumar Ghose, in the early period of the twentieth century, was editor-owner of the leading daily English newspaper of Calcutta, *Amṛita Bazar Patrika.* Mr Ghose was from North Calcutta. Mr Shishir Ghose, in his youth, was moderately sympathetic to the Indian nationalist movement for independence against British imperialism. In the later part of his life, he turned into a religious man, a devotee of Lord Gaurāṇga. He used his journalistic skill 'to acquaint the English speaking people of Europe and America with the Holy name and creed of Srī Kṛṣṇa Caitanya'. He wrote a book in English entitled *Lord Gaurāṇga* and encouraged others to write more such books in English. This was how a contemporary writer described the incident:

. . . a genuine desire was evinced in many religious circles of Europe and America—especially the latter—of learning more of the gospel of Salvation through Love preached by the Great Lord. Not only so, but a regular Vaishnava movement was started by some of them in the U.S.A. and Mexico culminating in the erection of temples dedicated to Shree Rādhā-Kṛṣṇa on Christian soil which witnessed their strong and growing attraction for the charming personality and noble creed of the Lord.

That account was written in January 1925, by a person who prepared a rather free English translation of *Srī-Caitanya-Caritāmṛta* (an authoritative biography of Caitanya by Kṛṣṇadāsa Kavirāja of the sixteenth century).

A brief reference to two other scholars of the nineteenth century, who were known for spreading the message of Indian wisdom and spirituality, may be made here, if only to show the contrast. They were Raja Ram Mohun Roy and Swami Vivekananda. Raja Ram Mohun Roy, a Bengali Brahmin, who first set himself the task of making his Hindu co-religionists give up crude and obnoxious practices such as idolatry and *satī*, deliberately adopted the Western scale of values, and cited Christian theology to prove the necessity of monotheism. Roy tried to prove that monotheism (and not just abstract monism) was the dominant trend of the Upaniṣads of ancient India! He was a Sanskrit scholar as well as a thinker. Besides, he had a great talent for preaching religious sermons. He first went to England, and then to America. He became associated with the Unitarian movement of New England, and delivered several lectures on the unity of the Bible and the Upaniṣads. His ideas might have influenced the New England Transcendentalists.

But unlike his successor Vivekananda, Ram Mohun Roy was more eager to reform Hinduism than to spread Eastern wisdom to counteract the so-called Western materialism. Back in Calcutta, Roy founded a group called the *Brahmo-Samaj*, which was partly a social and partly a religious organization. In fact, it consisted mainly of the elite of Bengal and was much like a newly religious society rather than a new religious tradition.

Towards the latter part of the nineteenth century, Swāmi Vivekananda came to the West. He contended that he had a new message for the whole world, specially for Western people—a message which he claimed to have learnt from his guru, the well-known Indian mystic, Srī Rāmakṛṣṇa Paramahaṃsa (1836–86). This was probably the beginning of the Hindu mystics' conquest of Western soil.

Vivekananda's message was for universalism in religious thinking. He thought that the common factors in all religions must be spirituality and a form of religious humanism which included moral concern for, and service to others:

Religion is the manifestation of Divinity that is already in a man.
God can be realized by everyone, for every individual is potentially divine.
Various religions are but different paths leading to the Divine Realization (See Vivekananda, 1977).

In May 1883, Vivekananda represented, along with two other Bengalis (one of whom was a representative of Ram Mohun's Brahma-Samaj), the Hindu religion in the World Congress of Religions held in Chicago. His Chicago lecture made him famous almost overnight in the West. He was described in the Chicago newspapers as a 'cyclonic Hindu'. The theme of his Chicago lecture was the unity of all religions. Vivekananda established two Vedānta societies in North America in his lifetime. His official philosophy of religion was Vedānta, Śaṃkara's Advaita Vedānta. He also lectured on *rāja-yoga*. In fact this religious doctrine was a blending of monotheism and monism. In practice, Vivekananda attempted a re-interpretation of Vedānta, inculcating the theme of the unity of all religions in his neo-Vedāntism.

But unlike some modern gurus and swāmijis, Vivekananda was not concerned with saving the Western world from the evils of materialism. In fact his major concern was the appalling poverty and sufferings of his own country and countrymen. He dedicated his life to a sort of an iconoclastic activity ripping off the shutters of poverty and illiteracy of India, the sloth, superstitions and sluggishness of its people, and age-old Hindu abominations practised in the name of religion. In the following words, he gave vent to his real feeling about his own role:

Let each of us pray, day and night, for the downtrodden millions . . . who are held fast by poverty, priest-craft and tyranny—pray day and night for them . . . I am no metaphysician, no philosopher, nay, no saint. But I am poor. I love being poor . . . *May I be born again and again, suffer thousands of miseries, so that I may worship the only God that exists, the only God I believe in, the sum total of all souls.*

The impact of Vivekananda's dynamic personality on Indian society was considerable. The above speech reveals him more as a humanist than a religious preacher. What a remarkable difference from a modern Oriental guru in the West today!

This brief incursion into the nineteenth century history about Ram Mohun Roy and Vivekananda provides only a background. Today's religious movements in Europe and North America are decidedly different.

The newspaper tycoon of North Calcutta, Mr Shishir Kumar Ghose (who was later called a Mahātma) and his followers tried to introduced Caitanya's message of love and devotion in the Western world, as we have already noted. The spiritual master, Mr A.C. De (or Prabhupāda) came from a similar background, which must have influenced his final decision to bring the message of Caitanya and Kṛṣṇa to the Western world.

To continue with Prabhupāda (*à la* Faye Levine), Mr De continued to be a family man and managed the pharmaceutical business for another eighteen years. To fulfil, however, his promise to his guru, he tried to publish a devotional magazine in English dealing with Caitanya and Vaiṣṇavism. He might have acquired the title 'Bhaktivedānta' during this period. But he did not become a monk or a Swāmi. It was only at the age of fifty-eight, in 1954, that he decided to become a Swāmi with saffron robes and shaven head. Four years later still, in 1958, he renounced all his interest in the pharmaceutical concern in Calcutta, and became a full-fledged *niṣkiñcana* (a proper monk). For about seven or eight years, he maintained the life-style of a Vaiṣṇava monk worshipping Kṛṣṇa and chanting 'Hare Kṛṣṇa' in ecstasy.

When you are a Vaiṣṇava monk, you become also a guru. Thus, Prabhupāda was successful in gathering around him a number of disciples, some of whom were monks while others were family-men. But in 1965, at the age of seventy, Prabhupāda found his long cherished dream fulfilled—the dream of spreading Kṛṣṇa's message to America. It has been said that a distinguished woman named Sumati Morarji was one of his Indian disciples. She was the owner of Scindia Steamship Lines, one of the largest shipping concerns in India. She paid for his passage from India to USA, Prabhupāda thus disembarked in Boston probably with very little money. And very little is known about how he fared in Boston in the first few months.

Prabhupāda came to New York after a few months, and rented a small storefront apartment at 26 Second Avenue, by the side of a Mobil gas station. The place had been an old curiosity shop before and the previous tenant had painted over the outside door: 'Matchless Gifts.' On that July morning of 1966, when the seventy-three-year-old Prabhupāda met Howard Wheeler and escorted him to this apartment, the latter saw these words on the door. Later on Howard Wheeler wrote in *Back to Godhead*, October 1969 issue: 'At that time I didn't realize how prophetic the words were.' Prabhupāda had put his own sign also in the window saying: 'Lectures on *Bhagavad-Gītā*, A.C. Bhaktivedānta Swāmi, Monday Wednesday Friday 7–9' (Dasa, 1985, p. 2).

The first impression of the 'storefront set-up' was negative upon Mr Wheeler. He wrote later about his impression (see account in Dasa 1985).

I knew he would not attract wealthy or influential New Yorkers downtown, but I thought the East Village hippies would be interested enough in Indian philosophy or whatever he was offering to give him some patronage.

To be nice and polite, Mr Wheeler left Prabhupāda that morning after promising to return to attend his 'class' one evening.

One evening, Mr Wheeler did return to attend one of his 'classes' along with four of his friends. He was instantly charmed by the chanting of 'Hare Kṛṣṇa' in accompaniment with 'kartals' (cymbals). They all joined in the chanting that was led by Prabhupāda sitting on a dais.

The 'transcendental sound vibration' finally proved to be successful with Howard Wheeler. He also learnt that 'Kṛṣṇa Consciousness' actually meant God-consciousness. But he was still not sure of Prabhupāda's 'mass' appeal. He asked him about the drug movement, about the widespread use of psychedelic drugs for self-realization. But Prabhupāda answered in significant language:

You don't need to take anything for your spiritual life. Now everyone is claiming God is dead or 'I am God'. You just chant Hare Krishna. Eventually you will have God dancing on your tongue. Dasa, 1985, p. 14.

Wheeler understood the full significance of these words. Chanting in this manner could very well bring on 'spiritual' ecstasy. A state of exalted consciousness can very well be achieved through constant emotional chanting in a group. The 'Beat' generation of the fifties had shown us the effectiveness of sound. In Howard Wheeler's own words, Prabhupāda appeared to him to be 'naturally in a state of exalted consciousness—a state many try to trigger via psychedelics.' What is more, Prabhupāda 'promised' that he could teach Howard and others the same.

Thus, Howard Wheeler became Hayagrīva (he did not become a monk, but only a disciple) and turned into his public relations man when Prabhupāda needed it. Wheeler's first thought was to enlist the support and help of the poet Allen Ginsberg. And it had to be Ginsberg. Ginsberg could be called Poet Laureate of three successive movements in North America—from the 'beat' movement of the fifties to the LSD movement and then the Hare Kṛṣṇa movement of the sixties. Timothy Leary, in his historic San Francisco lecture (in an LSD conference sponsored by the

University ɔf California in June 1966) greeted Ginsberg as the 'Beloved Guru' of the drug movement. Thus, Wheeler was right when he said: 'it had to be Ginsberg.'

Ginsberg was respectable as a poet. Hayagrīva 'tracked down' the poet in New York and sent him invitations to one of the chanting sessions of the group. Ginsberg started coming to the chanting sessions almost regularly, and eventually *The York Times* ran a story on Prabhupāda describing him as the new Lower East Side Swami. The article quoted Ginbsberg saying that chanting of the *mantra* Hare Kṛṣṇa was instant 'ecstasy'. This was the way, as Hayagrīva later observed, Prabhupāda's *Gītā* class was suddenly transformed into a movement that spread all over the world.

Hayagrīva, co-founder of the New Vrindaban, acted as an expert public relations man. He was in direct touch with the mood of the American youth. Here are some quotations from the evangelical handbills which he himself wrote and distributed at Tompkins Square Park during the early chanting session (Ginsberg suggested earlier that the daily chanting session be moved to Tompkins Square Park where the hippies were starting to congregate and that would help the movement spread.):

STAY HIGH FOREVER

No More Coming Down.

Practice KRISHNA CONSCIOUSNESS

Expand your consciousness by practising the

TRANSCENDENTAL SOUND VIBRATION

Furthermore: *'Turn on* through Music, Dance, . . .

Tune in: Awaken your Transcendental nature.

Rejoice in the ocean of bliss.

Drop Out of movements employing artificially induced states

of

self-realization and expanded consciousness

In fact, the Hare Kṛṣṇa movement offered something better to satisfy the 'spiritual' hunger of the western youth of the sixties. Prabhupāda had often said:

> Just vibrate Hare Kṛṣṇa once, and your spiritual life has already begun. There is no expense, and if there is some gain, why not try it?

Prabhupāda met Hayagrīva in July 1966. By 1967, the Hare Krishna movement was in full swing in New York. It became increasingly appealing to the Western youth of the sixties. Hayagrīva described one occasion in 1967 in these words:

> We splashed in the Haight pond with a mammoth *mantra* rock-dance at the Avalon Ball-room. Prabhupāda and Ginsberg danced on stage with upraised hands. Multicoloured light swirled across huge wall slides of Krishna and Rāma. The Grateful Dead, Moby Grape and Big Brother blared away. Even Tim Leary garlanded one of us and salaamed, 'A beautiful night, a beautiful night.'

The above outline of the development of the Hare Kṛṣṇa movement clarifies certain puzzles. One of the puzzles is 'Why did the Hare Kṛṣṇa movement become so popular within such a short period?'

It may be noted that the Hare Kṛṣṇa people spared no pains to utilize any current topic in order to advertise their movement. Even the title of the magazine is significant: *Back to Godhead*. It is further explained as 'Back to HOME, Back to our original existence of pure bliss.' What is the major problem with most young people today in Western, heavily industrialized society? A sociologist will tell us that most of these confused young people today have lost their HOME, their family surroundings. So what promise could be more welcome to these people other than the promise: Back to Home. Those who join the 'Kṛṣṇa Consciousness Society' do get back a home, a commune-like home, whatever be the value of such a home in absolute terms. The devotees are described by Prabhupāda as members of Kṛṣṇa's family.

In fact, Prabhupāda had seized every opportunity to propagate his movement. In 1968, when space travel and moon-landing were very much in the news and in the minds of the people, Prabhupāda wrote a new book to utilize the situation: *Easy Journey to Other Planets* (1968). He claimed that he was using the Vedic scriptural writings of India to make an important contribution to our knowledge of new, upper planetary systems and interplanetary space travel. Referring to the scientists' notion of 'anti-matter', Prabhupāda renders it as the Spiritual substance, and identifies it with Kṛṣṇa and his spiritual realm Vaikuntha. Only a few decades ago, some Indian leaders, suffering from foreign domination and from a sense of inferiority before the technological and scientific progress in the West, used to cultivate a sort of defensive position. They claimed that every new scientific truth can be found in the Vedas and epics. Only one had to know how to look for it there! Thus, airplanes, jets and atom bombs are all to be found in the mythological accounts of the epics—the *Rāmāyaṇa* and the *Mahābhārata*. Sometimes, even educated

Indians, without caring to look minutely into our past history and ancient texts, believed that their forefathers were much more scientifically advanced than modern Westerners. By now, perhaps, this belief has generally been abandoned with the exception of a few over-zealous traditionalists as well as some new converts who are influenced by such recent books as *The Chairot Of the Gods*. But Prabhupāda was different. He had come forward with his novel planetary system and a new theory about space-travel. And this scientific knowledge was all the time there in the *Bhāgavata-purāṇa*, in the *Gītā*, and in the Vedas. Prabhupāda claimed that the Sputniks and other man-made machines will 'never be able to carry human beings very far into interplanetary space' because 'in the higher planetary system the atmosphere in different'. One can travel to these 'anti-material' planets by yoga and only after death. One can prepare, according to Prabhupāda, oneself for such a journey after death by practising Kṛṣṇa consciousness under a 'bonafide spiritual master'. I am referring here to Prabhupāda's book on space-travel; Prabhupāda's merit as a spiritual master need not be discounted at all by his naiveté in scientific knowledge. One can easily see the point of his argument at a different level.

4. SANSKRIT AND THE INTERNATIONAL SOCIETY FOR KRṢNA CONSCIOUSNESS (ISKCON) MOVEMENT

Let us now switch to a different aspect of the movement. One can, I believe, make a similar argument regarding Prabhupāda's knowledge of Sanskrit and the 'Vedic' language. Whether or not he is an outstanding scholar, that is, Sanskrit scholar, can very well be doubted. Specially when he either translated or summarized many Vaiṣṇava Sanskrit texts, it would be plucky to doubt or to challenge his knowledge of Sanskrit.

Scholars may not always agree with the details of his translations and interpretation. But a religious leader or a spiritual master does not have to be a perfect scholar. It is true that the original followers of Caitanya, six Gosvāmins of Vṛndāvana, were first-rate Sanskrit scholars. This is well proven by their numerous Sanskrit writings. But there is also the following idea dominant among the Bengali Vaiṣṇavas:

> A fool may say 'Viṣṇāya' while a scholar would say 'Viṣṇave' (for Visnu, the supreme deity). The former is (grammatically) wrong, while the latter is correct. But Janārdana (i.e., Kṛṣṇa) accepts only the *bhāva* (mental intention), and ignores the outward utterance.

Thus, in my opinion, it would be unfair to combat the Sanskrit knowledge of Prabhupāda. For, as the above quotation shows, a spiritual master is not that much concerned with the grammar or syntactic techniques of the texts as he is with the 'spirit' and 'meaning' (i.e., inner meaning) of the texts. An example can make our point clear. It is all right for an automobile driver as long as he can drive well. It is not necessary for him to be also a good auto-mechanic so that he could understand and explain well the functioning of the automobile engine.

To turn to another important issue here. We may ponder over the nature of the Sanskrit language. Sanskrit, in my opinion, is one of the most flexible languages. And qualified Sanskritists can play games with this language. It is a fact that certain important texts like the *Bhagavad-Gītā*, the *Upaniṣads,* and the *Brahmasūtras* have been commented upon by about a dozen of commentators in different ages. Such commentaries often refute each other while each claims to be explaining the identical texts. This is possible only because of the flexibility of the language of these original texts.

Let us take typical example. The *Brahmasūtras* of Bādarāyaṇa were commented upon by Śaṃkara in the ninth century AD to prove his Monistic Vedānta philosophy, according to which the individual soul is identical with the Universal Soul or *Brahman*, the Ultimate Reality. This philosophical position is summed up briefly as follows: the Ultimate Reality is One without a second. Again, the same *Brahmasūtras* were commented upon by Bhāskara (*c.* tenth century AD), by Rāmānuja (c. eleventh century AD), by Madhva (c. thirteenth century AD), by Nimbārka (c. fourteenth century AD), and by Baladeva (an eighteenth century follower of Caitanya). Each of these commentators refuted Śaṃkara's interpretation as well as the interpretations of preceding commentators in order to establish his own interpretation. Each claimed his own interpretation to be authentic while disagreeing with others. And it should also be noted that every one of these commentators mentioned above was a Sanskritist par excellence. The question for us here is not to decide who was right and who was wrong in his interpretation. The moral to be derived is that each of these interpretations could be claimed to be valid because such is the nature of the Sanskrit language and such is the character of these crucially important Sanskrit texts.

Qualified Sanskritists can play games with Sanskrit. It is easy to create ambiguities, make up riddles and puns in this language. Poets in the middle ages had actually written long narrative poems in Sanskrit using only two or three sounds or letters. Sometimes two different narratives had been told in a single narrative poem, where each verse would admit of two or three different meanings. This will be enough to warn us against challenging anyone's interpretation of a Sanskrit verse from a text like the *Gītā* from a purely linguistic point of view. It is quite easy to lose oneself here in the quicksand of futile arguments and counter-arguments.

Prabhupāda had apparently looked for endorsement from scholars and academics. Thus, academics in North America were not always indifferent to Prabhupāda's movement. Professor Edward C. Dimock of the University of Chicago has written in his foreword to the *Bhagavad-Gītā As It Is* (1973):

> The scholar, the student of Gauḍīya Vaiṣṇavism, and the increasing number of Western readers interested in classical Vedic thought have been done a service by Swami Bhaktivedānta. By bringing us a new and living interpretation of a text already known to many, he has increased our understanding manyfold.

It is perhaps correct to say that Prabhupāda's interpretation of the *Bhagavad-Gītā* is new. But the very title of Prabhupāda's book contradicts the fact that this is only one among many interpretations of the *Gītā* by both the Vaiṣṇava and non-Vaiṣṇava sects.

This is an age where loud self-assertion is more effective than the Vaiṣṇava modesty and humility. Thus Prabhupāda may be justified in asserting himself. He has pointed out that 'mundane wranglers have taken advantage of *Bhagavad-Gītā* to push forward their *demonic propensities* and mislead people' (Preface to *Bhagavad-Gītā As It Is*; my italics, p. xix). His obvious opponent is a follower of Śaṃkara (who is called by him the Māyāvādi). According to the Vaiṣṇava tradition, it is not unnatural for a Vaiṣṇava to refute Śaṃkara's Advaita philosophy. Spiritual masters beginning from Bhāskara, Rāmānuja and Madhva had taken a similar stand before. But Prabhupāda never mentioned the interpretations of the *Gītā* by other Vaiṣṇava masters like Rāmānuja and Madhva. In fact, if he followed any standard Vaiṣṇava commentary, it was never mentioned. At the end of each chapter, Prabhupāda added, following the well-known practice and style of a Sanskrit commentator, a colophon in English in which the 'purport' is claimed to be his own, that is, 'the Bhaktivedānta Purport'. Thus it supports Professor Dimock's comment that it is a 'new' interpretation of the *Gītā*.

It should be admitted that unlike most Eastern gurus in the West today, Prabhupāda laid considerable emphasis, in the course of his preaching, on the importance of the Sanskrit tradition. This is a commendable stance on the part of a spiritual master.

That Prabhupāda encourages his disciples to study Sanskrit is a good thing, after all. For it is at least a move in the right direction for anyone who aspires, for whatever reasons, to understand and comprehend ancient Indian religion, culture and 'wisdom'.

5. 'VEDIC' ORIGIN—A CONTROVERSY

Let us then shift our attention to another aspect of the Hare Kṛṣṇa movement in the West. The Hare Kṛṣṇa people claim that their Kṛṣṇa Consciousness movement is the 'Genuine Vedic' Way. I am reminded here of a strange exchange of letters that took place between Prabhupāda and Professor J.F. Staal of the University of California at Berkeley between January and April in 1970. All these letters were later published by the ISKCON press as a booklet with the title: *The Kṛṣṇa Consciousness Movement is the Genuine Vedic Way*. What triggered off the discussion was an article in the *Los Angeles Times* of 11 January 1970, containing a remark of Professor Staal.

According to the *LA Times* reporter, Staal commented that modern young men who were turning away from Christianity, Islam and Judaism had usually lost faith with the personal god of these religions, and were looking for a mystical religion without absolutes. Thus, for Staal it was a puzzle to see that the Western young people in the Hare Kṛṣṇa movement had turned to a religion which was highly personalistic. Staal was quoted as saying:

> They [the Hare Kṛṣṇa people] accept a personal god, Krishna, and Christianity has that. I feel that they have transferred some of their Christian background to a Hindu sect (*LA Times*, 11 Jan, 1970, p. 22).

Staal's comments provoked criticism and a reply from His Divine Grace Prabhupāda. In the course of the prolonged dispute, Staal argued that neither the Vedas nor the *Gītā* did recommend constant chanting of Hare Kṛṣṇa as the *only way* to achieve the spiritual goal. Prabhupāda, in reply, quoted, among other things, a verse from the *Gītā* (Ch. 9, verse 14), where Kṛṣṇa is supposed to have said that constant chanting is the only way to God-realization. Prabhupāda also referred to *Brahma-sūtra* 4.4.22: *anāvṛttiḥ śabdāt* and interpreted it as: 'By sound vibration one becomes liberated.'

Interpretation of the above *Gītā* verse hinges upon the interpretation of a key term *kīrtayantaḥ*. Staal argued that this term in the said context need not mean chanting of the name of Kṛṣṇa. On the authority of the other respectable commentators of the *Gītā*, the word in question can be interpreted as 'glorifying', 'chanting', 'talking about' and so on. And *Brahma-sūtra* 4.4.22 obviously admits of an entirely different interpretation. *Śabda* in this context refers to the revealed Vedic scriptures, and Śaṃkara has explained the *sutra* accordingly.

In reply to Staal's explanation, Prabhupāda quoted several verses from texts like the *Bhāgavata-purāṇa* and the *Bhaktirasāmṛtasindhu* to *prove* that chanting of the name of Kṛṣṇa is the sole teaching of all the Vedas! But this was obviously a futile attempt which finally turned into an intriguing arguing in a circle. For no one disputes that the *Bhāgavata-Purāṇa* and similar Vaiṣṇava texts talk about Kṛṣṇa as the supreme Godhead and recommend chanting as one of the means, perhaps the best means (in their opinion) for conducting devotional services to God. But these texts are certainly not part of the Vedas. What Staal questioned was whether there was any sanction in the Vedas regarding chanting as the best means for attaining God. Such a sanction, in my honest opinion, can never be found in the Vedas. For most of the Vedic *ṛṣis*, if not all of them, were concerned with things (Soma drink, Agni hymns, Indra and Varuna) that were very different from Kṛṣṇa, God, devotion and chanting of the name of God.

I have, however, some difficulty in comprehending what is really at stake in such a dispute. I cannot understand, for example, why the sanction of the Vedas would be at all necessary for the cultivation of Kṛṣṇa worship. In sum, why are Prabhupāda and his devotees so eager to stamp their movement as 'Vedic'? Historical research shows that the Kṛṣṇa cult as well as devotional services to attain God was very ancient, perhaps pre-Vedic. In the course of time, when the lifeless and dry-as-dust rituals and sacrifices of Vedic India failed to satisfy the growing 'spiritual" and religious yearnings of the Indians, their emotional involvement with 'the inner world', the idea of God, worship, devotion, service and surrender—all entered into the Sanskrit tradition in the form of the Kṛṣṇa cult, Rāma cult, Śiva cult and so on. The rise of the epics, the *Rāmāyaṇa* and *Mahābhārata*, and various *purāṇas* dealing with such godheads as Viṣnu, Śiva and Brahmā can be taken to be an expression of this new trend in orthodox Hinduism.

It is true that in the past centuries religious leaders of India did seek some support or sanction from the 'Holy Scriptures', that is, the Vedas, in order to propagate their different religious doctrines, because otherwise it would have been difficult for them to reach the general people for whom the doctrines were intended. This fact was understandable, because the Vedas used to be held in the highest veneration by the people of India.

But ordinary people had very little knowledge about the contents of the Vedas. The scriptures were not supposed to be read except only by a few privileged persons. In any case, I can understand that the so-called 'Vedic' sanction or support was necessary for getting the message across. This explains partly why Śrījīva Gosvāmin in the sixteenth century took so much pains to skim through the entire Vedic and post-Vedic literature to find out and gather support for Caitanya's doctrine of love and devotion for Kṛṣṇa. But that was a different story. In modern times, it is difficult to see why it becomes necessary for the Kṛṣṇa worshippers in the West to go back to the Vedas and lean over backwards to derive some support of their creed. In the same manner, one can question the use of the word 'Veda' or 'Vedic' by the TM people to propagate their doctrine.

A second oddity has also been indicated earlier. Why are the modern Western Vaiṣṇavas so infused with messianic zeal to convert others?

6. THE POPULARITY OF ISKCON

Neither of these two, however, remains puzzling when we think a little deeply. Psychoanalysts today might use their diagnostic tools to identify the first phenomenon with such technical concepts as 'the return of the repressed' or 'displacement'. From a layman's point of view, I see the following thing happening.

When a person grows up developing some kind of 'faith' in a person or in a system and afterwards finds out rightly or wrongly that the person or the system is a fraud or 'has too many holes', his or her immediate reaction is to reject the too familiar and search for a replacement. This replacement usually comes through the substitution of another that is apparently different and not too familiar (and hence attractive). But in most cases, the selection of the substitute is guided by an unconscious desire to find at least the likeable aspects of the already familiar but (unfortunately) rejected object. It is commonly seen that a girl who finds it difficult to live with her father or relate to him, would finally select a husband who would resemble the father in more ways than usual, and live happily ever afterwards! Thus the search for a substitute in the place of the rejected object is not always a search for something entirely different or the opposite. It could be, and often is, a search for something very similar, although such similarities may not be consciously recognized by the person at the moment of the acceptance of the substitute. In fact, as the Indian aesthetician, Ānandavardhana would say, disguised similarities are often psychologically more attractive than undisguised and explicit ones.

Today's rejection by young people of a highly hierarchical and authoritative religion or an authoritative household (parents) is not always due to their being highly authoritative or suffocatingly hierarchical. It is sometimes due to an awareness and discovery of their (real or imagined) phoniness or hollowness. This rejection is usually followed by a very confused state of mind when it finds anything that is disorderly, chaotic, senseless and shocking as desirable. This is the revolt and outburst that is due to erosion of 'faith' in the familiar system the young people grew up with. This is not necessarily an expression of their erosion of 'faith' as such. Passing through the phase of recklessness and irresponsibility, paranoia and fear, some young people often look for a retreat into a more orderly and disciplined lifestyle, a life of continence with apparently meaningful justification for such continence. It is now natural for such young people to enter the Hare Krsna temples and change their names and appearances and embrace a hard, abstinence-oriented lifestyle. For now they seem to think that they have found the overall 'meaning of it all'. They find a purpose and a 'mission' in their life! Everything they do now would be done for the satisfaction of, and in the service of, God, that is, Kṛṣṇa! What more could one expect? Like a disturbed and confused child, a devotee of the Hare Kṛṣṇa movement looks for a Father-image to 'surrender' to and he finds such an image in the spiritual master, or in Kṛṣṇa. Thus, *Back to Godhead* means for such devotees only 'Back to *Home*'!

Just as alcoholism is said to be cured by certain drugs like LSD, recklessness, paranoia and fear may be cured by joining a movement like the Hare Kṛṣṇa movement. We should recall that the 3HO movement of Yogi Bhajan explicitly claimed to cure drug-addicts. Messianic movements of these sorts can, I believe, be substitutes for drugs. According to the reports of Faye Levine, who lived in the New York temple as a devotee for some time, most devotees in their past have had experience with psychedelic drugs. I believe that this report is somewhat exaggerated. But it is, at least, a pointer to a solution of the above puzzle.

Levine reports that as soon as a person has entered the Hare Kṛṣṇa movement he is asked to 'shake off' his past background. Admittedly in most cases, the past has been a painful one, and hence one is well advised to 'shake it off'. In a somewhat strange way, this practice of 'shaking off the past' is quite similar to the time-honoured custom of the Indian *śramaṇas* or ascetics. An Indian ascetic who leaves behind a family life to join a monastic order, is supposed to 'cut off' all connections, physical as well as mental, with his previous family or old environment. The Hare Kṛṣṇa people today not only shake off their past lives but also accept, of their own accord, a lifestyle which is strictly disciplined, highly puritanistic and full of hardship. Prabhupāda did not boast in vain when he said that all his devotees gave up 'the four principles of material sinful life', that is, 1. meat eating, 2. illicit sexual connection, 3. taking intoxicants or drugs, 4. gambling. They really do. (See Dasa, 1985, p. 131).

It is further reported by Levine that when Allen Ginsberg told Prabhupāda about drug-induced mystical states, the latter refused to accept it as a real liberation from man's material nature. Although the devotees live together in a commune-like home called temple, it would be wrong to assume that they indulge in illicit sexual connection. Prabhupāda was apparently able to introduce some form of discipline in these temples. But whether such abstentions make the Hare Kṛṣṇa devotees much 'nicer' and more desirable people of earth, I cannot tell. My ambivalence on this issue is caused by certain strong evidence to the contrary.

7. INTOLERANCE AND ISKCON

This brings us to the discussion of the second oddity mentioned above. Although the Hare Kṛṣṇa devotees are asked to abstain from sex and LSD, from meat-eating and gambling, and lead a well-regimented life, the movement nevertheless offers an outlet for the aggressive drive of its members through a different channel. This is somewhat paradoxical. The sexual instinctual drive of the devotees compensated by their overtly aggressive behaviour as well as by their 'delusion of grandeur' with regard to their own activities. Hare Kṛṣṇa devotees are not really almost 'angels' on earth.

Prabhupāda had written in his letter to Staal that his disciples had turned into rare *mahātmas* by vibrating the transcendental sound, Hare Kṛṣṇa. He said:

> Recently, there was a big procession of our students in Berkeley on the Advent Day of Lord Caitanya, and the public has remarked as follows: 'This crowd of men is not like others, who assemble to break windows and create havoc.' This is also *confirmed by the police*. . . . Similarly, in Detroit there was a big peace march, and our men were appreciated as 'angels' in the crowd (1973, p. 19).

The devotees may not be violent enough to 'break windows', but they are very vocal and violent when they enter into a debate or argument for the sake of propaganda about their Kṛṣṇa Consciousness movement. Terms like 'rascals', 'idiots', 'fools' and 'asses' are very frequently used by them to address their opponents who may happen to believe in Vedānta or Zen or Buddhism, but not in Kṛṣṇa consciousness. They call other people who follow different cults 'impersonalists'. I shall quote below three long extracts which will speak for themselves. Two of these extracts are from their official magazine, *Back to Godhead* and the last one is from an issue of *Time* magazine.

Back to Godhead, No. 29, 1969: Heroine Govinda Dasi (a girl devotee) reporting about *The Pleasure Fair*, a programme for young people held in the Waikiki Shell, Honolulu, on 20 and 21 June:

Toward evening, I was crossing the hill and, passing an enclosed tent, I peeked in to see an altar with a man's picture, flowers, candles, etc., and learned that it was a booth glorifying a prominent 'incarnation' of God. A young man inside was giving an informal [talk]. . . . He was speaking of love of God, and how this could be achieved by a process of elevation through sense gratification, yogic powers, etc. . . .

I was astonished to hear these things, so I questioned him. 'What scriptures do you follow?'

He said, 'His own writing.' 'What is this man you are worshipping?'

He said, 'He is an avatar of God, he is Rāma and he is Kṛṣṇa.'

The so-called incarnation he was speaking of actually had none of the qualifications of God, and I was becoming angry that such an ordinary mortal was being passed off as the Supreme Lord. I began to speak loudly so that all could hear: 'You have no scripture, you have no *disciplic succession*, you are blindly following the teachings of this RASCAL! What proof do you have that this man is God? Kṛṣṇa lifted Govardhana Hill as a child when he appeared on this planet, but this man has not done any wonderful thing. Rather, I see by this picture that he is old and wrinkled and ugly, ready for death to take him; and yet you so foolishly believe that he is God. In Vedas, the avatars' appearances are fully described along with the birthplace and philosophy of each avatar. There is no mention of this RASCAL!'

After a few lines, she continues:

The young man . . . tried to argue, but was defeated on every point. Appearing like a FOOL before many people, the boy was very upset and tried to compromise and stop the argument. He said, 'All right, I will come down to your booth and we can discuss it further.' . . . A girl in the crowd was upset because I wasn't 'emanating love'. I told her, 'How can I emanate love? This RASCAL is misleading so many people, and I am feeling compassion for them on account of their innocence' (pp. 30–1).

No specific comment on the above is necessary. Remember that this was the report of a female devotee. Numerous such reports had been published in almost very issue of the *Back to Godhead* magazine. Let us note what the so-called 'disciplic succession' means for these Western devotees. Let us also note how ignorant these devotees are about the contents of what they call 'the Vedas', and presumably on the basis of such ignorance they want to destroy (almost literally) their fellow spiritualists.

My second extract is from a lecture-cum-discussion by His Holiness Hṛdayānanda Dāsa Gosvāmi (a devotee in the renounced order of the Hare Kṛṣṇa society) at the University of Florida:

> HDG: If Kṛṣṇa was ordinary, why then did he act extraordinarily? Why did all the contemporary authorities say that Kṛṣṇa is extraordinary? People argue that these descriptions can be psychologically explained. But actually such faithless demons can be psychologically explained. These fools are simply envious of Kṛṣṇa (European Edition, Gosvāmi, 1973, p. 23).

My third extract is from *Time* magazine, 11 February 1974:

> Trouble is stirring in Nirvāṇa. A.C. Bhak[t]ivedānta, Swami of the Hare Krishna movement, at a news conference in Hong Kong last week denounced a rival guru: self-styled divinity Maharajji, 16, now counseling his disciples in California. The ascetic swami, whose followers constitute a kind of saffron-robed Hindu version of the Salvation Army, began by saying, 'You've got to decide whether he is God, or a dog' (p. 36).

This aggressive character of the modern messianic religious movement is contradictory to the principle of non-aggression and humility taught by Caitanya in the fourteenth century AD in India. One of the few verses that Caitanya used to repeat all the time to his disciples was:

> You should always chant the name of Hari, while considering yourself lower [humbler] than the grass, cultivating toleration like that of a tree, being yourself without pride but paying respect [regard] to others.

It is explained that exemplary humility is to be learned by the devotees of Viṣṇu from the grass and exemplary non-aggression and toleration should be learned from the trees which never protest when people pluck flowers, fruits or leaves or chop them down. This should be the ideal of a devotee who wishes to chant the name of Hari. Thus, Caitanya explained that a worshipper of Kṛṣṇa should also be an ascetic who has no family life (and no material pursuit). For it is possible only for an ascetic to practise this ideal of absolute humility and non-aggression. Otherwise, asceticism has no place in Caitanya's religion where emotionalism is explicitly recognized as the dominant trend.

Most Vaiṣṇava mystics in India tried to cultivate humility and modesty in an exemplary manner. I recall the remark of one Vaiṣṇava guru who said to me, 'You know why they call me guru? I am in the role of the guru not because I know more than they do, nor because I am more advanced spiritually than they are, but because I know that I do not know much while they do not know that they do not know much.' The point here is about the humility, honesty and modesty of a mystic or a religious man. Even some interpreters of Buddhism say today that the Buddha's doctrine of *anātman* (sometimes translated as the doctrine of non-ego) is supposed to be a doctrine of utmost humility, selflessness and non-aggression.

8. SENSUALITY AND VAIṢṆAVISM

Let me conclude with one further observation. Prabhupāda has consistently underplayed the sensuality and emotional eroticism of the Bengal Vaiṣṇavism in his preachings. He hardly mentions the fact that the highest form of love for Kṛṣṇa is emphasized by Caitanya to be like the love of a married woman with a paramour. The Vaiṣṇava masters call it the *parakīya rati*. Sex is a dirty word for Prabhupāda. Thus sex outside the marital tie would naturally be unthinkable to him. In the name of the Vedic culture, Prabhupāda has prescribed a very stereotyped puritanism and middle-class sexual ideas for his disciples. Paradoxically enough, this type of puritanism had a successful appeal for the people of this over-indulgent, and perhaps over-permissive, Western society. This explains also the growing popularity of Prabhupāda's creed.

Prabhupāda has refused to follow the paths of other gurus and Swāmis in the West today. He does not tell his followers that they can indulge in drugs and illicit sex or in any exotic pursuit of pleasure and still they will be *saved* and God will show mercy. He does not imply, as some other modern gurus obviously do, that people can indulge in whatever corruption and evil doing they like, and finally through some mysterious process of meditation or illumination, they will reach God, Heaven or the Ultimate Goal of Ecstasy, which is all that counts. In this respect, Prabhupāda's attitude is more like a Protestant's criticism of human sin than a Catholic's toleration of sin and human lapses with a forgiving gesture. The following are his comments about sex and enjoyment of human beings:

> The world is meant for enjoyment. Enjoyment is already present in my spirit soul, but we have come here to partake of contaminated enjoyment, just like a man who is on the Bowery and thinks he is enjoying. *Some animals enjoy by eating stool.*

According to body, we have different kinds of enjoyment. The basic principle of enjoyment is sex life. Therefore, you will find sex life not only in human society, but in cat society, dog society, bird society—everywhere. *During daytime, a pigeon has sex at least twenty times.* This is his enjoyment. The basic principle of material life is sex life (1973, p. 14).

The above quotation about sex and morality, I think, requires no comment. Unfortunately, the religious leaders who worry so much about sex have very little to say about the bigger sins of modern life, about hyprocrisy, cheating, persecution, domination, aggression and repression, about killing, murder and the complete undermining of human values. But this will lead us to a more general issue about religion and morality which I cannot discuss here.

In any case, the sensibility and emotionalism of the Bengal Vaiṣṇavism was so obvious that the later Vaiṣṇava masters betrayed an ambivalence and attempted a symbolic and mystical interpretation of the Kṛṣṇa Rādhā story. The ambivalence regarding Kṛṣṇa's sensuality and apparently illicit affairs with the Gopīs is even noticeable as early as the *Bhāgavata-purāṇa.* Thus, when Śukadeva, the reciter of the Kṛṣṇa story in the *Bhāgavata*, was asked the justifiability of Kṛṣṇa's amorous play with his adolescent girlfriends (some of whom were married), he gave an evasive answer. But the sensuality in the Kṛṣṇa story in unmistakable. We can refer to Jayadeva's *Gītāgovinda*, which was Caitanya's favourite text. Let me also refer to the verse from the *Gītāgovinda* with which we started this chapter. The *Mahābhārata's* image of Kṛṣṇa was that of a shrewd statesman with superior intellect. He was not universally accepted as the Supreme God in the *Mahābhārata.* Duryodhana, for example, used to describe him as a man with some magic or mysterious power (*indrajāla*), a man who used to trick other people. But Caitanya revived the image of Kṛṣṇa more as a divine lover engaged in eternal amorous sports with the Gopīs. In fact, in Caitanya's religion, the sex instinct was explicitly accepted as the highest human instinct, which was to be transformed or sublimated into a para-sensuous play with the divine being. Thus, a scholar like S.K. De noted:

The sex-instinct is thus acknowledged in this theology as one of the highest human instincts which finds a transfigured counterpart or ideal in the highest sportive instinct of the divine being (1961, p. 379).

Thus, if Prabhupāda tries to ignore the overt sensuality of the Bengal Vaiṣṇavism, he is somewhat away from the spirit of Caitanya.

But there is also a historical precedent for Prabhupāda's attitude. Let me explain. Vaiṣṇava masters who are more aesthetically and poetically inclined interpret the sensuality of Bengal Vaiṣṇavism quite literally except for the fact that they would substitute the word 'earthly' in 'earthly love-making' by the word 'divine'. Kṛṣṇadasa Kavirāja, one of the authoritative biographers of Caitanya, writes in his *Caitanya-caritāmṛta* that the distinction between earthly passion or *kārma* and divine love or *prema* is this:

> Earthly passion is the drive for the gratification of one's own sense pleasure. Love divine is the drive for the gratification of the sense pleasure of the Divine, i.e., Kṛṣṇa.

But this explanation is apparently not very satisfactory to the Vaiṣṇava masters who are less poetically inclined and more influenced by the abstract metaphysics of Vedānta. Thus, these masters try to interpret the love play of Kṛṣṇa symbolically and claim that this is but an allegorical description of the individual soul's yearning for the mystic union with the Supreme God or the Universal Soul. To put the same matter in another way, the artists prefer the literal meaning of the Vaiṣṇava texts while the metaphysicians, for reasons of their own, prefer the metaphorical meaning and ignore the literal meaning.

In the eighteenth century AD, Baladeva Vidyābhūṣaṇa was a metaphysician, who tried to link Caitanya's Vaiṣṇavism with the Madhva school of Vaiṣṇava Vedānta. But as already noticed above, Madhva's philosophy is very different in spirit from the sensuality and emotionalism of Caitanya. A follower of Madhva usually rejects the *Rasa* dance section of the *Bhāgavata-purāṇa*. Madhva's was a very speculative system of Vaiṣṇava metaphysics and theology where there was hardly any place for Rādhā and the Gopīs. Thus, it is hardly possible that Madhva's philosophy exerted any influence upon the original emotionalism and sensuality of Caitanya's doctrine. But Baladeva apparently started this conservative trend within Caitanya's Vaiṣṇavism. Thus, at least here, Prabhupāda is following some trend, though not the predominant trend, that was already in the tradition before him.

It should also be noted that side by side with eroticism in Caitanya's religion, asceticism was equally emphasized. Among the followers of Caitanya during his lifetime there were the six Gosvāmins of Vṛndāvana who became ascetics and devoted their lives to scholarship. And there were also many others who were close associates of Caitanya like Nityānanda and Rāmānanda but remained in their family life and enjoyed it.

Here we are probably at the central paradox of almost all forms of Hinduism, if not of all forms of religion in general. Śiva, for example, was both a severe ascetic and a great lover. This paradox of asceticism and eroticism was well expressed in the dual system of Yoga and Tantra and became the common property of not only different forms of Hinduism but also of Buddhism. Thus, Caitanya's religion was no exception to this paradox. Perhaps, the paradox is an expression of the human ambivalence between abstention and over involvement with regard to man's sexual drive. The ascetic tendency exerts a curbing influence on the erotic tendency, that is, our drive for sense pleasure. And a true Vaiṣṇava is one who is probably caught between these two streams. This is after all a human predicament. As Jayadeva has portrayed:

> Two lovers meeting in darkness
> Embrace and kiss
> And claw as desire rises
> To dizzying heights of love.
> When familiar voices reveal
> That one ventured into the dark
> To betray the other,
> The mood of love is mixed with shame. (Miller, 1976, p. 94) (Pt. V, 18).

The rather critical and debunking tone of my account of some new (Eastern) religious movements in the foregoing three papers is actually a preliminary to a discussion about what is admirable and acceptable even today in these religious doctrines. As regards to turning East, there is always, as is usual with many other similar matters, a distinction between how not to do it and how to do it. When we understand how not to turn East, we will have a better idea of how to turn East, as Professor Harvey Cox himself would testify.

Notes and References

Cox, Harvey (1977), *Turning East: The Promise and Peril of the New Orientalism* (London: Allen Lane).

De, Sushil Kumar (1961), *Early History of the Vaiṣṇava Faith and Movement in Bengal* (Calcutta: K.L. Mukhopadhyay).

Gosvāmi, Hrdayānanda Dāsa (1973), 'Avoiding Wrong Turns in the Path of Knowledge', *Back to Godhead: The Magazine of the Hare Krishna Movement*, 1973, no. 60, pp. 21–5.

Krṣṇadasa Kaviraja (1977), *Caitanyacaritāmṛta* (New Delhi).

Miller, Barbara Stoler, ed. (1977), *Love Song of the Dark Lord, Jayadeva's Gītāgovinda* (New York: Columbia University Press).

Prabhupāda, A.C. Bhaktivedānta Swāmi (1968), *Easy Journey to Other Planets* (Boston: Iskcon Press).

———. (1973), *Bhagavad-Gītā As It Is* (Los Angeles: The Bhaktivedānta Book Trust).

———. (1986), *Kṛṣṇa: The Supreme Personality of Godhead, a Summary Study of Srila Vyāsadeva's Śrīmad-Bhagavatam, Tenth Canto* (London: Bhaktivedānta Book Trust, new edn.).

Prabhupāda and F. Staal (1972), *Kṛṣṇa Consciousness is the Genuine Vedic Way* (Boston: Iskcon Press).

Vivekananda, Swami (1977). *The Complete Works of Swami Vivekananda*, 8 vols., 15th edn. (Calcutta).

PART V
Concepts in Indian Religions

24

On Omnipotence

1. INTRODUCTION

Child: Who is God, Dad?
Father: He is one who knows everything (because he sees everything) and *can* do anything.
Child: So, he is not only a know-all man but also a do-all man?
Father: Something like it, Son.

Conversations of this kind usually stop here. And surprisingly, even the most sophisticated arguments of the philosophers over the ages have not done any better. One useful point is clearly made even in 'kid-stuff' conversation of the above kind. Omniscience is not *really* analogous to omnipotence. A know-all being is at least conceivable: 'X knows everything' unpacks as 'far all *p*, if *p* then X knows that *p*'. Omniscience in this sense is an intelligible concept if not a totally coherent one.[1] For doubts have been raised against its compatibility with the notion of time or timelessness, with the doctrine of free will or indeterminism, and for the most part such doubts can be sustained in spite of the attempts of the theists of ancient as well as recent times. Kenny has summed it up as follows (1979, p. 87):

> If determinism is true, it is comparatively easy to explain how he can infallibly foresee free action, but impossibly difficult to show how he is not the author of sin. If indeterminism is true, the Free Will Defence can be offered to exonerate God from responsibility for sin, but no coherent account seems possible of his knowledge of future free actions.

The notion of omniscience has its own 'internal' problems, no doubt, besides its being in conflict with other traditionally emphasized characteristics of God, omnipotence, his essential goodness and his immutability. But as an isolated notion, omniscience may not be faced with formidable objections. Roughly, we can conceive ofa giant computer mind which contains all the information that is there. Or, as the *Yogasūtra* 1.24 defines it, the knowledge stores of each individual may be compared with straight lines of varying lengths and God's knowledge then would be like the longest line, that is, a possible straight line beyond which there is nothing longer. This does not resolve any problems, but it is at least an intelligible concept, if not a coherent one. In fact, the *Yogasūtra* idea of God, according to at least one standard interpretation, is that he is a know-all person although he is not a do-er, or at least, he does not do much. I have, however, promised to talk about omnipotence rather than omniscience, although later on both the concepts would need to be brought together, as we will see.

2. AN ACCOUNT OF DIVINE OMNIPOTENCE

Although it may be possible for God to know everything, it is not possible for him to do everything. For example, he cannot sneeze, nor can he sin. Omnipotence may be understood in terms of 'can do', that is, in terms of powers. But it is also possible to understand it in terms of explicit agency only. Agency can be direct or indirect. An indirect agency is usually a *causative* agency (or what the Sanskritists call *prayojakatva*). This causative agent 'causes' something or makes it happen, or causes somebody or something to do A, instead of doing it himself. God's agency is usally taken to be a causative agency. The traditional theist says, 'Whenever anything happens, there is God's hand in it.' This is an obvious reference to the kind of causative agency that I am talking about. Almost all of us, at some point of time or other, feel that we are being, or could be, manipulated by one other or others. If it happens once or twice, it is conceivable it can happen all the time. In popular and pejorative language, God is then the greatest manipulator of all.

We have not yet touched upon the controversies regarding omnipotence. The major issue is, of course, the problem of evil, to which I shall come later. To begin with, we may try to get clear about how much power we must attribute to God to be consistent with traditional theism. Must we say that for all *p*, God can bring it about that *p*? This would obviously attribute too much. For it is usually conceded that God cannot square a circle, nor can he bring about that both *p* and not-*p* simultaneously. But suppose we say, for all *p*, if *p* then God brings it about that *p*.[2] This is not very different from the causative agency that I have spoken of above. But do we then attribute too little to God, so that it would offend the theist? The tendency of philosophers has been to answer in the affirmative.

At this point we can introduce the paradox of the stone or what Mackie has called the paradox of omnipotence. 'Can an omnipotent being make things which he cannot control?' (Mackie, 1955, p. 210). Can he make a stone which he cannot move? Mackie has argued that either way we answer—yes, or no—we lose, or rather God loses, his omnipotence. Kenny (1979, p. 94) thinks that the right answer is 'No, he cannot', but this 'cannot' is not necessarily an admission of his impotence with regard to at least one thing. For, what would be that thing which he cannot make? A thing which an omnipotent being cannot control? If so, then we have a being who can control everything makes a thing which he cannot control. Is there such a thing? It seems analogous to ask where there is a barber who shaves all and only those who do not shave themselves. Kenny defines omnipotence, or 'complete omnipotence', as the possession of all logically possible powers, and argues that divine omnipotence, in order to be coherent, must be a narrower omnipotence, possession of all logically possible powers which it is logically possible for a being with the attributes of God to possess. The so-called power to make while remaining omnipotent a thing which he cannot control is not a logically possible power. Hence God does not lose his omnipotence by not making such a thing.

R. Swinburne has chosen the other horn of the above dilemma. He says that an omnipotent being *can* make something he cannot control (1977, p. 156). It is coherent to attribute such power to God, but obviously God cannot exercise this power without ceasing to be what he is, omnipotent. This 'cannot' again is not necessarily an admission of his lack of omnipotence. Could we say that exercising it would be like starting a war to end all wars, destroying to end all destruction? It is tempting to argue this point. But any way, such is the mystery of any power that possession of it does not necessarily mean exercising of it. Obviously, each one of us can have power to destroy himself or herself, but most of us do not exercise it. Some theologians argue that God has the power to do even evil but does not exercise it voluntarily, a fact which only adds to his greatness. Plantinga (1967) thinks that finding an account of omnipotence that is satisfactory to all parties concerned is an extremely difficult, if not an impossible, task. But Mackie's paradox can be resolved one way or the other even without such a satisfactory formulation of the definition of omnipotence. Geach, however, has despaired of any coherent formulation of the notion of omnipotence (1973, 7ff) and suggested that a theist would be satisfied with the notion of being almighty instead. For 'God is Almighty' means that he has power over all things, and this will be central to the religious yearning of the theist.

A coherent account of omnipotence is, I have suggested, possible. It can be either in terms of logically possible powers (as Kenny has argued) or in terms of causal agency in all that happens. The so-called paradox can probably be resolved one way or other by answering either yes or no, provided a suitable modification is made in our account of omnipotence. But the point is that if the so-called resolutions become a matter of arbitrary choice then we simply solve one problem only to make room for another. It may be conceded that the paradox is not a genuine paradox in the sense *that if it is true that God makes or can make an uncontrollable thing* then it is false and vice-versa. But we genuinely face a situation here which raises an undecidable question about omnipotence. It is, in fact, a situation which the Sanskrit philosophers call *prakaraṇa-sama* or *sat-pratipakṣa.* Of two contradictory theses, either has genuine evidence in its favour, but we obviously know both cannot be true. The power of the evidence for one is perfectly counterbalanced by that of the other. In a tug-of-war of this kind, there is no winner. This is apparently a very philosophically unsatisfactory situation, if not a paradoxical one. Taking a cue from one of my former students, I wish to call it a philosophically paralysing situation.

3. EVIL AND THE FREE WILL DEFENCE

A satisfactory account of divine omnipotence should be connected with that of divine omniscience, although the two notions are detachable. But traditional theism attributes not only omnipotence and omniscience but also total goodness to God, and hence faces what is called the problem of evil. The problem is an old one in both the Judeo-Christian tradition (the Book of Job), and the Indian theistic tradition (the *Brahmasūtra*). It is essentially a logical problem, or that is how, at least, it has entered into the discussion of modern philosophers (Mackie, Plantinga, Pike and many others).[3] The problem arises because there is evil in the world. If evil is thought to be a mere illusion (as some philosophers have suggested), then, of course, the problem disappears. Or, if it held that there is nothing really evil in the sense in which it is opposed to the kind of 'goodness' we attach to God, the problem is easily solved. But these views are not going to be our concern here. The logical problem is that the theist seems to hold a set of beliefs that are inconsistent with one another. For he holds that there is a god who is omnipotent, omniscient and wholly good and yet evil exists in the world he created. To show an explicit contradiction, all we need to do is to add the premise that good is opposed to evil in such a way that a wholly good being eliminates evil as far as he can.

Theistic philosophers have tried to circumvent the difficulties in various ways. The most promising defence of theism so far has been the Free Will Defence. A modern version of Free Will Theodicy (due to Plantinga) says that the freedom of man is good, and as long as the divine attributes do not logically entail that any free creature created by God does always what is right, it is possible that God with all his attributes in fact creates *free* creatures who sometimes do wrong. Freedom of the creature implies that he can choose between alternative courses of action. The defence thus boils down to stressing that God, in spite of his divine attributes, cannot create a *perfect* world with *free* creatures who can do wrong. For this is not *logically* possible.

This defence, however, would lose its strength as soon as it is shown that it is not impossible for a perfect world to be created by an omnipotent, omniscient and wholly good god, full of *free*, saintlike creatures who act always rightly. It is possible that a free creature would perform at least one morally wrong action. It is equally possible that he would not perform any morally wrong action. It is, therefore, not logically impossible for free persons always to choose what is right. It would have been logically impossible for free persons to choose always what is right, if the proposition 'a free person does not choose always what is right' were an analytic proposition (like 'a bachelor is not married'), or if it followed from the definition of a free person that he performs at least one morally wrong action. But as long as such a concept of freedom is not adopted, the Free Will Defence of Plantinga cannot make any further progress.

It has been said that freedom is good and this is the overriding consideration of God in creating men as free agents. But if it is not incoherent to say that such a free agent could always act well rather than badly, then we do not yet have a satisfactory explanation for the occurrence of evil in a world created by a perfect, omnipotent and omniscient being. One may object that such a perfect world would be dull or boring. In fact, this objection, or rather this defence of theism, can be made to look more serious than what it appears to be in the first place. It can be said that good and evil actually form an organic whole and hence the world as a whole is a better and more attractive place as it is, with some evil in it. I wish to call this defence the 'aesthetic' defence of theism,[4] which can allow an evil in the world created by a perfect being only as a *justified* evil, an evil that heightens the good by contrast and *on the whole* it does not matter. This view as a possible defence may succeed, provided it can show that all evils, moral or natural, ordinary folly or genocide, are simply part of the whole pattern, are *justified evil* in the above sense, and that this is the way God wants to play the game of his world-creating, and ultimately he absorbs everything within himself. This is not exactly the position that takes all evils to be illusory or unreal, but is not very far from it either. This position I have outlined is closer to that of Kaśmiri Śaivism, but I would not attribute it to that school only. It seems to me that a defence of theism of this kind may be sustained, although the God of the Judeo-Christian tradition would seem to undergo a distinct metamorphosis under this defence. Notice that he remains omnipotent, omniscient and a perfect creator, but he does not appear to be benevolent or wholly good.

4. GOD: THREE MODELS

The preceding paragraph opens up the possibility of discussing different models for an alleged transcendent creator of this universe. Generally speaking, we see that there are three distinct models by which God is said to have created this universe. The first is what I shall call the stage-magician's model. God creates the entire universe out of nothing, much as the stage-magician produces a rabbit out of an empty hat. This model, I suggest, is very dominant in Judeo-Christian tradition, although it is not the only model that is discussed there. The second is the model of a potter creating a pot out of pre-existent clay. In the Nyāya-Vaiśeṣika school of Indian philosophy, God is said to be the creator, only in the sense of being an efficient cause of the universe. The world is in a sense said to be eternal or 'beginningless' (*anādi*) there 'being no first creation, but only periodic dissolution and re-creation through the intervention of providence (in the form of *samjihīṣa* and *sisṛkṣā*; cf. Praśastapāda). The ultimate constituents of matter, the atoms, are indestructible and eternal; through God's will they can combine or remain separated from one another. Human souls are also uncreated and eternal. Some form of the potter's model is sometimes alluded to in the Western tradition, but nowhere there seems to be presented in all its details, which I shall describe below.

Uncreated souls are, however, free agents and they enjoy and suffer according to whether they act rightly or wrongly. Moral evils are understandably the creation of the free agents who even suffer from some initial or inborn imperfection and depravity in the form *mithyājñāna* and *doṣa* (cf. Plantinga's 'transworld depravity'). Even natural evils, earthquakes such as, are regarded here only as variations of moral evils, being simply results of some well-forgotten free actions of the victims. This part of the theory may be difficult for us to swallow, for we are gradually led into the controversial hypothesis of transmigration and previous births in our intense search for the relevant free action that is responsible for such misfortunes. But this seems to be no less implausible than what has been suggested as a modern version of the Free Will Defence. Those natural evils that cannot be ascribed to human choices at all can be ascribed to malevolent actions of fallen angels (Plantinga). To return to Vaiśeṣika theism, God is here the distributor of justice, reward and punishment, and he creates the world accordinlgy. Distribution of reward and punishment amounts to letting the souls enjoy and suffer according to acquired *karma* on the basis of their free actions.

The third model I wish to call the 'spider' model. God caused everything to emanate out of his own essence after the manner of a spider which spins its web out of itself. The analogy occurs in the Upaniṣads, but the name is suggested to me from some comments of David Hume. Hume (1960, p. 476) says that the metaphor 'appears' ridiculous to Westerners, for 'a spider is a little contemptible animal', but then goes on to add 'still here is a new species of analogy, even in our globe'. I have already given above a version of the spider model. In essential respects the model is reflected in the theism of Spinoza, the Advaitins as well as the neo-Platonists. The model avoids the logical perplexities of evil and omnipotence if only at the risk of (a) making God less familiar (and perhaps less 'real') to the ordinary believers and (b) urging a re-definition of 'good' and 'evil' that is perhaps remotest from that of common sense. It does not always invoke illusionism, but some sort of relativism or holism is nevertheless implicit in this position. Some even brought the charge of atheism against the position (Spinoza was excommunicated and called an atheist!). But notice how much can be saved of traditional theism: God remains the omnipotent, omniscient creator, but he is beyond good and evil, the ultimate reality.

The 'potter's model' seems to do more justice to the ordinary believer and at the same time tries to satisfy the logician-philosophers to some extent. God is a person and the transcendent creator of the universe. But he creates depending upon the pre-existent matter as well as the pre-existent destiny of man. He is also wholly good. Responsibility for inequalities (*vaiṣamya*) in creation and evil cannot be ascribed to him, although he has power over all things (*kartum akartum anyathākartum ca śaknoti*—'has power to do it, or not to do it or to do it otherwise'). In other words, he is almighty. His omnipotence is possibly curtailed not only by logical laws but also by natural and moral laws. Men are free agents, but he did not create their freedom, nor did he create their creaturely essences (souls). He then can be exonerated of the charge of being the author of evil. However, such curtailment of God's omnipotence would be hardly satisfactory to the Western theist. Leibniz, for example, argued that the omnipotent God could have created any possible world he wanted, provided that it was a world that contained God himself. Since God is omnipotent in this sense, as well as omniscient and wholly good, Leibniz concluded that the actual world must be the best of all possible worlds, or, at least, no possible world is better than this actual one.[5] This position can obviously be ridiculed by those painfully concerned for the evils of this world: witness Voltaire's *Candide*. Recently Plantinga has pointed out what he calls 'Leibniz's lapse', and convincingly argued that there are possible worlds which even an omnipotent God is not able to create. In the context of this, I think there are possibilities even in the potter's model which need not be easily dismissed with even if it tends to lower the strict standard of God's omnipotence. I shall develop this suggestion at the end.

The three models that I have discussed here do not, however, exhaust all the varieties of theism seriously considered by the philosophers of India. The *Yogasūtra* model of God is another distinct variety. This is developed in the context of the *Sāṁkhya* metaphysical system which is sometimes described as non-theistic. I have earlier alluded to the detachability of the concept of omniscience from that of omnipotence. This possibility seems to be reflected in the Sāṁkhya-Yoga model of matter, conscious souls and God. God, as I have already noted, is here a 'know-all' person, an omniscient being, but he does not do anything, or at least, does not do much. In fact, the Sāṁkhya dualism speaks in terms of two independent principles, the material principle which is the do-er of everything, but not know-er of anything and spiritual principle which is the know-er but not do-er. Individual souls belonging to the latter category are only know-ers, not do-ers. One is *lame* while the other is *blind*, and the individual life goes on through the cooperation of the two. God is regarded as the final goal of our religious life and spiritual aspiration. He is to be realised by such persons as seek after him. He is the prefect soul and it is such perfection that our religious life must seek. He can help us only in so far as we are bent on attaining such perfection. As for the rest of the universe or our action with regard to it, he seems to be indifferent and unresponsive. Here, therefore, the role of a benevolent and omniscient deity is reduced to a minimum. This is no doubt very remote from the Judeo-Christian notion of a transcendent creator God who is omnipotent and wholly good, but still it is one that is integral to a religious life and nourishes religious faith in the ultimate goal of salvation or freedom. The problem of evil does not usually arise in such a system and if it does at all, it is easily brushed aside since the objection would no longer be logical inconsistency with the divine attribute.

If the concept of God is loosened in this way, one can go even further and ask: can God be conceived as a person who has perfected himself? If the answer is yes, then we have come closer to such non-theistic religious systems as Buddhism and Jainism. For the position of the Buddha or Mahāvīra is not very different from this type of God, a being who perfected himself and therefore can help others to be on the way to perfection. A Buddhist or a Jaina might balk at the word 'theism', and rightly so, but at the same time, an ordinary believer in Buddhism or in Jainism certainly looks upon the Buddha (or the Mahāvīra) with supreme veneration and pays utmost homage to him in the way it is done by the ordinary believers in a theistic system. Hence I believe we are not very far from truth in our above comment about theism in Buddhism and Jainism.

5. IS A RESOLUTION POSSIBLE?

The above has been a slight digression into the varieties of theism. Let us return to the problem of evil and omnipotence. The theist has been accused of holding a set of inconsistent beliefs: first, there exists a creator God who has the divine attributes that are traditionally ascribed to him, omnipotence, omniscience and complete goodness; second, there are evils in the world he created. Contradiction arises because it is further believed that there are no limits to what an omnipotent being can do, and that good is opposed to evil in such a way that a completely good being eliminates evil as far as he can. What is the thrust of this argument? When two sets of beliefs are shown to be inconsistent with each other, the rational man tries to discard one of them or modify it drastically so as to make it compatible with the other. One way out, in the above case, would be obviously to discard the second belief and say that evil does not exist. Equally obviously it is much more difficult, if not impossible, to disbelieve that evil exists. We have seen that some philosophers made this move in spite of its difficulties; evil is turned into apparent, and comparatively unreal, reality, or it becomes instrumental to the ultimate good and hence not completely undesirable.

The other way out would be to discard or modify the first set of beliefs. In fact, the atheist thinks that he has definitely scored a point here over the theist. Since evil exists (and we have overwhelming direct evidence for this belief), God cannot exist. More clearly, such a God as has been described in traditional theology, does not exist. Hence, the search is on to find out a way to reconcile the two sets of beliefs by modifying the notion of divine omnipotence. The Free Will Defence connects all evils with the free choices of human beings and thereby tries to keep the divine omnipotence and goodness unaffected. It is to be obviously assumed here that freedom of man (or other creatures), which either God bestowed upon man (as in Western theology), or individual (uncreated) souls initially possessed on their own (as in Indian theology), is a higher good which God, despite his omnipotence, does not want to spoil by intervening. This amounts to saying (*à la* Plantinga) that there are possible worlds or states of affairs which even an omnipotent God is not able to create.[6]

In Plantinga's story, Curely Smith (and many others) suffers from transworld depravity which is a fact about his *creaturely essence.*[7] He misuses his God-gifted freedom and actualizes a situation, by accepting bribes, which even God for the goodness of him cannot eliminate. Two significant points emerge from this version of the argument and they ring a familiar bell in the mind of an Indian theologian. First, the actual world or the state of affairs that is actualized every moment now, has a dual agency, man who exercises his freedom and God who gave him his freedom. An Indian theologian says, as I have noted earlier, that God's power is conditioned by its dependence upon the materials and tools it has to work with, man's imperfections and depravity, that is, his congenital misconception about what is good and bad, his destiny (*karma*) acquired through the exercise of his freedom of choice. The only thing that he would not say is that this freedom was bestowed upon man by God, for it is assumed that he existed all along with freedom and imperfections.

Second, God in Plantinga's story, seems to be faced with a limited choice. He has to create, that is, actualize from a limited range of creaturely essences, most or all of which may be stamped with 'transworld depravity'. But the question is: how can an omnipotent god who created everything out of nothing in the first place (cf. the magician's model), allow himself to work with only a limited range of creaturely essences? Prior to the creation and prior to the presence of any being with free will, how can there be such a state of affairs, a number of depraved creaturely essences, which could limit God's omnipotence in the way suggested. Again God's alleged omnipotence is at stake, and particularly his creation of everything out of nothing seems to be incoherent with this suggestion.

In defence of the Free Will Defence, it may be said that God is not responsible for the 'depraved' creaturely essences, for they were already there. Nelson Pike made a similar concession when he criticized Plantinga, and he elaborated his point in another parable, his Edam story. In his version, God did not create the 'mouse set' or 'the person set' (comparable to the 'creaturely essence' in Plantinga version), but 'He found it'. In the version of the Indian theologian, 'free creature' possibilities or essences were never possibilities, but have been actualities all along. Hence the so-called limitation on God's omnipotence was neither self-chosen nor mysteriously put up with.

That the Free Will Defence is incoherent with divine foreknowledge has been pointed out by many (cf. Kenny). Plantinga's version is particularly incompatible with the 'creation out of nothing' interpretation of the divine omnipotence which is dominant in the Western tradition. The Indian theist may be in a slightly better situation by emphasizing the potter's model. For my part, I do not see a great deal of difference between acceptance of pre-existent actualities or free souls as far as the final thrust of the free will defence argument is concerned. Only God becomes a loser in this to some extent, for he cannot exercise his free choice of bestowing freedom upon creatures. But so much the better for him, for foreknowledge, prudence and goodness should have then prevented him from starting the creation, given the circumstances and the 'fine mess' that his creatures have made of their freedom. If his creative function is reduced to a simple 'divine nod' and it is for the sake of the imperfect and depraved beings to get a chance to work out their eventual perfection that the creation is started, then this theism has a slightly better chance of being coherent.

The Indian version of the Free Will Defence has, of course, its own problems. One of its weaknesses is the hypothesis of the *karmic* destiny and the transmigrational doctrine that it necessitates. The so-called freedom of the souls becomes almost meaningless if they have to carry always a back-log of *karma*. This type of freedom may be just a disguised form of a very hard determinism. (And no doubt the *karma* doctrine has thus been rightly criticized). But this weakness is also inherent in the Plantinga version of the Free Will Defence. The concept of creaturely essences and its built-in depravity must put serious constraints on the free actions of the agent. However, exposing weakness in both alternatives does not constitute an argument in favour of either.

Suppose God's omniscience does not involve knowledge of the future contingents. In this way too, the existence of evil can be explained, for

God does not know beforehand what free choices his creatures will make. This, however, would further diminish his powers which the theist, particularly the Western theist, would not be able to concede. In fact the Indian version of the defence can be criticized, from the point of view of the Western thism, as a camouflaged 'atheistic' position. For does it not try to re-define God out of existence? In reply, one can say that that is only the consequence of our attempt to make the fact of evil consistent with the divine attributes.

In conclusion, we must say, on the one hand, that coherence is not the only test of reality and hence even if the coherence of theism can be established it does not help the theist very much. On the other hand, the God of the philosophers should be distinguished from the God of religions. The philosopher's ideal is that a rational man must have a set of beliefs which are consistent with one another. But then the set of beliefs of the theist can hardly be shown to be consistent. But do we, as human beings, have *always* a set of consistent beliefs? Most probably we do not. And a religious man does not worry about the God of the philosophers and all members of his belief-set may not be consciously present to him at the same time to make the supposed inconsistency articulate and pronounced. This may be another part of our imperfection, or our transworld depravity.

Notes and References

1. It may be asked if a concept is coherent, how can it be claimed to be intelligible? I will so argue that coherence is a sufficient condition for intelligibility, but not a necessary one. A concept may be intelligible to common sense even if its coherence is in doubt. To cite some historical examples: The 'infinite divisibility' paradox (or Zeno's paradox) cast doubt upon the coherence of the concept of an atomic (lowest) magnitude or dimension, but through some stipulation the atomists of India (and also of the West) found the notion of the longest extension or ubiquity or all-prevasiveness. For like the notion of the highest number, they are also incoherent. But for a long time, some philosophers have maintained (and perhaps some still do maintain) that this is a possibility.
2. This is obviously not strong enough and hence unsatisfactory to many, unless we add some modality to it to bring in, within God's power, things which are not so but might or could be so. In modern discussion, usually a counterfactual is introduced to give an account of divine omnipotence. An account of minimal omnipotence could be formulated following this trend: If *p* were so, then God would bring it about that *p*. Similarly God's omniscience must make him capable of knowing more than what merely happens to be so. In the formulation, if *p* then God knows that *p*, *p* may be allowed to range over not only what happens to be so, but also over counterfactual conditionals. The concept

of omniscience becomes problematic for it involves God's foreknowledge of future contingencies. Is it possible to deny God such foreknowledge? Is it possible to deny God powers to do things which are not so but could or might be so? Would that make God less Godly than we are allowed to assume? I am simply raising these questions at this stage.

3. By 'logical problem', I mean, following Mackie, that the theist holds a set of inconsistent beliefs. If the theist believes that evil exists then it conflicts with his beliefs in the omnipotence, omniscience and goodness of God. One can also see this problem as one of disconfirming evidence for certain theological doctrines. A philosopher who is not committed to theism can see this as essentially a conflict between theory and evidence. Every test of any theory involves some such potential conflict. Thus, one may state the problem as follows: evidence for the existence of evil conflicts with the theory that there is a god who is omnipotent, omniscient and wholly good. But in recent discussions, the theological doctrine is not treated as a theory, not a hypothesis, but a belief (or a set of beliefs) which seems to run counter to another belief, viz., belief in the existence of evil. Later on, we will see that some theologians even argue that evil does not exist, or is not a reality, and hence there is no conflict in what is believed by a theist.
4. What I am calling the 'aesthetic defence' here is no doubt related to what is called generally 'the moral defence of theism'. Evils are created by God for corrective purposes. God is good and hence the world created by him is good even with some evil in it. This is roughly the moral defence for the existence of evil. The 'aesthetic defence', which allowing this possibility, goes on to say that even if it were possible for God to create a perfect world full of perfect beings, it would be dull, boring, mechanical and hence aesthetically inferior to what God has actually created, namely, this world with some evil in it, so that the imperfect beings can work for their eventual perfection or union with God. We, the initially imperfect beings, may be initially tormented by the evils he has created, but that is the way he wants to play his game or *līlā* (cf. *svatantrecchāmayaḥ īśvāraḥ*). It may be a 'cruel joke' to us, but he is, after all, only joking.
5. According to Leibniz, strictly speaking, the actual world must be *the* best, not merely maximally good. For, otherwise, God would not have a 'sufficient reason' for choosing this one. But a modern quasi-Leibnizian may be content with the actual world's being merely maximally good. Hence I have added this clause here.
6. Plantinga's story is first told in terms of a fictional character, Curley Smith, a mayor of Boston, who has accepted a bribe of 35,000 dollars to drop his opposition to a freeway (*The Nature of Necessity*, Oxford, 1974). Now the following counterfactual is considered:

   If Curley had been offered 20,000 dollars, he would have accepted the bribe. Now the theist has to admit that God should know all true counterfactuals about the free actions of actual and possible creatures. Hence, God should know in advance what Curley would do if created and placed under different states of affairs. Kenny has shown how Plantinga's argument here fails (pp. 67 ff). I state this view of Kenny. I simply wish to bring out certain minor implications of Plantinga's position.

7. If God created everything out of nothing, then there could not have been a number of depraved creaturely essences, prior to the creation. If the depraved creaturely essences were there already, then it is not a creation out of nothing, unless, of course, creaturely essences, which are already existent, are regarding as 'nothing'. The force of this argument does not, I think, vanish even when we re-name the creaturely essences as depraved 'free creature' possibilities (as in N. Pike's version).
8. It may be argued that since inconsistent beliefs cannot be true, it gives a reason, for some people, at least, for finding the actual situation. I conceded this point. But religious beliefs of religious people are, in fact, judged by such standards as outweigh their concern for consistency. It is difficult to articulate what these standards could be. They may be a group of 'bilks' following R.M. Hare's notable suggestion.

Brahmasūtra of Bādarāyaṇa with Śaṁkara's *Bhāṣya* etc., ed. A. Sastri, N.S. Press, Bombay, 1938.

Geach, P.T., 'Omnipotence', *Philosophy*, 1973, no. 48, pp. 7–20.

Hume, D., *Dialogues Concerning Natural Religion*, in *The Empiricists*, A Dolphin Paperback, New York, 1960.

Kenny, A., *The God of the Philosophers*, Clarendon Press, Oxford, 1979.

Mackie, J.K., 'Evil and Omnipotence', *Mind*, 1955, vol. 64, pp. 200–12.

Pike, N., 'Plantinga on Free Will and Evil', *Religious Studies*, 1980.

Plantinga, A., *God and Other Minds*, Cornell University Press, London, 1974.

Praśastapāda, *Padārthadharma-saṁgraha*, ed. D. Jha, Varanasi, 1963.

Swinburne, R., *The Coherence of Theism*, Clarendon Press, Oxford, 1977.

Yogasūtra of Patañjali, ed. J. Vidyasāgara, Calcutta, 1891.

25

Duḥkha, Nirvāṇa and Holy Men

Indian soteriology is, in general, based upon the thesis of universal suffering. This thesis can be expressed in the form of an equation: life or existence or life-experience equals *duḥkha*—'pain', 'suffering' or 'anguish'. This thesis was not a dominant trend in the Vedas or in the Upaniṣads. But it definitely became a predominant theme in later philosophical/religious traditions. Thus, Mircea Eliade has asserted:

> 'All is pain, all is ephemeral.' It is a leitmotiv of all post-Upaniṣadic Indian speculation. Soteriological techniques, as well as metaphysical doctrines, find their justification in this universal suffering, for they have no value save in the measure to which they free man from 'pain'. Human experience of whatever kind engenders suffering (1958, p. 11).

How this notion of universal anguish crept into the mind of the Indian thinkers is very difficult to say. But undoubtedly the theme dominated the scene in all early philosophical systems.

The first noble truth of Buddhism is equivalent to the thesis of universal suffering. In the *Visuddhimagga*, for example, three different aspects of *duḥkha* are mentioned. The first is called *duḥkha-duḥkha* under which all ordinarily unpleasant things and unhappy mental states are classified. The second group consists of what would ordinarily be known as pleasant objects and happy feelings. They are to be judged as *duḥkha* because they change and decay and do not stay long enough to impart happiness. Thus, the fluctuating character as well as impermanence of this world should persuade any wise man to judge it as the source of unhappiness or unhappiness itself. The third type of *duḥkha* is called *saṃskāra-duḥkha*, a more pervasive and abstract type of unhappiness. It is the realization itself, or our unhappiness resulting from the realization of the essentially conditioned existence of ours. Our psychosomatic existence of attachment is called suffering from this point of view. For, to a wise man, it appears to be a self-perpetuating imprisoned state dotted by craving, drive for pleasure, the agony of search, dissatisfaction and further craving happening in cyclic order (*Visuddhimagga*, 1969, p. 99).

Almost a similar thesis is propounded by Patañjali in *Yoga-sūtra* 2.15: 'To a person with discernment everything is pain because it co-exists with the three modes of *guṇa* (viz., happiness, unhappiness and ignorance), and causes pain due to change or fluctuation, due to mental anguish, and due to *saṃskāra* (conditioned state).' This threefold aspect of suffering is easily comparable with the threefold aspect of suffering found in Buddhism. If our worldly existence is essentially suffering and an imprisonment, then *nirvāṇa* or freedom (*mokṣa*) is worth striving for.

What is so unique about suffering that it should be given the status of the first Noble Truth? What is so novel about the fact of human suffering that we needed the Buddha to discover this truth for us? Is it not a commonplace idea that suffering exists in our life and that our moments of happiness are by far outnumbered by moments of unspeakable pain? The prevalence of suffering is obvious enough. As David Hume has expressed it so beautifully:

> Were a stranger to drop in a sudden into this world, I would show him as a specimen of its ills, a hospital full of diseases, a prison crowded with malefactors and debtors, a field of battle strewed with carcasses, a fleet foundering in the ocean, a nation languishing under tyranny, famine or pestilence. To turn the gay side of life to him and give him a notion of its pleasures—whither should I conduct him? To a ball, to an opera, to court? He might justly think that I was only showing him a diversity of distress and sorrow' (1779, *Dialogues Concerning Natural Religion*, 1935, part x).

Thus, if *duḥkha* is only suffering then there is much to be said in favour of the puzzlement of Professor A.C. Danto about the fact that the Buddha propunded it as a problem. Danto attempted to solve the puzzle as follows:

> It is characteristic of philosophy to find the commonplace puzzling. Everyone in a way knows the First Noble Truth, but it took a virtual act of genius to see it as the sort of truth that the Buddha did. Everyone suffers. But not everyone knows that he suffers. What the Buddha recognized is that knowledge of the fact can be a step towards its mitigation. The first, and in some ways the hardest, step for a certain sort of sick man to make is towards the knowledge that he *is* sick (1972, p. 68).

Danto obviously has the model of Freudian psychoanalysis in his mind. This is, however, not an uncommon sort of move on the part of modern interpreters of Buddhism. Even Patañjali's Yoga system has been explained with the help of the Freudian psychoanalytic model (see Ben-Ami Scharfstein, 1973, pp. 122–32). But I am not sure whether such comparisons explain the above puzzle satisfactorily. *Duḥkha*, a modern Buddhist scholar would assert, cannot mean only physical suffering, but denotes a mental state born probably out of frustrations due to the transience of the objects of craving. It is said that even a man who has acquired through *karma* about a million years in heaven should consider himself also suffering because his pleasures are, after all, finite in the infinite time-scale! Thus, suffering is here made equivalent to an awareness that the present state of pleasure will soon pass by—a theme that is commonly emphasized in many other religions. But I think this also fails adequately to explain the notion of *duḥkha*—the First Noble Truth which the Buddha emphasized in the context of his doctrine of *nirvāṇa*.

Duḥkha, in the ultimate analysis, is neither physical suffering nor mental frustration. It is also to be distinguished from the obsession that our pleasures will not last as well as from the state of paranoia about the loss of pleasure. In fact, it is not a hedonistic concept which could be contrasted with pleasure or happiness (*sukha*). For, remember happiness is also *duḥkha*. *Duḥkha* is thus a realization that we are essentially in a conditioned state (compare the *saṃskāra-duḥkha* of the *Visuddhimagga*), in a state where there is complete lack of freedom. We are supposed to be 'free' agents. We, at least, try to 'kid ourselves' that we are free. But we are really not. An awareness of this utter lack of freedom in our conditioned state is what makes *duḥkha* a profound realization. That we are necessarily in a conditioned state is not an obvious truth. The human situation is comparable to that of a man caught in a colossal traffic jam, who certainly has his 'free will' but cannot make it 'work', for his situation has already been conditioned!

The above seems to be a plausible interpretation of the concept of *duḥkha*. With such interpretation in mind, we can make good sense of the concept of *nirvāṇa*, the unconditioned state of freedom. Our everyday suffering is obvious enough, but that does not give us any insight into the nature of our condition. However, it is always our ordinary everyday suffering that sets us into worrying about the problem. Thus it is that Prince Siddhārtha began to ponder over the problem of suffering, that is, ordinary suffering, old age, decay and death, to be sure. But this is the place where one always starts—puzzling about the problem of suffering. In the case of the Buddha, however, this initial puzzlement gradually led him into the deep insight about the essentially 'conditioned' state of ours. The actual realization of this *truth* is gained through hard discipline of the mind and mystical insight.

It is, however, not easy to convince us, the common people, that our life-experience is just suffering and hence unacceptable. Different methods have been tried by different schools to drive this point home. The Buddhist indoctrination is based upon the following argument: Everything is suffering because everything is conditioned, is impermanence and in a flux. Are we not helpless in our attempt to stop something from passing away due to disease, decay and death? Is it not just a matter of a moment for ordinary pleasure to turn into pain? The Nyāya school, in its early phase, emphasized the same thesis of universal suffering. But their method of convincing people about its truth was a bit different.

According to Nyāya, everything is to be judged as pain because, strictly speaking, we do not have any experience of unmixed pleasure or joy. Even our most joyful moments are invariably shadowed by a feeling of pain. 'Even our sincerest laughter with some pain is wrought.' Thus each experience falls short of the ideal of *pure* joy or happiness. The ideal of happiness is envisioned here as similar to the logician's 'ideal' of truth. Each of our factual experiences is like a compounded whole with distinguishable components. Now, just as a truth-functional conjunct is false if one of the components is false, so also an experience is judged to be painful if it has just one painful component. Thus, Vātsyāyana has explained (under *Nyāya-sūtra* 1.1.2):

> Just as food that is mixed with honey and poison should be discarded, so also happiness that is tampered with unhappiness.

This theme of showing mundane pleasures to be really pains became very popular in India, and many religious and didactic literatures emphasized it. Even the Lokāyata materialists conceded that miseries and unpleasures of life by far outnumber the pleasures of life. They, however, argued that persistence of unpleasure should not provide sufficient reason to negate life and avoid pleasures, for that would be unwise. Thus, Mādhva says:

> The only end of man is enjoyment produced by sensual pleasure. Now may you say that such cannot be called the end of man as they are always mixed with some kind of pain, because it is our wisdom to enjoy the pure pleasure as far as we can, and to avoid the pain which inevitably accompanies it; just as the man who desires fish takes the fish with their scales and bones. . . . It is not therefore for us, through a fear of pain, to reject the pleasure which our nature instinctively recognises as congenial. . . . As has been said by the poet:

'The pleasure which arises to men from contact with sensible objects,
Is to be relinquished as accompanied by pain,—such is the
reasoning of fools;
The berries of paddy, rich with the finest white grains,
What man, seeking his true interest, would fling away because
[they are] covered with husk and dust?'
(tr. Cowell and Gough, 1882, pp. 3–4).

The Jains were probably concerned directly with the hedonistic concept of suffering and pleasure. They show that the object of pleasure does not really satisfy our drive for pleasure, for we wish to have more and more of it and thereby bring down pain upon ourselves. Food and drink may give pleasure up to a certain limit, but the further impulse to eat and drink beyond one's capacity produces only discomfort. Love-making imparts pleasure only by answering our sexual need, but it is, according to Umāsvāti, like scratching an itching pimple. Further scratching only produces pain. Wealth is no unalloyed blessing for the cares, and anxieties over possessing and protecting wealth make it impossible to enjoy it freely.

All these arguments were admittedly commonplace. But their sole purpose was to justify the soteriological techniques of different schools. The soteriology was based upon the following belief: our earthly existence, our profane life, our everyday routine, is not to be regarded as final. This is not all that there is. There must be another, and perhaps, a better, mode of existence, a sacred mode of being or living—a supermundane bliss or beatitude to look forward to. We should make efforts to advance towards that goal of sacred existence, for otherwise how can we boast of being humans as opposed to animals? This assumed distinction between the profane and the sacred, the conditioned and the unconditioned, is supposed to mirror the distinction between mortal existence and immortality. The latter, as I have shown, is the goal of all religious systems.

Why is *saṃsāra*, perpetuation of the birth-and-rebirth cycle, regarded as suffering in Hinduism? Danto, in his superb and admirable style, has given a very interesting interpretation of this concept. Referring to Nietzsche's idea that 'there is an eternal return in events', Danto has argued that it was the knowledge of the 'eternal recurrence' of the same, monotonous life-activities that was particularly 'nauseating' to the Hindu mind, and as a result it despaired of life:

Imagine having endless times to go through what we all have gone through once, the mastering of our bodies: learning to walk erect, learning to control our bowels and going through all the same stages of emotional awakening again and again with all of its embarrassments, all the torments . . . I think the knowledge would be shattering. The mere tedium of it all could not be borne. And it is this cosmic boredom, I believe, that underlies the Indian despair of life (1972, pp. 47–8)

This is a novel interpretation of what is called the Indian 'despair of life': that is, *saṃsāra* is *duḥkha*. And this, according to Danto, accounts for the prevailing other-worldliness of Indian religions, their 'exclusive' concern for *mokṣa*. This is, as I have noted already, an admirable attempt at cross-cultural understanding. But I wonder whether this can be true from the point of view of the Hindu mind. The concept of 'boredom' is of recent origin in Western literature. It is highly uncertain whether a Hindu in ancient India (where the concept of *saṃsāra, mokṣa* and Brahman originated) would actually despair of life because he was 'bored' by the 'mad repetition of life after life' (Danto, p. 51).

I have suggested above an interpretation of the concept of *duḥkha* in the context of Buddhism. The idea of '*duḥkha = saṃsāra*' will not be very different in the Hindu context. In fact, *duḥkha* in Hinduism should be interpreted in terms of desire or craving—but not just in terms of a desire *for something*. It is a dissatisfaction born out of a desire for something different, a desire for a sacred or higher existence which will offer a contrast with the profaneness of this world. Using Nietzsche's terminology, perhaps we can say that the Indian (or Hindu) other-worldliness is born of a deep-seated resentment against this world, this *status quo*.

Salvation is, according to some, a supermundane bliss; a beatitude or God-realization, according to others; an unconditioned existence, according to still others. But in all cases, it is regarded as an escape or freedom from the profaneness of existence which we are used to all the time. One evidence from a particular religious tradition will suffice. The goal is described in *Udāna* (a Buddhist text):

There is, monks, an unborn, not become, not made, uncompounded, and were it not, monks, for this unborn, not become, not made, uncompounded, no escape could be shown here for what is born, has become, is made, is compounded. But because there is, monks, an unborn, not become, not made, uncompounded, therefore an escape can be shown for what is born, has become, is made, is compounded.

Those who refer to the ultimate goal as being a supermundane bliss do not always think that this bliss is completely different from our earthly pleasure. Thus, while the ascetic traditions emphasize that the best way to achieve salvation is the withdrawal from the sensual world, detachment from possessions and ambitions, radical isolation or unconcern, there is another tradition which believes that earthly pleasure is a fragment of the ultimate bliss, and hence it is not altogether unacceptable. The implicit idea is that the ultimate bliss in salvation is only earthly pleasure multiplied a billionfold! While earthly pleasure is transient, supermundane bliss is eternal! The idea is, however, as old as the Upaniṣads. The *Taittirīya* Upaniṣad (2.8), for example, gives an elaborate account of how world pleasures are to be multiplied a billion times (in fact, an octillion times, by arithmetical computation) in order to approximate the ultimate bliss. The *Kaṭha Upaniṣad* (5.14) describes the ultimate bliss as 'the highest, indescribable happiness'.

The goal of all mystic paths is this highest bliss. A striking image has been used in *Bṛhadāraṇyaka Upaniṣad* (4.3.21) to illustrate the nature of this bliss:

> As a man, when in the embrace of a beloved wife, knows nothing within or without, so this person, when in the embrace of the intelligent Soul, knows nothing within or without. Verily, that is his [true] form in which his desire is satisfied, in which the Soul is his desire, in which he is without desire and without sorrow (Tr. R.E. Hume, 1931, p. 136).

This need not be taken to be just an accidental simile. In fact, there are numerous passages to show the Indian thinkers did see that there was an essential connection between the sexual and aesthetic pleasure on the one hand, and the ultimate bliss on the other. The writers on aesthetics, in ancient India, have argued that the enjoyment or aesthetic pleasure that we derive from a work of art or a piece of *kāvya* (poem, literature) certainly exalts our thought for a few moments, above the bounds or limitations of the empirical ego, and this aesthetic pleasure is nothing but a reflected splendour of the ultimate bliss. It is *rasa* (cf. *raso vai saḥ*). Some poeticians found here an argument to show that study and writing of poems would eventually lead to one's religious goal, and hence cultivation of art and literature was important! (cf. Masson & Patwardhan, 1969, pp. 24–34).

It is rather paradoxical in the ascetic tradition (in the ways of the *śramaṇas*) to describe the ultimate goal as a blissful, happy state, to assert that the 'sacred' existence is one of unlimited pleasure. The ascetic technique mainly lies in renunciation, and withdrawal. It is difficult to see how abstinence and continence should unlock the door of unbounded pleasure. Thus, the early Buddhists and the early Nyāya both emphasized consistently in unambiguous terms that the ultimate goal was the complete cessation of anguish and pain, in which both pleasure and unpleasure should vanish. But other schools nevertheless clung to the notion of bliss, beatitude, pleasure and happiness, as the goal, only by adding such all-important adjectives as 'transcendental', 'all surpassing', 'unsurpassed' and 'unconditioned'. In fact, most teachers who preached mystical consciousness to be the ultimate goal would invariably talk about bliss and beatitude in the ultimate state. A devotee of Kṛṣṇa talks about the climactic condition of sensuality and emotionalism when he describes his ultimate goal. A yogin similarly talks about unbounded pleasure in a slightly disguised language. Even a Mahāyāna Buddhist sets his goal as the ultimate calmness attended with perfect bliss.

The ascetic tradition became very influential in the post-Upaniṣadic period. This is the tradition of the holy men, monks, *swāmis*, *sannyāsis* and *bhikkhus*. How this tradition originated in India is very difficult to say. But by the sixth century BC, there was, alongside the hereditary priesthood, a class of religious teachers or 'philosophers', who repudiated the hereditary principles and the establishment of the *brāhmaṇa* priests. They were called *śramaṇas*, 'strivers', presumably striving after the truth. The *śramaṇas* were the forerunners of the 'holy men' (*sādhus*, *swāmis* and *sannyāsis*) of India today. A *śramaṇa* abandoned his former station in society (his family life) in search of the 'truth'. He was supposed to have voluntarily chosen to become a wanderer, giving up all his earthly possessions, and depending upon begging or on fruits in the forests to stay alive. He was supposed to devote his entire time and energy to soteriological technique, with salvation as his goal. Gradually *śramaṇas* established different schools of thought, and organized communities and monasteries. What was more interesting was that they also found themselves in the role of religious teachers and philosophers of the society which they originally had left. In this role, they had the priests as their rivals. They claimed to teach and encourage what may be called 'free thinking' as opposed to the traditional ritualistic orthodoxy. This was the beginning of the ascetic tradition of monks in India, and a large number of them were quite mystically inclined, and developed different techniques for generating mystical experience.

The contemporary society accepted them as 'spiritual' masters. In fact, ordinary people in ancient times would pay as much respect and heed to these monks as they did to their *brāhmaṇa* priests. That the monks abandoned their social life and mundane pleasures, and did not conform to the normal rules of life in society was counted as a great credit for them. For, while ordinary men were seeking pleasure, the monks of their own accord embraced hardship and a life of renunciation in search of the ultimate meaning of life. Hence, they were to be highly respected and honoured. This was (and perhaps, still is) the general feeling among the laity. There was another reason for the popularity of the monks among the laity. They were supposed to be invested with magical and miraculous powers. For the association of magic and miracle with religion and religious merit is almost as old as humanity. Needless to mention, in primitive societies priests were also regarded as witch-doctors and magicians. Even great religious leaders like the Buddha, Mahāvīra and Jesus were said to be endowed with miraculous powers (e.g., *daśabala*, the 'ten miraculous powers' of the Buddha).

Danto has rightly observed that 'the hope of miracles forms the vulgar basis of religious belief' (p. 61). This is not to be wondered at since magic and miracle were at the starting point of the human awareness of the spiritual world, and thereby at the root of the religious awareness of the human mind. Even the professed non-believers are rumoured to have been converted to religious belief as a result of experiencing some kind of magic and miracle (cf. exorcism, faith-healing, etc.). Thus it is that the position of a monk became, perhaps unfortunately, a very convenient tool for exploiting people. This was, in a sense, a paradoxical result of the *śramaṇa* movement, or the movement of the 'free thinkers' against the organized religious traditions. The *śramaṇas* originally attempted (quite successfully, I believe) to expose the *brāhmaṇa* priests in their exploitation of the weakness of the people. But when the priest was dethroned as a result of the teaching of the free thinkers of that age, the vacuum was filled by the *śramaṇa* 'monk' himself! Thus, since the same 'throne' was now occupied by the monk, the door became open for him for exploitation. That some of the monks did not succumb to this temptation was only an historical accident. It does not take much imagination to assume that many monks did exploit the situation to their advantage.

The role of a monk in Indian society is a very privileged one. He is, as Danto has rightly observed, 'a licensed Bohemian, relieved from ordinary responsibilities and duties' (p. 61). Besides, the profession of monkhood became very tempting for various reasons. Apart from 'spiritual' reasons, it was easy for the criminals to join the so-called 'vocation' in order to escape punishment from the society. The belief is persistent that being a monk you go 'beyond good and evil' and therefore you are automatically forgiven by the society. It was also easy for power-loving humans to join the 'organization' of monks to gain power and control. Admittedly these are not the right reasons for joining the order. But they were not the wrong reasons either. For the holy man becomes 'holy' because he has joined the order, not necessarily because he has become a *perfect* man overnight.

An outstanding story (a historical incident) from ancient India may illustrate our point about the organization of monks and its parallelism with the political organization. The story is told in the *Vinaya* II (Pāli recension) and in many other places (cf. Warder, 1970, p. 62). The Buddha was aware that many had joined the order for wrong and confused motives. Thus, despite his care in organization of the order, he was faced with serious internal problems towards the end of his life. Devadatta was a cousin of the Buddha. He joined the order, and had the ambition of eventually becoming the leader of the monks himself. Devadatta suggested to the Buddha that as he was then old he should retire and let Devadatta lead the organization. The Buddha refused to step down and warned the monks against Devadatta's intention. Devadatta was annoyed by the refusal and befriended Prince Ajātaśatru, who was waiting to become king when his father Bimbisāra would retire. Ajātaśatru and Devadatta plotted together to kill the king and the Buddha in turn so that the prince could become king without waiting, and the latter would become the Buddha. Ajātaśatru's attempt to assassinate his father was foiled by the ministers, but Bimbisāra voluntarily retired and Ajātaśatru became king. Devadatta then asked Ajātaśatru to have the Buddha killed. Attempts were made by the assassins, but they all failed. In the Buddha's presence the world-be assassins turned into his disciples. Then Devadatta himself made an attempt on the Buddha's life, but failed. The Buddha escaped with an injury to his foot. Later Devadatta was successful, however, in introducing a schism in the Buddhist community by proposing stricter disciplines. It is said that, at that time, five hundred monks followed Devadatta. Anyway, the story illustrates that not all the 'holy men' or monks were concerned for the Ultimate truth or salvation. And it is not just a metaphor that the Indian gurus are called by the honourable epithet, 'great king' (*mahārāja*).

Besides all these problems, there has always been the problem of distinguishing a phony organization of monks from a real one. A genuine organization of monks would be one where the so-called 'holy men', apart from facing all sorts of internal problems and power-struggles of the kind mentioned above, would at least believe, at the conscious level, in what they preach, that is, soteriology. But a phony organization is one where that belief does not even exist among the monks themselves. The organization actually becomes a façade. This problem is almost as old as human civilization. An example from Kauṭilya's *Arthaśāstra* (apparently reporting the socio-political picture of 300 BC India) will suffice. Kauṭilya discusses the espionage of the king and makes the following comments:

The king should appoint spies in secret service from the following: pupils, monks, house-holders, traders and ascetics. . . . The seeming monk: One who has relinquished the life of a wandering monk, but is endowed with intelligence and honest (as far as the king is concerned) is the apostate monk. Equipped with plenty of money and followers, he should get work done in a place assigned to him, for the practice of some occupation. And from the profits of (this) work, he should provide all wandering monks with food, clothing and residence. And to those (among them), who seek a stable livelihood, he should secretly propose, 'In this very garb, you should work in the interest of the king and present yourself here at the time of meals and payments'. And all wandering monks should make similar proposals to monks in their respective orders. . . .

The seeming ascetic: A hermit with shaven head or with matted hair, who seeks a livelihood, is the seeming ascetic. He should live in the vicinity of a city with plenty of disciples with shaven heads or matted hair, he should eat openly a handful only of barley or vegetable at intervals of a month or two; secretly, however, he can eat as desired. And assistants of traders (who are secret agents) should adore him with occult practices for becoming prosperous. And his disciples should announce: 'That holy man is able to secure prosperity for any one.' And to those who have approached him with hopes of gaining prosperity, he should specify events happening in their family, which are usually ascertained by means of the science of interpreting bodily marks (e.g. palmistry), but which actually he would learn secretly from the signs made by his disciples surrounding him. He should predict in this manner such events as some small gain, burning by fire, danger from thieves, the killing of a traitorous person, a gift of gratification, news about happenings in a foreign land, saying, 'this will happen today or tomorrow,' or 'the king will do this.' (All those will be regarded by outsiders as marks of his miraculous power.) Secret servants and agents should cause that prophecy of his to be fulfilled. To those among visitors who are endowed with spirit, intelligence and eloquence, he should predict good fortune at the hands of the king and speak of their forthcoming association with the minister. And the minister (at the secret instruction from the seeming ascetic) should arrange for their livelihood and work. (Book 1, chapter 7; tr. Kangle, partly changed.)

This is the other side of the picture. It shows in the least that as far back as the Maurya empire in India not all matted hairs or shaven heads were sure and unquestionable marks of saintliness and renunciation or of 'dropping out' and vagrancy. The problem is thus, I repeat, as old as human civilization.

Notes and References

Buddhaghoṣa. *Visuddhimagga*. Edited with Dharmapāla's *Paramatthamañjūṣā*, in Pali Granthamala 3. Three volumes. Varanasi, 1969–72.

Danto, A.C. *Mysticism and Morality*. New York, 1972.

Eliade, Mircea. *Yoga: Immortality and Freedom*. Translated by W.R. Trask. Princeton: Princeton University Press, 1958.

Hume, David. *Dialogues Concerning Natural Religion*. First published 1779. Edited by N.K. Smith. Oxford, 1935.

Hume, R.E. *The Thirteen Principal Upanishads*. 2nd edition, revised by G.C.O. Haas. Oxford: Oxford University Press, 1931.

Kauṭilya. *Arthaśāstra*. Edited and translated by R.P. Kangle. Bombay: Bombay University Press, 1960–65.

Mādhva. *Sarva-darśana-saṃgraha: Or Review of the Different Systems of Hindu Philosophy*. Translated by E.B. Cowell and A.E. Gough. London: Trübner & Co., 1882.

Masson, J.L. and Patwardhan, M.V. *Śāntarasa and Abhinavagupta's Philosophy of Aesthetics*. Poona, 1969.

Scharfstein, Ben-Ami. *Mystical Experience*. Oxford: Blackwell, 1973.

Warder, A.K. *Indian Buddhism*. Delhi: Motilal Banarsidass, 1970.

26

On the Universality of Suffering

The world is full of suffering and evils. But it is so obviously so that we do not need the wisdom of a Buddha or a Socrates as a philosopher to tell us that it is so in this way. Not everything is experienced as suffering, for there are moments of happiness, things of joy, and moods of ecstasy. There is love, pleasure, beauty. But still we can hardly question the thesis of the Universality of suffering. Let us listen to David Hume.

Were a stranger to drop in a sudden into this world, I would show him as a specimen of its ills, a hospital full of diseases, a prison crowded with malefactors and debtors, a field of battle strewed with carcasses, a fleet foundering in the ocean, a nation languishing under tyranny, famine or pestilence. To turn the gay side of life to him and give him a notion of its pleasures—whither should I conduct him? To a ball, to an opera, to court? He might justly think that I was only showing him a diversity of distress and sorrow.[1]

The *Sāṃkhya-Kārikā* starts as follows. There are three kinds of suffering, *bodily or physical, environmental* and *mental.* And they are all caused. Hence if the cause can be removed, they can be removed, but not permanently. So a search arises in man to find out means for the permanent removal of suffering, and so people turn to philosophy:

From the torment by three-fold misery arises the enquiry into the means of terminating it; if it be said that it is fruitless, the means being obvious to us, we reply *no*, since in such means there is no certainty or finality.[2]

Spinoza said in his *On the Improvement of the Understanding*:

After experience had taught me that all the usual surroundings of ordinary life are vain and futile; seeing that none of the objects of my fear contained in themselves anything either good or bad, except in so far as the mind is affected by them, I finally resolved to inquire whether there might be some real good having the power to communicate itself, which would affect the mind singly, to the exclusion of all else: whether, in fact, there might be anything of which the discovery and attainment would enable me to enjoy continuous, supreme and unending happiness.[3]

Almost all Indian philosophical and religious systems starts with apparently a very similar thesis of universal suffering, *sarvaṃ duḥkham*. The question is: is it the same obvious truth that can be empirically established? Some would answer this question in this way. Of course, the thesis of universal suffering that is entertained by different systems of India's religious philosophy is much more radical. For it is a (logically) universal proposition. In other words: its logical form is one of the two: For each thing *x*, if *x* is an item we have to deal with in our ordinary life, then *x* is or begets unhappiness; or, for each *x*, if *x* is an experience of life, then *x* is suffering. This means that we are not talking here about simply an abundance of unhappiness, an overwhelming presence of sorrows and pains in life; the claim is rather that even the so-called pleasures, happiness, joys and good things of life are nothing but *duḥkha*, suffering, sadness and unhappiness. And to make a bewildered listener understand, it may be added that all these may *appear* as pleasing, happy and desirable on the surface, but underneath they are simply varieties of unhappiness and suffering. And that is the realization of the truth, once we cut through the veil of appearance!

Some argument would also be added to support this line of understanding the thesis of the universality of suffering. For example, it will be pointed out that there is no unmixed, pure happiness. 'Our sweetest songs are those that tell of saddest thoughts.' Each honeycomb is contaminated with poison at the bottom. Or, in the manner of the Buddhist it will be said: happiness is so short-lasting, momentary and transient, that in effect it is more unhappiness than anything else. What causes unhappiness must be unhappiness also. The so-called happiness causes unhappiness (we lament the loss of such happiness) and hence should be only unhappiness. In other words, experiential happiness is only a variety of unhappiness, just as Hume said that a sad play was a variety of distress and sorrow.

I think this way of understanding the thesis of suffering is misleading, if not entirely wrong. Misleading because, as I have already mentioned, it then becomes a truth that is too obvious, and trivial and unphilosophical. It becomes misleading also because it is then inadvertently identified with an engulfing pessimism. If the truth is that we suffer invariably under any circumstances, then also we neglect the obvious. We are blind to the truly happy moments and good things in life. This rather unsound psychological state is one of pessimism and depression. This is a critique which simply means that there is really no good reason for us today to believe in such a thesis, and then the relevance of such Indian philosophical doctrines collapses for us. I say again that this is misleading.

One may counter this charge of pessimism in another way. One may point out that the theme of universal suffering was conspicuous by its absence in the early scriptures, the Vedas and the Upaniṣads. The early Vedic religion, it seems, was more concerned with life in this world, and much less with a life beyond. In its lack of overwhelming concern for the after life, the early Vedic Hinduism resembled early Judaism. But this defence by referring to history breaks down as we proceed further in history. With the rise of the *śramaṇa* school, the theme of universal suffering, whatever might have been the sociological reason for its origin, became dominant and persisted and permeated the entire spectrum of Indian philosophical thinking. It is upheld in its various ramified forms not only by Buddhism, Jainism, and Ājīvikism but also by Nyāya, Sāṃkhya and Mīmāṃsā. We know very little today about the socio-politico-historical causes or reasons that might account for the origin of the doctrine. Besides, even if we can find out a satisfactory historical explanation about the origin, it would be of little help in understanding the full implication and thrust of the doctrine, for it would fail to explain why and how the doctrine dominated the intellectual horizon of India for about two millennia. For certainly the socio-political condition that obtained in India in 500 BC did not exist afterwards and does not exist today. So why has the doctrine never been seriously challenged, repudiated or discarded? It stands to reason therefore to imagine that it contains some ingredients that survive the passage of time—some ingredients that can be variously manipulated to formulate an eternal truth! The question is: what is it?

I wish to emphasize again that this thesis must be distinguished from the psychological attitude called universal pessimism. Pessimism in an individual begets a crippling mental depression which precludes rational and positive behaviour. If a whole culture is under the spell of such a universal pessimism, its crippling effect would have rendered the culture bankrupt or would have made it extinct a long time ago. Indian culture on the other hand has shown its vitality and aggressiveness punctuated by material growth for about two thousand years, assimilating new ideas, changing and adjusting to the new situation as the new challenge confronted it from time to time. It is difficult for a culture infected with overwhelming pessimism to exhibit such vitality and adjustability.

It stands to reason therefore to dismiss the rather superficial pessimistic interpretation of the thesis of universal suffering. Some would say that Indian religious doctrines are not pessimistic for they defy pessimism by pointing to a goal of *nirvāṇa* or *mokṣa*, a goal of either unbounded freedom or unbounded bliss. This is presumably an escape route, and a truly pessimistic philosophy would have denied the existence of such an escape route. I think this defence of the thesis is also misleading, if not entirely wrong or false. For it presupposes a very *hedonistic* understanding of the thesis. A hedonist seeks the highest happiness in pleasure, regards pleasure as the principal good and demands that it should be the aim of our action. The attitude of the person who accepts the above defence is not very far from this. Noticing the overwhelming presence of suffering and pain and realizing the rather hollow nature and transience of ordinary pleasures of life, he would choose to act, accept a religious life, only to ensure a *perpetual happiness* or at *least a perpetual absence of pain* at the end. He gives up the unstable and fleeting happiness for the sake of the eternal bliss, as the saying goes. I concede that traditionally such a hedonistic *overtone* was present at certain levels. The Upaniṣads sometimes talk about immeasurable happiness as the goal, which the Buddha rightly criticized and ridiculed. In *Kaṭha* Naciketas rejected the offer of million years of happiness and pleasure from Yama; the argument being that in the scale of eternity, a million years would be insignificant.

I argue that this hedonistic understanding of the thesis may be popular at the ordinary level, but as a philosophical thesis it is *unattractive* and *unsound*. Psychological hedonism is an undeniable fact. We seem to assume that we have a *birth-right* to happiness, pleasures and joy. Hence, an abundance of suffering and pain in life is regarded as abnormal, even *genetically unsound*. We always ask why, why, why, why do we suffer? We try to explain with the notion of the original sin, or bad *karma*, and the quest for the ultimate good is justified. But a psychological tendency does neither generate nor guarantee the existence of metaphysical realities. Nor does it show, as a Freudian would have us believe, the *illusory character* of such assumed reality.

So far I have argued that all the standard interpretations and defences of the thesis of the universality of suffering fail. Yet I believe they are all attempts to express or explain something very difficult to express, but fundamentally correct.

Let me try another way. In recent literature there has been much talk about the meaning or significance of life, of our lives on earth. But the very question 'What is the meaning of life? Is there any?' is shot from the beginning. The psychological situation that makes it possible for such a question to arise demanding an answer, makes it, by the same stroke, either unanswerable or renders the whole question *rhetorical*. We call something a *rhetorical* question, if the answer is obviously implied by the asking of the question. Here the answer seems to be obvious and in the negative. There is *no* meaning to life unless we can invent one. It is part of our human predicament. Rats and ants do not ask the question. But we do. It is part of our being human that we can and so sometimes detach ourselves from the lives we are committed to live, step back in thought and survey ourselves. This is the human capacity of self-consciousness and self-transcendence. Once we have taken that crucial step backward, it takes very little to convince us of the futility, worthlessness, insignificance and absurdity of all our strivings, activities, hopes, aspirations and evaluations. This is not simply a *psychotic state*, as my friend Jeff Masson has argued,[4] for it is certainly more than what we usually identify as clinical depression. It is a self-conscious awareness which a rational man is privileged to have and, as long as it does not affect his rational behaviour, it does not amount to a psychopathological *state* in any derogatory sense. It can be called the Buddha awareness, for the Buddha had it. If it is argued that he was utterly depressed when he had this sort of mental state, I would point out that that does not usually matter. For as long as he used his rationality to find a way out of this situation, he was not behaving irrationally. Without making any judgement about the intrinsic value of the Buddha's prescription for a cure, one can claim that the self-conscious awareness of the absurdity of the human situation is a much deeper realization. If a psychosis or depression is associated with such realization of the most profound but discomforting truth, then let be it so. It is not my attempt here to distinguish between a saint and a psychotic, between sanity and lunacy. For (a) such a distinction does not matter here, and (b) ultimately such a distinction would be based upon some pragmatic considerations (is it harmful to many or not?) against the background of the acceptable standards of normalcy in a given society at a given period.

Let us consider the following broad theses:

1. Life is only suffering, *duḥkha*, an unacceptable state of affairs.
2. Life is devoid, empty, *śūnya*, of the substance that we attach to it uncritically.
3. Life is devoid of purpose, significance, meaning.
4. Life is devoid of sense, it is absurd.
5. Life is devoid of any ultimate value.

I do not wish to say that these theses are equivalent. They may not logically imply one another, but they belong to the same family. I am not saying that there is simply a family resemblance here. Rather I wish to emphasize that they are simply attempts to articulate and express a truth which dawns upon us from time to time and which it is very difficult to express adequately. As Thomas Nagel has put the matter about the absurdity of life:

> We cannot live human lives without energy and attention, nor without making choices which show that we take some things more seriously than others. Yet we have always available a point of view outside the particular form of our lives, from which this seriousness appears gratuitous. These two inescapable viewpoints collide in us, and that is what makes life absurd. It is absurd because we ignore the doubts we know cannot be settled, continuing to live with nearly undiminished seriousness in spite of them.[5]

'Life is devoid of any value' may be an evaluative statement. It may also be a factual one. I think it is both. And 'Life is *duḥkha* and it is utterly unsatisfying' belongs to the same category. For a mouse, 'Life is meaningless or devoid of value' is a factual statement and false. For those among us who have taken the crucial backward step and self-consciously searched for value, this is a factual statement and true. But for those among us who refuse to search for the ultimate values or meanings, those who envision a role or function in something larger than themselves and seek fulfilment in service to the society, the state, the revolution, sciences, religion and the glory of God, this is only a value-judgement. It is true for only such persons who do not doubt and question much larger purposes that confer meaning, value and justification to our life-activity. For theirs is the realization that such standards for conferring value and meaning can simply be called in question in order to be dismissed.

Let me explain the Indian context to clarify these comments. People among us have different natures, different inclinations and different 'tastes': *bhinnarucir hi lokaḥ*. We are all humans, but diversities among us can hardly be overemphasized. Pluralism is a well-recognized fact. Indian philosophers have argued that among such diversities there are two very broadly acceptable norms of life with divergent goals and values. One is called the path of activism (*pravṛtti*) and the other is path of renunciation (*nivṛtti*). This will dispel the misconceived idea about Indian religions that they are always other-worldly, life-negating obstacles to material progress and prosperity. As early as the *Ṛgveda*, we see hymns that ask humans to secure prosperity unabashedly side by side with hymns that glorify asceticism and renunciation. *Vedāntasūtras* 3.4.2.7 inform us that Jaimini contended that renunciation or self-mortification was no part of the normal 'Vedic' life. Sometimes this recognition of pluralism is regarded as the paradoxicality of Indian culture (asceticism and eroticism?). But instead of presenting it as paradoxical, I wish to underline this as a point of paramount significance, viz. the bold recognition that human nature is manifold and is expressed through diverse values, ways of thinking, acting and feeling.

If the thesis of universal suffering is interpreted in the above way as a thesis about the lack of meaning, value and significance of our lives on earth, a realization then dawns upon us sometimes, of a truth that is too discomforting to be accepted and yet at the same time too obvious to be ignored completely by everybody at all times. The absurdity of our situation is heightened by the fact that while we can take this view (maybe part of our original sin to eat of the tree of knowledge) and realize what we do in life is arbitrary and meaningless, we cannot disengage ourselves from life by this awareness. In Indian jargon, we realize the Truth while we remain, as we must, immersed in the ocean of untruths. This is not a practical joke but something very similar. As Nagel emphasized: 'the absurdity of our situation derives from a collision within ourselves.'[6]

No wonder some people would like to brush aside this awareness as some kind of madness, a psychosis when reason has given out. This awareness is utterly discomforting and dissatisfying and what else is the ultimate suffering if it is not this? What sustains us in this *unreason* is a mystery, maybe the 'inertial force' of taking the life and the world for granted, maybe the 'animal' way that dominates part of our being. (Remember that ants and rats do not face this problem and WE have eaten not only of the tree of Knowledge but also of the tree of Life.) For our lives and beliefs would collapse entirely—psychosis will actually take over, if we tried to rely entirely on reason and pressed it hard. 'How does the wise man behave?' The Indian mystic answers, 'The wise man behaves as the fools do. There is no difference in their external behaviour.'

Faced with the profundity of the truth that we discover in our self-imposed self-transcendent thought, what recourse is there left for us if we wanted to do something about it. Various responses are possible.

(A) We can declare it as an insane thesis, a psychotic awareness and try to shut it off in a lunatic asylum. We can feel complacent about it thinking that we have done our duty, our scientific duty: the awareness is shattering, so shatter the awareness itself or put a lid on it. Some philosophers suggested that we should play a game of backgammon[7] or grow vegetable marrows. Some would visit the lunatic in the asylum and then go for a swim; a cool refreshing swim will fix everything!

(B) Some have given the advice of being bold and taking it with a stride. Russell in his 'Free Man's Worship' talked about a similar kind of boldness and courage. We as human beings have our dignity (what else?) and hence we may abhor the escapist's routes. And it is a sort of escapism if we try to drop out of the 'rat race'. We may boldly go through it, taking in all the agony, absurdity, vacuity and unpleasure that life offers when it does not have a meaning. This is a sort of romanticism championed by the existentialists such as Camus.

(C) Some would counsel suicide.[8] But that may be too hasty. This is undoubtedly noted as another form of escapism. And, as Nagel has pointed out, must we not consider carefully whether the absurdity of our existence truly presents us with a *problem*, to which a solution must be found? Otherwise suicide would be another senseless act to be added to millions of others. Under a slightly different situation, the Jaina monks of India did recommend suicide in a slower, gradual scale, gradual withdrawal from food, drink and so on, slowly and coolly embracing gradual death, when you are absolutely ready to take it.

(D) Some would refuse to take the crucial, self-transcendental step backward in order not to land in a situation where the above awareness will dawn upon us. But are we really *free* to do this? We may be *free* in choosing various other things in life, but as humans, we have already eaten of the tree of Knowledge. Even if we want to refuse to take the other viewpoint, we have to be aware already about what we want to refuse. And hence it is a self-refuting position, for we have already gained the awareness itself. We cannot decide by will never to attain it any more!

(E) Finally some would respond by inventing a transcendental meaning and a transcendental value in the very same awareness which reveals our lives as arbitrary, trivial, hollow and purposeless. This is not a counsel of abrupt suicide or something like it. If no meaning or transcendental value of life can be discovered, let us *invent* such a value. It is a deliberate advice to undertake a course of action by following which we can slowly and gradually devalue and dissolve and decompose our animality, our 'inertial' force, that is, what makes us 'tick', what induces us to follow the ordinary course of life even with the awareness that this does not have any meaning, purpose or value. The process that is recommended is to slowly identify as completely as possible with the awareness that renders all our other doings meaningless in the way they first appeared to us. Life-experiences are pointless and hollow in the background of some *nirvāṇic* consciousness. It is true we do not *know* what the *nirvāṇic* consciousness will be like, for we have not experienced it. But let us assume that it is there. It will certainly be complete cessation of this absurdity, this meaningless, mad pursuit of pleasure. We might not have to pursue it in an aggressive and vigorous manner, for that will again be paradoxical. One can gradually let it happen, a process of self-etiolation. Practise the process of *niṣkāma karma*. Act but do not cling to it, for in this way acts would not cling to you and will gradually set you free. Free from what? The absurdity of our existence. Respond to your normal animal nature, normal impulses and gradually convince yourself about the hollowness of making the pursuit of animal needs a central aim. Go through the crowd and try not to be a part of it. This gradual disengagement from life will result in that complete dissociation from everything leading to the freedom of the awareness which made everything meaningless. This is not a defiant contempt, nor a courageous confrontation, nor a lunatic depression, nor an oblivious indifference, but an active, self-aware non-participation. It is again not a passive inertness, but an active non-participation—a state of mind, an attitude, call it serenity, in which you act and do what is expected of you, but you do not participate. It is like this: you act in a play but do not participate in the lives of characters. This *nirvāṇa* consciousness is a feasible, possible concept.

I conclude by saying this *nirvāṇic* consciousness seems to be a feasible concept, a possible idea, and one may actualize it.

Notes and References

1. Hume, *Dialogues Concerning Natural Religion*, ed. N.K. Smith, Oxford: Oxford University Press, 1935, Part x.
2. *Sāṃkhya Kārikā*, Verse I.
3. For details see *Works of Spinoza* (*On the Improvement of Human Understanding*). New York: Dover Publishers Inc., 1951, p. 3.
4. For further details see J.M. Masson, *The Oceanic Feeling: The Origin of Religious Sentiments in Ancient India.* Boston: D. Reidel Publication Co. 1980.
5. Thomas Nagel, *Mortal Question.* New York: Cambridge University Press, 1979, p. 14.
6. Ibid., p. 17.
7. D. Hume, *A Treatise on Human Nature* ed., L.A. Selby-Bigge. Oxford: The Clarendon Press, 1955, p. 269.
8. Nagel, op. cit., p. 17.

27

The Quest for Immortality

Then said Maitreyī: 'If now, sir, this whole earth filled with wealth were mine, would I be immortal thereby?'

'No,' said Yājñavalkya. 'As the life of the rich, even so would your life be. Of immortality, however, there is no hope through wealth.'

Then said Maitreyī: 'What should I do with that through which I may not be immortal?'

(*Bṛhadāraṇyaka Upaniṣad*, 2.4.2, tr. R.E. Hume)

'There is fire and storm, your palace is burning! Good sir, why don't you take care of your harem?'

Nemi replied: 'Happy we dwell, happy we live, who call nothing whatever our own. Though Mithilā may burn, nothing of me is burned!'

(*Uttarādhyāyana-sūtra*, 9: A Jaina Scripture)

A well-known parable—the parable of the man in the well—is found in a number of the religious texts of ancient India. The story, with variations, was shared equally by the Hindus, the Buddhists and the Jainas. It has been said that the story travelled to Medieval Europe (Haka Minaru, in correspondence). Here is an abridged version.

A certain man, oppressed by the woes of poverty, left his own home, and set out for another country. He passed through many cities and villages, and very soon he lost his way in a forest. The forest was thick with trees and full of wild beasts. All of a sudden he saw a mad elephant, charging him with upraised trunk. At the same time there appeared before him a most evil demoness, holding a sharp sword, and laughing loudly and shrilly. In utter fear, he looked in all directions. There, to the east of him, he saw a great banyan tree. He ran quickly and reached the mighty tree. But alas, he could not climb its high unscalable trunk. All his limbs trembled with terrible fear. He then saw nearby an old well covered with grass. Afraid of death, craving to live if only a moment longer, he flung himself into the well. The mouth of the well was full of reeds, and he clung to these reeds, for he saw below him terrible snakes, enraged at the sound of his falling. There was a black and mighty python at the bottom. He thought, 'My life will last only as long as these reeds hold fast. Then he saw two large mice, one white, one black, gnawing with their sharp teeth at the base of the reed-clump. Now the wild elephant, more enraged at not catching the man, charged time and again at the trunk of the banyan tree. At the shock of his charge a honeycomb on a large branch shook loose and fell. The man's whole body was stung by a swarm of angry bees. But just by chance, a drop of honey fell on his head, rolled on to his brow, and somehow reached his lips and gave him a moment of sweetness. He longed for other drops. He thought nothing of the python, the snakes, the elephant, the mice, the well, or the bees, as he craved for yet more drops of honey.

This grim little story underlines nicely two of the most fundamental instinctual drives of man: the drive for survival, or self-preservation, and the drive for pleasure. It also shows that the drive for pleasure, or desire for more may override even the fear of total extinction. Freud, at one time (Freud, 1905), postulated two groups of instinctive drives: the sexual instincts and the self-preservative instincts, although he did not clearly define the latter group in this context. Without going into the technicalities of psychoanalysis and the classification of instincts, it is probably safe to assume that man's will to live long (as well as his will to live forever) is derivative of his self-preservative instinct—an instinct that has led man to search for an immutable existence in which he may be perpetuated. This search has taken one form or another in history and upholds the promise of a deathless existence. At the material level, the search was for an elixir of life. At the theoretical level, it was for an assurance of self-perpetuation after physical death, that is, after the death of the body. This search has been at least one of the reasons for which man has engaged himself in constructing a system of beliefs as well as singling out a set of rituals, which in combination form the institution called 'religion'. Perhaps it will not be far from the truth if we say that concern for immortality is one of the basic concerns of most Indian religions, and perhaps also of most world religions. Perhaps the desire to be immortal is only an expression of one's inherent love for one's own self. A thirteenth-century Vedāntic text, *Pañcadaśī*, puts forward this proposition as follows:

> 'May I not cease to exist, but exist forever.'
> This is how everybody is seen to pray always,
> which is the perceptible evidence for one's love of one's own self (12.31).

If one of the many functions of religion is to uphold the promise of the immortality of one's own self, then the question naturally arises: what is the self? The most immediate answer would be to identify the mundane body with the self. But this position becomes highly unsatisfactory to us for we are, after all, looking forward to an imperishable existence! Thus, Indra is supposed to have said to Prajāpati, at the first stage of his instruction: 'If the body is the self, then it perishes immediately upon the perishing of this body. I see nothing enjoyable in this' (*Chāndogya Upaniṣad*, 8.9). Seeing that one's mundane body perishes, one tries to disassociate the notion of self from the body. One gradually conceives of a bodiless spirit or a soul and then identifies the self with this soul. Our body dies, but *we* continue to 'exist' as souls. A soul continues to eternity, and the self survives death being identified with the soul. The soul-doctrine in this way is a step forward in the direction of the promise of immortality.

The doctrine of self-soul identity is an expression of the belief that after a man's death, something of him outlives the decay of the body, and in this minimal sense, the doctrine becomes part of the fundamental teachings of almost all religions. How about the non-believers? There were in ancient India both materialists and sceptics—the followers of Cārvāka and the Lokāyata school—who denied the existence of a soul as distinct from the body, and thereby denied the possibility of an after-life or survival after death. For them there cannot be any survival of the self when the mundane body disintegrates. It is said:

> When once the body becomes ashes, how can it [the self] ever return again? (tr. E.B. Cowell & A.E. Gough, 1882, p. 10).

The materialists thus did not believe in any after-life and consequently did not preach any doctrine which would sustain the promise of immortality. For them, there cannot be any immortality. They declared in no uncertain terms that all religious doctrines about immortality and the Ultimate Bliss were nothing but the propaganda of the privileged priests. They said:

> Three types of persons concocted the Vedas; they are the cheats, the sly, and the goblins. (ibid., own translation).

In this way the materialists attacked all religions that preached immortality as the ultimate goal of man. For them mortality is reality and hence talk about an after-life is nonsensical.

If we generally conclude that the quest for immortality is an essential part of any respectable world religion, an apparent problem arises in the interpretation of Buddhism. For, all hopes of immortality are connected, in religions like Jainism, Hinduism (and, one might add, in Western religions too), with the conviction of the existence of an unalterable and imperishable soul. But Buddhism is well-known as a religion which teaches the no-soul (*anātman*) doctrine. It formulates a doctrine of transmigration without a transmigrating soul, a doctrine of perpetuation of existence without any entity persisting through the ever-fluctuating states. Thus, one might say that Buddhism, since it rejects the doctrine of soul, constitutes a counter-example to the general thesis about immortality.

But Buddhism is not really a counter-example, although it is arguable that the Buddha wanted his doctrine to be one. It does not take much effort to see that even Buddhism became a religion—an organized religion, to be sure—which tried to establish our faith in immortality and *nirvāṇa*. Whether or not the Buddha himself intended it to be that way, we cannot tell. The Buddha was greatly concerned with the problem of death, decay and old age. And his search was for a way (i.e., The Way) which will surpass or transcend this ever-dying and ever-decaying state. The Buddha, however, had the genius and the courage to discover that as long as we cling to a conviction in the existence of an unalterable soul, we will never have a true understanding of the nature of reality and *nirvāṇa*. And perhaps, the Buddha realized the futility of this search for immortality—a realization which itself was an experience called 'enlightenment'. Perhaps facetiously and paradoxically, it was pointed out that *nirvāṇa*, being cessation of decay and death, itself does not cease. But alas Buddhism turned into a religion. Buddhism became the Way that was supposed to lead to *nirvāṇa*. With the doctrine of *nirvāṇa* came the promise of a deathless existence, *de facto* promise of immortality. For *nirvāṇa* has often been described in the texts as a deathless state, an unchanging, undecaying existence. In fact, *nirvāṇa* is said to be the only way to avoid death and repetitions of death (cf. *punar-mrtyu*).

It would be worthwhile to quote from Asaṅga's description of the third Noble Truth of Buddhism, *nirodha*, that is, *nirvāṇa*. To explain the first Noble Truth, *duḥkha*, Asaṅga quotes a *buddha-vacana*, supposedly a direct quotation from the Buddha's dialogues: 'Whatever is impermanence, is *duḥkha* (suffering, unhappiness, or anguish).' Referring to the Third Noble Truth, the goal of Buddhism, Asaṅga describes it as follows:

Why is this cessation (*nirodha*) called unshaken? Because there is lack of motion in the midst of mobile objects. Why is this cessation (*nirodha*) called imperishable or deathless? Because there is lack of origination. . . . Why is it called unborn? Because there is no birth. . . . Why does it have the characteristic of cessation (*nirodha*)? Because there is disconnection with defilement (*kleśa*). . . . Why does it have the characteristic of tranquillity (*śānta*)? Because there is disconnection with pain. . . . Why does it have the characteristic of liberation (*niḥsaraṇa*)? Because it is the abode of the eternal bliss (Asaṅga, 1950, pp. 64–5).

One cannot be blamed if one interprets the Buddhist programme for *nirvāṇa* as a programme for immortality, although we should admit that the Buddhist notion of immortality was of a very different sort compared to the usual notions of immortality found in other religions.

Let us probe the Buddhist situation a little further. The concept of a permanent soul is so often associated with the notion of immortality that it is difficult not to construe, at first sight, the no-soul doctrine of Buddhism as the express rejection of immortality. But if the notion of immortality is carefully defined in such a way that it becomes independent of the belief in an unalterable soul-substance, then it is easy to see that the 'no-soul' doctrine would surely be compatible with immortality. In fact, Buddhism shows us that it is possible to maintain a doctrine of immortality without implying thereby a doctrine of an unalterable soul. Logically speaking, the conception of an unalterable soul is itself a derivative of the doctrine of immortality, which, I have maintained above, is an expression of the basic human drive for self-perpetuation. There are obviously other secular ways by which we try to fulfil this aim, such as perpetuation of the self through children, and attaining undying fame through good work. But we need not concern ourselves with secular means in a religious context. If the soul-concept is derived from the notion of immortality and not the latter from the former, then rejection of the soul-concept does not necessarily imply rejection of the immortality notion. It is then possible for the Buddhist to reject the soul-concept and still maintain the doctrine of immortality.

Historically speaking, the notion of immortality in India was prior to the notion of a permanent soul. In the *Rg-veda*, for example, we find frequent references to the idea of immortality, in the prayers for immortality. But the notion of a soul that is imperishable does not occur with such frequency. The *Rg-veda* is the earliest available document of Indian religious thought. I quote below some interesting verses that deal with the theme of immortality (translated by A.A. Macdonell):

Soma VIII. 48:

Wisely I have partaken of the sweet food
That stirs good thoughts, best banisher of care,
To which all gods and mortals, calling it honey, come together.
We have drunk Soma; we have become immortal;
We have gone to the light; we have found the gods.
What can hostility now do to us, and what malice of mortal man,
O immortal one?

Puruṣa X. 90:

MAN (*puruṣa*) is this all, that has been and that will be.
And he is the lord of immortality,
Which he grows beyond through food.
Such is his greatness, and more than that is MAN.
A fourth of him is all beings.
Three-fourths of him are
What is immortal in heaven.

It is significant to note that in the first hymn the Soma drink (a kind of drug or inebriant) is conceived as taking man beyond unhappiness, evil and death, to the goal of immortality. In the second hymn, the primeval Man is conceived as one that pervades both the mortal world and the world beyond, that is, immortality.

The Buddha himself repeatedly said that he had proclaimed and taught nothing but the doctrine of *duḥkha*, 'suffering', and its removal, *nirvāṇa*. He deliberately refused to answer or discuss any metaphysical or eschatological question that relates to the notion of soul or survival after death. For, he claimed, all such theoretical philosophizing would be only superfluous speculation and would therefore not help in the least the practical way to *nirvāṇa*, cessation of suffering. The state of *nirvāṇa* is also described here negatively, not as a condition of blessedness but only as a release or freedom from the suffering of existence and transmigration. In thus emphasizing the negative character of *nirvāṇa*, the Buddha successfully avoided discussion of such questions as: whether the Tathāgata exists after death or not.

But *nirvāṇa* is, after all, an escape from this conditioned existence which is full of suffering, constant decay and death. This existence is full of suffering because of its repetitious mortality. *Nirvāṇa* is an escape from this ever-changing, ever-decaying state of transmigration. At the threshold of *nirvāṇa*, the following knowledge arises: 'There is no more rebirth, the holy conduct is complete, the duty is fulfilled. There is no more recurrence in this world.' *Nirvāṇa* is not certainly annihilation but it is at the same time cessation. The Buddhist canons are eloquent on this point. The Buddha declared:

And I who thus speak and preach, monks, am accused by some ascetics and priests wrongly and falsely thus: 'This ascetic Gautama is a nihilist, he teaches destruction, annihilation, and ruin of the being that now exists.' These ascetics and priests falsely accuse me, O monks, of what I have not preached or taught. They say what I am not. Only one thing I teach you, monks, now as I have done before: suffering and the removal of suffering (*Majjhima-Nikāya* 22; 1888, I, 140).

One may suggest that the doctrine of *nirvāna* as described above is another instantiation of our universal quest for immortality. This does not, as we have seen, imply that the Buddha implicitly accepted a 'soul doctrine'. Some modern Buddhist scholars have argued that there must have been an implicit soul-doctrine in Buddhism and their argument hinges upon the point that the Buddha did not emphatically refute the notion of the soul. We need not agree with them. In fact, this has been a well-known controversy among modern Buddhist scholars. Our point is neutral, not being in favour of deciding the question one way or the other. Therefore I have chosen here a neutral concept, immortality (the negation of mortality that all human beings aspire to avoid in some way or other), which may be unfamiliar to neither the 'soul' philosophers nor the 'no-soul' philosophers.

The important question that might be asked in the context of Buddhism is the question of survival after death. If there is no permanent soul, what would survive death? We may again go back to the Vedic literature for an indication of the purported solution of the problem. Yājñavalkya, in one of the earliest Upaniṣads, was asked by Ārtabhāga in the court of King Janaka (where all the priests from all over northern India gathered together) about this question of survival after death:

'Yājñavalkya', said he, 'when the voice of a dead man goes into fire, his breath into wind, his eyes into the sun, his mind into the moon, his hearing into the quarters of heaven, his body into the earth, his soul (*ātman*) into the space, the hairs of his head into plants, hairs of his body into trees, and his blood and semen are placed in water, what then becomes of this person (*puruṣa*)?' 'Ārtabhāga, my dear, take my hand. We two only will know of this. This is not for us two [to speak of] in public.' The two went away and deliberated. What they said was *karma* (action). What they praised was *karma*. Verily, one becomes good by good action, bad by bad action. (*Bṛhadāraṇyaka*, 3.2.13, tr. R.E. Hume).

Yājñavalkya did not refer to the immortal soul in this context in direct answer to the question of survival after death. His answer, on the other hand, was similar to the answer given by the Buddha about two hundred years later: *karma* survives death. The conception of a persisting soul-substance is rejected in Buddhism, but the *karma* principle continues and accounts for re-birth and transmigration. How? *Karma* comes from craving, and creates in its turn more craving for self-perpetuation. How? Nāgasena helps our understanding here with a simile, in his discourse with the Greek king, Menander:

> 'Reverend Nāgasena,' said the King, is it true that nothing transmigrates, and yet there is rebirth?'
>
> 'Yes, your Majesty.'
>
> 'How can this be? . . . Give me an illustration.'
>
> 'Suppose, your Majesty, a man lights one lamp from another—does the lamp transmigrate to the other?'
>
> 'No, your Reverence.'
>
> 'So there is rebirth without anything transmigrating!' (*Milindapañha*, Trenckner, 1880, p. 71).

Our belief in the existence of a soul, a permanently enduring personality-essence behind all sorts of decay and death, is only a reflex of our quest for immortality. We are, it is true, ill-prepared to accept our death, decay and complete extinction. Hence we try to discover within us something that must survive this process of complete extinction. The Buddha, in his enlightened insight, saw the process of constant decay and extinction as the ever-conditioned-ness of this reality. But could we attach any significance to this fragility of existence, to this utter deterministic condition, in the absence of a comprehensive contrast with an unconditioned, undetermined freedom? To ask this question implies, at least indirectly, that the inquirer is expecting a positive, affirmative answer. Therefore, Buddhism posits an unconditioned reality, *nirvāṇa*, and in the all-pervasive context of such an unconditioned freedom only this conditioned reality is supposed to make any sense.

There is a common ground for divergent religious traditions found all over the world: concern for personal survival, the quest for immortality. We are, of course, aware that there are almost innumerable doctrines of personal survival, a fact that accounts for divergent religious and philosophical systems in the East and West. Moreover, faced with the problem of defending the notion of personal immortality against the overwhelming fact of universal mortality, philosophers in all ages have philosophized on the subject so much so that sometimes the doctrine of personal survival is transformed into a metaphysical doctrine that is no longer recognizable as one of survival. One may argue with proper justification that Aristotle's thesis of the Eternal Intellect is entirely different from the common belief that we humans shall continue to exist (forever) after our deaths. The same situation is found in a few other sophisticated versions of religious doctrine. But this is beside our point here.

In the West, immortality has generally been associated with the soul-doctrine, and this soul, in the Platonic tradition, is deemed 'incorporeal' (distinguished from body), and must be identical with the person, that is, the true or essential person. This essential soul is what is supposed to escape unharmed and unnoticed at death. Socrates insisted that after he had drunk the poison he would no longer remain with his friends, but depart to 'a state of heavenly bliss':

'We shall try our best to do as you say,' said Crito. 'But how shall we bury you?'

'Any way you like, replied Socrates, 'that is, if you can catch me and I don't slip through your fingers.'

He laughed gently as he spoke, and turning to us went on, 'I can't persuade Crito that I am this Socrates here who is talking to you now and marshalling all the arguments. He thinks I am the one whom he will see presently lying dead, and he asks how he is to bury me!' (*Phaedo*, 115d, p. 95).

The truth of the doctrine of personal survival depends on the premise that the person be identified with the supposedly enduring soul. It was one of the problems before the Upaniṣadic thinkers of ancient India: to identify the person with the soul. Thus, Prajāpati said in *Chāndogya Upaniṣad* (8.7.3, tr. R.E. Hume):

The Self (*Ātman*), which is free from evil, ageless, deathless, sorrowless, hungerless, thirstless, whose desire is the Real, whose conception is the Real—He should be searched out, Him one should desire to understand.

When Indra and Virocanā lived at Prajāpati's place as students for thirty long years, Prajāpati instructed (ibid., 8.7.4):

That person, who is seen in the eye—He is the Self (*Ātman*) of whom I spoke. That is the immortal, the fearless. That is Brahman.

'But this one, sir, who is observed in water and in a mirror—which one is he?'

'The same one, indeed, is observed in all these,' was his reply. Both Indra and Virocana misunderstood Prajāpati's doctrine at this time, confusing the soul with the physical person. But when Indra accepted Prajāpati's studentship for one hundred and one years, the latter instructed:

O Maghavan, verily, this body is mortal. It has been appropriated by Death. (But) it is the standing ground of the deathless, bodiless Self. Verily, he who is incorporate has been appropriated by pleasure and pain. Verily, there is no freedom from pleasure and pain for one while he is incorporate. Verily, while one is bodiless, pleasure and pain do not touch him. . . . As a draft-animal is yoked in a wagon, even so this spirit is yoked in this body.'

One recognized problem in the immortality-cum-soul doctrine in the West is the problem of individuation: how is one bodiless soul to be distinguished from another bodiless soul? This problem is reflected in the Christian tradition in its doctrine of resurrection of the body, which is sometimes interpreted as the reconstitution of the human person (St Thomas: *Summa Theologica* III, supplement). This seems to overcome the problem of individuation (for, how else can I be sure that what survives my decay and death is my own self?) But then this theory relies on God, on an act of sheer omnipotence to make the reconstituted person an immortal one.

Despite the resurrection doctrine in Christianity, the Platonic conception of soul (the soul is an incorporeal substance, identical with the person) has dominated the Western philosophic tradition. The Cartesian idea of soul is also of a piece with the Platonic notion. But Plato apparently believed in the pre-existence of the soul and he based his argument on the doctrine of reminiscence (an argument not infrequently used by the Indian philosophers):

They say that the soul of man is immortal. At one time it comes to an end—that which is called death—and at another is born again, but is never finally exterminated. On these grounds a man must live all his days as righteously as possible. . . . Thus the soul, since it is immortal and has been born many times, and has seen all things both here and in the other world, has learned everything that is (*Meno*, 81b–c, p. 364).

Socrates insisted on the doctrine of pre-existence when he tried to prove the theory that learning is nothing but recollection (see also *Phaedo*, 73a–77a).

But the pre-existence doctrine has never been accepted in the Western orthodoxy, probably because of the strong Christian influence along with its doctrine of creation by God. It is interesting to note that due, perhaps, to Western cultural conditioning, the Indian notion of pre-existence always appears much less credible to a Western mind than immortality or survival after death. It will not be fair to say that the Western mistrust of pre-existence is due entirely to the lack of credibility of Plato's argument in support of the doctrine. Admittedly, Plato's argument was weak. But so was his argument for an incorporeal, immortal soul. And this latter doctrine seemed acceptable to the Western mind for a pretty long time. One may further point out that Plato, in insisting on both pre-existence and immortality, adopted a less arbitrary position than those who accept immortality alone! As David Hume has put it:

Reasoning from the common course of nature, and without supposing any *new* interpretation of the supreme cause, which ought always to be excluded from philosophy; what is incorruptible must also be ingenerable. The soul, therefore, if immortal, existed before our birth: and if the former existence nowise concerned us, neither will the latter (1755, [1980, p. 92]).

There may be another reason for the popularity of the Platonic idea of soul and immortality in the West. Philosophers can see that the Platonic idea of immortality does not presuppose the existence of any sort of god. Thus, even the so-called atheist philosopher can affirm immortality without thereby running into any contradiction. But, on the other hand, at the popular level in the West, belief in God and immortality have always been tied together. For people have been led to believe that the main point about immortality or survival is to provide inordinate rewards and punishments. However, it is important to realize that there is no logical incompatibility between a belief in immortality and a disbelief in God, just as there is no incompatibility between a belief in immortality and a disbelief in an incorporeal soul-substance (a point I have already made in connection with Buddhism).

Of many arguments given by the philosophers in the West to prove immortality, let us take one in particular for the sake of illustration. This argument states that our belief in immortality is somehow evidence of its own truth: the existence of the universal desire for immortality calls for a fulfilment. Immortality is advocated along with the Divine purpose. But, as Hume has shown, this only proves the opposite—mortality:

All doctrines are to be suspected which are favoured by our passions. And the hopes and fears which give rise to this doctrine [the doctrine of immortality], are very obvious (1755, [1980, p. 96]).

A modern Freudian would welcome such comments. For, he can argue, it is just because of the presence of the universal desire for immortality that the doctrine should be suspect.

In today's world of science, the scientific evidence is very strong against not only transmigration but also any soul-substance or any survival of consciousness after death! In other words, the evidence of science that we can gather so far conflicts directly with the fundamental assumption of almost all religions. Some of the arguments are too well known to be repeated here. People usually put them under the rubric: opposition of science to religion. Let me refer only to two sets of evidence. First, there is the unquestionable dependence of mind or consciousness on the possession of a physical body and nervous system. There are ample facts to prove this dependence. An infant has an infant body and infant consciousness. As the body matures, consciousness matures. Injury to the brain may produce a disordered mental life. Therefore it would be unthinkable that there would survive a particular consciousness when the body disintegrates.

In ancient India, we have some remarkable formulations of this purely materialistic position, according to which the concept of soul or immortality becomes merely an academic myth. Glimpses of such forms of materialism are to be found in the epics and the Buddhist and Jaina canons. Let me refer to the views of a materialist prince, Pāyāsi. It is interesting to see how a 'philosopher' in those early days, with inadequate scientific knowledge at his disposal, would betray what we call today 'scientific outlook' and would try to reject the idea of the soul, immortality and the other world as 'unscientific'.

> I have had friends, companions, relatives, men of the same blood as myself, who have taken life, committed theft, or fornication, have uttered lying, slanderous, abusive, gossipy speech, have been covetous, of malign thoughts, of evil opinions. They have then fallen ill of mortal suffering and disease. When I had understood that they would not recover from that illness, I have gone to them and said: 'According to the views and opinion held, sirs, by certain wanderers (monks) and priests, they who break the precepts of morality, when the body breaks up after death, are reborn in the Waste, the Woeful Way, the Fallen Place, the Pit. Now you, sirs, have broken those precepts. If what those reverend wanderers (monks) and priests say is true, this sirs, will be your fate. If these things should befall you, sirs, come to me and tell me, saying: 'There is another world, there is rebirth not of human parentage, there is fruit and result of deeds well-done and ill-done.' . . . They consented to do so, saying, 'Very well,' but they neither came back themselves, nor dispatched a messenger. Now this . . . is evidence for me that there is neither another world, nor another birth which is not from human parentage, nor fruit or results of deeds well-done or ill-done' (*Pāyāsi-Suttanta*, trans. T.W. Rhys Davids, 1910, pp. 351–2, slightly notified).

Pāyāsi repeated the same request to the virtuous people who were dying. But they also disappointed Pāyāsi, for they too were unable to inform him about the existence of the other world, about survival after death. Pāyāsi continued with many crude forms of experiments. Thus:

Take the case of a felon who, having been caught red-handed by men, has been brought before me. They say, 'This felon, my lord, was caught in the act. Inflict on him what penalty you wish.' And I should say: 'Well then, my masters, throw this man alive into a jar; close the mouth of it and cover it with wet leather, and put over that a thick cement of moist clay, put it into a furnace and kindle the fire.' They, saying, 'Very good,' would obey me and . . . kindle a fire. When we knew that the man is dead, we should take down the jar, unbind and open the mouth, and quickly observe it, with the idea: 'Perhaps we may see his soul coming out!' But we do not see the man's soul coming out! This is evidence for me that there is neither another world, nor rebirth or birth other than by parentage, nor fruit or result of deeds well-done or ill-done (ibid., pp. 358–9).

There is today the scientific doctrine of the evolution of human consciousness out of animal consciousness, which religious people have tried to discredit in various ways. But, if the theory of evolution is true, then the doctrine of survival of consciousness after death becomes an absurdity. For, it is hardly compatible with the Western theory of individual survival or with the Indian theory of transmigration of consciousness. In the West, man has been said to be a 'special creation' of God, and he is supposed to have a soul while the animals are soulless. This cannot be held, if it is agreed that man evolved out of animal. The Indian religious people do not worry so much about the theory of evolution because the predominant view is that even the animals have souls. (Jainism goes to the extreme and says that everything, animate or inanimate, is endowed with a soul—a classic support for the animistic doctrine of the origin of religion.)

The Indian mystics, however have tried to refute this doctrine of 'suffocating' materialism. They point out that immortality, or survival, means only reabsorption of the individual consciousness into the ultimate or universal consciousness. They cite, as a convenient analogy, the space delimited by the four walls of a room, and the space outside. Consciousness is like the space that is boundless, and the demolition of the body is comparable to the demolition of the four walls. I do not know whether this analogy holds, or whether this interpretation is really satisfactory. But it seems to be a very ingenious way out of the problem about the theory of survival under any circumstances.

Religious philosophers set themselves the task of finding conclusive proof that will show that consciousness is independent of the body and nervous system. But this does not seem to be an easy task. Perhaps the possibility that consciousness is separable from the body was first suggested to man as he saw that through ingestion of some drug or through partaking of the Soma-drink one could surpass or forget pain and physical encumbrances. Remember our *Ṛg-vedic* Soma-drinker thought Soma could stir good thoughts, banish evil and bestow 'immortality'. And, perhaps, the mystics discovered many other ways to 'alter' consciousness. But this may lead one to the essential connection between body and consciousness. The mystical philosophy of India explained the mystical experience as an absorption of individual consciousness into the universal consciousness—a state which was asserted in the early Upaniṣads to be phenomenologically indistinguishable from deep sleep, death or final release. The modern drug-cultist also seems to uphold the same theory of absorption in mystical consciousness. But it is rather paradoxical that the little scientific knowledge that we have today about consciousness-manipulating (i.e., psychedelic) drugs proves, if anything, the dependence of consciousness on body-chemistry—a truth that might prove fatal to the fundamental assumption of consciousness as entirely separate from body and nervous system. The answer or answers that we would like to have, and the way we would like to have them, are not forthcoming. The chief division among mankind today, as it has always been, is between those who *believe* they have (or may have) an answer and those who *know* they do so. And, of course, there are those, a third group probably, for whom the question of understanding the self is either self-defeating or self-fulfilling.

Notes and References

Asaṅga, *Abhidharma-samuccaya.* Critically edited by Pralhad Pradhan. Santiniketan: Visva Bharati, 1950.

Freud, S., *Three Essays on the Theory of Sexuality.* Standard Edition of the Complete Works of Sigmund Freud, volume vii. London, 1905.

Hamilton, E. & Cairns, H. (eds), *The Collected Dialogues of Plato.* Princeton: Princeton University Press, 1961.

Hume, David, 'Of the Immortality of the Soul', in R.H. Popkin (ed.), *Dialogues Concerning Natural Religion.* Indianapolis: Hackett Publishing Co., 1980, pp. 91–6.

Hume, R.E., *The Thirteen Principal Upaniṣads.* 2nd edition, revised by G.C.O. Haas. Oxford, Oxford University Press, 1931.

Macdonell, A.A., *Hymns from the Rigveda.* Calcutta: Association Press, 1922.

Mādhava. *Sarva-darśana-saṃgraha: Or Review of the Different Systems of Hindu Philosophy.* Translated by E.B. Cowell and A.E. Gough, London: Trübner & Co., 1882.

Mādhava [Vidyāraṇya], *Pañcadaśī: A Treatise on Advaita Metaphysics.* Edited and translated by H.S. Shastri, London: Shanti Sadan, 1954.

Majjhima-Nikāya. Volume 1. Edited by V. Trenckner. London: Pali Text Society, 1888. Translated as *Middle Length Sayings* by I.B. Horner, London: Pali Text Society, 1954.

Pāyāsi-Suttanta. Translated by T.W. Rhys Davids, *Dialogues of the Buddha*, part ii. London: Henry Frowde, 1910, pp. 349–74.

Trenckner, V., *The Milindapañha.* London, 1880.

28

Karma and the Moral Order

Why should the good suffer and the wicked prosper? We do not know. Why is there inequal distribution of misery and happiness in this world? We do not know. The Fatalists usually answer such questions by referring to Fate: Fate has written down everything and not a word of it can be changed. Omar Khayyam says in his *Rubaiyat*; ch. LII):

> And that inverted Bowl we called the sky,
> Lift not thy hand to it for help—for It
> Rolls as impotently on as Thou and I.

All these questions can be re-phrased and transformed into religious questions, to which different religions have tried to find possible answers over the ages.

To simplify a very complicated issue, let us analyse the above problem into *three* basic questions. The first question is usually discussed under the name 'the problem of evil.' The traditional formulation of this question within a theistic religious tradition (like Christianity, or Vaiṣṇavism in India) can be stated as follows: if our Creator, God, desires to save all his human creatures, he should be able to do it, unless, of course, he is really limited in his power (i.e., not omnipotent). If, on the other hand, he does not desire salvation for all, he should be considered limited in his goodness. We have formulated the question already in a roundabout fashion, for our formulation here assumes a perplexing dualism, between God and evil (Kṛṣṇa and the demons in Vaiṣṇavism, Ahura Mazdah and Angra Mainyu in Zoroastrianism, God and the Devil in Christian mythology). We can reformulate the question in the form of a dilemma: if God is omnipotent, he must then be capable of preventing evil. If he is, again, essentially good and just he must want to prevent evil. But evil exists. Therefore, either God is not omnipotent, or he is not essentially good or just. In other words, the unlimited goodness of God is difficult reconcile with his omnipotence. These two qualities are difficult to reconcile with each other just because evil exists. A modern Indian poet has expressed the problem in the form of a popular question:

> O God, at every age, you have sent your messengers on earth again and again.
> 'Have mercy for all,' they said. 'Love all beings,' they taught, 'and rid thy mind of the poison of hatred.'
> They are honorable persons, they deserve to be remembered.
> Yet I turn them out today with a fruitless salutation from the outside door.
> For I have witnessed how secret hatreds,
> Concealed in the darkness of night, attack the helpless.
> I have heard the voice of justice weeping secretly and silently,
> When the strong commit crimes for which there is no redress.
> I also see young boys running in frenzy
> Strike their heads in vain against the stone wall,
> And die in unspeakable pain.
> My voice chokes today, my flute loses its music.
> The prison-house of the dark moonless night
> Has wiped my own world in a nightmare.
> Therefore, I ask you, my lord, in tears:
> 'Have you yourself shown mercy to them?'
> 'Have you yourself loved these people,
> Who poison your clean air,
> And put out your light?'

(Rabindranath Tagore: *Question.* Own translation from Bengali).

Thus, at one level of Hinduism, we find the notion of a personal God as an independent creator and responsible director of the universe, and there is also an insistence on the maintenance of complete individuality of man. Hinduism, at this level, may be comparable with the Judeo-Christian tradition. But the notion of a personal God is progressively weaker at other levels of religion and philosophy where Hinduism tends towards either some form of pantheism, or monism, or mysticism. And at such levels, there is gradual tendency toward putting the responsibility on man rather than on God. As W.E. Clark had remarked of Hinduism:

> If life is a 'vale of tears' the responsibility rests with man's weakness, not with God (1934, p. 29).

In Mahāyāna Buddhism or Advaita Vedānta, the well-known dilemma arising out of the prevalence of evil does not seem to exist. For the phenomenal world along with its evil is described here as a 'transcendental' illusion or, at best, a provisional state of affairs. If Advaita Vedānta accepted a Creator God, he was regarded as one who was subordinate to the Ultimate Being, Brahman. Mahāyāna Buddhism, however, rejected the idea of a Creator God and redescribed the problem of evil in order to dissolve it. Evil, suffering, unhappiness, cannot be final or ultimate in this system. The goal in this system is to reach beyond good and evil, to the unitary ultimate reality.

Our *second* question is related intimately to the first. This question is about the moral responsibility of man for human pain and suffering. This also falls under the general problem of evil. But it is useful to distinguish between different types of evil. There are what we call the 'natural' sources of evil, such as disease, earthquake, flood and storm, for which we cannot blame anybody but the Creator God (if there is such a God). There are also evils in the form of torture, injustice, wars and many other forms of 'man's inhumanity to man'. Another type of evil can be distinguished only if we accept the premise that man is a creature endowed with free will. This is the evil which consists in the form of man's suffering, pain and agony caused through an exertion of his own free will—the pain that we cause to ourselves because of our own mistakes and wrong doings.

Our *third* question is eschatological: what happens to us when our body dies? Does everything end with death? Is there an after-life? I have discussed this issue in another article, 'The Quest for Immortality'. Let us concentrate now on the first two questions.

In the Christian tradition, the problem of evil as well as the problem of moral evil or sin (and hence moral responsibility) have often been treated together. It is believed (and it has generally been urged by theologians like St Augustine and Calvin) that the origin of sin or moral evil is due to the culpable fall of man from the Garden of Eden. It is the freely acting will of men (and, of course, angels) that has ushered evil into the creation of God, which is intrinsically good but, perhaps, corruptible. Thus, it solves the first question, the problem of evil, by saying that nothing is really evil within God's creation. Natural evils like disease and disasters are divinely ordained consequences of 'man's first disobedience' at the Garden of Eden. All other evils similarly originate in man's misuse of his own freedom. We are free agents, and through free will we turn away from the higher good (what God wants us to do) and turn to what is only lower good, and thus we become corrupted. In short, we are responsible for our own sins and should suffer the consequence.

A more enlightened formulation of the Christian position is sometimes given as follows. Man's Fall from the Garden of Eden is not a historical or prehistorical event but it represents man's present condition of 'estrangement' from God. Man in the pre-Fall state was like an *apparently uncorrupt but corruptible* child (a child of God). Man is created as imperfect but perfectible. In other words, just as man was corruptible, so is he now perfectible. Since God bears the ultimate responsibility of this situation, he has entered 'into human life' in Christ, to bring about man's redemption. The eschatalogical question is answered here by referring to a final day of judgement and Christ's resurrection, followed by God's decree of eternal heaven for the chosen few and eternal damnation for the rest. The doctrine of eternal damnation or hell-fire, however, creates another obstacle in Christian theology. It leads to the unsatisfactory dilemma: either God is not all-powerful or he is not all-good and not impartially just.

What was the situation in ancient India? In a word, India offered a variety of theologies and soteriologies. There was the notion of self-redemption through the mechanism of retribution and causality of *karma*, and there was also the notion of a redemption through the grace of some divine power. There are also varied interpretations of the highest goal of the religious life in India and it is wonderful to see how most varied hopes and yearnings of the human heart have been reflected in their conceptions of the final goal. One finds here salvation in the individual survival that is devoted to the constant service of God (cf. Vaiṣṇavism), or to the development of the highest activity for the welfare of mankind (cf. Bodhisattvahood). There are others here who talk about the complete dissolution of the ego or merging of the personality in the all-One Absolute (cf. Brahman). Again, for others, the final goal is eternal life with sensuous and supersensuous ecstacies (cf. Śaivism, Tantra). For some, it is clearly going back to the 'arms of the Divine Mother' (cf. Śāktas). For still others, it is a state of calm and tranquillity devoid of anything else (cf. Yoga). The ancient Indian thinkers thus produced an astonishing variety of religious ideas, a study of which can be highly rewarding provided we have the proper spirit and right attitude. Besides variety, we may say that the coexistence of opposite views which are expressly recognized by each other, and the prevalent awareness of the multiplicity of religious paths and goals, added a special charm to the ancient Indian situation—a situation that was not easily matched by other parts of the ancient world. This is, however, not to say that all these religious ideas are viable today in the modern world-situation, and that therefore, we should be respectful to the modern jet-propelled gurus, swāmis and masters who are preaching them to the Western world. In fact, most religious ideas, be they eastern or western, are not viable doctrines in the world today. But that certainly would not make study of any such doctrine or belief a less interesting subject.

The Indian mystics say that just as there are men of different natural dispositions and constitutions who need different sorts of nourishment, similarly there are men with different spiritual yearnings who need different sort of spiritual food. Thus, they explain the necessity for a variety of paths, a variety of religions. Whether such an explanation is acceptable or not is beside the point here. This attitude of the mystics certainly indicates their deeper insight into the natural diversity of taste, and also the conditioned state of all religious experience. Like religious leaders elsewhere, the ancient Indian thinkers tried to answer some of the great questions of mankind. Whether their answers are valid or useful today or not is not our concern here. One would naturally be disappointed if one looks for permanent and happy solutions to these almost unsolvable questions. As Arthur Danto has said: 'No one can save us but ourselves.' (1972, p. xi). But I venture to add that a careful and open-minded study of these answers aided by proper information and understanding is bound to be useful and educative for us.

On the problem of evil, it would be instructive to discuss first the Lokāyata materialist's view. The Lokāyatas were referred to both as *brāhmaṇas* (belonging to the class of priests) in the *Rāmāyaṇa*, and as *śramaṇas* (belonging to the class of monks) in the Pāli sources (Kaviraj, 1966, pp. 47–9). The Lokāyata materialist gives a naturalistic interpretation of the origin of the evil. Good and evil, happiness and misery, exist naturally side by side in this world like the bones and meat in a cooked fish dish (Mādhva, 1882, p. 4). The problem before man is to avoid one and obtain the other just as the problem before the fish-eater is to eat the meat without the bones. There is no Creator God because the world is only a natural development out of material elements. The Lokāyata maintains a complete scepticism in anything that is immaterial such as a bodiless soul or spirit and an after-life. Here is how Ajita's materialism has been described in *Dīgha Nikāya* I. 47:

> Man is formed of the four elements; when he dies earth returns to the aggregate of earth, water to water, fire to fire, and air to air, while the senses vanish into space. Four men with the bier take up the corpse; they gossip (about the dead man) as far as the burning ground, where his bones turn the color of a dove's wing, and his sacrifices end in ashes. They are fools who preach almsgiving, and those who maintain the existence of immaterial categories speak vain and lying nonsense. When the body dies both fool and wise alike are cut off and perish. They do not survive after death (tr. A. Basham, in Bary, 1958, p. 43).

Here we find, as early as the time of the Buddha, the clearest materialistic answer to the eschatological question. Even Naciketas, in the *Kaṭha Upaniṣad*, most probably referred to the Lokāyata view when he asked a question about the after-life to the God of Death:

> [Naciketas asks Death]: This doubt that there is in regard to a man deceased:
> 'He exists,' say some; 'He exists not,' say others —
> This would I know, instructed by thee!
> Of the boons this is the third (I. 20, tr. R.E. Hume)

The question of sin and moral responsibility is answered by the Lokāyata by denying the possibility of moral causation. Nothing exists except the material world as we see it. Here a particular action can generate certain particular (material) consequences which the agent might enjoy. For example, if we sow the seed we can reap the harvest. But there is no moral responsibility in the form of merit and demerit that the religious people talk about: No reward or punishment from any supermundane source. Tradition, indeed, has it that Ajita, a materialist of the time of the Buddha, consoled the despot King Ajātaśatru of Magadha (who committed parricide) with such a view of morality. The question of why some people are in a position to enjoy life more than others, was answered with reference to the notion of 'chance' or 'accident'. Thus providence or *karma* played no part in it.

Next, we can note the view of the Ājīvaka monks, who developed a doctrine of Fate or *niyati*. They agreed with the materialist about the natural development of life and the universe, there being no Creator God to create them. And thus the problem of evil, as it has been formulated above, does not arise in this case. But unlike the materialists, they believed in the unchangeable soul as distinct from the body, and also in the possibility of the final release or salvation. Life-experience is regarded in this system as decidedly painful and everything is full of suffering. Souls are said to be transmigrating in this system through innumerable births before salvation, a painless, deathless existence, is reached. The series of transmigrations is like the unwinding of a ball of thread which ends when and only when it runs its full course.

But the interesting part of this doctrine was the theory of 'non-action' (*a-kriyāvāda*). The question of moral responsibility is avoided by denying emphatically the efficacy of human action. The notion of human beings as free agents is a myth as far as the Ājīvakas are concerned. Theirs was a theory of complete determinism, which was just the opposite of what was understood as the *karma* doctrine of other schools. The inexorable world-process goes on in its course in accordance with the predestined *niyati* or Fate. Gośāla, who was the leader of the Ājīvaka sect, agreed with the materialists that morally good deeds had no non-material effect which might affect the future of the doer. Gośāla's doctrine is described in the *Dīgha Nikāya* I. 47 as follows:

> There is no deed performed either by oneself or by others (which can affect one's future births), no human action, no strength, no courage, no human endurance or human prowess (which can affect one's destiny in this life). All beings . . . are developed by destiny, chance, and nature. The cycle of birth or rebirth is measured as with a bushel, with its joy and sorrow and its appointed end. It can neither be lessened nor increased, nor is there any excess or deficiency of it. Just as a ball of thread will when thrown, unwind to its full length, so fool and wise alike will take their course, and make an end of sorrow (tr. A. Basham, in Bary, 1958, pp. 42–3).

In short, everything that is predestined to happen will happen: 'What will be, will be.'

It was in opposition to this absolute determinism and fatalism that the *karma* doctrine was propounded in ancient India. The *karma* doctrine was formulated in Buddhism, Jainism as well as in other brahminical schools. It is to be noted that since the idea of a transcendent Creator God was not the dominant trend in the Vedas and Upaniṣads, the problem of evil in the form of the dilemma stated above was not a major problem for the Upaniṣadic thinkers or the *śramaṇa* philosophers. Monism gradually became a dominant doctrine in the Upaniṣads. Thus, when the problem of evil in its generalized form made its appearance before these thinkers, a monistic solution was possible: good and evil both belong to the phenomenal reality behind which there is the Ultimate Reality, and this Ultimate Reality is beyond good and evil. This is the doctrine that finally paved the way for mysticism. The *karma* doctrine, however, was an early substitute for fatalism and recognized human beings as free agents. Since the rotion of a Creator God was not prevalent (in fact, it was explicitly rejected in systems like the Sāṃkhya, Jainism and Buddhism), the *karma* doctrine became very important in ancient India to explain the problem of evil as well as the problem of creation. In fact, a ninth-century Jaina teacher, Jinasena, argued that the formulation of the problem of evil itself would be sufficient for the repudiation of a Creator and Transcendent God:

> And God commits great sin in slaying the children whom he himself created. If you say that he slays only to destroy evil beings, why did he create such beings in the first place? (tr. A. Basham, in Bary, 1958, p. 80).

What creates mountains, rivers, springs? The Lokāyata answer was: Nature. What creates man's happiness, unhappiness, misery and pain? The Lokāyata answer was again, Nature. The Ājīvaka answer was: Fate or *niyati*. The upholders of the *karma* doctrine answered: man himself as a free agent creates his own misery.

The historical evolution of the notion of *karma* is interesting. In the Vedas and Brāhmaṇas, *karma* usually meant rituals and sacraments. In the Upaniṣads, *karma* in the sense of moral action (ethical acts) was in the ascendence. In fact, *karma* stood for both moral acts and rituals, both being believed to be responsible for our future existence in some way or other. In this respect, the Indian belief was not much different from the Christian belief. Thus, Helmuth von Glasenapp has pointed out:

> . . . Indian religions have never separated, any more than other religions have, the sacral-magic sphere from the moral. Thus, 'puṇya' (transcendent merit) that is acquired by carrying out definite ceremonies, by building temples, by gifts of charity to priests, etc., is put on an equal footing with ethically conditioned merit. So also, according to Christian belief, not only is the ethical life the preliminary condition for bliss, but the sacraments too have the effect of blotting out sin, and baptism is a necessary assumption for salvation (1963, p. 26).

Much has been said and written on the *karma* doctrine as well as its eschatological counterpart, the *saṃsāra* doctrine or metempsychosis. Most of these writings have been very confusing and misleading. It is to be noted that these two terms have been in use in Indian literature through the ages with many shades of meaning. Even the modern Indians today use them in a multiplicity of senses. But very few really care to critically examine these terms or investigate about their origin or their original intention. I would like to underline here some simple assumptions and considerations implied in these concepts, some simple points which are too often omitted in the relevant discussions because they are too obvious!

The *karma* theory in its simplest form means that every act, whether good or bad, produces a certain result or consequence which cannot be escaped by the perpetrator of the act. The doctrine is posited in a religious context as a *moral necessity*. It is an attempt to answer the question of moral responsibility in man. Metaphysically, it is based upon the doctrine of physical causation, according to which each effect has to be accounted for by its causal precedents. It is a kind of extrapolation or extension of the doctrine of causation from the physical realm to the moral realm. Originally, the doctrine attempts to answer three essential problems:

(a) It is a theory that refuses to admit that the world is arbitrary; (b) It is opposed to the theory of Fate, and determinism, and accepts human beings as free agents; (c) It also attempts to explain the world process and inequalities of good and evil without resorting to the whims or grace of a transcendent, all-powerful Creator God.

It was not conceived as a mechanical law, as most modern people now assume it to be (see, e.g., Danto, 1972, p. 27: '. . . the karmic system is, as it were, a moral mechanics, with a predetermined output for any given input.'). Nor is it an experimentally verifiable principle obtained through induction (as some over-enthusiasts today try to prove). It is at best a hypothesis for the explanation of certain empirical facts, and at worst a supposition. But it is, perhaps, the best possible defence so far given to justify the moral responsibility of man's action.

Let us further note that the *karma* doctrine as such does not imply the unfortunate caste system that existed (or, still exists) in India. Buddhism and Jainism both uphold the *karma* doctrine but argue against the caste system. The caste system which crept into Indian life and society for many socio-economic reasons in the early period of Indian civilization was later defended by the priests (brahmins, to be sure) very conveniently and effectively by using the *karma* much in the same way some westerners (even today) try to justify racial distinction or anti-semitism by appealing to Biblical statements. The important point to remember is that the caste system is neither to be identified with, nor a necessary conclusion from, the *karma* doctrine, as it was originally envisioned. But this issue is sometimes confused. A.C. Danto has written a very interesting book on oriental thought and moral philosophy. Such a book is more than welcome because it is one of the few attempts by a serious-minded Western philosopher to discuss Indian ethics. But it is rather unfortunate that Danto, in his criticism of *karma* and caste (1972, pp. 22–45), has overlooked the essential difference between the two doctrines. Most of his criticisms here are undoubtedly directed against the caste problem and 'the pollution-craze' of modern India (and, of course, I join Danto in his condemnations of the caste system). But the impression one can get is that the author has been critical of the *karma* doctrine.

This, however, does not mean that there is very little in the *karma* doctrine which can be criticized. The *karma* hypothesis, like some of its rival hypotheses, does not answer satisfactorily a number of facts, as we shall see presently. But our point is that the obvious merit of this *karma* hypothesis should not be made obscure by modern misconceptions and patent misunderstandings.

The varieties and inequalities of life and human experience were accepted in ancient India as empirical facts standing in need of some explanation, that is, some causal explanation. The short-cut way would have been to posit an all-powerful God and then make his 'mysterious ways' responsible (i.e., causally responsible) for all these empirical facts. But most of the early philosophical systems hesitated to accord omnipotence to God. The Sāṃkhya system rejects the idea of God as Creator (*Iśvarakṛṣṇa, Sāṃkhya-Kārikā*, verses 31, 56). The *Vaiśeṣika-sūtra* forgets to mention God as an existent being. Even later, when Praśastapāda incorporates God in the Vaiśeṣika system, God's will or God's grace appears to be more or less an inessential appendage to the Vaiśeṣika theory of natural creation and destruction in terms of atomic conjunction and disjunction. The *Nyāya-sūtra* considers only the possibility of God's being essentially causally responsible for the creation of the universe, but ends on a sceptical note (*Nyāya-sūtra* 4.1.19–21; Ingalls, 1957). Even the *Vedānta-sūtra* poses the question: how can God be causally responsible for this universe unless he is also thought to be unjust and partial, or full of whims and caprices (*Vedānta-sūtra* 2.1.34–6). The dilemma has been solved there by making God dependent upon man's *karma* for his creative activity. This was the situation with the Vedic schools. The non-Vedic schools like Buddhism and Jainism were avowedly atheistic but accepted the *karma* hypothesis as a viable alternative.

The *karma* doctrine requires that man's own 'character' be his own 'destiny'. His past actions are responsible for his present joys and sorrows. The present is determined by the past, but since human beings are free agents, the future is not necessarily determined by the present. For man as a free agent can do *something* to attain a desirable future. What man can accomplish is, perhaps, very little, but it is this theoretical admission of man's freedom of will that makes the theory so interesting. It is a doctrine of self-responsibility. Man is free to work his way out of this 'mess' in which he finds himself. In the context of overwhelming and disheartening determinism, such a theory had certainly its charm and appeal. Thus, reduced to its bare essentials, the *karma* theory, as I see it, breathes a rather healthy spirit of self-determination and looks at the facts of life with a much straighter eye, instead of explaining things away by appealing to some 'mysterious way' or Providence.

In fact, due to a strong belief in *karma*, and insistence on the idea of regularity and law in the universe (compare the *Ṛg-vedic* conception of *Ṛta*), the theology and philosophy of India have never been able to find any satisfactory justification for theism. The thought of an inscrutable

Providence thus brings no comfort to the Indian mind. Being acutely aware of the sufferings and imperfections of the world, the Indian philosophers believed that all these must be ascribed to the acts of the individuals themselves, and not to an all-wise, all-good God. It is another 'factual belief' of the Indians that man is not the centre of the universe. Man is merely a stage higher than plants and animals (and, perhaps, a stage lower than the gods!). These beliefs are undoubtedly foreign to the general scheme of things that prevails in the Western religious tradition. But, contrary to Danto, I think that a study of these beliefs may be as sober as the study of modern astronomy as well as modern ecological and environmental problems. It was W.E. Clark who said in 1934:

There are logical difficulties with the doctrines of *karma* and transmigration, but these logical difficulties are no greater than those which attach to the Christian solutions of the problem of good and evil. The doctrines of forgiveness of sin and of death-bed repentance might result most disastrously from a moral point of view. Should we ask whether these doctrines are absolutely true or false, or should we ask whether they are psychologically satisfactory to the people who have faith in them? It was Macaulay, I think, who argued that Protestantism was true and Catholicism false because Protestant countries were more prosperous than Catholic countries (p. 24).

Danto has claimed that 'The Indians have made no arguments to speak of that "prove" the existence of *karma* and certainly no efforts to explain the mechanisms whereby it works' (1972, p. 41). After this remark, he goes on to enumerate some 'popular' arguments given by 'the ordinary man in India' (p. 42) in defence of their uncritical belief in what they call the *karma*-cum-*saṃsāra* doctrine. It is not clear whether Danto wants to say that the ancient philosophical/theological texts of India do not present any argument in favour of the *karma* doctrine. In fact, there are several texts which try to 'prove' the existence of *karma* (give as much 'proof' as one can hope to gather in favour of such a hypothesis), and 'explain' its mechanism. One may mention such texts as Śaṃkara's *Brahmasūtra-bhāṣya* (*sūtra* 2.1.34–6), the *Sāṃkhya-sūtra* 5.20 and 6.41, and the Jaina text, *Karmagrantha* of Devendrasūri. The so-called 'mechanism' has been discussed in detail from the Buddhist point of view by Vasubandhu. Several Vaiśeṣika and Nyāya authors beginning with Praśastapāda have discussed the mechanism from the non-Buddhist point of view. This 'proof', however, has the characteristic of a 'theological' proof, for the hypothesis can hardly be called a verifiable one. I shall quote below excerpts from Śaṃkara's argument since it is quite well known (Commentary under BS 2.1.33–6):

God cannot be the cause of the world. Why? For, otherwise, he would be reproached for lack of impartiality and lack of compassion. Some beings, viz., the gods (or kings) and others, he renders eminently happy; others, as for instance the animals (who are slaughtered by man), eminently unhappy; to some again, as for instance (ordinary) men, he allots an intermediate position. A God who brings about such an unequal condition of things must be accused of passion and malice, like any common person acting similarly. And this would be contrary to the essential goodness of God affirmed by the scriptures and relevant secondary literature. Moreover, as the infliction of pain and final destruction would be part of his dispensation, he would be charged with great cruelty, a vice abhorred even by low people.

Śaṃkara's solution is that God creates everything depending necessarily upon the *dharma* and *adharma* (the residual forces of *karma*) of the living beings. In other words, creation is guided by the principle of *karma*, while God is the creator of everything only in the same sense that rain is the creator of all vegetation. To quote Śaṃkara again:

Just as rain is the common cause for the production of rice, barley and other plants, while the difference between various species is due to the various potentialities of respective seeds, so the Lord is the common cause of the creation of gods (kings), men, etc., while the respective merit (*dharma*) belong to the individual souls. Hence the Lord, being bound by such limitations, cannot be reproached with lack of impartiality and cruelty.

To put it simply, the argument is that we can 'solve' the problem of evil and inequalities of individual happiness and unhappiness in a theistic system only if we assume the *karma* hypothesis.

In a non-theistic system like Buddhism, *karma* is posited in order to explain the same inequalities between one man's potential and another. This is how Nāgasena answers King Menander:

'Venerable Nāgasena,' asked the King, 'why are men not all alike, but some short-lived and some long, some sickly and some healthy, some ugly and some handsome, some weak and some strong, some poor and some rich, some base and some noble, some stupid and some clever?'

'Why, your Majesty,' replied the Elder, 'are not all plants alike, but some astringent, some salty, some pungent, some sour, and some sweet?'

'I suppose, your reverence, because they come from different seeds.' 'And so it is with men! They are not alike because of different *karmas*. As the Lord said, 'Beings each have their own *karma*. They are born through *karma*, they become members of tribes and families through *karma*, each is ruled by *karma*, it is *karma* that divides them into high and low (*Milindapañha* tr. A. Basham, in de Bary, p. 110).

It is, however, highly paradoxical that the *karma* theory led, in fact, to conservatism and inaction in India, that it favoured an acceptance of the status quo rather than a vigorous attempt to remedy injustice and interfere with the 'consequences' of *karma*! This is a historical fact. To understand the paradoxical situation one needs to analyse cautiously and carefully many other contributing factors. One needs to investigate many sociological, psychological and environmental problems in detail—a worthy undertaking which we cannot go into here. It is simply highly intriguing to see that the *karma* doctrine, which was originally propounded to oppose fatalism and encourage free will became later only a plea for disguised fatalism. The blind force of Fate or *niyati* stole its way into the *karma* doctrine under the guise of the 'unseen' (*a-dṛṣṭa*) residual forces of actions perpetrated in the previous births!

This unusual about-face of the *karma* doctrine was brought about with the help the *karma* hypothesis received from another closely associated hypothesis, that of *saṃsāra* or transmigration. If the varieties of our experiences, the inequalities in our situations, births, environments and potentialities, cannot be explained with reference to our own actions in the present life, the full-fledged moral causation theory, as it is envisioned in the *karma* hypothesis, seems to dwindle away. We particularly face a problematic situation when, for example, we wish to rationalize the 'bad luck' of newborn babies and their apparently unaccountable sufferings. It was in this way, I believe, that the hypothesis of pre-existence of the soul was forced upon the *karma* theory, so as to avoid the unwelcome alternative, that of chance or 'bad luck'. In much the same way, I believe, the idea of post-existence, or after-life, was recognized in the Indian religious tradition. Once the 'transmigration' hypothesis was fully developed, it began to reinforce and sustain the *karma* hypothesis. Thus, we have here a combined doctrine which rendered the Creator God hypothesis somewhat inessential and the 'chance' hypothesis as well as the 'Fate' hypothesis generally unacceptable.

Initially the *karma*-cum-*saṃsāra* doctrine was supposed to be a simple hypothesis to justify our belief in moral responsibility. But obviously it was ornamented with many fanciful mythological details and humorous combinations when the principle was explained to satisfy the feeling of the masses. Examples of such fanciful details are numerous in the *Purāṇas*, *dharmaśāstras* and Buddhist and Jaina texts. It is said that a man was covetous and cruel, and was born as an elephant. Another, who committed murder out of greed, was born seven times as a fish (to be easily killed by fishermen), then seven times as a mosquito and so on. A good man who shares food with others is rewarded with a good memory and intelligence. Another who digs a pond for others reaches the heaven of gods. But obviously such fanciful statements should not be understood literally. If they have any significance for us, it would be in underlining the general principle that was part of the belief in *karma*: good works beget good results, bad works beget bad ones. Some modern critics of the *karma* doctrine ridicule such fanciful stories. But this is wrong. Thus, von Glasenapp has pointed out:

> It is clear that the entire greatness and depth of such a view is to be found in the idea as such that all attempts to systematize and work it out casuistically are individually bound to have a crude and arbitrary effect (1963, p. 30).

This may explain the reason why Danto has not been able to find an explanation of 'how the mechanism of *karma* works'.

Obviously, there are many unsatisfactory consequences of the *karma*-cum-*saṃsāra* doctrine. Critics who are seriously minded usually point out the following defects:

1. *Karma* leads to fatalism in the way I have indicated above. It does not, thus, give any incentive to social reform. It accounts for the general apathy of Indian society towards natural, social and political evils.

The above is only partially true. For one has to consider also many other factors in the situation. When a man is disinclined to work, he tries to find some excuse. When a man is strong and wicked and wants to exploit others, he also looks for some excuse to justify his behaviour. If such excuses are readily at hand, for example, in something like a *karma* doctrine, people will use them. And if the excuses are not readily at hand, they can easily be invented or forged. Thus, the question is: whether the total effect of the *karma* doctrine generated such evils in Indian society, or whether the society itself degenerated and allowed such evils to persist, probably receiving a helping hand from the *karma* doctrine of the priests? For, distortion and misinterpretation usually come from the motives of the interpreters, in this case, the priests, the privileged classes, and the strong. A devil may quote the Bible in support of his devilish act, and certainly it is no fault of the Bible. Similarly, one may argue, it is no fault of the *karma* doctrine.

2. There is the perplexing question of free will and determinism in ethical philosophy. The *karma* doctrine, as we have seen already, first endorsed free will and then led into determinism. The deterministic doctrine states roughly that human actions like all other natural events are determined by preceding conditions, by the immutable laws of

nature. Our belief in the doctrine of physical causation intensifies our belief in determinism. The physical science of the seventeenth and eighteenth centuries supported the doctrine of determinism. With the rise of the Freudian school of psychoanalysis, determinism has been further strengthened. Even the Socratic doctrine of 'virtue is knowledge and vice is ignorance' implies determinism.

Briefly speaking, the problem with determinism is that it reduces the concept of moral freedom into an absurdity, and hence the laws of punishment and reward in the courts of justice become meaningless. To take a simple example, a murderer cannot be tried with fairness under the deterministic principle because he did not act as a free agent. Thus a clever lawyer can save many guilty persons from the gallows. Faced with this type of difficulty, some philosophers have argued for what may be called 'soft determinism'. Hobbes, for example, preached a soft determinism and tried to reconcile moral freedom with determinism. Freedom was defined by Hobbes as just 'freedom from constraint'. It is difficult to say, however, whether the expositions of 'soft determinism' available so far can successfully reconcile causal determinism with man's moral freedom. The evidence is that such a reconciliation is a remote possibility. Similarly, we may say that the *karma* doctrine did not solve the problem either. A modern writer, T.G. Kalghatgi, has tried admirably to interpret the Indian *karma* doctrine as a form of 'soft determinism' (1972, pp. 33–5). But it shares, along with other forms of 'soft determinism', the same ambiguity regarding the concept of freedom of choice and human responsibility.

3. A most disturbing argument against the 'transmigration' hypothesis is the gradual increase in the world's population (cf. J.E. Sanjane, 1954).

The multiplication of the species goes against the idea of pre-existing eternal souls. Modern writers like P.V. Kane have tried to answer this objection, but unfortunately these answers are too inadequate to require any comment here (Kane, p. 1611, Kalghatgi, p. 63). One thing is at least clear: belief in transmigration can hardly be a justified belief because of the predomination of evidence to the contrary. But the *karma* doctrine, or, perhaps a modified form of the doctrine of moral responsibility, still seems to me to be a viable hypothesis, which shares the same inconclusive status as the hypothesis of an all-powerful, all-benevolent God.

Notes and References

Bary, Th. de (ed.), *Source of Indian Tradition*. (Part Two: 'Jainism and Buddhism,' by A.L. Basham.) New York: Columbia University Press, 1958.

Basham, A., *History and Doctrines of the Ājīvikas; A Vanished Indian Religion*. London: Luzac, 1951.

Clark, W.E., *Indian Conceptions of Immortality*. Cambridge, Mass., 1934.

Danto, A.C., *Mysticism and Morality: Oriental Thought and Moral Philosophy*. New York: Basic Books, 1972.

Hume, R.E. *The Thirteen Principal Upanishads*. 2nd edn., revised by G.C.O. Haas. Oxford, Oxford University Press, 1931.

Ingalls, D.H.H., 'Human Effort versus God's Effort in the Early Nyāya', *Felicitation Volume Presented to S.K. Belvalkar*, edited by S. Radhakrishnan et al., Banares: Motilal Banarsi Dass, 1957, pp. 228–35.

Kalghatgi, T.G., *Karma and Rebirth*. Ahmedabad: L.D. Institute of Indology, 1972.

Kane, P.V., *History of Dharma-śāstra*. Poona: Bhandarkar Oriental Research Institute, 1930–62.

Kaviraj, G., *Aspects of Indian Thought*. Burdwan: University of Burdwan Press, 1966.

Mādhava, *Sarva-darśana-saṃgraha: Or Review of the Different Systemms of Hindu Philosophy*. Translated by E.B. Cowell and A.E. Gough, London: Trübner & Co., 1882.

Śaṃkara, *Brahmasūtra-bhāṣya*. Edited by J. Shastri. Delhi, 1980.

Sanjane, J.E., *Dogma of Reincarnation*. Bombay, 1954.

Von Glasenapp, Helmuth, *Immortality and Salvation in Indian Religions*, trans. by E.F.J. Payne, Calcutta: Susil Gupta, 1963.

29

A Note on *Śaṃkara's* Theodicy

Theodicy is an old and worn-out issue. Probably nothing new can be said about it. It is also believed that theodicy was not a problem for the Indians, specially for the Hindus, because evil was, according to them, an illusion. Particularly, it is urged, in Śaṃkara's Advaita Vedānta, the whole world is an illusion along with its evil, and hence the problem of evil is resolved. This belief is partly based upon a misconception. It is true, however, that the problem of evil did not dominate the field of Indian philosophy of religion, although the problem existed; that is, it was formulated and discussed. A resolution was suggested along different lines. Besides, the rather pervasive, but uncritical and unexamined assumption that in Śaṃkara's philosophy the world along with its evils is simply an illusion, leads to misconception and false ideas about Indian philosophy in general and Śaṃkara's philosophy in particular.

Śaṃkara propounded a new cosmology by reconstructing or, to use a modern jargon, by 'deconstructing' the old Scriptural texts on creation (*sṛṣti-śruti*). The world is identical with *Brahman*, the so-called creation is identical with its creator, for 'creation' is, in a nutshell, the imposition or superimposition of diverse names and forms on reality on account of what is called *avidyā*, the cosmic misconception, the congenital false belief of creatures. (I am somewhat allergic to such translations as 'nescience' or even 'ignorance'.) Under 2.1.33 of the *Brahmasūtra*, Śaṃkara reminds us:

na ceyam paramārtha-viṣayā sṛṣṭi-śrutiḥ avidyā-kalpita-nāma-rūpa-vyavahāra-gocaratvāt, brahmātmabhāva-pratipādana-paratvāc caitad api na vismartavyam.[1]

This is, in the briefest terms, Śaṃkara's reading of the 'Creation' texts of the Vedic scriptures. The author of the *Brahmasūtra*, however, has raised the problem of theodicy in unmistakable terms, and Śaṃkara explains the problem at that level too, without bringing in notions from his new cosmology. He does not say, for example, that since creation is nothing but superimposition of diversity through false belief, the question of the creator's being unjust and cruel (cf. *vaiṣamya-naighṛṇya*, BS 2.1.34) does not arise. On the other hand he finds it important and necessary to justify the realist's (or the popular) notion of creation and the Creator God. One may wonder why. I believe that he did not reject realism outright, but having a firm footing in the realist's world he argued that the ultimate truth transcends the realist's view of diversity and shows its ultimate unity with Brahman. Hence a defence of the ordinary notion of creation is also necessary. It is, perhaps, what he called *sthūṇa-nikhanana-nyāya* (BS 2.1.34). When we dig a hole to plant or fix a flag-pole (*sthūna* = sacrificial post), we try the base of the hole at various points so that the pole may be firmly planted on the ground. The ordinary notion of creation is the base or infrastructure upon which the edifice of Śaṃkara's new cosmology is built. So the digging of the base must be supervised as well.

I shall be concerned here with only three *sūtras*, BS 2.1.34—36, and Śaṃkara's commentary upon them. 2.1.33 says that God, the creator, cannot be unjust or cruel, for he is *not* independent in his act of creation, and the Scriptures show His dependence upon other factors such as *karma*, or the creatures' *dharma* and *adharma*. The world *karma* is not mentioned in this *sūtra*, but found in the next one. Śaṃkara supplements it and quotes in support from the *Kauśītakī-brāhmaṇa* and *Bṛhadāraṇyaka Upaniṣad* as well as from the *Bhagavad-Gītā*.

It seems that the problem of evil must have been a well-known and well-formulated issue at the time of the composition of the *Brahmasūtra*. The contemporary Buddhist and Jaina texts clearly raised the issue. It is said that even Nāgārjuna wrote a short tract to refute the idea that Lord Viṣṇu was the sole creator of the universe. In his *Twelve-Door Treatise*, it is said:

> If God is the maker of all things why did He not create all happy or all unhappy? Why did He make some happy and others unhappy?[2]

This is a clear formulation of the *vaiṣamya* argument, that is, the lack of equality, the injustice consisting of the lack of equal distribution of happiness and unhappiness. The *Mahāpurāṇa*, a Jaina text of probably the ninth century AD, says among other things:

> And God commits great sin in slaying the children whom He Himself created. If you say that He slays only to destroy evil beings, why did He create such beings in the first place?[3]

This is the *naighṛṇya* argument, that is, the cruelty of the omnipotent creator. David Hume's oft-quoted lines have the same resonance:

Is He [God] willing to prevent evil, but not able? Then He is impotent. Is He able but not willing? Then He is malevolent. Is He both able and willing? Whence there is evil?[4]

Leszek Kolakowksi has, in a recent book, *Religion* (1982, Fontana) underlined the problem of theodicy in the phrase 'God of Failures'. The idea is that theodicy has not so far had, and in fact cannot have, any satisfactory solution, except the old, old resolution found in the Book of Job in the Old Testament. In reply to the problem posed by the persistence of evil as against a Creator God's omnipotence and benevolence, it was said:

[Zophar said]: Wilt thou seek to fathom the inscrutable Godhead?[5]

This is the oldest resolution and as yet still the best, perhaps, in the Judeo-Christian tradition. Professor H.A. Wolfson once said:

Does anybody know of a better solution, and is not resignation out of faith better than resignation out of despair?[6]

Turning to Śaṃkara, we must see what resolution he offers. If creation is *ex nihilo* and if the Creator is omnipotent, as it is generally said in the Judeo-Christian tradition, then no satisfactory reconciliation can take place. The author of the *Brahmasūtra* clearly repudiates the two antecedent conditions. First, creation is not *ex nihilo*, as BS 2.1.35 underlines. *Ex nihilo* presupposes a beginning, but here it is said that creation has no beginning, it is *anādi*. Second, BS 2.1.34 emphasizes that creation is *sāpekṣa*, the Creator is not independent. He does not have free choice. Śaṃkara adds another dimension to the causality of God: *parjanya-vat* (comm. on 2.1.34). Rainfall is the common cause for the production of rice, barley and so on Rainfall does not show any favour or disfavour to the various seeds that are sown. God is likewise the common cause of 'creation'. The varieties and inequalities of the creatures are due to God's dependence upon special factors in each case, the particular *nature* of the creature, which is usually determined by the accumulated *karma* of the creature itself.

The next *sūtra* 2.1.34, raises and answers the obvious objection to this position. In the very beginning of creation, no *karma* existed, so whence the diversity? Answer: there was no such beginning, just as time has no beginning. 2.1.36 tries to justify this notion of beginninglessness. First, the question is raised: if *karma* is the factor on which creation depends, then creation is also a factor on which *karma* depends, and so which one was first? This is ruled out as an idle question. For it is exactly like the chicken-and-egg (or, in the Indian context, the seed-and-sprout) controversy. Second, had there been a beginning to creation, it would have started by a pure accident or 'causelessly' (=*akasmāt*, comm. on 2.1.36). This seems to be reminiscent of the 'why not sooner' argument which is tackled by the Greek and scholastic philosophers in the West.[7] Besides, creatures would have to suffer a lot for which they are not at all responsible (*akṛtābhyāgama*), and varieties and inequalities of the creatures' happiness and unhappiness would be unaccounted for. To avoid such *absurd* consequences, one has to admit the beginninglessness of creation. Śaṃkara adds: *anāditve bījāṅkuranyāyenopapatter na kaścid doṣo bhavati*—'If beginninglessness is accepted, since it follows the process of seed-and-sprout regularity, no fault will arise.' However there seems to be a way out even without our conceding the 'beginninglessness' hypothesis. If there was a beginning and the beginning was a happy one, but *free* creatures were created, and if through the exercise of *free* will they brought about inequalities upon themselves, then the alleged absurdity vanishes.

A number of important questions, however, arise for us moderners, and we may discuss only some of them here. Before we turn to them, we must note the later part of the *sūtra* and Śaṃkara's comment on it. The hypothesis of beginninglessness is supported by a sort of *reductio ad absurdum* (cf. *prasaṅga*). However, what stands to reason on pain of absurdity may be a possibility but not a certainty. In other words, truths are not established simply by *tarka* or such *reductio* or *a priori* argument on pain of absurdity. This has been elaborately discussed under BS 2.1.11. In fact, Indian philosophers were well aware that the *reductio* arguments by themselves cannot establish anything beyond any reasonable doubt. Hence to strengthen the hypothesis which the *reductio* suggests, an evidence, a *pramāṇa*, needs to be cited. The author of the *sūtra* and Śaṃkara both cite a scriptural passage as such a *pramāṇa.* A line in the *Ṛg-Veda* signifies that there was creation before creation, and hence no first creation. And in Vedānta, the authority of the scriptures overrides all other evidence: it is a *pramāṇa* par excellence.

Let us now raise some more substantive issues. First it seems that the Hindu idea of a Creator God is decidedly different from the same in the Judeo-Christian tradition. The traditional view, which underlines Judaism, Christianity and Islam, regards God, if we follow Spinoza, for example, as independent of the world, and it makes the world dependent upon God. This means that the existence of God does not necessarily imply the existence of the world, for the world came into existence after having not been in existence. This also implies that prior to its existence there was a God without a world and it is further believed that some day the world will end but God will continue, again without a world. If this even remotely represents what is commonly believed in Judaism, Christianity and Islam, then the 'beginninglessness' hypothesis of the Hindus is contradicted. However, the existence of time 'prior' to the creation is not universally accepted by all Christians. Besides, as Sorabji points out (in a private correspondence) it was an important Judeo-Christian view that God would create 'a new heaven and a new earth' (Isaiah 65.17). The idea of eternity or even pre-existence was, in some sense, present among the Greeks (cf. the conception of the eternity of the world), although the Hindu idea of 'beginninglessness' maintains its uniqueness. In fact, some believers in the revelation maintain that any form of eternity of the world would be a restriction on the power of God. This is not, however, universally held—on the other hand, we may note here another point. It may be pointed out in this connection that creation at a certain point of time and annihilation at a certain future date, minus the idea of a Creator God, is quite in keeping with the spirit of the modern natural science.

Second, in the Judeo-Christian tradition, the divine omnipotence has very seldom been compromised. In recognition of the problem of evil, both physical and moral evils, various explanations have been suggested since the early days of Biblical scholarship. However, for the remaining problem, some sort of incomprehensibility of Providence has been appealed to. This has been the root of scepticism in the Western tradition. Spinoza called it 'the asylum of ignorance' (*Ethics*, I, Appendix) and J.S. Mill described it as 'an ignominious failure', (*Three Essays on Religion*, New York, 1878, p. 192). And yet those who have firm faith in revelation theology can hardly give up the divine omnipotence. The old philosophical way of understanding omnipotence is fourfold (I follow H.A. Wolfson's exposition): (1) God, if he willed, could have created a different world with different laws, and (2) if he wills, can undo this world and create a new one with a difference; but (3) he has created this world and implanted in it certain laws of nature by which it is run; and (4) he can, if he wills, override these laws and create miracles. Suprisingly, one notion of omnipotence in India is very similar: *kartum a-kartum anyathākartuṃ ca śaknoti* (he can do it, or undo it, or even do it in another way).

This seems to answer most of the problems in the notion of divine omnipotence. One problem is that there exists a clearly discernible distinction between what we call a logical truth or a logical law and a law of nature. Squaring a circle would represent a violation of the former kind and flying in the air like Superman in the comic books or like Hanumān, the monkey chief in Indian mythology, would represent a violation of the second kind. Most miracles reported, or God's reported interventions in many religious lores, fall in this latter category. Factual impossibilities lie within God's power, but he chooses not to exercise it. How about logical impossibilities? Can God square a circle? This has been discussed over the centuries in the West. And usually it has been conceded that he can, but chooses not to, or he cannot, but, such a 'cannot' does not detract from his omnipotence. However, the *sāpekṣatva* 'dependence' thesis which BS 2.1.34 underlines and which Śaṃkara amplifies as God's dependence upon the *karma* of the creatures, seriously delimits or restricts God's omnipotence, and so will not be shared by any of the Biblical religions, Judaism, Christianity or Islam.

Third, in the Judeo-Christian tradition, God as creator is either an artisan or a begetter. The Jewish conception is that of an omnipotent artisan who is in no need of *material* for any of his acts of making. St Thomas, and the Christians in general, chose the begetter model after the analogy of natural procreation. The begetter model may have some superficial similarity with popular Hinduism. There is also a pronounced from the procreation analogy in the Śiva-Śakti model. As the poet Kalidāsa says:

> *Jagataḥ pitarau vande pārvatī-parameśvarau.*
> I bow down to the parents of the Universe, Śiva and Pārvatī.

The idea of a self-sufficient artisan has a distant resonance with the spider model of God, which is well known in the Upaniṣadic tradition. The spider weaves a web out of itself, much as God does. This spider analogy of the Hindus was even mentioned by David Hume (*Dialogues Concerning Natural Religion*, Part VII). Hume comments on this with half-hearted irony: 'But still here is a new species of analogy, even in our globe.' However, it was not as new as Hume thought. The notion of a self-sufficient artisan carries the same sense, as far as the analogy is concerned. Incidentally, the spider model must have been well-entrenched in some Hindu thought, so much so that Śāntarakṣita found it necessary to comment upon it and refute it in his famous book *Tattvasaṃgraha* (Part I, verse 154).

The Judaic artisan analogy is, however, very different from another Hindu 'artisan' analogy. This is the analogy of a potter who makes pots with pre-existent clay. This model is favoured by the Nyāya-Vaiśeṣika and would presumably be favoured by Śaṃkara also when he explains the ordinary notion of creation at the *vyāvahārika* level. Matter in the form of atoms pre-exists any creation. The pre-existence of matter is also a Platonic idea. A potter is an artisan who depends upon separate and independent materials for creating whatever he creates. Here, divine omnipotence is further curtailed, for God has to 'depend upon' (cf. *sāpekṣa*) both the atoms of matter and the *karma* of the creatures. Since the eternity of creation is still maintained, for the beginninglessness thesis is not given up, 'pre-existence' here means persistence between periodic (and partial) creation and dissolution. Such a position is diametrically opposed to the Biblical tradition of a unique and sudden creation through God's wilful intervention into history.

It is implied by most of what Plato says that matter existed beginninglessly, but in a chaotic state, until God formed it into the orderly universe we know. And it was also God who installed the celestial clock and created (measurable) time as we know it. This would mean that the ordering of matter had a beginning, while the existence of matter is beginningless. However, matter according to Plato, is still not eternal in the fullest sense of being outside time in the way the Forms in Plato are eternal.[8]

Aristotle criticized Plato on the grounds that the world could not have had a beginning (and some Platonists reinterpreted Plato's lines to answer that even the orderly world, according to Plato, existed beginninglessly). By eternity, Aristotle meant endless time, not being outside time.[9] However, in one passage, *On the Heavens*, 1.9.279a 11ff, Aristotle does seem to mean timelessness by eternity (I owe this information to a private correspondence from Richard Sorabji). The Indian notion of eternity is akin to the first; something is eternal, for it has no beginning and no end. 'Timelessness' is not talked about usually, but probably the very notion of time was different. God is often identified with Time (e.g., in the *Bhagavad- Gītā*). However, a distinction was made from a different point of view. Eternity can be either ever-changing everlastingness (like the flow in a river, *pravāha-nityatā*) or unchanging everlastingness (*kūṭastha-nityatā*). Hence, one may argue, since ordinary time and change are intimately connected (one measures the other), an eternal entity can be unchanging, that is, changeless and hence by implication, timeless. The point is, however debatable.

It may be noted in passing that neither Plato's gods nor Aristotle's God, who was merely a philosophical thinker, would be faced with the problems that arise out of the concept of divine omnipotence. Plato believed in reincarnation, but he exonerated Providence by insisting that we *choose* our next life (*Republic* X, 619–20) and that our subsequent incarnations will depend on our behaviour in the present ones (*Timaeus* 41A–42E). Besides, God is exonerated because we entrusts the creation of the bodies of the creatures as well as their irrational souls to lesser gods.

In any case, the beginninglessness of the universe has been upheld by almost everybody in European antiquity outside the Judaeo-Christian tradition. Although Aristotle argued against infinite causal chains, it was decidedly in the context of generating motion. He argued against infinite chains of movers.[10] However elsewhere he asserted his belief in infinite chains of fathers and sons. The anomaly was explained by the Aristotelians by calling the chain of fathers and sons an *accidental* causal chain. Even some Islamic philosophers (as Thomas Acquinas informs us, noted by Sorabji in a footnote, *ST*. I., q. 7 a 4) endorsed the idea of infinite 'accidental' causal chains. However, as Richard Sorabji has argued, there does not seem to be any real logical objection to infinite causal chains, accidental or not (1983, pp. 230–1). The Indian version of the acceptable and 'provable' (*prāmāṇikī*) infinite causal chain of seeds and sprouts seems to be harking back to a similar argument. And this supplies the rationale for the *anāditva* 'beginninglessness' argument.

This excursion into non-Indian philosophy has been made simply to underline the point that beginninglessness is not a stupid or unintelligible notion. And there is no real logical difficulty in conceiving it, in the absence of any definite knowledge about how the creation began. The second point is to question whether it is absolutely necessary to resort to the 'beginninglessness' hypothesis in order to account for the inequalities and differences in the suffering of creatures. The Indian philosophies along with Śaṃkara seem to assume it. However, if with Plato we assume reincarnation, and if we assume further that the first incarnation was happy (I owe this point to Sorabji), inequalities and differences in happiness of the *free* creatures would not be unaccounted for.

Fourth, the *karma* doctrine has its own philosophical problems. The rational defence of *karma* seems to be based very much upon inadequate evidence and *a priori* assumption. Hence if one depends on *karma* to explain inequalities and presence of physical and moral evils rather than on the inscrutability of Providence, is one not flying from one 'asylum of ignorance' to another? This is a more substantive issue. Besides, the *karma* doctrine faces some well-known objections. First, it cannot be sustained without the hypothesis of transmigration. How can it be believed, as the Hindu, Buddhist and Jaina mythologies declare, that humans are born as birds, beasts and insects? Besides, it leads to fatalism, which makes people passively accept their destiny and discourages them from making sincere efforts to change the world. At worst it would support an argument in favour of keeping the caste-orientated society intact and go against any doctrine encouraging change of the status quo.

I have noted elsewhere how Max Weber thought of the *karma* doctrine, which was in his words 'the most consistent theodicy ever produced' in history.[11] While I do not share Weber's enthusiasm, I believe the connection between *karma* and theodicy should not be lightly dismissed. Immanuel Kant described theodicy as 'defences of the highest wisdom of the creator against the complaints which reason makes by pointing to the existence of things in the world which contradict the wise purpose'. Using this idea, my friend Arthur Herman has argued that all religions are failed theodicies.[12] Herman, however, illustrates his point from various facets of Indian religions. Indulging in a generalization, which may not be an illicit one, we can say that the Hindus, the Buddhists and the Jainas all try to uphold the idea of retributive justice in creation, by making the existence of inequalities and differences dependent upon and conditioned by the *karma* doctrine. The causal paradox that is then generated is avoided by an appeal to the beginningless nature of the creation process.

Fifthly, *karma* is to be regarded as a hypothesis formulated to explain certain recalcitrant features in our conception of the creation of this universe. Hence the weakness or the strength of this hypothesis should be judged on the basis of its explanatory power. The doctrine or rebirth or transmigration is only an extension of the original hypothesis, and hence it is not impossible to uphold the *karma* hypothesis without the excess baggage of the rebirth hypothesis. The *Śvetāśvatara Upaniṣad*[13] enumerated a number of rival hypotheses: nature, chance, destiny, Matter, Time or human *karma* (the word *puruṣa* in the verse, I take it, has all three meanings suggested). Of these, *karma* is only one, and eventually this was thought to be more acceptable by the Indians. However, as time passed, in the popular tradition, the original *karma* doctrine went through a metamorphosis, where the supposedly acquired *karma* of previous births was virtually lumped together with the unseen destiny, Fate or *niyati*, which became as inscrutable as God's Will, or the writing of

Vidhātṛ, on the newly-born baby's forehead. In this mixture or conflation, the original doctrine's idea of moral responsibility for one's own deliberate moral action is lost, and the whole point of the morality that the original doctrine tried to sustain is unconsciously given up.

We may note that although Fate is sometimes called *Daiva* ('of gods') in the popular literature of India, it is also recognized that God often cannot control it or stop its operation. Thus, God is said to be more powerful than all of us, but still not omnipotent. In the *Mahābhārata*, Lord Kṛṣṇa was regarded by most as God Almighty, but he himself admitted more than once that he was powerless before the operation of Fate or time (*Kāla*). He acknowledged, for example, before the sage Utaṅka, that he did not have the power to stop the most disastrous bloody battle of Kurukṣetra. His power had its limits. Rāma, in the *Rāmāyaṇa* (who is also regarded in popular literature as God Almighty) also had to surrender before *Kāla* or Fate. That was how the abandonment of Sītā as well as of Lakṣmaṇa at the end was explained, and that was why all the four brothers, Rāma, Bharata, Lakṣmaṇa and Śatrughna, had to die. This idea is not entirely unfamiliar in Western literature; for example, in Greek myths, Zeus was said to be not superior to Fate.

Sixthly, even if we reassert the original spirit with which the *karma* hypothesis was propounded, the hypothesis faces other formidable objections. Let us deal with only one. A significant objection from the point of view of a westerner is that a sincerely held belief in the *karma* hypothesis confuses and conflates two very different domains, sharply distinguished in modern Western philosophy: fact and value. One may summarily reject the doctrine as unintelligible for it violates Hume's principle of distinguishing fact from value.[14] The separation is important and calls for significant methodological considerations in the pursuit of material science: causal explanation of factual events must be in terms of other factual events and their interconnections, not in terms of 'subjective' values. The question, however, is much discussed today. As far as our present purpose is concerned, it does not matter a great deal whether or not evaluative statements or moral prescriptions can be derived from factual statements. I believe they can be, within limits. The more pertinent question is how to justify the move to obliterate the distinction between a natural law like the law of gravitation and a prescriptive law, a law involving the domain of value, which the law of *karma* inescapably implies. For the essence of the *karma* doctrine consists in actions being evaluated as morally good or bad, and justice, reward and punishment being distributed accordingly, in an automatic regularity. And to ask us to believe in it is, in fact, going against the current, that is, the acquired wisdom of the 'scientific' Western civilization.

In plain language, how can we extend the law of natural causation of physical events to the domain of ethics, and speak in dead seriousness about moral causation, unless the latter is only a metaphor? If I eat a lot one day, I might have indigestion as a result, which may be my punishment, but it is by and large, physically accounted for. But if I am a compulsive liar and clever enough to cheat most people with impunity, there are very little factual grounds on the basis of which one may say that I will receive my punishment no matter what, unless of course it is presumed that nature has a teleology, or there is retributive justice in creation, or the natural order has a purpose and a direction, or, to use the Indian term, there is *Ṛta* in our cosmos. Even if we become hard-headed moral realists and treat moral qualities as objectively as physical qualities, it would be too much to imagine that such qualities of my action would punish or reward me by sending me to hell or heaven. 'Lying is wrong' may be true, but it cannot be true in the same sense as the Law of Gravitation or Heisenberg's Uncertainty Principle; at least, that is the received wisdom of our age. Natural law, one may contend, is nothing more than a given sequence, unless, of course, we imagine a divine mind who can be made responsible for the assumed teleology, or we imagine such a teleology to be immanent in the natural universe.

It seems that the Greek Stoics believed in a similar teleology immanent in the natural universe: as materialists, they gave an entirely physical explanation of our unhappy states. Providence, then, was not clearly separable from the natural law, according to the Stoics. However, this was argued differently. Here we may have a contrast, and it may be philosophically fruitful to explain it.

In sum, I have focused upon two significant aspects of Śaṃkara's theodicy. Whether this theodicy fails or not, its intelligibility depends upon these two aspects: the 'beginninglessness' argument and the dependence of creation upon *karma*. It has been shown that 'beginninglessness' is not at all an unintelligible concept. If creation has a beginning, the theist will have more problems to face and resolve. The *karma* doctrine is intelligible only if we assume that nature has a purpose and a direction. However, if we are unable to concede this, the *karma* principle may be taken to be a religious proposition, an article of faith. In fact, few arguments are given there in the vast philosophical literature of India. It is the *given* in Indian religions. It is not a fully worked-out theory. It is given as the general guideline that is supposed to shape the Indian way of life, the Indian social and moral behaviour. Not to believe in it would be taboo. And there cannot be a culture without taboos. As Leszek Kolakowski has said in *Religion*:

> . . . culture *is* taboos, or to put it another way, a culture without taboos is a square circle.[15]

Notes and References

1. Śaṃkara, *Brahmasūtrabhāṣya*, ed. J. Shastri, Delhi, Motilal Banarsidass, 1980, under 2.1.33.
2. See H. Cheng, *Nāgārjuna's Twelve Treatise*, Dordrecht, Reidel, 1982, ch. 9.
3. The *Mahāpurāṇa* of Jinasena, 4.16–31, 38–40. Cited in *Sources of Indian Tradition* (Revised ed. Ainslie T. Embree), New York, Columbia University Press, 1988 (first edn., 1958), pp. 80–2.
4. D. Hume, *Treatise on Human Nature*, ed. L.A. Selby-Bigge, Oxford, 1951, x, p. 490.
5. *The Book of Job*, ed. Buttenwieser, New York, Macmillan, 1922, 11.7.
6. H.A. Wolfson, *Religious Philosophy: A Group of Essays*, Harvard University Press, Cambridge 1961.
7. R. Sorabji, *Time, Creation and the Continuum*, Duckworth, London, 1983, pp. 232–8.
8. Ibid., ch. 17.
9. Ibid., pp. 125–7.
10. Aristotle, *The Basic Work of Aristotle*, ed. R. McKeon, New York, Random House, 1941, 7.1, 8.5.
11. Max Weber, *The Religion of India*, tr. & ed. H.H. Gerth and D. Martindale, New York, 1958 (original edn. 1920–21), p. 121.
12. A. Herman, 'Peligions as Failed Theodicies: Atheism in Hinduism and Buddhism', in *Indian Philosophy of Religion* (ed. R. Perrett), D. Reidel, 1988, pp. 35–60.
13. *Śvetāśvatara Upaniṣad*, Ch. I, verse 2.
14. See Terence Penelhum, 'Critical Response', in *Karma and Rebirth* (ed. R.W. Neufeldt), SUNY, Albany, 1986, pp. 339–45.
15. L. Kolakowski, *Religion*, Oxford, Fontana, 1982, p. 196.

Index